CHARLES V
FATHER OF EUROPE

CHARLES V AT THE BATTLE OF MÜHLBERG
Titian, *The Prado, Madrid*

[*Frontispiece*

CHARLES V

FATHER OF EUROPE

by

GERTRUDE VON SCHWARZENFELD

LONDON

HOLLIS & CARTER

This translation from the original German, Karl V: Ahnherr Europas
(Marion von Schröder Verlag, Hamburg), was made by

RUTH MARY BETHELL

MADE AND PRINTED IN GREAT BRITAIN BY
HAZELL WATSON AND VINEY LTD., AYLESBURY AND LONDON, FOR
HOLLIS AND CARTER LIMITED
25 ASHLEY PLACE, LONDON, S.W.I

First published 1957

SUMMARY OF CONTENTS

INTRODUCTION
(p. ix)

I. EL ESCORIAL
(p. 1)

II. MADRID
(p. 17)

III. TOLEDO
(p. 31)

IV. FROM MADRID TO ANDALUCÍA
(p. 97)

V. GRANADA
(p. 103)

LIST OF ILLUSTRATIONS

INTRODUCTION

This book was originally intended as a journal, the diary of a journey in Spain which I made between February and April, 1948. But wherever I went the personality of Charles V met me and impressed itself so vividly on my mind that my notes gradually evolved into a kind of history.

My first plan, to do a volume of *Pictures from Spain*, might have been dropped at that point, but it became evident that Spain belonged to Charles V, intrinsically. In Spain he spent his happiest years; that essentially Spanish quality, tenacity, became second nature to him; the spirit of Spain sustained him, and Spanish money supported him in his fight for the unity of the Faith, a cause that repeatedly called him away from Spain to Germany.

Spain was his base, Germany his battle-field; Spain signified continuity, Germany, change. His was a great life, lived in perpetual tension between the eternal values and the spirit of the times. And loyalty to the former was to mean his defeat by the latter.

So it is more than a coincidence that in the following pictures the background is Spanish.

And it is certainly no coincidence at all that the last great European Emperor has in our day regained his significance: his personality appeals to us because today the idea of universality once more makes sense. His failure grips us because we know he was fighting for a basic principle of Europe's. His lifelong endeavour to give precedence to a conception of the whole over the component parts, with their self-centred interests, takes on a new meaning for us, today, too, for Europe has to be put together again and welded into a whole, loyal once more to the old common Christian values.

True enough, the tendency is still centrifugal, that is to say, splintered by nationalistic and individualistic forces hitched exclusively to this world—forces which asserted their independence in Charles V's time and are still dividing and subdividing the peoples of Europe. But it may be true, as Fichte held at the beginning of the nineteenth century, that 'in the process of achieving full expansion egoism has met its doom', and that the new era of which we are experiencing the birth-pangs will no longer be wholly under the sign of materialism. In the old cathedrals, the mediaeval wall-paintings whitewashed by the Reformation are coming to light again, and simultaneously the Christian idea is once more finding its way to the surface of our minds; now, in the midst of our ruins and lurking perils, we may be on our way to a renaissance of the *universitas Christiana*.

That, however, would be a theme exceeding my capacity. But any survey of Charles V's life, even one strictly limited in scope like this present one, is a contribution to the study of that turning-point in history when the modern view of the world was formed—a view which today cries out for revision.

GERTRUDE VON SCHWARZENFELD

Paris, 1953.

I

EL ESCORIAL

> . . . always there is a yearning for
> what is boundless. But much has
> to be preserved. And not least,
> loyalty.
>
> *Hölderlin*

SAN LORENZO DE EL ESCORIAL

The Castilian landscape is empty and barren, but it has a rare heartening effect of its own. The sky reigns undiminished over the high plateau which appears to stretch out into infinity. The light over it is uncommonly clear—one wonders, is it indeed but light, and not, rather, spirit? It arouses new forces within us, very necessary ones if the great purity of it is to be borne at all. Of a sudden we understand the commandment, let thy yea be yea, thy nay, nay—and appreciate that provocative 'be hot, or be cold', admitting that, after all, absolute truth does exist and here is what we seek, here we stand on firm ground.

The royal monastery of San Lorenzo de El Escorial, the home of Philip II, lies at the foot of a cliff that rises like a protective wall above it.

It is a massive building with a number of towers and a dome, severely simple in style. But after several visits and wanderings through the many interior courts, passages and rooms, the bare structure began to blossom from within like the page of a book that proved difficult at a first reading, till its meaning gradually dawned. For in those walls a secret treasure lies hid: Philip II's dream.

His dream was the sovereignty of the Catholic idea, a dream which here, in a limited sphere, for the space of a few years, took on form and substance.

Philip's living-quarters are reached by crossing a flight of rooms which the Bourbons, the Habsburgs' successors in Spain, adorned with colourful tapestries and baroque ornamentation; to move on into Philip's unpretentious quarters is like hearing, after an empty jangle of voices, one single voice with something real to say. His study is roomy and pleasantly proportioned. There are small Flemish pictures on the whitewashed walls and a portrait of Philip in the black clothes he wore as widower in his latter years. His face is pale, his eyes blue, with a gentle look; this is not the gloomy tyrant of the history books, but a man grown mature in the performance of difficult duties.

The dark, rigid furniture is what Philip actually used. On one small chair he propped his gouty leg, his state papers lay strewn over the writing-table, and there he sat many hours a day, carefully scrutinizing in turn the various documents he was brought.

The study window overlooks the wide, consecrated landscape of New Castile. Towards evening the ruddy earth glows like the gold ground of a mosaic, and the saffron sky becomes transparent and clear as though heaven were nearer here than anywhere else.

The dark alcove which served him as bedroom is alongside the monastery church; a small connecting door opens on to the high altar, so that Philip could follow Mass from his bed when he was in too much pain to get up.

The immense structure of the Escorial seems to have been put up solely to protect this cell, with its view of the altar, from the outside world.

It must have been a consolation to Philip to think that, here, the Blessed Sacrament was guarded by strong walls. Here, the perpetual light glowed in peace. Philip saw to it that, in Spain, the sacred light burned on in all tranquillity, to the ever-renewed consolation of the living and of those to come.

SPANISH HABSBURG

To the left of the high altar in the Escorial church there are a number of gilded bronze statues representing the kneeling figures of Charles V, Isabella his wife, his daughter Maria, and his two sisters Leonora and Maria; and to the right, Philip II, his fourth wife Anna of Austria (mother of his son and heir, Philip III), his third and first wives, Isabella of Valois and Maria of Portugal, and last of all, his first-born son, Don Carlos.

All these figures face the altar with folded hands, as though they turned to bronze at their prayers, like those other figures in the tomb of Maximilian I in Innsbruck: that Emperor stands in effigy in a small church in the heart of the Tyrol, 'the last knight', the noble hunter 'whom an angel rescued when he lost his way on the rock-face of St Martin'; he was Dürer's friend, holding his ladder steady while he worked—the 'gentle and tender' Emperor, with his wife, Maria of Burgundy, whose rich dowry brought the Netherlands to Austria.

> *Bella gerant alii, tu felix Austria nube,*
> *Nam que Mars aliis, dat tibi regna Venus.*

'Let other lands make war; you, happy Austria, make marriages,' as we learnt at school. How heartening it sounded. How the lutes of Burgundy and Brabant re-echoed it! *Tu felix Austria nube*: the children of the marriage of Maximilian I and Maria of Burgundy were Philip the Fair and Margaret.

Almost simultaneously, those two married another brother-and-sister pair: Margaret became the wife of Prince Don Juan, only son and heir of the Catholic Sovereigns of Spain, and Philip married Don Juan's sister, Joanna.

There was a remarkable affinity between the Spanish and Austrian couples; Juan and Margaret found such delight in one another that the young prince burned out in the fires of his marriage-bed—in popular parlance in Spain he is 'the prince who died of love'. And his sister, Joanna, loved her husband, Philip the Fair, to distraction, and even to the point of madness. Charles V was their son.

Charles V, in whose realm 'the sun never set', is for me, here in Spain, a link with an Austria that *has* set. The Habsburg double-headed eagle, smashed to pieces at home in Bohemia, here occupies a place of honour, and the ground I tread on is firm, is like home.

The history of the Habsburgs in Spain concerns me personally as a sort of family history—a determining factor in the formation of character. It is on account of Habsburg loyalty to the Faith that I am at home in a Catholic church, in much the same way as I was at home in my parents' home in the old days. Through 'Mad Joan', there was Spanish blood in Ferdinand's veins—and with Ferdinand, brother of Charles V, Spain came to Bohemia.

Ferdinand was crowned King of Bohemia in St Vitus' church in Prague on 24th February 1527, and on 24th March 1558 he was made German Emperor. Thus the German line of the House of Habsburg took rank among the European powers, a position it was able to maintain, despite setbacks, till the downfall of Austria in 1918.

During Ferdinand's reign Bohemia was still suffering from the aftermath of the Hussite Wars, when many of the villages and churches had been plundered and burnt to the ground. Ferdinand brought in Italian builders and German craftsmen, and put spiritual reconstruction into the hands of the monastic orders and, in particular, the Jesuits, 'so that they may form a bulwark against Hussites, Wycliffites and other heresies and sects that abound in this land', he wrote. Cistercians, Franciscans, Carmelites, Brothers of Mercy, and Ursuline nuns came to Prague and founded religious houses.

Under Ferdinand, Bohemia became Spain's second spiritual home. The Old Faith revived in the form given it by Ignatius of Loyola, churches were built in the Jesuit style, with rich gold ornamentation. The Spanish spirit and the Austrian melted and merged in the fire of the Counter-Reformation.

One of the most enduring effects of Spanish religious influence in

Central Europe came about through the simple fact that Philip II took his nephews, Rudolf, Albrecht and Wenceslas, to Mass with him in the Escorial. Philip's sister Maria, the wife of Maximilian II, Ferdinand's eldest son, entrusted her sons to her brother for their education, because in Spain they were safe from the Protestant influences that prevailed in Maximilian's entourage. Philip II personally supervised his nephews' schooling. He taught them Church observances and gave them a personal example of Catholic living. Like Ignatius of Loyola, he knew how important it was 'to draw water from the source and attack disease at the root, for a vessel takes on the taste of the first liquid that is poured into it'. The boys learnt to serve at the altar and to keep the Church's feasts with due reverence. This liturgical initiation impressed their religion indelibly on their minds. Rudolf, the elder, as Emperor Rudolf II, was to stand for the Catholic Faith in a Bohemia seared by dissensions, and his successors remained true to the Old Faith throughout the centuries.

Emperor Francis Joseph, whose sense of duty, as ruler of the Austrian territories at the heart of Europe, was as keen as Philip II's when he governed the world-wide Spanish realm of the sixteenth century, remained loyal to those same Christian principles right into the time of the First World War—principles for which Charles V and Philip II had lived and fought. Corpus Christi, Charles V's favourite feast-day, was a high-water mark of the liturgical year in modern Austria: in old age Emperor Francis Joseph, in his red-and-white general's uniform, still walked in procession through the streets of Vienna, behind the Blessed Sacrament.

THE LIBRARY

In the Escorial library the books are placed with their backs to the wall, turning their gilded edges to the visitor. I asked the librarian the reason for this curious arrangement. He replied it had to do with the preservation of books—they could the better be dusted that way round, and the light and air to which they were thus exposed protected the paper from the worse effects of damp. And it looks better, he added.

Indeed, the long room glows warmly with the gold of the page-ends, and pure contemplation ousts desire for knowledge. There are some remarkably fine manuscripts lying open under glass, among them the valuable *Codice aureo*, of 1000 A.D., exquisitely illuminated in the byzantine style, and many other mediaeval manuscripts ornamented with flower

6

tendrils and golden lettering—including manuscripts of St Teresa of Avila whose clear handwriting speaks out as frankly as her words.

The librarian told me that St Teresa once visited the king in the Escorial. It is known that she requested an audience of him, but there is no reference anywhere to an actual meeting. However that may be, people of such spiritual affinity as those two have no need to come face to face: their minds correspond and they travel along the same road, for their goal is the same.

A letter from Teresa to Philip has been preserved. It is dated 11th September 1577 and contains a plea for mediation on behalf of a priest accused of heresy by the Inquisition. Actually it would not have been surprising if Teresa had pleaded for herself: at that very time the diocesan authorities of Plasencia issued a decree forbidding her to carry her reforms through. The court of inquiry called her 'a restless female always on the move'.

The Spanish clergy observed the activities of the mystically inclined religious with some mistrust, suspecting their mysticism of being a new form of Protestantism. The *Alumbrados*, the 'illuminati' who preached in many parts of Spain and claimed to have direct contact with God, were as a body suspect of heresy.

Philip stopped the Inquisition's case against Teresa. He appreciated that the nun's reforming activities had nothing whatever to do with heresy but sprang from a real desire for a renewal of religious life.

Teresa used to speak of 'our holy King Philip' and she understood him better than any of her contemporaries. And Philip gave Teresa's work his support, in fact the great interest of her life was shared by him: San Lorenzo de El Escorial was mainly a monastic foundation.

The king and the mystic had the same cause at heart—the defence of the Catholic Faith and the purging of its external forms. Philip was able to arrest the spread of Protestantism in Flanders and to preserve Spain intact as a true hearth of the Catholic spirit. Meanwhile his missionaries were spreading the Old Faith in the new Indies.

Philip was a scrupulous ruler. He was also a lover of books and pictures, a connoisseur and collector of beautiful things and a patron of scholarship and the arts. The monastery of San Lorenzo de El Escorial was to be a centre of culture with its own art collection, 'a well-head of all forms of learning', as he called it.

The Escorial library bears witness to his desire to endow religion with the whole range of contemporary scholarship: the Escorial schools were to be capable of providing material for a 'Summa', an all-inclusive commentary on modern scholarship, like St Thomas of Aquinas' schools at just such another turning-point in history.

Between the bookcases there hangs a life-size portrait of Philip II by Pantoja de la Cruz: Philip at the age of about seventy-one. He stands in his black widower's clothes with a small white ruff framing his pale face, and the Order of the Golden Fleece gleams faintly on his chest.

His gaze betrays acquaintance with suffering and is very still. A deep careworn furrow divides his brows, a painful line runs from his nostrils to the corners of his lips. It is a face revealing depths of abnegation and disillusionment, together with a beauty and pride born of infinite patience. St Teresa springs to one's mind, 'praying often for a great lord of this world who was deserving of pity because of all the distressing things he had to endure.'

Opposite the painting of Philip II hangs a portrait of Charles V, a copy of a lost Titian, representing the Emperor at the age of forty-nine, in a black coat-of-mail adorned with gold. His plumed helmet lies on a chest to one side, as though he had discarded it as superfluous. His face is pale and he seems bowed down by the weight of his armour, bent under the burden of sovereignty. But an intensity of will-power is conveyed even through the inanimate medium of the copy; indeed, it was Charles V who began the fight for the Catholic tradition: self-constituted champion of the Old Faith, he, first and foremost, made a stand for the basic religious values of Europe. 'Much has to be preserved. And not least, loyalty.'

SIGUENZA: CHARLES V AT YUSTE

Ever since the Order of the Hieronymites, to whom the monastery was originally entrusted, died out, the reading-room of the Escorial library has been run by Augustinian monks. I asked for the history of the original Order, written by Fray Joseph de Siguenza for Philip II. A monk in a black cowl handed me a large volume bound in pigskin: *Historia de la Orden de San Geronimo*.

I could have wished to put it all on record: the remote, quiet atmosphere of the monastery reading-room, the old book so heavy in my hands, the great brown letters on the yellowed pages, the dignity and solemnity of the Spanish words—those round rich sounds of a more animated Latin. As I turned the stiff leaves my eye fell on the name 'Carlos

Quinto'. I read on. 'After the Emperor Charles V had vanquished his opponents, the enemies of Christ, the rebels against his Church and the foes of his lands and his empire, there only remained for him to conquer himself, and this victory was very much greater than all the others.

'The idea came to him in Brussels where he was suffering from an attack of gout in feet and hands—to give up reigning and go to Spain. To renounce the majesty of the world. He had all the accredited authorities of Brabant and Flanders assembled. (The abdication took place on October 25th in the year 1555, on a Friday at three o'clock in the afternoon.) The Emperor took ship with his two sisters, Dona Leonora, Queen of France, and Dona Maria, Queen of Hungary, and came ashore in the harbour of Laredo.... The road was bad, he had to be carried on a chair over numerous passes. His Majesty said, I shall travel no other way in my life but the way of death: and it is not too much that a place as good and wholesome as Yuste cost such a price to reach.

'Imperator Charles V entered the monastery of Yuste to end his days in the practice of holiness.

'... In came the Emperor, carried by hand. They set him down on a chair. The community issued in procession to receive him. At the church door the Brothers began to intone the *Te Deum*—set to fine music, with the organ playing.... The church was full of lights and decorated as well as the community could manage it.... Then came the Brothers to kiss the Emperor's hands. Here his serving people shed many tears, breaking out into sobs with cries of anguish and tenderness—some, because they were to leave him; others, because they remembered the handsome endowments, the negotiations and victories in which they had seen this great prince engaged, now to see him surrounded by poor Brothers whom he embraced and welcomed as his equals. They uttered words of great love and much feeling and praised God on seeing so holy and humble a demeanour.... Then he had alms distributed to the villages of the neighbourhood, as far off as the town of Plasencia. The place called Quacos, the one nearest the monastery, obtained the largest share of these favours as lying nearest to the source. Some of the people of this village are people without regard—ungrateful, selfish, unmannerly and malicious. Later on they achieved something that the brave and strong foes of the Emperor never did: they exhausted his patience and forbearance: so great was their lack of due regard.'

Then Padre Siguenza describes the Emperor's living-quarters next the church, where he could look down upon the high altar from his bedroom.

'On the west side the windows looked over the garden which was adorned with many flowers, an abundance of orange and lemon trees and cedars and a beautifully wrought fountain. To the east there was another garden; it too was full of a great variety of flowers and plants of distant provenance, all well tended. The Emperor's rooms were surrounded by orange and lemon trees that grew up to the windows, very pleasant with their scent, their colouring and their green leafage. This was the cell of that great monarch—somewhat roomy for a monk, but narrow for one who comprised so much in himself. . . .

'The Emperor punctually and faithfully observed the daily ritual and humbled himself as though he were a monk and not the Emperor. On the days he received Holy Communion he was not content with his Low Mass, but he attended High Mass too. Vespers he usually heard from his window on to the high altar.

'These rules were inherited by his son Philip.

'Corpus Christi was observed with great solemnity, the Emperor's joy was evident and the country people came from far and wide to celebrate the feast with their holy Emperor. . . .

'On Good Friday he washed the feet of twelve paupers; he gave rich alms. . . .

'Sometimes a boy (later Don Juan of Austria) paid him a visit and the Emperor's eyes rested on him at length.

'His health improved on account of the equable climate, the good air and the fresh spring water. The Emperor experienced a new sense of well-being. He said he felt "cheered and rested". "Now that I am cheerful and contented," he said to his father confessor, "I should like to assist at a requiem ceremony on behalf of my dead parents, in order to find myself anew in them now God is giving me good health." Then he begged his confessor to let him take part in his own funeral service. The performance of this ceremony brought forth from all who were present as much sighing and grief as though he had really died; for often the imagination of an evil is worse than the occurrence of it. After the Mass he handed the priest the lighted candle he held as though he were yielding his soul to God, for in olden times this was the usual symbolic act on such an occasion.

'After the ceremony he told his confessor he was very happy and felt great consolation in his soul which seemed to be full to overflowing—a fulness he felt in his body even.

'On the same day, which he spent in lengthy converse with his confessor, he had the Empress's portrait brought him and gazed at it a while. Later he asked for the painting of "The Prayer on the Mount of Olives". After contemplating it for some time he said, "Bring me the picture of the Last Judgement". Before this picture his meditation lasted even longer—so long that his physician, Mathys, told him he should not continue, it did no good to put such strain on his strength. The Emperor turned to his doctor trembling all over and said, "*Malo me siento*"—"I feel unwell."

'That was on the last day of August, at four in the afternoon.' Siguenza then describes 'the Emperor's holy death, which took place on September 21st 1558, at Yuste, after he had lived there two years and fifteen days, withdrawn from the world and all earthly affairs, wholly taken up with the salvation of his soul—a happy space of time in that monarch's life and its highest peak.'

In the following pages Fray Joseph tells of the 'purity and clarity' of his spirit, 'in all he did taking counsel with God in direct prayer'. He terms him 'a prince of great patience'. Repeatedly he praises the 'candid mind of the Emperor, from whose body there sprang that flower which to all nations, Latin, Greek or Hebrew, is symbol of Hope; and all those nations look to him'.

The word Caesar, which Fray Joseph uses as synonymous with Emperor, in Charles V's day still had something of the world-wide, unique resonance that it had possessed in the time of the Roman Empire. It was a mighty word, alive in all its implications in the European mind. There were, of course, a number of monarchs, but only one Emperor. He alone was Caesar—the personification of that supreme system of justice which had once held the Roman Empire together and now gave moral consistency to the loose structure of the European states.

. . . that is why a shudder ran through the western world when its lord and master laid aside such great sovereignty. Charles V's abdication put in question the whole Renaissance with its new conception of life. The news rang out like a warning cry, a challenge to consciences—a call from beyond: *My kingdom is not of this world.*

Spain understood. For Charles, here in southern Europe was a land where the soul of man could feel at home. 'Give up governance and go to Spain': his decision was as natural as a flower's turning to the sun. He went to Spain as a creature goes to its natural habitat. 'Every creature is happy in the place in which it belongs', said Master Eckhart. In remote Yuste the Emperor found what he had longed for throughout his fighting days: purity and clarity and peace of mind. The clear light, the wide skies of Estremadura were nourishment to his soul—he was now at home.

PANTHEON

'The Kings' Pantheon' of the Escorial is reminiscent of the tomb-chambers of the Egyptian Pharaohs: everything in it symbolic of duration—black and dark-green jasper, bronze and iron, telling of earthly durability.

But the forest solitude Charles V elected for his last refuge is far away. The granite, marble and lead of his tomb cut him off sharply from all contact with Mother Earth—jealously bent, it seems, on safeguarding him from those final nuptials of our terrestrial existence.

But perhaps it is we living who alone see things as separate from one another; for the dead, maybe, all is unity and happiness.

Next to the Kings' Pantheon are the tombs of the royal family. Before the tombstone of Don Juan of Austria I meditated on the fate of this natural son of Charles V, who completed his father's work as though pre-destined to it in his decisive victory over the Osmanic fleet on 7th October 1571, delivering Italy from the menace of a Turkish invasion.

When news of the Christian fleet's triumph reached Pope Pius V, he exclaimed, 'There was a man sent from God whose name was John . . .', and Cervantes, who fought in the Spanish ranks at Lepanto, named this sea-battle 'the most glorious event that the present and the past ever saw or ever will see'.

The victory of Lepanto was a real turning-point in history, from that day on the great tidal wave which Mohammed had set in motion re-ceded; for centuries it had required unflagging vigilance on the part of the defenders of Christendom to keep it at bay. But now new storms broke out within Europe itself, storms that crushed Philip II's Invincible Armada and overthrew the supremacy of the world of the Old Faith.

Don Juan would doubtless have commanded the Spanish fleet more efficiently, but when Philip began to equip the Armada Don Juan was no longer among the living.

In 1575 Philip II appointed his half-brother Regent of Flanders, which was then in revolt. For two years Don Juan conducted a cold war there and the antagonism grew steadily worse. By the end of 1577 military action was inevitable. He built up his army with the assistance of the Pope and the Catholic Guises. And as at Lepanto, he held up a Cross in front of his troops and on his banners were the words, *In hoc signo vici Turcos, in hoc vincam hereticos.*

Don Juan and his loyal soldiers fought against forces far superior to his own, to the point of complete exhaustion. In July 1578, when he was entrenched in Bouges, awaiting reinforcements from the Catholic lands of Germany, a typhoid epidemic broke out, and like his namesake and contemporary, Juan de Dios, Don Juan spent himself in succouring the sick and dying. As he wrote to Philip, 'I assure Your Majesty there is work enough here to undermine any man's natural constitution and do every life to death'.

Whilst looking after his men he succumbed to a heavy fever. In delirium he was borne out of his damp tent and placed in a wooden shed where at least he was secure from the mud and moisture caused by the autumn rains. A field-altar was erected by his bedside so that he could lie and follow Holy Mass. He was anointed, and divided his possessions among his faithful followers. To his confessor he said he had never possessed a handful of earth of his own.

On 10th October 1578, Don Juan died the Christian death of a Habsburg. His last wish was to be buried in the Escorial beside his father.

El Greco: San Mauricio

In the sacristy of the Escorial hangs Greco's great painting of 'San Mauricio'.

It is a wonderful picture in the way it conveys harmony of spirit through gestures.

The subject represents that moment in the legend of the Thebaic Legion when the Christian group refused to worship the heathen gods. The Emperor commanded that they be decimated—in the background to one side we see the execution of the Christian legionaries.

In the centre of the picture stands the Roman ambassador with his back turned, commanding Mauritius to submit. But Mauritius has no ear for the voice of the world now, and he and his companions appear to be overhearing the hymns of the angels rejoicing above them in heaven. These doomed men appear so gentle and resigned. To love, all is easy. Where love reigns, all is harmony. Observe how those graceful expressive hands, those shapely limbs, the clothing and clouds, are lifted on the breath of divine affluence, forming but a single movement of issue into light. The light that shines above the heads of the men radiates from their faces too, as though the state of blessedness was already present within them. Their determination to lose their life rather than deny their faith has won them true life.

Such concord of faith and being, will and feeling, sheds a glory of its own on our discordant human condition.

'They refuse to worship the heathen gods . . .'—their decision is self-evident for their own God is alive within them. They are happy because the meaning of it all is unmistakably clear.

. . . for in the decisive hour even the weak and doubting will see what really matters and say with the others, Yes, I stand firm, this is my faith, here art thou, my God. . . .

The painting owes its existence to Philip II, who had ordered it for one of the basilica chapels, but he did not care for it and had another picture hung in the church instead. (It is curious that Philip should have turned down a work that was so much after his own heart, but it is not always true that 'like calls to like'.) Greco was not appointed royal court painter, and he remained in Toledo where a few years later he painted his master-piece, 'The Burial of the Count of Orgaz'.

El Greco: 'Philip II's Dream'

We do not know whether Greco's other picture in the Escorial sacristy pleased the king any better. It is 'Philip II's Dream'. Greco is said to have painted it at the same time as the 'San Mauricio', that is, in 1579; another view is that he did it between 1594 and 1604, but it does seem to belong to the same period as the 'San Mauricio', for it glows with the same sense of confidence and does not betray that unsatisfied striving for possession of his vision that characterizes his later pictures. 'Philip II's Dream' is a small and curiously tender work, despite the fact that purgatorial fires to one side wreak punishment on the sinners they engulf. The picture depicts the bliss of the elect and the tortures of the damned, but the heaven of the blessed is of such splendour that its radiance overlays the pangs of the underworld.

For sheer passionate religious feeling, this surpasses even a St Ignatius, for the assurance of salvation is deeper here: in fact it is early Christian in conception.

Philip kneels in his simple black dress among the enraptured clergy and faithful, as still as a mediaeval figure in his humble absorption in God, though the Counter-Reformation seethes in all its intensity around him— a solitary solemn figure reminiscent of Gothic art, or of the Icon, as though the schism that separated Eastern Orthodoxy from Rome had healed; for a basic unity is present here in the soul of a man humbly contemplating its God.

Philip's composed attitude is the expression of a will relaxed, confidently resting in pure Being and filled with a presentiment of the Four Last Things.

This is the most authentic picture of the Catholic King, who remained unerringly at home in the old calm depths of the Faith and stood in no need of the rousing emotions of his time.

The symmetry, the peace of soul that Greco managed to express in this kneeling form, make it the most byzantine thing that he ever painted: its true source of inspiration lies not in Hieronymus Bosch's system of ideas, but in the traditional gold ground that stood for transfiguration.

SILLA DE FELIPE SEGUNDO

Today I walked to the *Silla de Felipe Segundo*, 'the seat of Philip II', a hill of which legend relates that the king often had himself borne to the summit in order to see from the top of it how the building of the Escorial was progressing.

The road to this hilltop leads through a landscape of great antiquity. Large stones lie scattered all around as though the Flood had swept them here to await the Day of Judgement. Some are piled high to form a cliff standing lofty and airy before the brown hills called *Los Eremitanos*, rising to their solitary heights sheer from the very plain itself, bare of vegetation and very solemn and severe in their naked state. They are long in shape and rounded at the end; millions of years have left their mark, they are older than the later Alpine ranges. Here they stand, in utter composure, like creatures that have matured and learnt to keep silence over the tribulations to which they owe their integrity.

So it is probable that from this prominence Philip watched the progress of the building that meant so much to him. And he may well have come to enjoy the view.

From 'Philip II's Seat' the Escorial appears independent and self-contained, yet obedient to the higher authority of the mountains. Clear as a well-considered thought, the structure lies in the heart of the landscape, a focus determining the order and placing of the things around it. The front of it shines out yellow in the evening light, as does the earth itself; the blue-green roof-slates reflecting the colouring of the cliffs behind.

In the distance the snow-covered range of the Guadarrama fades away to the south like a fugue emerging into the basic harmonies of its theme.

The theme is Castile, that high plateau which raises the heart nearer to God.

The Escorial reposes on the plain like an ark, and an ark it is, where in a stormy century a devout spirit rescued from annihilation all that needed to be rescued. Here it is, safe and sound.

FAREWELL

I lived for a fortnight in the shadow of the royal monastery of San Lorenzo de El Escorial, held in the spell of the personality of its founder. But my reading in the monastery library led me from Philip II to Charles V—a step back in time, but a step from narrow passes into wide fields; a step from the close strictures of the post-Tridentine world into the hopes, though unfulfilled, of the Reformation period.

The Escorial as it stands here is like a deliberate statement of fact, an expression of certitude postulated once for all. It is rigid and exclusive.

The Escorial—seen from the heights in the pale blue light of morning, bedded among green firs.

The Escorial—under the noon sun, hard, in sharply contrasted light and shade.

The Escorial—in the afternoon, granite, hewn out of the granite of the rocks.

The Escorial—at night by starlight, under the great, close, gleaming stars of the Spanish sky—dark and unyielding, guarding the great conception of its creator.

But in the morning the distant horizon of Castile speaks of a candour still beyond our reach.

Impediments of spirit remain, to be encountered and to be dealt with, if all that is still captive in structure and stone is to find release.

San Lorenzo de El Escorial is a challenge, a charge, a seed that fain would flower and issue in life and wind, space and light—a breath of life for our times too.

II

MADRID

Let us depart from here and fly
to our Father's wonderful land!

Plotinus, Enneades, I, Book VI

Titian: *Charles V at the Battle of Mühlberg*

Madrid means, to me, the Prado, a picture-gallery with the intimate atmosphere of a private collection where impeccable taste has accepted only the best works obtainable. And indeed a personal approach was the decisive factor here. The paintings of the Prado were formerly the property of the Spanish kings, and Charles V's liking for Titian was the basis of this collection of masterpieces, with valuable additions from Charles' great-grandson, Philip IV.

It was this Philip who commissioned Velázquez to purchase in Italy the finest works he could discover. So it is to Velázquez that we owe many of the pictures that hang in the Prado to this day. In 1681 the Prior of San Lorenzo de El Escorial wrote: 'It is thanks to Velázquez that the royal palace has become one of the greatest royal palaces of the world in regard to its collection of paintings.'

This time I hurried through the galleries with only a passing greeting for familiar pictures—Velázquez' 'Infanta Margarita', Greco's 'Nobleman with his hand on his chest'—a glance of recognition, as between old friends. But they did not respond, time had altered them, increasing their depth, and they were silent, full of mystery like people one does not know, like new lands waiting to be explored.

With the feeling of having come here on pilgrimage, I sank into one of the plush seats, absorbed in Titian's great painting of 'Charles V at the Battle of Mühlberg'.

A wonderful stillness and a remarkable twilight effect are the dominant notes of this picture—a twilight as between two epochs, two different moments in spiritual life. The Emperor is on horseback, fully armed, alone in the evening landscape. So it was he rode ahead of his troops during battle, firing them by his example: it was his own battle, the fight against the foes of the Faith who had disdained his efforts to reach an understanding, so that he had to combat them in person, lance in hand.

The noise of battle died away, victory was his and the victor felt himself secure in the hands of God.

It is this repose in a higher will than his own that lends this picture its peculiar attraction: rider and horse, tree and shrub appear as though under the spell of higher powers. Evening wind and falling light seem to linger: the goal is reached and a lifetime has come to fulfilment, reason enough for time to pause and for the Emperor to hold his reins so lightly, his lance so effortlessly; the trance-like figure merges into its surroundings.

The Angel of Providence guided the Emperor's lance to victory, but there remained one foe . . . and in his very act of thanksgiving he already passes beyond the sphere of achievement and his mind turns to questions of another order and to a new dawn, promising happiness.

In the evening light of Mühlberg, Yuste and all it was to mean in the way of renunciation are already faintly apparent. As Fray Joseph de Siguenza put it: 'Now that the Emperor Charles V had conquered all his adversaries, the foes of Christ and of his Church, there still remained the conquest of himself. . . .'

Titian was aged seventy when he painted this picture. To please the Emperor, for they were old friends, he came to Augsburg to do it from April to September 1548. It is a work in which the wisdom of his old age and the perfect craftsmanship of his latter years perfectly match the Emperor's own spiritual maturity. With all the intuitive insight of an understanding friend he recorded that moment between two worlds when the natural man ceded to the spiritual man; hence the picture's awe-inspiring twilight, for one light is going out, but a new awareness is dawning: the first Adam was made a living soul; the last Adam was a life-conferring spirit.

'We shall not all sleep, but we shall all be changed.'

Titian's 'La Gloria'

Opposite 'Charles V at the Battle of Mühlberg' hangs Titian's great picture of 'La Gloria', also called 'The Last Judgement', which he painted for Charles V in 1554. It accompanied the Emperor to Yuste. Indeed it was on this picture he was gazing in such absorption, that afternoon before his last illness, when his doctor begged him 'not to subject his mind to such a strain', and he trembled and said, 'I feel unwell'.

It is a representation of the Last Judgement with the triumphant resurrection of the Dead, the Holy Spirit soaring radiantly above the Souls of the Just. At the feet of the exalted Judge kneels Charles in a white tunic, raising folded hands in supplication, with the imperial crown he renounced on a cloud beside him; close by, in a similar attitude, is his spouse Isabella, both with attendant angels; behind them are their son, Philip, and the two Infantas. (Of this group Philip is the only one not facing towards God the Father, not raising his eyes, as though centred not on God but on himself, like a Lucifer-type of being, that is, a child of modern, individualistic, self-determining times. . . .)

Titian included himself in the picture as an old man, on one side, hoping that he, too, might be among the Blessed.

Titian: The Empress

In this same gallery hangs the portrait of the Empress Isabella, Charles V's wife. This picture went to Yuste too, and he gazed on it on that fateful afternoon.

It shows the Empress in all her youth and beauty, her fair hair combed back and held with strings of pearls, her pale face cool and proud, her attitude reserved and a little forbidding. Her blue-green eyes look steadily into the distance, but she has full lips. Charles V loved his wife tenderly. 'My dearest beloved wife,' he wrote at the beginning of the Tunis campaign, '. . . I kiss this sheet of paper with the same tenderness and the same warmth that I would kiss your lips, were I with you. . . .' Two months later he received Isabella's reply: 'Isabella . . . who has the happiness to be the servant and wedded wife of so magnanimous a prince, prays he may have health and length of life, for the well-being of Christendom and for a happy homecoming into her arms. . . .'

'The Emperor loved his wife and held her in high honour, and she loved him more than her life,' wrote Santa Cruz the chronicler, 'and she always shed many tears when she thought of the long time of separation.'

Wars and affairs of state often parted them for years on end. But distance could not divide them in spirit, for Charles and Isabella were united by that *amor amicitiae* over which time and distance are powerless, for it has anchorage beyond their reach.

While the Emperor was busy at the wars, Isabella ruled in Spain in his stead and faithfully reported to him all that went on in the land. But bent over a piece of fine needlework intended for the Chapel of the Redeemer in Jerusalem, she awaited her husband's return from battles in distant lands like the wives of crusaders of old, and watched over the play of her children, Philip and Maria—ever plying her needle and waiting, waiting....

Titian: The Bologna Portrait of the Emperor

In the same gallery there hangs another portrait of Charles V, in the white gold-stitched Renaissance state-dress in which he was crowned King of Lombardy at Bologna, on 22nd February 1530.

Here the Emperor is young-looking, he is the fortunate prince in whose cradle good fairies laid all earthly power. A large she-dog nestles up to her master affectionately, while he gazes reflectively into the distance.

Here he is 'the monarch of the earth', *Imperator Caesar Carolus V, Hispaniorum Rex, semper augustus, . . .* yet one is somehow aware of the hesitant start he made, and of that lethargy the young duke's contemporaries called *abulia*.

Emperor Maximilian, who was always in good spirits, was disappointed to find his grandson so quiet and apathetic. He said Charles was 'as imperturbable as an idol'. He was brought up an orphan and as a child was very quiet and reserved. The doctors called him *tendre et délicat* and did not expect him to live beyond adolescence. Pedro Martyr the chronicler wrote of him, 'Charles is sixteen years of age but he has the solemnity of an old man'. Contarini, the Venetian ambassador, reported, 'his temperament is mixed with sanguine traits but he is by nature melancholy'. All who saw the slender boy with his long straight legs praised the natural dignity and majesty of his bearing.

At fourteen, Charles was declared by Emperor Maximilian to be of age, but he still had many years to go before he attained the coming-of-age of his will-power.

Dante has it that young people of high character suffer from a sense of personal inadequacy on first surmising what perfection may mean: life's great ideals overwhelm them with *stupor* on first acquaintance and they are dazed. But with the sense of wonder there is born in them a reverence for exalted things and an urge to know them better. Here we owe 'faith and obedience', said Dante, and he esteemed youth's surrender to what it recognized to be worth while a nobler trait of character than self-willed precocity.

This idealistic trait accounts for Charles' attitude to his chancellor, the Lord of Chièvres: all observers at the Brussels court noted that Chièvres 'dominated' Charles. His attachment to his counsellor was, however, the devotion of a pupil to his revered master. Years after Chièvres' death Charles told Contarini he had given Chièvres his entire confidence because he recognized that he was 'able'. Charles, who served faithfully in his youth, when he grew up required faithfulness and obedience of others.

Titian painted the portrait of the Emperor with his dog at Bologna, between December 1532 and the end of February 1533. When Charles came to Bologna in the autumn of 1532, Titian was presented to him as 'the best painter alive today', and the portrait was begun soon after. Mutual esteem was to unite Emperor and artist from then on. When he returned to Barcelona the Emperor raised Titian to the knighthood and granted him an annuity (which was, however, very irregularly paid). To the courtiers, envious of the honours conferred on the painter, he replied: 'There are many princes on earth, but there is only one Titian,' and a well-known legend recounts how he bent down and picked up a paint-brush Titian had dropped, with the words: 'Titian is worthy of being waited upon by the Emperor'. 'The art of painting,' said Charles on one occasion, 'must be reckoned above all learning and all the arts, it must be given the palm,' and he himself gave Titian the palm among all the artists of his period.

In December 1532 Charles had the Diet of Augsburg behind him; he had tried to solve the religious problem by personal intervention; on 21st September 1532 he entered Vienna, then menaced by the Turks, and his presence had induced the great Sultan Suleiman to withdraw—the task of defending Christendom had come very near him; now, at Bologna, he stood still for a moment before taking the next step—the right step. . . .

And that is how Titian saw him: as one waiting; diffident about going forward before the direction was plain, hesitating to break the magic circle in which he stood.

I let my eyes roam from one to the other—the Bologna portrait and the painting of Charles at the battle of Mühlberg. What a tremendous evolution they testify to! So many semi-dormant and half-hearted traits in the earlier work are declared and assured in the equestrian picture; at Mühlberg the Emperor's features were drawn taut, a sign that achievement was costly. Indeed it was his very life that was at stake, for he dedicated himself unreservedly to the task which he recognized as his mission.

But a vocation is a fulfilment, too. Titian's art also reached the heights of fulfilment here. That is why the contemplation of those two pictures is by right a form of mystical experience.

It was quiet in the Titian gallery at the Prado. I found myself thinking of St Teresa's 'seventh chamber of the inner castle', 'in which all is ac-complished in an utter quietness resembling the building of Solomon's Temple where no noise was heard: so it is in this seventh chamber, where God and the soul take pleasure in one another in deep silence'.

Titian: Philip II

In the Titian Gallery there is also the portrait of Philip II at the age of twenty-three, in a short, gold-ornamented coat-of-mail, his shapely legs in ivory-white stockings. Like a shadowy flower his figure shines out upon the nearly black background, and the eyes of the young prince are dark too: he is a widower.

This full-length portrait of Philip was painted at the beginning of 1551, when he was on his German tour of introduction and stayed with his father in Augsburg. Two years later the picture was sent to England to woo Queen Mary Tudor. It was a successful wooing. Mary, at thirty-seven years of age, fell in love with Philip's portrait and opposed the wishes of parliament which wanted her to marry a fellow countryman. In spite of all, Mary's marriage to Philip was fixed for July of the year 1554.

The Spanish noblemen who accompanied Philip on his bridal visit had no illusions as to the reception that awaited them in England. They advised Philip to wear a steel shirt under his doublet all the time. But from the moment Philip met the Queen in Winchester, he won the favour of the English court.

At their first meeting Philip kissed Mary on the mouth, and the bridal pair chatted the whole evening in French (which Philip knew only imperfectly), while Philip's retinue conversed in Spanish with the Queen's ladies-in-waiting, who, understanding no word of Spanish, were but the more susceptible to the demeanour and voices of the Spaniards. Mary taught her bridegroom-to-be to say 'good night', and as Philip took his leave of the court, the last trace of prejudice vanished—it is always a heart-warming occasion when a foreign visitor takes the trouble to pronounce a word or two in the native tongue, though it fall from his lips as awkwardly as the stammering of a child.

The wedding took place next day, on 25th July 1554, in Winchester Cathedral.

Antonio Moro: Mary Tudor, Queen of England

In another room at the Prado there hangs the portrait of Mary Tudor painted for Prince Philip by Antonio Moro. It gives an impression of extreme plainness. We see a woman no longer young, dressed in a closely fitting sixteenth-century dress, sitting stiffly on her chair and holding a rose as though it were a sceptre. With its broad brow and slightly slanting eyes (in shape and expression reminiscent of her grandmother, Isabella the Catholic), her face reveals an indomitable will and absolute integrity, her thin lips lit with a shy, half-expectant smile.

Poor Mary! She fell desperately in love with her husband, eleven years her junior. (All four of Philip's wives loved him to the last; three died in

24

the effort of presenting him with longed-for progeny, and Mary was consumed with distress at her barrenness. This devotion of the women with whom Philip was intimately connected should be enough to dispel the legend that he had a cold, gloomy disposition.)

In spring 1555 Mary had hopes, but they were quickly dispelled, it was a mistake. At the end of August 1555 Philip was summoned to Brussels where his father was waiting to hand the reins of government over to him. Mary accompanied her husband as far as Dover. On bidding farewell she cried her eyes out and was not to be drawn away from the window where she watched the departing ship bearing Philip to the Netherlands.

In March 1557 Philip came back to England once more and spent a few months with his wife. But the marriage remained childless. Mary's tears over her barrenness were likewise tears at the miscarriage of her intention to bring back the English Protestants to the Catholic Faith.

Mary's endeavours to restore unity of faith in England broke on the antagonism of the reformed element. Their resistance only increased Mary's and Philip's zeal: in January 1555 the royal couple promulgated a law ordaining death by burning for those who persisted in the reformed faith. Soon after, Cranmer and many other reformers were burned alive on account of their 'persistence in heresy'.

From Brussels, Charles V saw with increasing anxiety how Mary's harshness imperilled the Catholic cause in England: for the return of England to the Catholic communion was the great plan that Philip's marriage with Mary was to bring to fulfilment. Only with Rome as its centre of gravity was the island to be retained in the European orbit. Were England to become irretrievably separated from Rome, then centrifugal forces would draw her away into the ocean, to become an *alter orbis*, increasingly distant and foreign. . . . The attempt to re-convert England came to an end after three years only, when Mary died. Her half-sister, Elizabeth, mounted the throne of England and the suppression of the Catholic faith was completed when the break with Rome became absolute.

IN THE VELÁZQUEZ GALLERY

What would Velázquez have become, had he not been made court painter? Ortega y Gasset raised the question and one remembers it in the

Velázquez Gallery. He said: 'It would have been rather like Goethe without Weimar'.

But that distinction of his, that unapproachability and sense of quality we connect with the name of Velázquez, are not dependent on the courtly setting of his pictures nor on the stiff costumes of his aristocratic models, they are due to the artist's own remoteness from his subject. In Velázquez' pictures the subject is remarkably indifferent: whether it is a princess, a dwarf or a court fool, his economical brush-stroke incorporates it into his conception of his picture.

Take his great painting of 'The Surrender of Breda', also called 'The Lances'.

The theme is treated traditionally. But if we stop to consider it, the patent content dims and we are left with a scaffolding of colour-tones and lines as significant in structure as an abstract painting.

It represents an early phase in the Thirty Years War, one of the last acts in the Spanish struggle to retain a hold on the Netherlands. Archduke Albrecht, Viceroy of the Netherlands and husband of Philip II's favourite daughter, Isabella Clara Eugenia, died in Flanders in July 1621, thus putting an end to the truce with the northern Protestant provinces of Holland, which then rebelled against Spanish rule. The young king, Philip IV, charged his General Spinola with the task of recovering North Brabant. Spinola laid siege to the fortress of Breda, 'the bulwark of Flanders', which yielded only after a long and stubborn resistance, and accorded very honourable terms of surrender to the aged governor, Justin of Nassau: his troops were to withdraw 'as beseems brave warriors, fully armed, colours flying and drums beating, equipped and mounted as though riding into battle'.

In the centre of the picture we see the two figures of the conqueror and conquered. Justin of Nassau is handing Spinola the keys of the fortress with a look of trusting, grateful devotion, and Spinola bows to him and lays a hand on his shoulder with warm-hearted generosity.

The upright lances of the Spaniards stand out sharply to the right. The sky is clearing and here and there a blue patch breaks through the racing clouds. It is a sky after storm, full of hope for peaceful days to come.

A sense of solemnity fitting to the occasion fills the picture; neighbourly love is present in the way the victorious warrior embraces his vanquished foe, paying respect to his human dignity and thus restoring a balance that was lost. Thanks to this generous gesture, a fresh start can be made in establishing peace and concord.

A mysterious rhythm enfolds the two groups, knitting them together: the Flemish backs balance the Spanish front; the head of Spinola's mount, turned towards the Spanish lines, is matched by a Flemish horse looking our way. And at the heart of it all our gaze discovers a clear path through into light and distance, beyond the events of the moment. In colouring, too, the picture is conducive to harmony and concord. The tones are few in number and form a closing chord: bluish green, golden brown, grey and rose are set down in simple beauty, as though all would be simple and well on earth if only good-will prevailed, and kindness, and courtesy.

Philip IV

Velázquez painted Philip IV at different stages, but we always find the same smooth, impassive face, unfurrowed by fate. But after the death of Balthasar Charles, his son and heir, his expression of melancholy grew more marked.

This melancholy was inherited from his ancestress Joanna, and in the last members of the Spanish line of Habsburgs it acted as a deterrent to any capacity to make decisions. Philip IV watched his kingdom perish with composed features—a kingdom which Philip II had defended at great cost.

But why hold fast to things that would rather go their own way? It was lands disinclined for Spanish unity that slipped from Philip IV's loose grasp. In 1648 he recognized the independence of the Netherlands; and Portugal, which Philip II acquired in 1580 as an heirloom from his mother, rose against Spanish rule too, and achieved its independence in 1668 with the help of English troops under a French general.

It was, moreover, in this period of political decline that occurred the golden age of Spanish art, the *Siglo de Oro*.

During the reign of Philip III, Cervantes wrote his *Don Quixote*; under Philip IV, Calderón, Lope de Vega, Molina, Quevedo and Góngora were all at work, artists who gathered up the very quintessence of the Christian and chivalric ideal of Spain, so soon to stand alone and poor in the world, a strangeling among nations that had turned away from the basic principles once common to all Europe.

Philip IV met the news of the revolt and loss of his provinces with sheer indifference, he was far more interested in what his artists and poets were doing. . . .

A Habsburg child in a stiff Spanish court dress, holding her rose and lace handkerchief as lightly as Habsburg held his dwindling sovereignty—a child whose fair hair gleamed in the darkness of the Alcázar like a reflection of Austrian springtimes—a pale child, of an ageing lineage the final blossoming.

The Infanta Margarita was the first child of Philip IV's second marriage which he contracted in 1648 with his niece, Maria Anna of Austria, thirty years younger than he, in order to provide Spain with an heir to the throne. His son by his first marriage, Balthasar Charles, had died in 1645. And the Infanta Margarita's first brother, the Infant Philip Prosper, died in childhood, too; but five days after his death the Queen gave birth to a second son, Don Carlos, who acceded to the Spanish throne as Charles II, 'the Bewitched', whom the people believed to be possessed by evil spirits. That was the end of the House of Habsburg in Spain. The portrait of the Infanta Margarita is deemed to be the last picture Velázquez painted and is said to have been completed by his pupil, Mazo. But the treatment of the silvery-grey silk dress is unmistakably by the hand of the master, an example of how in the last decades of his life he let the representation of things dissolve into elements of colour.

Consider the Infanta's dress closely, and we observe a confusion of grey, white and reddish flakes, but if we recede a step or two, order appears and a shape emerges. How is it possible, we exclaim, and proceed to a still closer inspection of the canvas, like a scientist bent over his microscope to discover the secret of life, who sees, instead of a unit, mere dancing cells. Thus Velázquez' canvas quivers in the rendering of an impression in terms of light-waves. We can appreciate how this road leads on to French painting in the nineteenth century.

IN THE MILITARY MUSEUM

A visit to this museum reawakens an awareness of Spain's great tradition which is so integral a part of the European heritage. Old flags and standards, weapons and trophies of victorious campaigns, make us reflect how today mechanical warfare can destroy in a few seconds all that a thousand years defended with streams of blood, over and over again.

Here are crusaders' coats-of-mail with the red dagger-cross, the cross of Santiago, patron and guardian of Spain. The old flags are faded and tattered. Here is the double-headed eagle, honoured and revered, here is the tent Charles V used on his campaigns, here is the armour he wore. . . .

There is something indescribably elegant about Charles V's armour: the part that covered his heart is rounded as though that valorous man had bent the steel with his breathing. The black cuirass adorned with gold is the very one he had on at Mühlberg, the one in Titian's portrait of him. It looks like a shell, a sea-shell distantly chanting of another life and other times.

On the walls hang the pictures of the kings of Spain, beginning with the Goths: Athaulfo, first king of Spain.

It was the Visigoths who in Spain linked kingship and justice together. *Rex eris, si recta facis: si autem non facis, non eris* are the words with which they were consecrated.

Under the Visigoth kings, who learnt from the Roman Catholic clergy the principles that were to determine their conduct, the Christian faith became the keynote of Spanish life.

Spain is completely herself only when she follows this guiding principle. Then she is truly European.

It is all very interesting—banners and swords and lances once used to defend men's lives—but they make an odd impression, like the weak points of something once strong.

Is it conceivably possible today to defend the old heritage sword in hand?

Is a nation free today in any sense, if it has not at its disposal an arsenal of technical weapons? Surely the very words 'freedom' and 'independence' are losing their old meaning, for there is not a single country in Europe that can stand alone, and all have to set about joining one or other of the two halves of this divided world of ours.

It may be that Europe no longer exists, politically speaking, and that its soul is departing from its body, like the soul of Athens from Hellas after the Peloponnesian War. Then we must the more ensure the integrity of our own souls, so that our true being may become strong enough to survive.

THE ARCHAEOLOGICAL MUSEUM

Stone-Age pottery: the very pots and jugs that Spanish women carried to the wells. Weapons and tools of bronze and iron. A model of the town of Numancia which was levelled to the ground by the Romans in 133 B.C. after an heroic defence by the Celtic-Iberian inhabitants. Torsos of Roman statues of divinities, found in Spanish earth. An altar from Merida dedicated to the goddess Venus. On remnants of Visigoth sculpture, for the first time, simple and clear, the Christian Cross. A reproduction of the animal drawings in the caves of Altamira.

Those drawings, many thousands of years old, are astonishingly modern and alive: in one unbroken line a likeness is conveyed, and this outline confines the creature two-dimensionally. The powerful aurochs must have been a dangerous foe to men armed merely with arrows. Perhaps the Spanish bullfight recalls bygone victories over that once ferocious beast, hence the ceremonious setting of a bullfight in Spain: the bull must have *bravura* in order that the fight may be dangerous, as of yore. And often the beast conquers the man, now as then.

The richness of contemporary Spain consists in the accumulation of cultures that swept across the land and left their traces as essential elements of life.

Thus the Celts were conquered but their spirit lives on. The Romans succumbed to the Goths, but it was the Roman mind that informed the Visigoth kings. The Goths went under, but the Cross to which they paid allegiance maintained its hold under Moorish rule. The Moors were driven out, but they left their stamp behind them.

The Habsburgs came as strangers and ended as Spaniards. They came powerful and ended weak. *Sic transit. . . .*

III

TOLEDO

The valiant river came in all its power,
in all its might;
and found itself confined in rugged narrows:
a mountain confronted it—this it would subdue,
and had it nearly surrounded
and encircled;
but the effort was too great,
and so it gave up and flowed on
smoothly, content with what was done.
And on the lofty mountain-side
there sits enthroned that limpid dream,
that heavy dream:
old buildings crowning the crest of it.
Thence, the Tajo follows the falling land
and waters fields and woods,
gently flowing on, ripple on ripple.

after *Garcilaso de la Vega*,
Églogia Tercera (201–216)

TOLEDO

On first seeing Toledo I found myself thinking of Rilke's Second
Duineser Elegy and murmuring the words, 'every angel is terrible'.

Every angel is terrible because our souls fear the unknown. Every angel
is a stranger because he belongs to a different order of being.

> And yet, woe is me,
> I sing you, birds so nearly
> deadly to the soul!

Toledo is frightening. It oppresses; one longs to understand and it re-
fuses to give itself away. It remains dumb and shrinks from every form of
contact. Such aloofness, such obduracy are quailing to the spirit.

The city is a rock and a fortress. The rock rises sheer from the desert,
almost encircled by the bed of the River Tajo and cut off from the surrounding world; crowded into its walls, the fortress is tense and stark in
its will to self-preservation. Keep watch! Never yield! Hold out for ever!
Its dour determination glowers down upon the approaching traveller.

The city is so old that in human reckoning it is as good as timeless.
Legend tells how God made the sun and placed it above Toledo, for
Toledo is the centre of the round earth, it is the Imperial City, the seat of
the Romans, the capital of the Goths, the residence of the Emperor 'on
whose Empire the sun never set'.

As a young Emperor, Charles V said he was never so conscious of
sovereignty as when he mounted the steps of the Toledo Alcázar. The
Alcázar ruins tower high above the city roofs, a symbol of endurance: as
though dogged perseverance in a way of life had inspired sturdy resistance and won again.

Toledo made its first appearance in history in the year 193 B.C. When
the Roman legions under Marcus Fulvius had subdued the tribes of the
plateau, they found on the banks of a river a fortified place. 'It was
Toletum,' wrote Livy, 'a small city, but strong on account of its position.'

Christianity reached Spain in the first century A.D. Under the Caesars'
Governors, and especially under Diocletian, the Christians were merci-
lessly persecuted and Spain honours many martyrs from early Christian
times. In A.D. 311 Caesar Galerius issued a decree ordaining toleration
of the Christian faith in Spain, and henceforth Christianity became
the dominant religion.

In A.D. 400 the first Christian Council was held in Toledo, and established the tenets of the Christian faith as laid down at the Council of Nicaea in A.D. 325. In A.D. 409 the Goths swept into Spain and conquered the whole peninsula. The second Council took place in 527 under Visigoth rule. King Leovigildo raised Toledo to the status of capital city in about 554; he was Arian, but during the third Council in 589 he was reconciled to the Roman faith. From that moment, the partnership between Church and Throne lent the Spanish monarchy a theocratic character which became dominant again under the Catholic sovereigns of the fifteenth and sixteenth centuries.

Between 709 and 711 the Arabs invaded Spain and vanquished Roderic, the last Gothic king, who, as legend relates, was treacherously murdered by men of his own clan, and by 718 nearly the whole peninsula was in the hands of the Moors, all but that impassable tract of land beyond the Cantabrian range, where the survivors among Roderic's followers fled to safety. The reconquest of the land began from that hearth, the moment the Moorish invasions were apparently over. In 718 the Christians gained their first victory over the invaders at Covadonga.

Within the walls of Toledo—erected by the Iberians, destroyed and rebuilt by the Romans, levelled and raised anew by the Goths, torn down and put up again by the Arabs—within those fortress walls the Christian faith survived four centuries of Moorish rule.

For the Arabs, Toledo was too rugged a place and too far away from the coast to be their capital, and they made Córdoba the seat of the Califate.

The centre of Christian resistance lay in Asturia; the capital was first Oviedo, then León, and at times Burgos. In 1085 Toledo was reconquered by Alfonso VI of León and Castile, who triumphantly termed himself *imperator totius Hispaniae*, though it was another four hundred years before the Arabs were finally driven out of Spain; Toledo, however, was Christian—Toledo was the rock on which Spain could found her unity.

The Archbishop of Toledo was the spiritual leader of the land, as in Gothic times. Cardinal Jimenez de Cisneros, confessor to Queen Isabella of Castile, played a decisive part in the final eviction of the Moors. He became Archbishop of the diocese of Toledo in 1495, and the spirit of mystical union, which of old the Roman Catholic clergy had inculcated in the Visigoth kings, was now a guiding principle of the reign of Isabella of Castile and Ferdinand of Aragon. They well deserved the title of 'Catholic Sovereigns' which Pope Alexander VI accorded them in 1494. In the century of the *Reconquista*, faith and state-government were thus in full accord.

At the age of eighty-one, Cardinal Jimenez, Archbishop of Toledo, Regent of Spain, set out to meet the young King of Spain, Charles I (later, as Emperor, Charles V). He disembarked at a small harbour in Asturias. The aged defender of the Faith was eager to perform the ceremony of consecrating the new monarch, but the journey over bad mountain roads proceeded slowly and was deliberately impeded by the Lord of Chièvres, Charles' first counsellor, who was determined the young king should not come into contact with the Cardinal, renowned for his powers of personal persuasion.

Cardinal Jimenez fell ill on the way and was unable to continue his journey. He wrote Charles successive letters filled with good advice, entreating him to take only Spanish counsellors, for the archbishop, alert for news, had already heard that Charles' entourage was entirely Flemish.

The Cardinal died in Roa on 8th November (eight days after Luther had posted his ninety-five theses against indulgences at the castle-church of Wittemberg). He died on the threshold of a new age, and before he could assure himself that the cause he upheld so tenaciously—the cause of Spanish unity—was in safe hands.

(It was said that the archbishop died of distress over a letter from the young king, in which he thanked him in formal terms for his services and relieved him of his office on account of his advanced years. Charles wrote the letter, but the archbishop did not live to receive it.)

The young king cast the archbishop's advice to the four winds and nominated as his successor the twenty-one-year-old nephew of the Lord of Chièvres, Monsignor William of Croy.

The appointment of a young Flemish nobleman to the rank of Archbishop of Toledo was proof enough that the old Cardinal's fears were fully justified, as was the complaint of the Spaniards that their king was wholly under the thumb of his chancellor. Pedro Martyr, the humanist, gave expression to the general discontent with the feudal Burgundian government, bemoaning 'the exploitation of the country by the ruling minister, the Lord of Chièvres, and his Flemish friends'.

The Spanish chroniclers are unanimous in their complaint that King Charles' courtiers were only interested in growing rich at Spain's expense; but what was really the matter was not so much the acquisitiveness of the Flemish courtiers as the clash between two cultures and the bitter feeling aroused by the presence of the foreigners in Spain. The traditional magnificence of the Burgundian court, which, as the Belgian historian Pirenne observes, 'made the Burgundian Age comparable to one long festive parish fair', was bound to cause offence among the frugal Castilians who were accustomed to a very parsimonious mode of life. The splendid tournaments, the multiplied courses at banquets, the rich attire of the courtiers, gave rise to the notion that Spain had to pay for it all.

The displeasure of the Castilian nobles and the people grew steadily: sympathies went to Charles' younger brother Ferdinand, who was born and brought up in Spain and was Ferdinand of Aragon's favourite nephew. During a meeting of the Cortes (the States General) in Valladolid Charles was given a pronouncedly cold reception, whereas his brother was greeted with jubilant cheers. The Lord of Chièvres took quick action: the young prince was suddenly ordered away on a journey, he had to leave his Spanish following behind, and on 27th March 1518 embarked for Flanders in the company of a Flemish nobleman. (So it came about that a few years later Ferdinand took over the Austrian inheritance and was the instrument whereby Spanish Catholicism spread throughout Hussite Bohemia.)

Charles' first personal act in Spain was to visit his mother, who since her husband's death lived in a state of profound melancholy in the Castle of Tordesillas. Charles went in to his mother's darkened rooms together with his sister Leonora who had accompanied him from Brussels. A courtier offered to carry a candlestick ahead of them but Charles snubbed him: 'We need no light.'

Mother and son did not need a light to find the way to each other through the veil of melancholy and the years of separation.

ERASMUS AND CHARLES V

In the wake of Charles V and his Flemish following, humanism invaded Spain (Cardinal Jimenez had prepared the way with his polyglot Bible, which was regarded as a great humanistic achievement at the time). Among Charles' following there was a number of preachers and secretaries of state who had been in contact with the ideas of Erasmus of Rotterdam at the Burgundian court in Brussels; Charles himself came to Spain with the reputation of being an 'erasmista'.

Erasmus (like Charles) was born in those same Netherlands where a century earlier a famous book of Christian piety was written: Thomas a Kempis' *Imitatio Christi*, preconizing a personal approach to God termed *devotio moderna*. It aimed at a deepening, a spiritualization, of Christian belief. Erasmus' teachers belonged to the brotherhood that promoted it and the stress he laid on genuine devotion in his later writings originated from this movement.

It was after his first journey to England, in 1498, that Erasmus began writing on this theme. Before that he had been a humanistic aesthete whose rule of life was founded on a remark of Petrarch's: 'Christ is indeed our Lord, but Cicero is the prince of our culture. I admit differences but can see no discrepancies.'

But in Oxford Erasmus heard Colet lecture on St Paul's Epistles, and at the height of the Renaissance he re-echoed the challenge of the Middle Ages: 'Christ is Master'.

Christum ex fontibus praedicare: 'To preach Christ from the sources' was now his aim.

It was a desire to promote the renewal of Christian doctrine that provoked the writing of his most influential work, the *Enchiridion militis christiani*, a 'Handbook for the Christian Fighter'.

In this work he attempted to retrace the relevance of Christ's teaching to life, with the intention of providing a 'method of holiness' to turn warriors into Christians and Christians into fighters for the Christian cause. 'The Christian,' he wrote, 'must be armed all the time, for he must fight all his life long.' Life is one long battle against the inclination to sin; the fight is a hard one, but the Christian must never give up the hope of improving himself with the assistance of divine grace and by his own efforts. A man's worth consists in conquering sin. Prayer, study, and above all knowledge of the holy Scriptures, self-knowledge and integrity are the weapons of the *militia Christi*.

This book paved the way for the Reformation in Germany.

In Spain it roused to action in the Church's battle-ranks that great soldier of the Counter-Reformation, Ignatius of Loyola.

Ignatius read the 'Handbook of the Christian Knight' (the Spanish title) at the time of his conversion. 'True, he soon threw it into a corner,' his contemporary biographer, Ribadeneyra, remarks, 'because as he read he felt his zeal grow cool, till at the end all his fire seemed to be frozen away and his spirit dulled.' Nonetheless, the work had such an influence on him that he became a fighter for Christ's cause and called the Society he founded '*militia Christi*'. The original framing of the phrase was St Paul's

—echoed by St Bernard with his *De laude novae militiae*, a work in praise of the Templar Knights.

The reawakening of the Christian ideal of the Middle Ages brought together three men, each very unlike either of the others: Erasmus, Ignatius of Loyola and Charles V.

Erasmus' connection with Charles V began in the year 1516, when he was appointed to the young Duke of Burgundy's Council. For Charles he wrote his treatise, *Institutio principis christiani* in which, in contrast to Machiavelli's *Il Principe* (which appeared in the same year), he gave moral questions precedence over practical interests. Like a mediaeval 'mirror of princes', Erasmus' work gave an idealized portrait of the Christian ruler:

'A prince loves virtue above all things and detests wickedness, avoiding it at all costs.' Unlike the heathen *tyrannus*, the *princeps christianus* has to guard and guarantee the freedom of the individual. Just as Plato desired kings to be philosophers and philosophers kings, so the *princeps christianus* must first of all be a *philosophus christianus*. 'Unless you are a philosopher, you can be no prince—at most, a tyrant.' The imitation of Christ was not only a matter for priests and monks, but for all Christians, and above all for princes, who had to be models of Christian virtue. When by reason of his sovereignty a prince had to face a decision involving an infringement of justice, he should lay down all his power, his very life even, rather than act unjustly, and should prefer to be a just private person rather than an unjust prince. The *princeps christianus* ought always to do what is *honestum*, and he must preserve *publica utilitas*, the common good; for the sake of the common good he should avoid war, but if war is inevitable he must take care to mitigate it and to end it as soon as possible. In his dedication, which Erasmus addressed to Duke Charles, he pleads earnestly in the name of peace:

'. . . You were born heir to a marvellous realm and are destined for great things. Just as Alexander set out to conquer, so it may be your mission voluntarily to renounce a part of your realm rather than hold fast to it. You owe it to heaven that sovereignty fell to your count without bloodshed and without hurt to anyone; it is now a matter for wisdom on your part, to hold it equally without bloodshed.'

True, Charles was frequently at war, and in order to keep his inheritance intact and to assert his authority, he was to use methods more in accord with Machiavellian practical politics than the Erasmian ideal. But on decisive questions his actions were determined by the Christian ethic preached by Erasmus, and towards the end of his life he was to choose

CHARLES V WITH HOUND
Titian, *The Prado, Madrid*

QUEEN ISABELLA
Titian, *The Prado, Madrid*

living as 'a just private person' in preference to giving his consent to conditions which he considered bad.

'Erasmus' Christian idea can be summed up in two words,' wrote M. Bataillon, '*pax et unanimitas.*' Peace and unanimity: an ideal state of things which for thirty years Charles V endeavoured in vain to bring about.

In the great conflict with Luther, Charles, like Erasmus, often stood between the two parties. A feeling of sympathy for the Evangelical effort, which prevented Erasmus from making an unconditional stand against Luther, was a factor in Charles V's dealings with the Lutherans; neither condemned the Reformation out and out, for the purging of conditions in the Church was a heartfelt concern of both. And it was a concern they felt to be imperilled by the hardening of the extremists on either side: Emperor and humanist both desired a more conciliatory attitude.

When, as a result of the success of the 'Handbook of the Christian Knight', the Spanish Dominicans began to accuse Erasmus of heresy, he found in Charles V 'a powerful patron'. In the Netherlands, too, the Emperor defended the great humanist from the attacks of the Louvain theologians and termed him 'a man who has merited well of the Christian community'. Charles knew that Erasmus was no 'enemy of religion'. Men who love Christ have a natural affinity.

This is explicit in a letter Erasmus addressed to the Emperor in September 1527, at a time when he was the butt of both sides, and when Charles, too, was in a politically ambiguous position:

'. . . We are both fighting for Christ, not for human interests, and as far as I am concerned, I shall defend the cause of Christian piety unflinchingly to my last breath. But it is Your Majesty's mission constantly to support those who fight honourably and bravely for the Church of God. I serve under Christ and under your banners and under these will I die, but I shall die the happier if I can foresee how, through your wisdom, your felicitous intervention, tranquillity may be restored to the Church, indeed to all Christendom. That Christ, our Highest and Best, may through you bestow this on us, is my constant prayer. May He guard your Majesty and guide you ever onward.'

MACHIAVELLI AND CHARLES V

'Three books only the king read with great delight and had them translated into his native tongue; one for the ordering of society: *Il Cortegiano*, by Conte Baldassare de Castiglione; one for its relevance to affairs of state: *Il Principe* and the *Discorsi* of Machiavelli; and the third on the conduct of war, Polybios' history and all his works.' So Sansovino (natural son of a famous Renaissance sculptor) reported in his work, *Simolacro di Carlo Quinto Imperatore*.

Thus Machiavelli was something of an influence in Charles V's life.

The contrast between Erasmus' and Machiavelli's notion of a prince witnesses to the tension to which Charles was a prey, a tension between the Christian ideal and a dechristianized world, between the claims of God's kingdom and the demands of the worldly kingdom, between the desire for justice and the will to power.

The *lex aeterna*, St Augustine's name for the law of divine reason in man's soul, was written indelibly on Charles' heart; but his participation in worldly government exposed him to the temptation to act despotically. In the very process of upholding authority he would find himself compelled to resort to measures more in accord with Machiavelli's opportunism than Erasmus' basic principles.

Erasmus the moralist wrote from the seclusion of his study, whereas Machiavelli the politician composed his *Il Principe* after years of office in the Florentine chancery of state. Erasmus was an onlooker, Machiavelli had personal experience of practical politics. Erasmus sketched his prince 'as he should be', Machiavelli described the authorities of his day 'as they really were'. 'To grasp what is, is the task of the philosopher,' wrote Hegel, 'for what is, is reason.'

To grasp what is, was Machiavelli's object, as it was to be Karl Marx's. A remark of Marx in his youth might well serve as a motto for Machiavelli's *Il Principe*: 'It is the mission of history, once other-worldly truth has disappeared, to establish the truth of this world.' Machiavelli observed that other-worldly truth, that is, the Christian ethic, had disappeared from political life. The truth of this world was, as he saw it, a matter of self-seeking and fraud, disloyalty and violence. As a young man he had witnessed the seizure of his beloved city of Florence by Charles VIII of France; the battles for the possession of northern Italy knew no end; the Papacy participated in the general struggle for power. Pope Alexander VI 'did nothing but deceive men', said Machiavelli. Only the violent methods of a Cesare Borgia appeared to hold any promise of success, amid the prevailing state of corruption. Machiavelli wished to provide the ruler of a small state—i.e. an exposed one—in the heart of disordered Italy, with arms for self-defence: the weapon he proposed was an unflinching sense of reality.

In the fifteenth chapter of *Il Principe*, he wrote: 'My purpose is to put useful material at the service of whoever wants it, and it is right, in my view, to go by the truth of things as they are, rather than by appearances. Many ideal forms of princedoms and free states have been dreamt of, which no one has ever seen realized nor ever come across in fact. For between the way one lives and the way one ought to live there is such a tremendous gap that anyone who stops doing what is commonly done in order to do what he ought to do, is asking for trouble rather than doing himself any good. A man always wanting to do right is sure to be ruined among so many who are not good. Therefore a prince who wants to make the most of himself must be capable of acting well, or not well, and doing what is good, or not, according to the need of the moment.'

It is the train of thought indicated in this last sentence which has brought down upon Machiavelli's head accusations of cynical disdain for the Christian ethic. But the key-word to the sentence is often overlooked: it is the word *need*. To do what is good or not *segondo la necessità* is what he wrote. Only under pressure of necessity at a given moment is it permissible for the ruler to act 'not well'. The terms 'good' and 'bad' are far from having lost weight, and precisely because they are used not as abstract ideas but as facts of life, they are subject like all that is human to the pressure of circumstances.

Machiavelli assumes that the Christian moral law rules men's consciences. He therefore counsels his prince 'to appear all sense of duty, all loyalty, all integrity, all religion' when unfavourable times make it impossible for him to be good. *Necessità* creates an emergency-right which justifies action incompatible with loyalty and integrity.

The pressure of necessity is an essential element in Machiavelli's work. Extreme necessity drives a man into depths where the mainspring of *virtù* is found like a source of life. *Virtù* means both virtue and capability; in Machiavelli it has the old classical ring of courage and strength: necessity and strength are interdependent. 'The more *necessità*, the more *virtù* there is,' he wrote in the *Discorsi*, and 'there are many things reason is not strong enough to make us deal with, but necessity does it'—or, as we say, 'necessity is the mother of invention.'

This 'virtue born of necessity' of Machiavelli's must not be taken out of its context, which is Italian Renaissance humanism.

Words like *umanità*, *bontà*, *pietà*, *liberalità*, even the word *carità*, bloom unexpectedly in Machiavelli's writings—all of them words with roots in the Christian ethic. 'A kind heart is all the more deserving of admiration in this age for being so rare,' we read in the *Discorsi*. The very tone of his concern, his sympathy for Italy in her chaotic condition, his deep sense of reality, all go to show that his work has not abandoned the ethical plane.

'We must beware of contrasting politics and morals,' wrote P. Lachance in his *Humanisme politique de Saint Thomas*, 'as though in pondering over man's social activities we were not at the very heart of the moral question.'

The Renaissance conception of *umanità*, 'humanity', lies at the root of all that was written in that last period before the Reformation. If the Christian moral law was no longer observed in Renaissance society, it still influenced behaviour and had a beneficial effect on human relations.

Later generations, for whom the climate of pre-Reformation Catholicity was foreign, found Machiavelli's ideas 'machiavellian', for by then the reconciling elements—*umanità*, *bontà*, *pietà* and *carità*—had faded out of the picture.

It is necessary to distinguish.

That Machiavelli's intended political humanism should come to stand for a form of conduct devoid of ethical sanctions, was only possible because of the Reformation's break with the Catholic way of life.

In Catholic thought, sin by no means excludes virtue; according to the Vulgate, though men's thoughts and actions are inclined to evil, they are not intrinsically evil. It was Luther who first said human nature was corrupt through and through, incapable of choosing to be good on its own account; and Zwingli held that all men's feelings and actions were evil. This belief that all that is natural is corrupt caused Machiavelli's ideas to degenerate into Machiavellianism, for Luther set up a dichotomy between God's world and Satan's world, and between private and public morals, thus legitimizing the split between ethics and politics and leaving politics to the devil.

It might be objected that the rift between a kingdom of the world without hope of salvation and a perfect kingdom of God was in St Augustine's mind, if we so interpret a sentence from *De Civitate Dei* (IV, 4): 'For if justice fails, what are kingdoms but great robber-bands?'

But St Augustine never identified the State as such with the corrupt *civitas diaboli*: it was only diabolical when it excluded justice. *Pax* and *justitia* should reign on earth, and that is how St Augustine presented his vision of the *Civitas Dei*, to draw men from what is human to what is divine and change the earth-world into God's world. This ethical impulse of St Augustine's was responsible for giving the western world its spiritual bias, and exalting the Papacy till in the eleventh and twelfth centuries it had actual and real supremacy.

According to Meinecke, Machiavellianism is 'the doctrine of the primacy of political over ethical principles'.

The primacy of politics over morals need not necessarily mean giving precedence to selfish interests over the common good.

In St Thomas Aquinas' conception of the State we find the primacy of politics over morals too, but in his mind there was no discrepancy between them, they were, rather, complementary to one another. St Thomas gives positive value to politics as a function of ethics: as energy, for politics is the idea in operation. 'It is necessary,' he wrote, 'that politics be regarded as the foremost of the practical sciences, the one which determines the structure of all the others and has in view the highest good.' In mediaeval political thought, and in St Augustine, the highest good is justice. But his platonic tendencies made St Augustine's conception too remote, placing it in a super-secular borderland, whereas St Thomas, with his sense of right proportion (which he learnt from Aristotle), conceived it as the interrelating of the secular and the divine.

Through its concern for the common good and for peace, secular rule should bring about Christian conditions on earth.

The decline of the two powers entrusted with the administration of *pax* and *justitia*, the Papacy and the Empire, paved the way for the coming decadence of politics and morals. Dante already bemoaned the anarchy of his time and called for reforms in both the ecclesiastical and secular spheres. At the beginning of the sixteenth century Machiavelli's diagnosis pointed to the same process of disintegration, but his political insight did not rouse any reforming zeal in him.

Machiavelli is a product of his times, of that late mediaeval tendency for nations to split apart. He saw no alternative to the revolt of component parts at the cost of unity and accepted the existing state of affairs as a necessary evil, instead of seeking a way out. It is this attitude of conformity to things as they were that paved the way for Machiavellianism, which is simply a misfire, a failure to comprehend the necessity of the Christian idea of life, an incapacity to restore the lost equilibrium between politics and morals and to see them as interdependent.

Machiavelli's critical but inactive attitude is typical, showing the moral impotence of secular humanism when the Renaissance cut itself adrift from 'truth's other world'. Without truth's other world it is impossible to cope with this world. Life needs ethics to support it and keep it going. By turning away from Christian ideas in order to devote himself single-mindedly to worldly practice, Machiavelli, like Karl Marx after him, was, because of his failure to do justice to the spiritual side of human nature, to become an inhibiting force: he drove truth's other world out of the world.

At the beginning of the sixteenth century there was a general desire for the renewal of Christian order. Erasmus, who sought to make his own contribution to a renaissance of the ideal of justice, and Charles V, who tried to counteract the centrifugal tendency and to reunite the disparate parts of Christendom, embodied not backward-looking forces but a form of progress that is effective when the special need of a given hour produces a renewal of ethical concern.

For Charles V, who, as Sansovino wrote, *si dilletava di leggere*, delighted in reading Machiavelli, politics and ethics were not to be parted. He was a statesman and therefore political practice took precedence over principles, but it was principles that gave the impulse to practice and kept it on the right lines.

Charles V's political activities show him not averse to following certain of Machiavelli's counsels. Thus he endeavoured to lead his army himself, for Machiavelli advised the ruler to be his own field-marshal; he read historical works to acquaint himself with methods of conducting warfare, for in Machiavelli's view the best safeguard for a prince was mastery of the art of war; he also took to heart Machiavelli's counsel to build up a national army, for mercenaries were not to be relied upon. As Sansovino reported, 'The Emperor Charles V took a great interest in the art of war, which he held to be the basis of sovereignty, and he believed he knew more about conducting warfare than anyone else in the world. As regards artillery he had practical experience and he had a great gift for putting an army in order.' If at times Charles followed Machiavelli's advice on methods of government (when the need of the hour demanded harshness) he nonetheless remained unfailingly faithful to those mediaeval ideas which Machiavelli dubbed illusions.

It is on account of their different attitude to the mediaeval Christian ideal that Machiavelli's and Charles V's conception of the state differ. Machiavelli discarded Christian metaphysics as immaterial for worldly success, if not positively harmful; Charles, on the other hand, found the ultimate motive for his actions in supernatural ideas. He refused to set the sails of his ship of state to the wind of circumstance alone. *Plus ultra!—*

there is more to it than that! Still, the storm of his times wrecked his ship of state. But his failure served to stress the Christian ideal, and his personal dedication to it gave it fresh endorsement.

THE IDEAL OF CHIVALRY

What Machiavelli called an illusion was the ideal of a Christian society.

Once, it came true. Some say it never took shape in real life, dismissing the Crusades as mere military actions against the Turks, business interests and a spirit of adventure being the main motives that fired the knights to undertake those perilous expeditions eastwards.

Doubtless, religious and material interests were closely interwoven— and all the time a distinction had to be made between 'genuine' and 'false' crusaders, but the element of self-interest never wholly eclipsed the live ideal which lit up the eleventh and twelfth centuries. This really was a period when the gap between the Christian ideal and plain reality was closed, for a time. The ruling caste of warrior-knights put their swords at the service of the Church and took their orders from the Church: it was the age of chivalry.

An age when the spirit of Christianity united Europe. As a chronicler of the First Crusade said: 'Even though we spoke different languages, we were like brothers in the love of God, and as those most close together, of one heart.' In Germany, St Bernard preached the Second Crusade in Latin; few of his hearers understood him, but they caught the drift of his words: he was a Christian speaking to Christians.

The ideal of the spiritual orders of chivalry was an ideal of service: *La saint Eglise salver et garantir* was their motto, first formulated in French. The knights who set forth to deliver the Holy Sepulchre from the hands of the infidels pledged themselves to defend the Christian faith with their lives. The Knights of St John, the Templars, the Teutonic Knights, took monastic vows of obedience, chastity and voluntary poverty: they were fighters for Christ and at the same time defenders of the weak and help-less, guardians of the sick and poor, and deliverers of the oppressed.

Even the rules for the secular knighthood were drawn up by the Church: obedience to Emperor and Pope, defence of the Faith, the pro-tection of widows and orphans. A high conception of honour and loyalty, a sense of justice, practical charity, unconditional integrity, a detestation of lying and hypocrisy, were among the knightly virtues.

'What would a Christendom be like that had not become incarnate in human society?' asked Péguy, that valiant forerunner of our twentieth-century Christian renaissance.

A desire to abolish the gap between the ideal and the realization of it is the mark of every renewal of basic morality. When the things our faith requires of us are conceived as obligations laid upon us, it follows that belief and action should tally. The knights set out to realize that ideal, hence their motto: Thou shalt practise what thou dost believe!

One of the documents setting out the obligations and functions of the knighthood is from the pen of the Spanish mystic, Ramón Lull, who wrote his 'Book of the Order of Knighthood' in 1275 (at a time when a decline had set in). His account of the foundation and functions of the knighthood was intended as a challenge to the barbarism of his own age:

'What the world lacked was love, loyalty, justice and truth; hostility, disloyalty, contempt, dishonesty, set in, and thence error and unrest arose among God's people which was created in order that men should love God and know Him, honour, serve and fear Him. While in the world disdain of justice was on the increase because love of neighbours had declined, it was needful that by means of fear justice should be re-established' (in Lull's mind, 'fear' means the fear of God and is something like 'necessity'; thus the need of the times gave birth to the virtues of chivalry).

To the service of God and service to their secular lord, the worldly knighthood added service to women. The 'Minne' (courtly love) sweetened court society through and through, said the German poet of that period, Walther von der Vogelweide. France was the cradle of chivalry, but in Germany, too, the Christian ideal infused life. But as early as 1200, Walther von der Vogelweide found cause to mourn the decadence of culture and of justice:

> Grounds for complaint there are on another score:
> Loyalty, breeding, honour are no more.

The Christian ideal only came to life for a moment in time; it was too exalted for earthly forces to submit to its control for long. After the great upsurge of fervour that accompanied the First Crusade, devotion to the Christian ideal broke down, a spent force. The old Adam returned claiming his old prerogatives, as truculent and intransigent as ever, and the law of the mailed fist prevailed.

Translated into terms of real life, even the highest ideal cracks under the strain and becomes flawed.

The heretical movements of the twelfth and thirteenth centuries were at first nothing but a desire of the broad masses to integrate to themselves the Christian ideal that flourished in the monastic houses and in chivalric society. But the good seed fell on untilled ground and thistles grew instead.

The accusation of heresy was levelled against the Knights Templars, too. How far it was justified has never been elucidated. In actual fact the Templars soon gave the lie to the observance of obedience, chastity and poverty, their behaviour was autocratic, they were pleasure-loving and lived opulently. They abused their political independence (they were answerable to the Pope alone) and came into conflict with the secular powers. Philip IV of France (that ambiguous figure between the sinking Middle Ages and the rise of absolute national power) accused the Order of adopting the Manichaean heresy—i.e. belief in evil as an independent force. In 1307 the king confiscated all the Order's property; in 1310 the first knights were burned as heretics, and Pope Clement V abolished the Order in 1312. With the end of the Knights Templars, the ideal world of chivalry fell in ruins.

The ideal of knighthood was henceforth an illusion. Only an echo of it is heard in the late mediaeval romances—it lived on as a 'code of honour' in court society, but its Christian essence had vanished, it was merely a matter of form.

The ideal of knighthood survived longest at the Court of the Dukes of Burgundy.

In 1430 Duke Philip the Good founded the Order of the Golden Fleece, on the model of the mediaeval Orders of knighthood, laying moral obligations on the individual holders of it. But the requirements of the Order were seldom observed and its roll soon had to register serious transgressions committed by members. Philip the Good also wished to renew the ideal of the Crusades, and the fantastic oath taken on the occasion of a banquet by the 'Knights of the Round Table', laid on them the obligation to go and fight the infidels. However, neither Philip the Good nor his nobles stirred beyond the borders of Burgundy.

In 1453 Constantinople fell to the Turks.

The collapse of that most easterly pillar of Christendom, in a defeat which cut off the Balkans from the Christian community for centuries, no longer roused the princes of Europe to common action. Philippe de Commynes, the French historian and *gentilhomme* whose memoirs were among Charles' favourite books, called this indifference by its proper

name: *Ce fut une grande honte à tous les princes crestiens de la laisser perdre*—
'it was a great disgrace to all Christian princes to let it be lost'.

Charles V was the first to think seriously of fighting the Turks. In childhood, at the Burgundian court, he had imbibed the spirit of chivalry, and his devotion to the Christian ideal called the 'illusion' back to reality.

THE CATHEDRAL

One walks along the narrow streets of Toledo, like gullies, dark in shadow, and never sees it. Then suddenly one comes face to face with it, towering up like a great cliff; and inside there is breadth and space, a quiet strength, and power.

Pillars soar heavenwards like immense tree-trunks spreading their branches on high. After a while, in the dark of this forest one discovers an abundance of blooms, a prolixity of blossoming.

A sacristan took me from altar to altar and showed me the sacristy, displaying treasure upon treasure, gem upon gem. *Para Dios todo oro*, he said, 'for God, all gold', and showed me the monstrance wrought of the first gold that Columbus brought back from the New Indies; he brought out crosses and chalices set with precious stones, twelfth-century Madonnas of silver, richly embroidered vestments, the standards of the Catholic Sovereigns from the battles with the Moors, the faded blue flag of Lepanto. . . .

Then, picture upon picture, all of deep significance, a delight to the heart. Here the Christian ideal lives on, here is real Europe, here the Cross is alive.

EL GRECO AND TOLEDO

The inside of Santo Tomé's church is low; Greco's famous painting of 'The Burial of the Count of Orgaz' takes up the whole of a wall under an arch.

The sacristan pulled back the cloth over the picture and I involuntarily held my breath, expecting a revelation. But my first impression was a divided one, and while the sacristan went on with his account, I was uneasily conscious of cold, dull greys and sharp, hard black and white.

The picture represents the miracle that is alleged to have taken place at the burial of the Count of Orgaz. The pious count had the church of San Tomé rebuilt and founded a monastery in the parish of St Stephen in honour of St Augustine.At his funeral, legend recounts that the two saints descended from heaven in full regalia in order personally to lay the meritorious count in his last resting-place. This astonishing occurrence is depicted quietly and soberly in the lower part of the picture, and there faith is alive in the faces of the noblemen and clergy watching the saints performing their act of mercy—faith in the reality of supernatural events; one priest, quite unperturbed, goes on reading the Office for the Dead, while angels bear the soul of the dead man to heaven, which opens up immediately above the heads of the gathering.

In spite of the unity of intention, however, the picture falls into two distinct halves: the faces of the hidalgos and prelates are painted with scrupulous, masterly skill; the heavenly scene, on the other hand, is but hastily thrown together, the clouds are more like featherbeds than atmospheric shapes, the figures of the Blessed appear fantastic, livid. Here it is clear that the artist was above all a distinguished portrait-painter, and that he deliberately transgressed the limits of his powers, and indeed the limits of art, by such excursions. The heavy heaven has too arbitrary an effect on top of those accomplished portraits of men all dignity, goodness and compunction.

Now this dividing line running through the picture, parting the human and the divine portions of it, may be the echo of a rift in Greco's own soul, due perhaps to a dichotomy of will and feeling—a symptom of his times. The narrow pointed faces of those noblemen betray an impotence like a personal confession of inadequacy. Greco may have desired to be a mystic, but he remained nonetheless the prisoner of his ego. Like the promoters of the Counter-Reformation, he bent his will to the utmost in a vain endeavour to capture what only God can give.

St Teresa often warned her Sisters about *sequedades*, aridity of the soul, a drying-up of the flow of love.

The shallow painting of the upper portion of this picture reveals something of the despair of a soul that at the moment of highest endeavour encountered an inner drought where emotion silted up. When this occurs the soul flares up in reaction, but where grace is lacking the effort is but convulsive, wilful self-enhancement.

In Greco's house (a house he never lived in himself, but where a number of his pictures live on) there is a little inscription attached to his 'Prospect and plan of Toledo', explaining why he elongated the limbs of his saints beyond all natural likelihood. The inscription refers to Our Lady and St Idelfonso descending from heaven, and states why they are painted larger than the houses in the picture:

'I made use of the fact that in a certain sense they are heavenly bodies, as we see in the sun, moon and stars, which look small from a distance however large they may really be.'

It was not faulty eyesight that made Greco distort and exaggerate— his portraits could not be more true to life—but rather a reaching out in vain towards an unattainable goal.

Later Greco paintings are like those 'groaners' of whom the Arab mystical writer, Aben-arabi, tells, 'whom God sanctified through the sighs they emitted, feeling their impotence in striving for spiritual perfection'.

Greco knew *esta sed del supremo*, that thirst for the highest, and knew, too, the torment of not being able to quench it, nor to possess what he longed for: mystical union.

We are told that once, in the course of a lawsuit, he was asked why he came to Toledo. He did not answer. But at the end of his life he gave his answer in his loveliest landscape picture: 'Toledo in a Storm.'

Toledo in a storm. It was always in a storm of light or of darkness, a storm of tension between heaven and earth.

When Greco lived in Toledo, Philip II had already transferred the Spanish capital to Madrid. Greco was left behind in a city where life stood still.

Toledo's fate was his own: rejected by the king, he sank out of mind in the evening shadow that descended upon the city. He painted 'The Burial of the Count of Orgaz' in the years 1586–88. From those pictured faces there speaks the sadness of men whose powers were diminishing. With increasing exasperation he sought to force inexpressible things from his exhausted spirit; he became more and more deeply enmeshed in his barren ecstasies. He died forgotten within the old walls of Toledo. And to this day his city lies stranded and phantom-like on the banks of the Tajo.

FIRST DEPARTURE FOR GERMANY

Old views of Toledo show the Alcázar towering like a portent over the roofs of the city. Here, civilizations lie like geographical strata one above the other, intersecting, sometimes overlapping, but with every epoch guarding its own characteristic formation intact. The castle bears the Moorish name *Al-Kasr*, the Palace. But the building which, since the summer of 1936, has towered a ruin over the roofs of Toledo, goes back to Charles V's time.

Like the beginnings of Toledo, the beginnings of the Alcázar are lost in the dim past. The remains of a Roman fort lie sunk in its soil. Legend recounts that St Leocardia died a captive within its walls. From this centre the Visigoths ruled over the Iberian peninsula. The Arabs reconstructed the old fortress. After the liberation, King Alfonso VI built the royal castle on the same spot. In 1521 the rebel Comuneros sought refuge within its walls, and with the siege of the castle by the royalists the Alcázar entered Spanish history.

An insurrection broke out in Toledo, a demonstration in support of the Cortes' protest at the young king's intended departure, after only two years in Spain: he was to be crowned Roman Emperor in Germany. In January 1519, on receiving news of the death of his grandfather, Emperor Maximilian, Charles' determination to stand for the imperial crown became adamant. 'There is nothing I more desire,' he wrote to his Aunt Margaret in Brussels. 'I have told my agents not to economize, it is my reputation and honour that are at stake.'

In his last years Emperor Maximilian had expended his whole fortune on ensuring that his grandson Charles should obtain the throne. When he visited his beloved Innsbruck for the last time, he had to enter the old Tyrolean capital without any pomp and circumstance, for he had no means to pay for it. He lamented that 'a great deal of money' was the main prerequisite for the imperial election—golden florins, too, for only with ready money were the 'dreadful practices' of the French to be counteracted: the French king was a rival candidate.

The fact that not only the King of France but also the King of England had it in mind to stand for election to the imperial throne shows how, in the age of humanism, the super-national character of the imperial idea was once more admitted. With the rediscovery of antiquity men remembered the old Roman Empire, an empire which had bound the countries of Europe together in one comprehensive state. It was an ideal which had revived under Charlemagne, which accounts for the fact that Francis I of France, as heir to the Frankish kingdom, considered himself eligible for the title of Emperor. Francis' mother, Louise of Savoy, used to call her son, *mon fils, mon César*.

In spite of the French moneys received by the Archbishops of Mainz and Trèves, and in spite of the sum of more than half a million ducats which Jacob Fugger had advanced for Charles' election, the Electors offered the imperial crown to Duke Frederick the Wise, of Saxony, who, however, withdrew in favour of Charles.

On 28th June 1519, Charles was unanimously elected German Emperor. On 22nd August the Elector of the Palatine arrived in Barcelona to receive Charles' acknowledgement.

At that time, the High Chancellor Gattinara, a Dante scholar, addressed a memorandum to Charles: 'Sire, God has granted you this great grace, raising you above all the kings and princes of Christendom to a power that hitherto only your predecessor, Charlemagne, had possessed, and you are now on your way to world sovereignty and the gathering of all Christendom under one shepherd.'

But the Spaniards were not pleased, they resented that their king should be leaving the country, and that he wanted money from the Cortes to pay for his journey and coronation. The Cortes' reaction to the imperial election took the form of a three-point resolution, demanding, first, that the monarch should not leave Spain; second, that he took neither gold nor silver out of the country; and third, that no foreigner be given public appointment.

On 7th November 1519, two citizens of Toledo, Juan de Padilla and Don Pedro Raso de la Vega, raised these three points in a letter to various cities of Castile, exhorting them to press their claims.

But King Charles was determined to go. In Castile the atmosphere was so hostile that when he went to Tordesillas to say good-bye to his mother, the excited mob almost prevented him from riding out of the city gates. There were shouts of 'Long live the King, death to his bad counsellors', and the Lord of Chièvres, who accompanied him, must have felt very queasy in his skin.

The next Cortes was called in Santiago, for the journey money was still lacking. And this assembly, under the presidency of Chancellor Gattinara, again refused to sanction the king's application for money. Whereupon the Cortes were transferred to La Coruña, the port of embarkation. This time Dr Mota, Bishop of Badajoz, opened the session. He was a member of the royal council, the third in rank after Chièvres and Gattinara. He knew how he would have to speak to his Spaniards to gain their support for the king's cause. Stage by stage he worked on his audience, and broadened out their horizon: he knew that words like *imperator, caesar*, were sure of an echo in Spanish hearts, so intrinsically a part of their own history as they were.

King Charles is not a king like other kings, said Mota, he alone on earth is 'king of kings', for he received the *imperium* from God. This *imperium* was, however, a continuation of the old one, and as those men said who used to praise Spain (a reference to Claudius)—when other nations sent tribute to Rome, Spain sent Emperors, for it sent Trajan, Hadrian and Theodosius—'and today the Empire comes and seeks its Emperor in Spain, and our King is by God's grace Roman King and Imperator of the world . . . King Charles did not accept this Empire in order to gain new territories, for he has enough by inheritance; he accepted it in order to fulfil the very heavy duties it entails, in order to safeguard the Christian faith from great evil, and in order to proceed against the infidel foes of our holy Catholic faith, in which enterprises he will, with God's help, engage his royal person. . . . In this imperial mission Spain is the heart of the *imperium*. This kingdom is base, protection, strength for all the others.' Therefore Charles was resolved 'to live and die in this kingdom, and he will persevere in this resolve all his life long. The garden of his joy, the castle of his defence, the power of his attack, his treasure, his sword must be Spain.'

Viva el Rey! Long live the King! All money for him who is Emperor, Caesar.

A majority voted to give the king the required sums.

On 20th May 1520, Charles took ship for Germany at La Coruña, with four thousand Spanish ducats in his treasurer's money-bags. . . .

THE CORONATION AT AIX-LA-CHAPELLE (1520)

Aix-la-Chapelle. On 22nd October 1520, in Charlemagne's Cathedral, the solemn Coronation Service was celebrated according to the old rites. The ceremony was a religious one, not unlike the ordination of a priest, conferring grace worthily to perform the duties of office. During the ceremony the Emperor lay prone on the altar steps, his arms stretched out in the form of a cross, as a sign of his total dedication in Christ. Then he swore to defend Church and Justice, to protect the weak and defenceless, and to fight infidels. Whereupon the Archbishop of Cologne turned to the assembled princes and representatives of the people and said: 'Will you have this King Charles as Emperor and King of the Romans, and will you be obedient to him according to the words of the Apostle?' Nobles and people answered in one voice, 'Yes, yes, yes!' Like 'I will' in the marriage service, the oath was binding and indissoluble. Then the Archbishop of Cologne and the Archbishop of Trèves anointed his chest, head, shoulders, elbows, wrists and hands. After the anointing they arrayed him in Charlemagne's coronation robes, put the sceptre and orb into his hands, and the Archbishop of Cologne placed on his head the old imperial crown with which the great emperors of the Middle Ages were crowned. The Emperor said: 'I swear to safeguard the law, justice and peace of the holy Catholic Church.' Seated on Charlemagne's throne he then received the homage of the whole company.

At the end of the ceremony the Archbishop of Mainz read a letter from Pope Leo X, according King Charles the title of 'King of the Romans and Elected Emperor' (he was not 'Roman Emperor' till he was crowned by the Pope).

The sacramental character of the coronation made an indelible impression on him, imprinting a permanent mark on his soul. In the highest sense he knew himself to be the guardian and defender of the faith of Jesus Christ. From now on, all the irresolution of his youth vanished. The consecration had bestowed on him the strength he needed to carry out the duties of his high office.

EVE OF THE REFORMATION

From Aix-la-Chapelle the Emperor went on to Cologne to meet the Princes of the Church and States and confer with them on ways and means to combat the religious crisis which the writings of the Augustinian monk, Martin Luther, had brought about.

Erasmus, too, was in Cologne, with the intention of influencing the young Emperor and furthering reconciliation, for he wrote an anonymous pamphlet for him entitled *On peace in the Christian Religion*.

It is necessary to stop at this point and consider the course of events that led up to the Reformation. It was foreshadowed as early as the twelfth century, in the endeavour to introduce a way of life wholly committed to the Christian ideal, an endeavour in which the miscarriage of the later attempt was already prefigured.

The Papacy had not succeeded in setting up God's kingdom on earth;

PHILIP II IN ARMOUR
Titian, *The Prado, Madrid*

MARY TUDOR, QUEEN OF ENGLAND
Antonio Moro, *The Prado, Madrid*

the Orders of Chivalry had not been able to establish the rule of Christian morality in daily life; ideal and fact fell asunder yet again.

In that period of crisis, due to the incipient disintegration of the universal culture of the Middle Ages, man found himself thrown back upon his own resources; mysticism sought its solitary way to God.

In Germany whole districts, often for decades on end, lay under the ban of excommunication, which brought all religious life to a standstill. The clergy became worldly, and often it was devout women who attended to the duties which the clergy neglected.

'The Lord's vineyard has no one to tend it, for its head is sick, its members are dead,' said the twelfth-century mystical writer, Elizabeth of Schönau, in a letter to Hildegard of Bingen, called 'the Sibyl of the Rhine'. She hoped Hildegard would be able to incite a renewal of religious fervour.

Hildegard foresaw the impending split in the Church: 'the time will come,' she wrote, 'when princes and people will forsake the Papacy, finding no religion in it. . . .'

In the thirteenth century St Mechthild of Magdeburg lamented in these terms: 'O glorious crown of the Church, how thy splendour is dimmed by hideous rust. Thy precious stones, holy living and suffering, have fallen from thee. Thou art become poor as a beggar, for the most precious jewel of all, Love, is lacking.'

A deep longing for an improvement of Church conditions filled the latter Middle Ages. In Calabria, the monk Joachim of Flora proclaimed that the age of the Father and of the Son was drawing to a close and that soon the age of the Holy Spirit would dawn.

The high quality of religious devotion among the people showed up the worldliness of the clergy all the more sharply. Visits to shrines, wayfaring flagellants, pilgrimages, the honouring of relics were expressions of general concern for the cure of souls. As spiritual leadership was lacking, faith often turned into superstition. A sense of portent and impending disaster hung over the close of the Middle Ages. In art, the Dances of Death and Dürer's engravings of the Apocalypse were signs of a time awaiting the onset of a new age.

The *vita nuova*, the 'new life', first made its appearance in Italy. There, in view of the prevailing religious and political confusion, poets and writers resorted to a new independence of thought. 'I will gather together the fragments of my soul and in all earnestness hold commune with myself,' wrote Petrarch in the mid-fourteenth century, and he founded the *studia humanitatis* which offered his period the ideal of a humanity enhanced by education and right behaviour. Christian mysticism encouraged the growth of private devotion—the Italian Renaissance aroused a new sense of life; and now the gap between the eternal and the temporal remained to be bridged, to provide room in life for spiritual things and to spiritualize human existence. And that was what humanism proposed to do.

In Renaissance humanism, temporal and eternal concerns, reality and the ideal, were united. The world of ideas was a wide one, embracing Antiquity and Christianity. The humanists echoed Justin, the Church Father: 'Whatever is lovely is ours'. Cicero and Senaca are ours, for they taught the Christian virtues, Plato prepared the way of the Lord, Plotinus led men up the same steep path as Christian mysticism. 'Holy Socrates, pray for us,' wrote Erasmus; and the words are not a symptom of a pagan turn of mind, but witness to the humanistic desire to integrate within Christianity the total spiritual and intellectual heritage of the western world.

'Of the Dignity of Man' is the title of the chief work of the Italian humanist, Pico della Mirandola. He taught that the dignity of man consists in freedom of choice. Man can degenerate into a beast and he can mount up to God. In his vocation to be more than man lies the dignity of *homo humanus*.

At the Platonic Academy of Florence, the humanist Ficino revived the Christian idea of man being made in the image of God, the temple of God, indeed—God on earth. (A notion rife with Lucifer's temptation. And Italian humanism was to succumb to this temptation, in its adoration of nature forgetting the supernatural. Then, in the name of the supernatural, Luther was to debase nature and part the divine from the human.)

But in pre-Reformation humanism, an equilibrium between divine and human things did exist. 'As much as we once loved God in what is good, we now love Him in what is beautiful,' wrote Ficino in his Phaedrus commentary. He translated the Areopagita with its mystical theology into Latin and dedicated it to the Archbishop of Florence, later Pope Leo X.

The Papacy of the Renaissance, so often denounced, is in reality splendid and colourful. To it is due the reconciliation of the Church with the lay world, and the crowning achievement of scholasticism, the integration of the wisdom of the ancients within the Christian body of ideas. Humanists occupied the See of Peter. The Pope was patron of the arts and friend of 'good learning'. He was *il Santo Padre* not only to the devout but to scholars, too. The humanists came to him to present their works in the guise of special offerings. Ficino and Erasmus dedicated to him their Greek books, Reuchlin his Hebrew studies, for the impulse of humanism towards universality would gladly have swept Judaism, too, into the main Christian current. Nothing human is foreign to the Church. She embraces the whole of life, in all its diversity and paradoxical complexity.

If at that time divine and earthly things were brought very close together, the earthly predominated. The Cardinal's purple could be purchased, and even the tiara succumbed to simony. The excesses of Pope Alexander VI were a scandal even to pleasure-loving Rome; his son Cesare was *condottiere* in the papal army. In a time of violence, the papacy used violent means to assert itself. 'Formerly,' wrote Machiavelli, 'no baron was too insignificant to despise papal power; now, even the King of France respects it.' Erasmus was pained to see the militant Pope Julius II enter Bologna fully armed. The monk Martin Luther contemplated with horror the pomp and magnificence of the papal court. From the living-quarters of Pope Leo X, strains from stringed instruments were to be heard. . . .

It was an ambivalent new period, the threat of pestilence hung over it, riots and revolts made it perilous. It was shaken to its foundations, and yet, at bottom, still one.

'O century, O learning, it is joy to be alive,' cried Ulrich von Hutten. The humanists felt they were torch-bearers, they were a new community of *homines spirituales*. Their claims were taken seriously, too, for the things of the mind were regarded with reverence. The need to communicate and share broke down all barriers of rank, and thinkers and poets spoke to popes and kings in all familiarity. The common culture created a wonderfully friendly atmosphere that bound all Europe together, from England to Italy and from Spain to Poland. The German Reuchlin wandered through the orange-groves of Lorenzo il Magnifico, Hutten was welcomed with open arms in Venice, and Erasmus found Oxford very much to his liking.

Erasmus' experience in England, where he encountered the Gospel, is a sign of transition, it belongs to the years between the Renaissance and the Reformation, which were years of revived interest in the problem of divine grace.

Erasmus used a disguise of buffoonery to speak out his dismay at Church abuses. His reforming zeal wore cap and bells to avoid destroying or being destroyed. His *Praise of Folly*, published in 1509, is an implicit condemnation of the abuses of religious and secular authorities, the presumption and pride of ruling circles, the sensuality and superstition of prelates and monks. The pamphlet was given the form of a jest, but the young sixteenth century was in no mood for laughter, it hungered for justice. The truth behind the puppet-show was all too apparent, and Erasmus' pamphlet thus contributed to enhance the general feeling that 'things must change'.

Change for the better. . . .

For humanism, it was the hour of crisis, the great moment when mind and spirit were at last to lay hold of life and transform it. The word of God no longer languished behind monastic walls, it was present and actual for all to see, a burning bush that set hearts afire. Indeed the German humanists had the feeling that a new Pentecost was at hand, with tongues of fire descending from heaven upon their own heads. 'But when the Spirit of Truth shall come, He shall guide you into all truth.'

Dawn was about to break, the dawn of a world founded on truth. The outward form of truth is—reality. The German humanists were immensely interested in reality, and their talk was of what was uppermost in their minds. Now the great concern of the day was the reform of the Church; but the needs of the kingdom were also omnipresent, and it was among these German humanists that the Renaissance tendency to consider worldly questions as quasi-spiritual ones was most sharply evident. Wimpheling, Hutten, Sebastian Brant were first and foremost ardent patriots. In Italy, the same tendency was apparent in Machiavelli: 'I love my country more than my soul,' he wrote in a letter to the historian Guicciardini.

This shift of focus, from love of God to love of Fatherland, took place in Germany under pressure on the border. For the centre of German humanism was Alsace, and Strasbourg, Schlottstadt and Colmar were conscious of the acquisitive eye of France upon them. Wimpheling wrote his polemical pamphlet *Germania* as a retort to King Louis XI's intention of extending the French frontier to the Rhine. In his *Germania nova*, Thomas Murner lamented the weakness of the Empire and ascribed it to the disobedience of the Princes.

Another humanistic centre was Silesia; it was laid waste by the Hussites, and German culture there was permanently on the defensive against Polish and Czech infiltrations. German national feeling and the accompanying hatred of all that was 'Welsh', i.e. foreign, were symptomatic. But the great counter-pole was Rome. Italian scorn of 'German barbarians' only served to touch up German pride in the 'Fatherland'. The heavy money-levies made by the Pope were regarded as exploitation by a foreign power. In 1511 Wimpheling published a series of accusations against the Church, the so-called *Gravamina of the German Nation*, in which he demanded that the sums sent to Rome be retained in the country to feed deserving priests, widows and orphans. Passionate participation in the questions of the day turned German humanism into a revolutionary movement, forestalling Karl Marx's remark that 'the philosophers have only explained the world in different ways, but the aim is to change it'. Like the earlier Orders of Chivalry, like Hegel later, they demanded that reality and the ideal should tally. As they saw with their own eyes, reality and the ideal were poles apart. The Gospel taught poverty and humility— but in Rome wealth and pride were dominant.

In a pamphlet published in 1519, Hutten concluded that the Pope was 'wholly and utterly the devil'. He attributed all the troubles of the day to Rome, and never sought for possible causes nearer home. Under his influence German thinking became fixated, to the exclusion of any concern for eternal values, serving the spirit of the times alone.

In England, Sir Thomas More saw deeper into the real sources of the troubles in Europe. In his *Utopia*, published in 1516, he compared the misery of the poor to ideal conditions on a happy isle, where, as in Plato's Republic, good prevailed. Between this satisfactory state of affairs and reality, the contrast was all too evident. More complained of endless wars, broken alliances, military expenditure, loss of time and money spent on forging instruments of destruction . . . and he concluded that man must first improve himself before the world can be any better. But in Germany, Hutten had no idea of a reform of the human heart. Luther's teaching was a tool for fighting Rome. And Luther was less concerned with renewal of the inner man than with transforming the ecclesiastical scene. It was a projection of the reform question from inward outwards, turning the religious problem into a political one, and this admixture of political ends with the Gospel brought not only Hutten but also German humanism to a disastrous end.

In Erasmus' letters we can follow the course of the Reformation drama as it unfolded, from the first upsurge of humanism, aiming at restoring the old cultural heritage, intellectual as well as spiritual, in all its purity, to the ultimate disintegration of the old unity of the Faith.

Sir Thomas More's martyrdom symbolized the failure of the true, intellectual and spiritual, reformation—the humanistic one.

On 31st October 1517, Luther posted his ninety-five theses on the door of the castle church of Wittenberg. They opened with a fine flourish: 'For love of the truth and in the endeavour to bring it to the light of day . . .'

The 'truth' Luther had in mind concerned the abuse of trafficking in indulgences, which at the time had become a sort of tax which the Roman Curia collected all over Christendom. The building of the new church of St Peter in Rome required gigantic sums of money, as did the maintenance of the papal court; the sale of indulgences proved a convenient source of income.

At the time of the Renaissance the system of indulgences still flourished as in its mediaeval form. It originated in the twelfth century when Pope Urban II granted remission of punishment for sins, that is, 'indulgences', 'to those who journeyed to Jerusalem solely for the salvation of their souls and the liberation of the Church, pledging their lives and property for the love of God and their neighbour'.

The idea that gaining an indulgence entailed some form of self-sacrifice was, then, a *sine qua non*, and participation in the arduous venture of a Crusade was regarded as penitential, a means of getting rid of sin.

The belief that every evil act must be atoned for is common to all the great religions of the world. The Brahman holds that by his actions in this life man creates good or bad conditions for himself in his reincarnation. The Christian conception of the far-reaching effects of any action stresses the uniqueness of human existence: every act has its own place in time and helps to determine the soul's eternal destiny.

It was, however, into this world, where cause and effect follow so relentlessly on each other's heels, that Christ came and suffered. 'Behold the Lamb of God, who takest away the sins of the world.' And the merits of Christ are so infinite, they form as it were a treasure-house for sinful humanity to draw on. This supernatural treasury has constant increments coming into it from the merits of the saints: their spiritual achievements mount up to a sort of capital investment, with interest paid out in the form of blessing and strength to all the community of the faithful.

Now the Church claimed the stewardship of this treasure-house and the right to distribute its benefits in the form of remissions of punishments due for sins in this life or the next, the penitent paying off his term of punishment in cash.

Wycliffe had already attacked this abuse, but Luther put in question the very belief people had in this form of remission of sins, i.e. in indulgences. In his Wittenberg theses he declared it was idle hope to suppose one could achieve blessedness by gaining indulgences. It was a merely human invention that 'as soon as the coin clinks in the money-box the soul springs out of purgatory. One thing is sure: when the money clinks in the money-box, gain and greed are on the increase. But whether the Church has success with her intercessions or not, is a matter for God to decide'—and he dubbed the sale of indulgences 'a net for catching people's money'.

And indeed so it was, and therefore Luther's words awoke an immense response. His battle-cries of 'Evangelium!' and 'Freedom for the German Nation!' spread like wildfire.

Luther did not stop there. In his work, On the Babylonian Captivity of the Church, he attacked the Pope, whereas he paid respect to him in the Wittenberg theses, quoting the Emperor, Charles V: 'What he (the Pope) lays down must be borne, even though it be hard.' And now he denied the validity of the seven sacraments. In On Good Works, which appeared in 1520, he turned against the idea of merit gained by good works and thus attacked the very core of Christian moral teaching. His most thoughtful work is On the Freedom of the Christian Man, in which emphasis on the religious side of the problem of freedom foreshadows his later non-participation in politics; it has a sentence containing the essence of his 'justification' doctrine, a doctrine which defied all Charles V's efforts to bring about a settlement: '. . . faith alone, without any works, justifies a man, making him free and blessed. . . . That is Christian freedom, faith alone—not meaning us to go idle, or to do evil, but that we need do no particular works to do what is right and to attain to blessedness.'

Luther found the ground well prepared for his 'justification' doctrine: for centuries the preachers of indulgences had laid their emphasis not on the act of penance as such, but on trust in Christ's merits. Luther went further in teaching that 'peace is assured in faith'.

Paradoxically, Luther in fighting his vanguard action against indulgences fell a victim to the indulgence-complex: his justification doctrine is at bottom a total indulgence (unpaid-for), relieving the sinner of any transcendental consequences for his actions.

'Only trust and believe,' said Luther to his contemporaries who were athirst for absolution from sin. 'Your sins are all forgiven you.'

All those uneasy consciences accepted only too readily a total absolution so freely offered them. Now, it seemed, nature could be given free rein, seeing that all sins were 'vanquished in Christ'.

Luther had the more need of his trust in the saving power of faith for his deep conviction of the impotence of the will. 'Lust is wholly insurmountable,' he declared. Human nature was rotten through and through on account of the Fall; every good work was useless, for 'all our doing, feeling and thinking are utterly nothing'. 'It is man's nature to sin. Man is in his very essence sin. Man is sin itself.'

The fact that Luther despaired of human nature and created a new doctrine out of his own need for consolation, a doctrine that was to part him from the Church, is a tragedy that—like all great and painful events—has a double face and is open to various interpretations. But the then impending tragedy of the break-up of Christianity should not be allowed to cast its shadow over those earlier years, 1517–21, when Luther, full of audacity, 'for love of truth' made his stand against ecclesiastical abuses.

There is a woodcut by Hans Holbein the Younger showing Luther at this period as a *Hercules Germanicus* cleansing the world of unworthy priests—and so he appeared to his followers: as the man who purged the Church and cast out hypocrisy and a time-serving pseudo-Christianity; as the representative of the spirit of truth, as opposed to a debased clergy and degenerate forms of religion.

It remains a mystery why Luther, possessed of the desire to restore the eternal truths to the light of day, nonetheless became entangled in the worldliness of the period. And why, desiring to make 'love of neighbours' a living thing, he took it not in the sense of selfless service but as an untrammelled will-to-freedom and boundless self-assertion.

The explanation lies no doubt in his rejection of the ascetic strain in Christian mysticism.

Mediaeval mysticism had shown up the perils of an inflated, self-centred ego. John Tauler, whom Luther was fond of quoting, preached that it was essential to cleanse the very ground of our being of all self-seeking before we could expect to find ourselves again in God. Tauler would have been the first to spurn as madness Luther's notion that man was justified by faith alone. For Luther would not have anything to do with the idea of self-control. Though at the head of his Indulgence theses he set John the Baptist's and Christ's cry for penance (Mt. 3. 2 and 4. 17), he himself closed his ears to the call which demands of a man: Metanoia! Repent! Change yourself! Transform yourself through and through, turn away from sin, turn back to God.

True, Luther did give the best of his mind to divine matters, but without taking steps to divest himself of his egoistic, self-centred self. He wanted to reach the goal without adopting the right road. His assurance of salvation was his safety-anchor on the sea of 'insurmountable lust'. He caught at a phrase of St Augustine's, 'Love, and do what you will', and used it as a justification for increasingly risky flights of fancy. *Pecca fortiter*, 'sin strongly', he wrote to his fellow reformer, Melanchthon, on 1st August 1521, 'but believe more strongly still, and rejoice in Christ who is victor over sin and the world'.

Erasmus observed that people had not stopped sinning on account of Luther's preaching, only that their sins now went unpunished.

ERASMUS AND LUTHER

'Erasmus produced the egg, Luther hatched it,' said a Franciscan monk in Cologne. 'I laid a hen's egg, Luther hatched quite a different kind of chick,' Erasmus retorted. He never wearied of denying being a parent to Luther's writings. In fact he observed with positive horror how his own endeavours to establish the authenticity of the Church's tradition were endangering that very tradition. 'Luther is completely unknown to me,' he assured his friends in 1519. 'I have not read his books.'

But he answered a letter which Luther addressed to him, saying, '. . . it is still not possible to eradicate the entirely false assumption that your works were written with my assistance and I am the standard-bearer of the party. . . . I wish to maintain my integrity so as to make my own contribution to the expansion of learning. In my opinion, wise reticence can accomplish more than impetuous personal intervention. When things are so deeply rooted that they cannot suddenly be torn out of heart and mind, it is better to proceed with sound and effective argumentation than to make blunt assertions. One must always be on one's guard not to speak or act in a presumptuous or prejudiced manner; this, I believe, is in accord with the mind of Christ.'

Thus it was the Christian spirit that Erasmus desired to serve and to preserve alive from ill-considered fixations, rescuing it from cramping formulae and obsolete turns of phrase to give it full present efficacy. Yet his endeavours to put the teaching of the Church in a contemporary form, as *philosophia Christi*, met with no response in Catholic circles. The intolerant traditionalism of the University of Paris served but to heighten Erasmus' resolve not to take up arms as champion of the Church.

'Why do we narrow down our acknowledgement of Christ, when He intended it to be broad and accessible to all?' he wrote in August 1518 to Abbot Paul Volz.

Erasmus had a horror of any constriction of spiritual things. His appreciation of the superb abundance of the truth made him avoid anything conducive to limitation or lopsidedness. And having firmly planted himself at a middle point, he was bound to be caught between two extremes—Luther's blunt assertions and the anti-reform attitude of the orthodox theologians.

But it became more and more difficult for Erasmus to maintain his position; he was assailed from right and left and challenged to define his attitude to Luther. In that autumn of 1520, in Cologne, Erasmus found himself in a delicate situation; agreeing on the one hand with Luther's devotion to the Gospel, on the other hand he deplored the extravagance of his views. He deeply desired to avoid a break with the Church, but the monks' attacks on sound learning antagonized him. He feared that if opposition to Luther was successful, it would sweep away in its train all humanistic achievement, too.

On 5th November 1520, Luther's protector, the Elector Frederick the Wise, of Saxony, enquired of Erasmus, through his secretary Spalatin, whether Luther was right or wrong. Like the Delphic Oracle, Erasmus replied ambiguously. 'The best plan would be for the Pope to entrust the matter to a few men worthy of confidence . . . the world is thirsting for the true Gospel, and the tendency of the moment is in that direction. One ought not to oppose the spirit of the times in such an ill-willed manner. . . .'

Erasmus regretted the Papal Bull, *Exurge Domine*, which Pope Leo X had issued against Luther in June 1520, condemning forty-one articles of Lutheran doctrine as 'respectively heretical, or giving scandal, or false, or wounding to pious ears, or conducive to misleading simple people and contrary to Catholic truth'; under pain of excommunication, Luther and his followers were summoned to revoke the errors named within sixty days, and to send their recantation to Rome within a further sixty days, failing which they would be treated as notorious and hardened heretics. Luther had not recanted and was becoming daily more violent in his writings.

Erasmus advised Luther to be more moderate and more prudent in the expressions he used. But Luther made a reconciliation with the Pope impossible, on 10th December 1520 publicly burning the Papal Bull in Wittenberg.

The Pope issued another Bull on 3rd January 1521, in which he declared Luther and his followers liable to excommunication. This new trend brought Erasmus further over to the Catholic side: 'If it comes to the worst,' he wrote in January 1521, 'and the whole stability of the Church be threatened, I shall meanwhile take anchorage on that firm rock (Mt. 16. 18), till peace is re-established and it becomes clear where the Church stands. And Erasmus shall always be found only wherever the peace of the Gospel is. . . .'

In England, King Henry VIII became an active opponent of Luther's. With the assistance of Sir Thomas More, he drafted a document, 'The Confirmation of the Seven Sacraments', in which he defended the teaching of the Church and the supremacy of the Pope, and received the title *Fidei Defensor* for his services.

Thomas More recognized the danger that lurked in a denial of papal supremacy; he wrote that if Luther fostered a disdain for authority, people would not be content to question the authority of the Pope only but would have doubts as to Luther's authority, and as to the secular authorities, too: 'The people will throw off the yoke of their rulers and take their property away from them . . . till finally, with neither government nor law, without either justice or reason, nation will rise against nation and they will come to grief in dissensions, as the earthborn brothers once did.'

In Germany the excitement engendered by Luther's writings had grown so intense that a public declaration was not to be avoided. Charles V summoned the Diet (*Reichstag*) for the beginning of 1521 to discuss the question.

It was a novelty for a gathering of the States General to deliberate on a religious problem on which the Church had already pronounced. But in Rome there was still one door open for the return of the prodigal. Charles V acted in accord with the Pope in offering Luther an opportunity to renounce his opposition to Rome. Had Luther himself not stressed the duty of obedience in his Wittenberg theses? 'Let your conscience guide you, Martin, where your duty lies,' was the counsel many of his followers gave him.

The Papal Nuncio, Aleander, pressed the Emperor to outlaw him, but Charles replied: 'Luther shall not be condemned until he has been heard', and he sent a herald with a letter to Wittenberg, summoning 'his honest, dear devout Martin Luther' to come to Worms, promising him a safe conduct.

Although Luther had the example of John Huss before him, who in spite of the Emperor Sigismund's assurance of safe conduct was burnt at the stake by the Council of Constance, he undertook to come. He told Spalatin 'he would go to Worms even if there were as many devils there as tiles on the roofs'—'and though a fire were to stand between Wittenberg and Worms, I shall go!'

Erasmus was invited, too, but in his reluctance to take sides he stayed away.

He was not unaware of what was expected of him, but he remained passive. He was like the man referred to in St Luke's Gospel (6. 49), who listens but does nothing. Not that he did not see keenly enough what was amiss, but he evaded the responsibility his clear-sightedness laid on him. He was, it seems, imbued with the Greek disinclination for exact formulation, and preferred the paradoxical—often a symptom of inner tension. But like the first Christian Bishop of Athens, Areopagita, he felt that truth lies beyond all our assenting and dissenting. His mind was prone to search for the link (*connexus*) between contrasting things and to foster a process of formation, but now he was caught at the point of stress and unable to release himself or stand out for one party against the other. His Catholic awareness of universality was a factor in his reluctance to declare for the papal side at that moment when it was intent on blindly rejecting reform as such.

Thus in the critical year of 1521 Erasmus recoiled from becoming what is now termed *engagé*, and his freedom-loving spirit remained without influence on subsequent events through inability to take on an obligation. So the shaping of the future lay in the hands of those totally 'engaged': Luther, and Charles V.

ULRICH VON HUTTEN AND CHARLES V

Another man who committed himself heart and soul was Ulrich von Hutten. He had an extraordinarily strong personality and found existence an overwhelmingly powerful experience. *Febris* is the name of one of his Dialogues—'a discussion between Hutten and his fever', meaning a kind of ecstasy of awareness, and he desired that the whole world might equally be awakened to reality. In the Dialogue, his fever begged him to show it another place to assault, and Hutten referred it to the courtesans who, blind to the need of the time, lived in extravagant luxury: those were the people to tackle and rouse.

Sinceriter citra pompam: 'honest and without pomp' was Ulrich's first motto. His manner of speech was honest and downright, but his indignation at the 'Welsh (i.e. foreign) tyrants' possessed him so entirely that it made him unjust and unscrupulous. In 1520 he published his 'Complaint and admonishment of the excessive and un-Christian power of the Pope in Rome and his unspiritual clergy', in which he 'revealed many crimes' and 'exposed the shame of the Romanists'.

Hutten desired to transpose Luther's ideas into action. But Luther wrote in dismay to the Elector of Saxony's secretary: 'You see what Hutten is up to. But I do not wish the Gospel to be fought for with murder and deeds of violence.' And he finally denounced his all-too-zealous disciple, saying Hutten was a 'proud, insolent, blasphemous man'.

When a mind possessed of strong ideas turns to action, it is apt to be outrageous if it discards its religious ties. In striking out for freedom, Hutten forgot his Christianity. Though he wrote to Luther, 'Christ be with us, for His teaching was much darkened by the additions the Pope made to it, and we would bring it into the light', he ended his letter with 'let us fight together for the freedom of the Fatherland and free our Germany that was so long and so utterly oppressed. If God is for us, who dare be against us?'

In reality, Hutten was but little concerned with God. In his case there was neither the *pietas ecclesiae* represented by Charles V nor the *pietas Dei* for which Luther contended, but only *pietas patriae*. The fever that burned in him was love of the Fatherland. His whole devotion went to the Emperor's earthly realm.

But the Emperor, Charles V, was deeply anchored in eternity, and his manner of thinking and acting was strictly traditional. His realm was not, as he saw it, a mighty independent entity, but an ordered structure based on the Roman Catholic Faith. The defence of Church and Faith was a duty he accepted on becoming Emperor.

Hutten wanted to win him over to the national cause. He observed with distaste that 'Charles had as many masters as there were Cardinals' hats and Bishops' mitres crowding about him'; he wrote a disappointed letter to Luther: 'We must not rely on the Emperor, for he has so many priests (*Pfaffen*) around him to whom he feels he owes an obligation, and who take advantage of his youth to give him all kinds of damaging

67

counsels.' So he determined to place himself at the head of a national movement, 'for he could no longer bear to see how the German nation lacked its freedom'.

The national movement he instigated seems to have struck Hutten as likely to serve the Emperor's interests, in that it was to combat the autocratic trend of the individual States' ecclesiastical or secular rulers—all so many impediments to imperial power. In the summer of 1520 he went to Brabant to lay his plans before the imperial court.

Then the die was cast. The Papal Bull, *Exurge Domine*, was published, excommunicating Luther and his followers—of whom Hutten was one. He fled from Brussels, for he had heard that the Pope wanted to have Hutten brought to Rome in chains—a nauseating thought to the old knight that Hutten was, because it was time-honoured custom not to put captive knights in chains. Hutten had no intention of becoming a papal prisoner. In his distress he wrote to the Emperor as follows:

'Charles the Fifth, Emperor of the Germans and King of Spain, the German Knight Ulrich von Hutten presents his homage. They demand your consent to letting a German knight be led away in bonds, a member of that great body of which you are the head—because I asserted Christian truth and denounced the fantastic additions to it made by the Pope, because I showed Germany her rights and reminded her of her dignity. Above all, you, upon whom the whole hope of Germany depends, should be most careful not to let it appear as though you were withdrawing your protection from those who look up to you, whom it is your first duty to help to rise. What is to become of us Germans, what is to become of our freedom, our bravery, when with one's honour at stake and with the best intentions for the Fatherland, one is no longer safe? What will become of our religion, our piety, if one may not present the teaching of Christ but is compelled to prefer human patchwork to God's commands? The counsel I proffer you and the Fatherland arises from a sense of duty and love. But you, Charles, must not allow the eternal foes of our land to penalize me. You are our Emperor, that is, the guardian of the life of all of us. Therefore, invincible Charles, defend us, uphold your dignity, pave our way to freedom, open up the road to the truth that is struggling to arise. And keep me safe, my Emperor, for, as you will see, it would be greatly to your discredit if I were ruined. I desire nothing more fervently than to see you at the head of this enterprise, then I should not be concerned about myself any longer. I should think to have lived long enough, on seeing you go into action for the cause I upheld in writing and by word of mouth. Meanwhile you must hear my case and judge it! Any other judge but you I dare not and cannot abide. For what has a German knight to do with a Roman Bishop? But you will decide. In the meantime I will not tolerate that anyone, whoever it may be, should treat this realm and the German name with derision. Farewell, great Emperor, may you be at our head as our beacon for many years to come!'

That is undoubtedly the most 'democratic' letter that ever a German wrote to his sovereign lord. The bold tone of it sprang from the confidence and conviction of its author. Emperor and knight were parts of an organic whole, and the member of a body had the right to tell his head what troubled him. The letter's natural mode of address came from that sense of fraternity characteristic of humanism, a feeling that all thinking people belonged together, united by devotion to truth—as the early Christians were. 'My Emperor,' said Hutten, just as the Apostles said 'Brother' to one another.

If Hutten addressed Charles V as 'Emperor of the Germans', it was because he misunderstood the universal character of the idea of Empire, which extended far beyond national frontiers and embraced the well-being of the whole *respublica christiana*. But in Hutten's view the worldwide Empire ought to be confined to the nation to which he belonged.

At that time the Old and the New confronted one another. In 'To the Christian nobles of the German nation', Luther called upon the Emperor to rise against the Pope. Hutten desired most fervently that Charles should give ear to this summons. In March 1521 he wrote to the Emperor again, in *Pro Luthero exhortatoria*, imploring him not to be carried away by the Pope's wishes and not to condemn Luther without a hearing.

'This we entreat of you, with the trust we put in you as Emperor. And while no one is ignorant of all that is entailed in Luther's cause, you can believe that the whole of Germany together is prostrate at your knees, begging you weeping, imploring you with tears, entreating you to use your power, your good will and good faith, and calling upon you to save the land and restore it to itself, free it from slavery, guard its right from tyranny; in ever-sacred memory of those who once did not submit even to the Romans who ruled the whole world; and whom you must not abandon to be the servants of that weak and effeminate people. . . .'

This appeal evoked a response in Charles for the simple reason that he wished to come to terms with Luther. Cajetan, the Papal Legate, was charged to give Luther a 'fatherly hearing': in Rome there was still a hope that he would revoke his writings at the Diet. Pope Leo X sent the

Emperor a letter dealing with the possibility of Luther's return to the fold, adding in his own hand, 'We shall receive this same Luther as a dear son and reward him with honours'.

Charles V intended to prepare for a kindly reconciliation in all quietness. He sent an embassy to the Ebernburg, the 'Haven of Justice', where Hutten enjoyed the hospitality and protection of a knight, Franz von Sickingen. The spokesman of the delegation was the Emperor's confessor, John Glapion (in the opinion of the Papal Nuncio Aleander, 'the most important personality in the Emperor's entourage'); he was a Franciscan friendly to reforming views, who originally approved of Luther but took exception to his 'Of the Babylonian Captivity of the Church'. Glapion intended by means of direct conversations with the more important representatives of the new ideas to draw a line between their reforming demands and their doctrinal errors. Thus the Ehrenburg was the scene of a sort of secret council, a *rencontre international*. The spokesman for the Roman Catholic and Spanish point of view was the Frenchman Glapion, the German Protestant view was represented by the Lutheran theologian Martin Bucer, for Hutten was not versed in matters of doctrine.

All present were agreed on the necessity for a renewal of the Church. Glapion foresaw for Germany a reform on Spanish lines: the purging of unworthy elements among the clergy, the purifying of monastic life— but without interfering with doctrine. He anticipated a later remark of Charles to the Landgrave of Hesse: 'To reform is not to take on a new faith.' All agreed that it was most important to keep apart the Lutheran demands regarding Church practice and the erroneous articles of faith. Sickingen declared that he would defend Luther with his life in the cause of Church reform, but that he would be the first to burn those writings of Luther's that were contrary to Christian truth. Hutten agreed. Glapion therefore concluded that the most important question was settled, having won the consent of the leaders of the reforming party to deal with the reform problem apart from Luther's dogmatic assertions. He let it be known that the Emperor was raising Sickingen's and Hutten's remuneration (the latter drew it since his participation in the Swabian campaign) to four hundred gold ducats. Hutten accepted and for the time being he retained the imperial favour, although Luther's friend.

This equivocal loyalty of Hutten's did not receive a jolt till the spring of 1521. Luther's teaching had not as yet produced any practical changes and in Wittenberg holy Mass was still being said. A generally satisfactory solution of the reform question still seemed to be within reach. And

TOLEDO IN A STORM
El Greco, *Metropolitan Museum, New York*

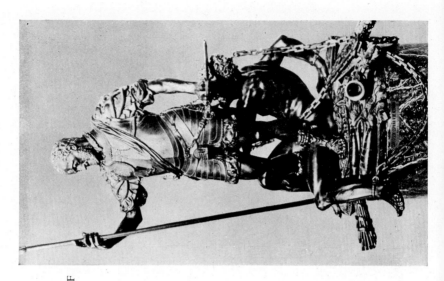

Glapion even considered a conversion on Luther's part to be within the bounds of possibility. In Worms, Luther was to be asked to recant only the part of his teaching that differed from the truths that were articles of faith in the Church—for all good Christians were at one with him in his demand for a renewal of faith in the spirit of the Gospel. Glapion had many kind words for Luther.

In an account of the meeting on the Ebernburg which Hutten sent Erasmus, he said: 'Glapion admitted that as far as he was concerned Luther had opened the way to an understanding of the deep mysteries of Holy Scripture; he had hitherto considered Luther a defender of true evangelical doctrine, and in Luther's teaching he had recognized the old authentic teaching of the Church.' Soon the rumour spread in Worms that the Emperor's confessor had been won over to Luther.

On the other hand, Aleander, who had been kept minutely informed of the course of the Ebernburg talks, recounted how, after a few words, Hutten had been won over by Glapion and had become 'tame as a lamb'; he said he did not represent Luther's point of view but only demanded that the ecclesiastics should be taken in hand and renounce their colossal wealth, which was the source of their vicious conduct, and that he himself only attacked the outward conditions of the Church and had not set himself in opposition to Church dogma.

Thus on the Ebernburg the two sides found a considerable amount of common ground. As yet, no fear of being false to one's belief strangled the desire for understanding, and no anxious clinging to the letter paralysed the common will to reform.

The preparatory work for Luther's appearance before the forum of the world and the Church was now completed. It remained to be seen whether he possessed the critical power and the insight necessary for a revision of his opinions, and whether he would be able to sift truth from falsehood in those articles of faith he had thrown out in the heat of battle: whether self-scrutiny would prevail over self-assertion.

Before Luther made his appearance on the stage of the Diet, Hutten sent him a letter saying: 'Have courage and be strong! You see what a turning-point in things depends on you!' At Worms Luther recanted none of his writings.

Hutten was delighted with his staunch stand. He saw political freedom within sight, and that was his own aim. But the Edict of Worms, in which Charles V decreed state proscription for Luther, put an abrupt end to his hopes. He rose in wrath and wrote to Charles that as the Emperor had taken the decision to persecute Luther, he himself was determined to defend him in the cause of evangelical freedom; and as the Emperor's will and his own were totally opposed, he could and would no longer remain in the Emperor's pay.

After this break, Hutten chose another slogan: *Jacta est alea*, 'the die is cast'. He composed a 'new song':

> I deliberately dared it,
> And have no remorse . . .
> . . . . . .
> A heart is not downcast
> That knows it is right. . . .

There is no doubt about the courage and vitality of Hutten's views; but the rightness of them is another matter. Hutten never considered whether his opinions were errors, he 'had no remorse'—Luther taught his self-assured disciples to live without remorse.

The Emperor's most loyal servant, Ulrich von Hutten, was now a rebel against the ordered structure of the realm which the Emperor stood for, and he exhausted himself in anti-Roman polemics. He inveighed 'against the Pope and his Romanists' and against the 'idle priests'; he called the popes 'God's enemies', and Rome he termed 'that godless Babylon'.

Hutten wrote in German to rouse the people:

> Formerly I wrote in Latin,
> Which was not known to everyone,
> Now I write for the fatherland,
> The German Nation in its tongue,
> To bring down vengeance in these things.

Napoleon on St Helena said: 'Do you think it was Luther who brought about the Reformation? Oh, no, it was public opinion that was opposed to the Pope.' The creation of this public opinion was in large part Hutten's work.

THE DIET OF WORMS (1521)

On 27th January 1521 the Diet was opened with High Mass in the body of the old romanesque Cathedral of Worms.

It is usual to see in this great Diet the first political manifestation of the

Protestant faith; and the encounter of Charles V and Luther is seen as the clash of the Middle Ages with modern times, the confrontation of the reactionary and the progressive spirit. Luther's followers believed that in Worms they experienced an encounter between the supporters of Antichrist and the champions of Christ.

Luther was desired to revoke those of his writings that 'sowed unrest and dissension in Germany'. But in the speech he made at the Diet of Worms on 18th April 1521, before 'the most gracious Lord and Emperor, the most illustrious Princes and gracious Lords' of the Empire and the dignitaries of the Church, he refused to recant and ended his speech with words in which some saw the courage of conviction, others mere obstinacy: 'Recant I cannot and will not, for it is neither safe nor wise to do anything against one's conscience. So help me, God. Amen.'

The Emperor intervened twice during the proceedings: first, when Luther spoke of the 'wickedness, avarice and tyranny of the Papacy', he broke in and commanded him to keep silence on that point; and again, when Luther denied the authority of the Council, he said, that was enough; since this man rejected the Council he would hear him no further.

Thus Luther threw the Emperor's favour to the winds, though the latter still hoped he would submit to the verdict of an ecclesiastical commission—which would have meant the solving of the doctrinal problem.

At the end of the session, Charles said he wondered that the man wrote such books. But his encounter with this monk who was so powerfully convinced of his own rightness made a profound and lasting impression on him.

If it was true that the young Emperor had hitherto been led 'like a child' by his counsellors, he came to himself when confronted with Luther's determination. He was barely twenty-one years old, his light-brown hair framed his pointed face page-fashion, in appearance he was still almost a boy. But his eyes were alert and for all his youth he bore the weight of the centuries and the memory of generations of ancestors loyal to the Church. His ancestral consciousness made him tradition-conscious. The faith that Luther attacked was the faith of Isabella the Catholic who went to fight the Moors, Cross in hand, it was the faith of the Dukes of Burgundy in whom lived the spirit of the Crusaders, the faith of Rudolf of Habsburg who on a stormy night met a priest hurrying to a sickbed with the Blessed Sacrament, and lifted him on to his horse to convey him over a rushing torrent—and he, Charles, was also to be the bearer of that sacred trust, the Faith, over the stormy seas of his time.

That very evening, after the Diet was over, Charles shut himself up in his room and wrote all night long, in his own hand, a memorandum addressed to the German nobles:

'You know that I issue from the Christian Emperors of the noble German nation, from the Catholic Kings of Spain, the Archdukes of Austria and the Dukes of Burgundy, who all to their death were loyal sons of the holy Roman Church. They defended the Faith for the glory of God and spread it for the salvation of souls. They bequeathed us a reverence for holy Catholic observance and the customary forms of Church rites, in which we, in faithful emulation of our predecessors, have lived till this day by the grace of God. I am determined to keep to them, as my predecessors did, and as I have hitherto done, and especially what was laid down by those predecessors of mine at the Council of Constance and other Councils; for those directives were right, and it is a great provocation that a single monk of erring opinions should rise up against the Faith which Christendom has practised for a thousand years, and would teach us that all Christians up till today have been in error. Therefore I am determined to pledge for this cause all my realm, my friends, my body, my blood, my life and my soul. For it would be for me as for you, who belong to the noble and renowned German nation, we who are called by priority and special prerogative to defend the Catholic Faith and guard it, a very great ignominy if in our time not only erroneous belief but even the mere semblance of heresy or a diminution of religion were to be ascribed to our negligence, remaining in people's hearts after us, to our eternal shame and calamity and that of our posterity. You heard the defiant answer Luther gave me yesterday in your presence. I tell you that I regret to have hesitated so long before taking action against the said Luther and his false teaching. I am determined never to listen to him again. He will be conducted back to his country under my protection, but he will be forbidden to preach his bad doctrine and to lead the people astray with his call to rebellion. I am determined to take proceedings against him as a notorious heretic. I beg you to declare yourselves in this matter, as good Christians, and in accord with your oath of allegiance.'

The memorandum is a wholly personal statement of Charles V's, it breathes with the solemnity that filled the young Emperor, as for the first time he made a pronouncement on his deepest convictions. One can picture Charles' expression at that moment, set, with a glow of determination playing on his face, lighting up his youth, telling of will and emotion both bent the same way.

From Worms we may date the birth of Charles V's personality, and at the same time the birth of the Counter-Reformation.

Now Charles V is by no means to be identified with the Counter-Reformation. He was to spend his latter years striving to bridge the antagonisms which he helped to create in Worms. For decades on end he was to represent the 'progressive' conciliatory movement as against the orthodox papal party.

However, in Worms Charles did in fact represent 'reaction' as against 'progress'. But the question arises, what meaning are we to give the word 'reaction' in this context?

A reaction is a natural spontaneous retort on receipt of a given impression, and it is inevitable in history. Charles' memorandum was the retort to Luther's challenge, it was—to adopt Hegel's proven terminology —the antithesis to Luther's thesis, and it had to be formulated in order to make a future synthesis possible.

A synthesis is only possible when a proposition and a counter-proposition have crystallized into clear definition.

At moments of high tension in history, it is chiefly a matter of clearing the atmosphere. But that process cannot start merely by bringing opposites together, but requires a wholly unambiguous statement of either case. That is the service rendered by Charles' memorandum: as a single-minded declaration of the Catholic standpoint it could not be improved. If Luther stuck resolutely and obstinately to his own opinion, the young Emperor replied with no less resolution and obstinacy; the Spanish-Burgundian royal prince was as unconditional as the Saxon peasant's son. Steel had met steel. And it was well that it was so, so that men should know where they stood.

It is an axiom of Protestant history-writing that at Worms Charles V lost the Reformation cause.

But he did not spurn the Reformation cause as such, only Luther's revolt against the authority of the Church.

He recognized by instinct, conditioned as he was by tradition, that Luther's attack upon the Church shook the very foundations of Europe. At Worms the young Emperor set himself to oppose this attack, ready, for the defence of the Old Faith, 'to pledge his realm, his friends, his body, his blood and his soul'.

For Luther's revolt against Rome was at the same time a revolt against the whole Christian tradition. It was a revolt against Albert the Great, and St Thomas Aquinas who had made Aristotle a part of the Christian heritage; it was a revolt against the humanism of the Renaissance which introduced Plato into the Christian field of thought; it was a relapse—in Étienne Gilson's words—'into what was darkest in that period called the Dark Ages'—a relapse into unreason.

Luther, who wished to see 'the whore, reason' driven out of the sphere of faith, struck a mortal blow at the very heart of Christian humanism by attacking the harmony of reason and faith, causing the breakdown and ruin of the great work of the Renaissance, which had consisted in uniting the old religion and the new learning.

It is worth noting that Luther made his attacks on the Roman Church from Wittenberg University; that university was first founded in 1502, that is to say, it had no roots in the high Middle Ages. Now Luther's defection from Rome also meant a break with mediaeval scholarship and its endeavour to reconcile the *theologia rationis* with the *theologia fidei* so as not to breach the fundamental unity of *Logos* and *Theos*.

Luther's assault on Scholasticism endangered the work of more than a thousand years, for Scholastic philosophy had incorporated Greek wisdom into the Church's body of doctrine. But Luther deplored the fact that in the universities 'there reigned the blind, heathen master, Aristotle', and his advice was to do away with his works altogether, for 'the damned deceitful pagan led so many of the best Christians astray'.

Luther attacked Scholasticism at the very time Erasmus dedicated to Leo X, the humanist Pope, his translation of the New Testament from the original Greek text into Latin. Erasmus rejected in Scholasticism only its desiccated formalism, not the living philosophical work as such, and his new translation with its exalted dedication paved the way for a renewal of theology within the framework of the Church. But Luther's defection destroyed this newly established and still precarious balance between tradition and research; Luther's thesis that reason stood in opposition to faith must be reckoned as a main cause of that dichotomy of mind and heart which has impoverished European thought ever since.

In his report on the Diet of Worms, the Papal Nuncio wrote that when he left the hall Luther 'raised his arms, as the Germans do in fencing, as a sign of victory'.

Sandoval tells us that 'next morning the Emperor did not wish to take part in the Diet, but had his Declaration read out. And great was the satisfaction and applause of the Catholics and all the greater the dissatisfaction and the disparaging murmurs of the Lutherans. The Catholics lauded the Emperor's steadfastness in loyalty to the true religion and said that he was indeed the worthy son of his forebears; the Lutherans, however, said he was young and badly counselled, that his friends did what they liked with him. Everywhere, written on the walls, appeared the words, *Vae terrae cujus Rex est puer* (Woe to the land whose king is a child). Four hundred German knights planned to kill the Archbishop of Mainz. In the proclamations, a taunting word of Luther's appeared again and again: 'defiance—defiance——'

In defiance of Pope and Emperor, Luther's followers elected the path of defection from the Catholic community. They went out of the body of the Church in which Christendom had grown up, at the very time when it was urgent to unite, in order to repair the old structure, and to enlarge and broaden its scope. The rejection of it as an entity by a fraction was the beginning of the end for the old Empire—the opening of a period of conflict, distress, fire, pestilence and turmoil.

THE EDICT OF WORMS (1521)

The Edict condemning Luther was published on 26th May 1521. Aleander reported to Rome that the Emperor signed the document in church, after High Mass, and said to him with a smile, 'Now you will be pleased with me' (for Aleander had wanted to see Luther condemned from the beginning). The Edict ran as follows: '. . . now that it is no longer hidden how far the errors and heresies depart from the Christian way, as taught by one named Martin Luther—destroying the seven sacraments—scandalously sullying the laws of holy matrimony—stating that holy anointing is an illusion—discarding confession, which is of such assistance to hearts sullied or laden with sins—denying free will—teaching a licentious, self-willed way of life exempt from all law and wholly bestial—he himself being a licentious, self-willed man who condemns and suppresses all law—therefore all writings of the said Luther are forbidden, as being evil, suspect, spurious, the work of a professed and hardened heretic, and it is prohibited to follow his opinions, to hold, preach or protect them, even when some good may be contained in them——'

The Edict was not given to the States General to confirm but was read out as the Emperor's decree. Charles V acted as absolute monarch and with youthful intolerance. He acted out of his own conviction, not on the Pope's directives, for Leo X was himself surprised at the severity of the Edict. He wrote a Brief in which he praised the 'more than human insight and wisdom of the Emperor': 'What greatness of soul! What steadfastness! God protect this King.'

Charles V believed he had finished with Luther's doctrine by proscribing him. 'In a well-ordered state, that would have sealed the fate of the new doctrine,' wrote H. Baumgarten. But in the German Empire the Emperor's word had lost its power long ago. The Edict was duly published, but it was not observed. The imposing of it would have demanded hard, radical measures. But Charles believed his word was deed, and he returned to Spain.

He was to remain away from Germany for eight years. During those years the German princes were to establish their power in the realm under the banner of 'evangelical freedom'. Soon they would seize hold of Church property. According to the chroniclers, 'the princes had gold and silver vessels, monstrances, pictures, relics and gems fetched from the churches and monasteries, to sell them and pocket the proceeds'. The Lutheran preachers roused the people against the clergy and inspired them with hatred of the Church. The war cry of 'the pure word of God', beside which all Church forms and rules were said to be mere 'human prescriptions', undermined the people's devotion to the old Catholic practices that had lent such dignity and dedication to daily life. Philip, Landgrave of Hess, compelled the inhabitants of his territory 'either to confess Christ or to emigrate'. The successor of the loyal Duke George of Saxony 'went reforming like a Turk or a Tartar'. In 1524 Magdeburg, Breslau, Nürnberg and Strasbourg abolished the Mass. The Papal Legate, Campeggio, wrote at that time from Württemberg, that the land was *lutheranissimo* and for three hundred years no such disorder had been known. It came to street-fighting in the cities, to peasant risings in the countryside, and monasteries were stormed.

Meanwhile, Charles was in Spain. What was the spell that held him so far away from Germany during those years of crisis? In 1523 Ferdinand wrote to his brother: 'The Lutheran sect rules in this whole German land, so that good Christians are afraid to stand out against it.' The situation in Germany called out for strong action, but nothing was done. Charles expected that a Council would settle the religious difficulties. With his own counsellors he discussed his wife's dowry. He pondered the recovery of Burgundy, the land of his ancestors.

In those years the threads were spun that bound Charles to Spain. 'He began to enjoy hunting,' Sandoval wrote; 'on the Toledo heath, more than once he went so far afield that no one could hear his horn and some sort of Morisco had to show him the way, when in the cities lights had already been placed in the windows and the bells were rung in order to look for him.'

Lost in remote Castile, the young Emperor forgot the world and its cares.

SOCIAL UNREST IN SPAIN (1519–21) AND IN GERMANY (1522–25)

While Charles was in Germany, Spain had undergone a period of serious disturbances. Charles left Cardinal Adrian of Utrecht (later Pope Hadrian VI) as Regent of the Spanish lands. In his Instructions there stood the phrase: 'The imperial throne is so great and exalted that it overtops all other offices of this world.' Spain still had no ear for this supra-national language. But Charles was in process of binding Spain to Europe; he was to extend the horizon of the Spanish lands over Europe and across the ocean, and he would cultivate in Spain a sense of universality corresponding to the idea of Empire, the Empire 'on which the sun never set'. The first, harsh lesson consisted in the suppression of rebellion in the Castilian boroughs.

The demands of the rebels, who called themselves Comuneros, were modest at first; they wanted each city to have two representatives in the *Cortes* elected by the borough. Hitherto they had usually been noblemen whom the king nominated. But now the city middle classes also wanted a voice in the direction of public affairs. The rebellion was not against the monarchy in the first place, but against the nobles who took advantage of Charles' absence to assert their right to be sole rulers. A part of the nobility gained control of the Comuneros movement and the rebellion turned into a common revolt of the cities, and some grandees, against the super-imposed monarchy.

It is worth noting that Padilla, the leader of the Comuneros, followed the same course, at first, as Franz von Sickingen was to pursue three years later in Germany: a fight of the lesser nobility and the cities against the higher nobility. In both cases it was a class struggle: the 'noble proletariat' and the middle classes wrestled with the princes for social recognition. Padilla and Sickingen both had in mind a form of democratic monarchy and both came into conflict with their lord and master only through pressure of the current they had let loose.

In Germany, a limitation of the independence of the regional princes was long overdue. Sickingen desired to realize a plan that Nicholas of Cusa had thought out a century earlier. In his work *On Catholic Unity*, Cusa wrote that the saving of the realm depended on a strong imperial throne; and it was the avarice and selfishness of the princes that were responsible for the decline of the realm, as of the Church. 'Whatever, in justice and equity, strengthens the power of the Emperor, strengthens the whole community and is best for the people,' he wrote; 'on the other hand, whatever weakens imperial power strengthens injustice.'

From this point of view Sickingen and Hutten believed they were fighting for the freedom of the German nation and for the power of the Emperor when they started their feud against the autocratic secular and ecclesiastical princes. Sickingen, captain of the Swabian union and leader of the knighthood, still enjoyed imperial favour. 'Most loved and loyal', Charles called him when he wrote to acknowledge his services in warding off French attacks; but when Sickingen proceeded on his own account against ecclesiastical princes and laid siege to the archiepiscopal city of Trèves, the Emperor proscribed him and the staunch knight fell in the fight for the social renewal of the old realm.

The fall of Sickingen and Hutten meant the end of the old German knighthood.

This culmination is usually regarded as 'historical necessity', the victory of the princes having liquidated a degenerate and socially superfluous class.

But every violent dispatch of a section of the nation's body-corporate is an injustice damaging to the whole. The end of the knights held up the growth of a politically influential middle class which would have filled the gap between the high nobility and the ordinary citizen. The intended marriage of Hutten to the daughter of a Frankfurt burgher was a symbol of the merging of the knighthood, in its decline, with the rising middle class. And Hutten's scholarly leanings prefigured a parallel merging of the lesser nobility in the new intellectual aristocracy of the humanists. In the cities, the law scholars saw themselves as successors to the knights and competed for knightly insignia. Emperor Sigismund had held learned men in high esteem and Emperor Maximilian had greatly strengthened the social position of the humanists; Charles V encouraged learning and intellectual pursuits, too, together with knowledge and skill: his most intimate collaborators, Valdés, Gattinara, Granvelle, van Male, all came from the burgher class, but the fact that he showered distinction on certain men could not counterpoise the reversal the middle class suffered through the newly acquired powers of the princes.

For the victory of the princes over the knighthood was a serious setback to the whole German middle class. The autocratic princes hindered the free development of German society and cheated the rising burghers of participation in the ordering of public affairs—a participation which had become a reality for a short moment, thanks to the social influence of the humanists. And the success of the Reformation (which was really a victory of the Protestant princes over the Emperor) reduced the burgher class to tutelage and suppressed the intellectual leadership of the humanists. The German burghers of the Renaissance were men of world-wide views and experience; the post-Reformation burgher was a small-minded man, servile by nature, a subject of princes with an all-too-narrow range of interests—and thus the idea of Empire died. The wide-flung national feeling that had animated knights, burghers and peasants on the eve of the Reformation expired. In the cities there grew up a generation which—to borrow an expression of Fichte's—'had lost its previous self and its previous time and world'. The splitting up of Germany suppressed the mediaeval notion of the common good: the German burgher was now intent on his personal interests alone. Participation in politics, and that sense of common responsibility, which had spoken out so urgently in the writings of the humanists, were heard of no more. The German became 'unpolitical', his convictions were henceforth 'his private concern'. The decline of the Empire began in the sixteenth century with the assertion of that self-centred mentality which, since Martin Luther, has characterized the German people.

The social evolution of the peasants was suppressed by the princes, too. It is significant that Marx and Engels dated their social theories from the German Peasant War, as though the period between 1525 and 1848 had never existed. For it is a fact that the defeat of the peasants brought the evolution of the underprivileged part of the population to a standstill and reduced the landworker to serfdom for centuries.

The crushing of the peasants would not have been so terrible had not the fanatical Anabaptists taken up their cause and made a radical issue of it. A political movement turned radical is apt to take on a momentum of greater or lesser violence in proportion to the tension involved. The more abstract the principle at stake, the more extreme will the concrete working out of it tend to be. 'Theory, too, becomes a material force as soon as it lays hold of the masses,' said Marx.

The peasants' lot was harsh enough to justify their complaints, and at the beginning of the Reformation they were greatly affected by evangelical preaching. Luther was—in Marx's words—'the lightning flash of thought striking into the midst of that naïve people'; the Gospel became their battle-cry.

At the beginning of the rising the peasants sought only to be rid of the unbearable burden of taxation and the perpetuation of debts; and (like the knights around Sickingen and Hutten) they desired 'to serve no other lord but the Emperor'; their political interests were, like the knights', based on a democratic monarchy. But the revival of the Gospel by Luther stirred them deeply: they declared that all charges not mentioned in Holy Scripture were 'ungodly', and they demanded 'that in accordance with Holy Scripture all things be in common and no distinction of rank exist': the basic Christianity preached by the reformers brought about a state of utter confusion.

Thomas Münzer, at one time a follower of Luther's, later the leader of the Anabaptists, found a faithful following among the dissatisfied peasants. His demands were akin to those of the Communist Manifesto: the Empire should be transformed into a single undivided republic; the whole community should have the right to bear weapons; the final goal was a social state without private ownership and without class distinctions, preparatory to bringing about the 'kingdom of God' on earth.

Once roused, the peasants were raw customers (their burly bodies may be seen in Dürer's engravings), ready to impose 'God's justice' with clubs and scythes. They were fired by Gospel texts and believed that 'the godless shall be thrown from their seats and those that are lowly be raised'. All their pent-up fury against their feudal lords exploded in a spate of violence; castles and monasteries were demolished, churches were ransacked and burnt to the ground. Around the year 1524, utter lawlessness reigned in many parts of Germany. As later in the French Revolution, in the German Peasant Rising complaints that were originally justified, and a reasonable desire to establish freedom and justice, led on to unreason and injustice, terror and the overthrow of the existing order.

Luther, the real author of all this unrest, disowned the phantoms he had conjured up. Erasmus retorted: 'You do not know those trouble-makers, but they know you.'

Luther advised the territorial princes to 'beat down the thieving murdering bands of peasants' like 'a mad dog'—'if you do not beat him, he will beat you'. He and Charles V, who tolerated the draconian action of the territorial rulers, both stood for the maintenance of the *status quo* against the revolution and gave the death-blow to a movement which had at first striven for human rights for a depressed class; its cause was, basically, nothing short of total reformation, that is, a reformation not of religious life only but also of social life in Germany.

In his attitude to the revolutionary movements of his time, Charles may well be accused of belonging to those who—in Marx's words—'declare every appeal of the serfs against the stick that beat them an act of rebellion, so long as the stick was a time-honoured one, a pedigree one, an historic one'. In those critical hours Charles V acted merely as was to be expected of a prince of his times. Indeed, the sovereign power of rulers was on the increase everywhere and the age of absolutism was nearly due.

News of the revolt of the Spanish Comuneros reached the Emperor at Worms, where he was detained by the Diet. He ordered the suppression of the rebellion. During his absence the movement had developed a revolutionary character. In Segovia, the rebels hanged a delegate who had voted in favour of paying tribute to the king, and they had taken possession of the town and castle of Tordesillas and appointed Charles' mother, Joanna, Queen of Castile. Joanna proved equal to the occasion: first she raised Padilla to the rank of Captain General of the rebel Junta. He declared it was his object to drive the Flemings out of Spain, and Joanna hated the Flemings. But when he brought her a manifesto sanctioning all the actions, present and future, of the Junta, she managed to postpone signing it.

Whether it was a whim of hers, for she always hated being forced to do things, or whether it was a piece of political sagacity on the part of this king's daughter, not wanting to bind herself to the king, her son's, opponents, we shall never know. The fact is, Joanna's procrastination saved the throne for her son Charles, the foreigner.

Soon after, the loyalists drove the rebels out of Tordesillas and defeated them in April 1521, near Villalar. Padilla and other inciters of the movement were taken captive and executed in the market-place of Villalar. The rebel cities surrendered, with the exception of Toledo where the remnant of the Comuneros withdrew.

Padilla's widow entrenched herself and her followers in the Toledo Alcázar, but was soon forced to yield. Thus ended the last open protest of the times against absolute monarchy in Spain.

Here the defeat of the Comuneros was not the prelude to a return to serfdom, as in Germany. The fact that the immediate lords of the people, the Spanish Grandees, submitted to the Emperor, meant that great and small alike bowed to the same overlord, and thus, in Spain, a liberal slogan held good: *Del Rey abajo, ninguno!*—No lord have I beneath the King. Here, a strong Emperor strengthened the case for the individual. Whereas in Germany, his weak position reduced the lower levels of the population to utter dependence on their territorial rulers.

CHARLES V'S ALCÁZAR

The Toledo Alcázar was to be an expression of the idea of *imperium*. In July 1522 Charles V came back to Spain accompanied by a strong Flemish following and four thousand Germans. In M. Bataillon's words, he came 'as the arm of the universal Church', as Caesar almighty. Those of the rebels who had reckoned the king would not return now had serious misgivings. But in October a general amnesty was decreed and thus peace was restored to the land. Then Charles imposed on Toledo, the rebel stronghold, the building of a huge palace. The conception of the universal Empire had won the day. Toledo was capital of the Empire on which the sun never set.

The imperial coat-of-arms shows Charles' entry into Toledo. His imperial title now took precedence of that of King of Spain. The Spanish lands and those overseas were parts of one and the same realm.

Charles had a new gateway built in the old city walls, the *Puerta de Bisagra*. Over the archway, the double-headed eagle spreads its wings as confidently as over the entrance to the Hofburg in Vienna.

The word *Bisagra* comes of a telescoping of *via sacra, via sagrada*, the holy way. In former days it was the road to the sanctuary; later, to the castle. For from earliest times the castle stood next to the church to guard and defend it. Every ruler of Toledo added his quota to the fortress, which commanded a wide stretch of the plain. Charles V had a wholly new structure erected on the old foundations: a square building, flanked at the corners by massive towers, around a central inner courtyard called the *Patio Carlos Quinto*.

The building began in 1537. The Emperor never saw the completion of it, though it bears his stamp.

In 1525 the Emperor called the Cortes to Toledo, for he was in need of money for his North-Italian campaigns. The Cortes suggested he should marry, and proposed Isabella of Portugal, 'for she is of our tongue'. Also, the dowry of the Portuguese princess was considerable, for since the discovery of the 'Spice Islands', Portugal was a prosperous country.

The Emperor had been betrothed to Mary Tudor of England since 1522; she was sixteen years his junior and he was waiting till she grew up. Now he gave up the idea and asked King Manuel of Portugal for his daughter's hand.

The wedding took place in Seville a year later.

Toledo pleased the young Empress. Here she could see the Tajo whose green waters flowed on to Lisbon, her home.

But the responsibilities of government constantly tore the Emperor away from his much-loved wife; he felt a compulsion to be on the spot when decisive action was taken, as though conscious of being the instrument of Providence determining the course of destiny through his person. 'Oh, if I were there . . .' he cried, on receiving news of the outbreak of a new conflict, and departed soon after in order to be where danger loomed, in spite of distance, the difficulties of travel, lack of money, and the pangs of gout which tormented him in his latter years: it was the call of duty.

This continuous campaigning was costly. In November 1538 the Emperor once more called the Cortes to Toledo to discuss means of raising yet more financial assistance. He proposed a new tax which was to consist in reducing the quantity or weight of certain foodstuffs without altering the price. The Cortes angrily rejected the measure. 'That time I understood how little power I really have,' said the king some years later.

In his *Historiae*, Paolo Giovio (Jovius), chronicler and bishop, describes with all the sensitive appreciation of an Italian for a difficult political situation, an incident that laid bare the underground seething in Toledo—a city only superficially tamed.

During the session of the Cortes, the Duke de l'Infantado injured an imperial guardsman on account of some accidental misdemeanour; all the Grandees took the Duke's part; the atmosphere was so tense that the Emperor did not dare oppose them and even went so far as to declare himself ready to punish the guardsman.

The unfortunate man served as lightning-conductor to the Grandees' dissatisfaction with the Emperor's rule.

Jovius found this dissatisfaction not only among the nobility but among the populace, too. The grounds for it were the growing burden of taxation, perpetual warfare and the export of money. 'The fine gold

Taler which were so precious to Ferdinand and Isabella were no more to be seen. The land was impoverished and depopulated, the men went elsewhere. What did it matter to the masses that a few soldiers made their fortune, that government officials grew prosperous in lucrative posts and that the Spanish legions won fame on the battle-fields of Europe and amassed immense wealth in the lands of the new world? Neither peace nor welfare would return so long as Charles commanded the Christian armies.'

This statement of Bishop Jovius', written in the Emperor's life-time, provoked Charles to call him 'his liar'. According to Sandoval, during the negotiations the Emperor told the recalcitrant Constable of Castile he would throw him out of the window. The Constable retorted: 'Be careful, Your Majesty, though I am small I weigh heavy.'

It was at the Toledo Cortes of 1538–39 that the Castile representatives expressed a wish they had already once laid before the Emperor—regarding the keeping of records. 'We entreat your Majesty to appoint qualified persons to have the old and the earliest chronicles superscribed, so that the memory of the great deeds of your predecessors and your subjects be not forgotten.'

There spoke Spain, in all her awareness of tradition and her belief that written history is the record of a nation's memories. Historical awareness is a source of power, endowing passing events with permanence and the fleeting moment with a form of eternity. No condition of life can be taken as absolute and final when it is seen as a stage in an unbroken evolution. Each moment is supported by its relationship to the remote past and distant future: thus seen, the present is always the fullness of time, and history is both memory and hope.

It was probably under the sway of a Spanish sense of continuity that Charles decided to have the events of his life-time written down, so that no link should be missing in the chain connecting past and future.

The Emperor raised the Toledo Cortes in February 1539 without having accomplished anything.

A few months later the Empress died after giving birth to a stillborn son.

In deep grief, the Emperor withdrew to the monastery of La Sisla, where he remained for a time completely cut off from the world.

After that he paid only short visits to Toledo. The building of the Alcázar was continued by his son, Philip, who also carried on there the tasks initiated by his father.

CHARLES V IN 1520
Anonymous master of the 16th century, *The Louvre, Paris*

ERASMUS OF ROTTERDAM
Holbein the Younger, *The Louvre, Paris*

In January 1560 the building of the Alcázar was so far advanced that Philip II and his third wife, Isabella of Valois, could spend the first weeks of their married life in the new part of the castle. This serious monarch appeared to take pleasure in music and dancing again, and he himself drew up a detailed programme for the festivities, but they had to be cancelled because the young queen got chicken-pox.

Philip summoned the Cortes to Toledo to take the oath of loyalty to Carlos, the heir to the throne; at the same time the state finances were to be broached, and also the religious question. Luther's doctrine had cropped up again in Seville and was to be stamped out with the same severity as Calvinism in the Netherlands.

Philip II spoke like his father when he said: 'I have asked the Supreme Pontiff for the resumption of the Council of Trent and for the reformation of the clergy and monasteries in Spain, so that they may serve God with more integrity, purity and perfection . . .' and '. . . to make laws to reform what is bad and bring about better things. Very few laws will do, but they must be kept. They should be just and not make impossible demands, they should be adapted to the nature of our subjects just as medicine is adapted to the disease and the physical condition of patients. . . .'

At the end of his speech the king asked for money, 'in order that my armies may advance against the Turks and Moors, and in order to equip a fleet to defend the shores of the Mediterranean. . . .'

Thus within Toledo's narrow walls there rang out anew a summons calling for the defence of the entire Empire. But the city found such far-reaching appeals distasteful; shut up within its ramparts, irrevocably determined by the course of the River Tajo, it was incapable of expansion. It withdrew into its shell more stubbornly than ever when the king gave vent to his fateful utterance: 'I see Toledo as unfit to be a capital city.'

Philip III and Philip IV continued the building of the Alcázar. Various outbreaks of fire prevented its completion. In 1810, when Napoleon's troops abandoned Toledo, the Alcázar burned for three days on end. The rebuilding was completed in 1887. Later the royal palace served as a training college for cadets.

From 21st July to 27th September 1936 the national cadets heroically defended it against the assaults of Red Toledo.

We may well inquire into the meaning of what the Spaniards called 'red' in the summer of 1936.

Charles V would undoubtedly have considered every rising against his authority as 'red'. For Dante, the inhabitants of the Inferno were 'red', and to St Catherine of Siena her 'false self' was, no doubt, 'red', reckoning it as she did among the 'enemies of God'.

'Red' is a form of self-assertion, it is a sullen hatred for what is elevated, it is a denial of the kingdom of grace. Today, 'red' comes to us disguised as progress. But what passes for progress in our sluggish temporality is in truth but a hampering lop-sidedness, nothing alive. Thus at night we see stars that went out long ago.

In the summer of 1936, when the Red Revolution shook Spain to her foundations, the union of conservative interests in Navarre (the home of Ignatius of Loyola) published a little book which addressed itself to the individual in Loyola's own tones: 'The cause you are defending is God's cause. Consider yourself as a soldier on a crusade whose goal is God, relying on Him for victory. Think that you will give back to Christ His favoured nation which the sects have torn away from Him.... May your actions be performed in all piety, a piety founded on prayer, self-conquest and love for Jesus Christ.'

It is important to recognize the religious forces which were at work in Spain during that time, and it is important not to confuse those forces with any aspect of the contemporaneous movements in Italy and Germany. Precisely the anti-Catholic character of National Socialism proves how incorrect it was to apply the same norm to all the various forms of counter-action to the action of the extreme left in central and southern Europe. Spain alone reacted to the claims of militant atheism from the very heart of her unbroken Christian tradition, that fact has to be frankly admitted, and, with the passing of an historic age in Europe, must not be buried under the rubble: it contains the essence of true renewal.

In that summer of 1936 Toledo, self-willed, autocratic, Moorish Toledo, the Toledo of the Comuneros, beleaguered the Alcázar, that one-time stronghold of absolute monarchy; incarcerated within the old fortress, the cadets under the leadership of General Moscardo remained loyal to old Spain and defended the Alcázar under machine-gun fire and exploding mines and bombs for ten weeks long, till on 27th September they were relieved by the national troops under General Varola.

A veteran of the defence led me through the great ruin, through the mined passages, through the cellars that served as a military hospital, into the half-ruined inner courtyard, the *Patio de Carlos Quinto*, now *Patio de los Martires* in honour of the hundreds who met their death here.

In the midst of the rubble there stands the bronze statue of Charles V as victor of Tunis, with *Furor* in chains at his feet; he gazes unconcernedly upon the ruins around him and the pillars bearing the Habsburg arms. The Alcázar fell, but the soul of Spain was saved.

I found General Moscardo's room intensely moving. Here, on a table, stands the old field telephone through which he spoke to his son, a prisoner of the Reds who said they would shoot him if the Alcázar was not given up. The general refused to yield and his son was shot. On the wall there is a tablet bearing the words of their last conversation: 'My son, God receive your soul, cry "Long live Spain", and die like a patriot.'

I was overcome and could scarcely hold back my tears. It was not just the emotion we all feel on hearing of noble deeds, taking us back to our childhood when stories of knights and heroes who stood out for the right caused us such delight; it was the sorrow of knowing the sacrifice was, in a sense, in vain. The heavy sacrifices of the Catholic and conservative forces in Spain were insufficient to chain up the *furor* of world revolution.

That great relic of national defence, the Alcázar, is an historic monument. But if we wonder why the antitheses that were fought out in those walls still stand unreconciled today, it is because the world misunderstood the sacrifice made here. The retort was the right one for the times, but it was turned down by the bulk of the intellectuals of the western world. And that has constituted a handicap to the proper course of things. The western spirit remains dumb in the face of the undiminished claims of revolutionary doctrine for world domination. Incapable of spiritual counteraction, incapable of solving its divisions, incapable of creating that synthesis for which our time longs.

Indeed, those are glorious ruins, and the resistance they enshrined was a necessary one. But we do not want to maintain a permanent state of antagonism, and may we be preserved from having to seek in unholy wars a solution that has to be worked out in the spiritual sphere. Let us all consent to change, then we may shape a new world together. I thought of a word of Schelling's, the last sentence in his book *On Human Freedom*: 'This is not the time to stir up old quarrels but to seek what lies above and beyond all disparity.'

TOLEDO: THE BRIDGE

Siesta-time in Spain, with its darkened rooms. . . . When I returned to my room after the midday meal, the blinds were drawn down and the light that reigns over Toledo only shot in through the cracks. All life was at rest. The hour of the *siesta* is a holy hour. At that time of day the Arabian spirit of the city seems to pierce a way through the walls like the sunlight that slowly penetrates into a room.

It is odd to realize that the first contact of the European Middle Ages with the old forgotten Greek ideas took place here, in Toledo. But if we remember the church of *El Christo de la Luz*, where the Christian liturgy is celebrated among narrow Moorish arches, or the juxtaposition and mingling of architectural styles which give Toledo its distinctive character, it is easier to understand the effect and counter-effect of the Christian and Arabian spirit the one upon the other.

The Berber dynasty of the Almohades was a tolerant one and the set forms of Islam were blurred: it was held there was no great distinction between religion and philosophy, both being based on the same fundamental truth. Theologians and philosophers were free to go their own ways and—as the great thinker, Ibn Tufail, expressed it—'withdrawn in quiet contemplation, to live in princely libraries'. The Spanish-Arabic philosopher, Avempace of Saragossa, taught a mysticism of reason: by penetration into the active *Logos* of the world, human reason participated in the divine spirit. Averroës, the greatest of the Spanish-Arabic thinkers, also propounded the harmony of philosophy and religion, whose truths could not be in opposition for they issued from the same ground. These were the ideas of Plotinus and the Neo-Platonists that Averroës knew in the Arabic translation of the original Greek texts. Averroës was known as the highest authority on Aristotle: his ideas, together with the work of the Jewish philosopher Maimonides, made such an impression on Thomas Aquinas that he wrote his *Summa contra gentiles* to counter the influence they exerted.

In his *Introduction to the History of Mystical Literature in Spain*, Don Pedro Sáinz Rodríguez wrote the following passage: 'Since Renan demonstrated in *Averroës et l'Averroïsme*, that the reappearance of classical culture in the Toledo translations divided the history of mediaeval philosophy into two halves, there is no longer any doubt as to how much Arabic scholarship influenced the West. The development of this school of translators under Archbishop Don Raimundo leads to the conclusion that there was a long preparatory period during which earlier translations were done privately and subsequently lost, while research in oriental learning was carried on with religious devotion. It was a cult that grew steadily, scholars from many lands collaborating: Adelard of Bath, Hermann the Dalmatian, Alfred de Morley, Gerardo de Cremona, Michael Scotus and Hermann the German formed the nucleus of the groups of foreign scholars who worked hand in hand with Spaniards like Dominico Gundisalvo, Juan Hispalense, and Arabic and Jewish converts.'

The Jewish contribution to this work of mediation between East and West was considerable: the Jewish translators and publishers helped the wandering scholars who came to Toledo from Oxford, Paris, Cologne, to decipher the Arabic manuscripts and to retrieve from beneath the unfamiliar script the Greek wisdom it held concealed.

The exchange of ideas that this hive of activity fostered between Spain and the rest of Europe began with the reconquest of Toledo by Alfonso VI in the year 1085; and during the next two centuries Toledo was a spiritual centre for Spanish Christians, Arabs and Jews, and for pilgrims from France, England, Germany and Italy. The views of the philosophers Cordobas, Averroës and Maimonides were expounded and discussed at the Toledo School.

Averroës shared the opinion of the Gnostics that philosophy is only the concern of an enlightened minority; the elucidation of revealed religion being the business of scholars, not of ordinary people. Only those capable of philosophical thought should be permitted to explain Holy Scripture; they should, however, be given complete freedom. And they should only express their views in learned circles, in order not to confuse the masses nor disturb the peace of mind of simple people. Ideas were dangerous powers which had to be kept firmly under control, for if they made their way out into the open they condensed, and if they were not of the purest kind, they inevitably did much harm. . . . Erasmus constantly recommended 'that the matter be handed over to a few honourable learned men', and he lamented 'that the Germans must always be putting ideas into the heads of the common people'. On 8th June 1529 he wrote from

Freiburg: 'As for themes such as "Of the Free Will" and their like, there is much to be gained, from the religious standpoint, when they can be disputed in circles of learned men, but on condition that the enemies of Truth remain absent: I mean stubbornness and hatred, which cloud all powers of judgement. . . .'

GARCILASO DE LA VEGA

Marañón wrote that in the opinion of Nieremberg, of the Society of Jesus, it was Garcilaso de la Vega, the poet, a native of Toledo, who taught Charles V Spanish. 'Few men experienced as Charles of Habsburg did what a new language means to the soul; and the speech of Castile was planted in his mind by this wonderful gardener, with purest seed from Castilian soil.'

As his familiarity with his mother's tongue increased, the Emperor gradually acquired an understanding of his Spanish lands; his was a many-faceted personality and now the Spanish features came into evidence: steadfastness, perseverance, powers of resistance, strength of will, and thus Garcilaso's influence is not an unimportant one in Charles V's life.

Garcilaso, only a few years younger than Charles, entered his service in 1519. Charles, who picked his people with a sure eye, took him into the Royal Guard in 1520. In the same year Garcilaso's brother, Don Pedro Laso de la Vega, became a leader of the Comuneros rebellion. Thus civil war parted the brothers. Garcilaso remained loyal—a Ghibelline who followed his lord over all the battle-fields of Europe, fought at the Emperor's side in Tunis, was wounded by a Moorish spear, and shortly after his recovery, a year later, met his death at the storming of a citadel in Provence.

Garcilaso was not alone in his steadfast loyalty. Charles de Bourbon the Frenchman, Andrea Doria the Italian, served Charles devotedly. Spaniards and Germans, Dutch and Austrians often fought for their Emperor without pay. Garcilaso frequently spoke of his 'devout and valiant Caesar' and his admiration witnesses to the natural authority Charles V exercised over those around him and to the power of attraction of the Catholic ideal he stood for.

Although Garcilaso dedicated his whole life to the Emperor's service, his poems betray a deep weariness of wars (Jovius noted this in 1538, on the occasion of the Toledo Cortes), and also the melancholy that emanated from that old, disillusioned Toledo that declined to squander its blood and money on distant battle-fields. In his first Elegy occurs the following passage:

> More heavily than ever, now, Misfortune
> Weighs down upon our time, disfigures it,
> Turns it from bad to worse.
>
> And who is not
> Affected by these wars—
> By constant warfare, danger, banishment?
>
> And who, this year, is not exhausted too?
> Who has not seen his blood on a foe's spear
> —And by a hair's breadth
>
> Eluded death. And so much is at stake,
> House, home, wife, property.
>
> What is the meaning of it all?
> A little glory?
> Pay, or promotion? Or some other gain?
>
> He will see who reads, in the great plan,
> The fate whereby like dust in wind
> All our toil dissolves and our illusions too.

This elegy is akin in feeling to the lamentation of Andreas Gryphius in Germany, a hundred years later: 'So now we are utterly, more than utterly, laid waste . . .'

Charles V's battles may look like knightly tournaments compared with the horrors of the Thirty Years War. But war is always 'fire, pestilence and death that strikes through heart and mind'. And Garcilaso composed his poem 'among the weapons of bloody Mars'. In the second Elegy we find him 'in wild Germany' (*la fiera Alemaña*) and we see Charles in Regensburg, where he had called a Diet in March 1532; at that time the loyal knights of the Empire were assembling there to join the Emperor's advance upon the Turks.

Garcilaso, too, made haste to arrive in time for the campaign. But he had incurred the Emperor's displeasure during his stay in Spain: he had in

Emperor and his knights were waiting 'till the Danube was favourable' to travel by boat to Vienna and free the city from the Turkish menace.

Thus Danube and Tajo both flow through the landscape of this poet's mind, a poet who had all Charles V's realm for his imagination's playground.

Garcilaso fell in battle for his Emperor at the age of thirty-four, and it was the Marquis de Lombay, Duke of Gandia, later a Jesuit, Francisco de Borja, who consoled him in his last hours. '. . . and coldly and numbly he watched the speaker's inspired delivery, garb of the most cultured flowering of learning and oratory. . . .'

TOLEDO AT NIGHT

After sunset the streets of Toledo are deserted. In other Spanish cities the children play, sing, laugh, scream, dance around till midnight; the men sit before the coffee-houses, talking and talking; the women lean at the windows and watch the life of the street go by. But the narrow roads of Toledo are empty at ten o'clock and night falls upon a city gone dead.

This nocturnal silence is uncanny; as though an unfamiliar way of life had deliberately retreated behind closed shutters and went on brooding there in its impervious otherness.

Only the full moon lights up the gloom of those narrow, gully-like ways. But some are roofed over with wood, Moorish fashion, and remain dark even by moonlight. At night the oriental character of Toledo emerges, narrow and enclosed like a ghetto.

The high cloister walls are windowless; the church, too, seems to be on the defensive, taciturn and inscrutable.

This negative attitude, this crouching density, this pugnacious insistence on being itself, are typical of Toledo: that is why Garcilaso, its poet, called it *aquella ilustre y clara pesadumbre*, 'that illustrious and clear nightmare'—a vivid but heavy dream. . . .

At night a frightening dream. In the morning uncomprehended, secretive and distant.

from that old, disillusioned Toledo that declined to squander its blood and money on distant battle-fields. In his first Elegy occurs the following passage:

> More heavily than ever, now, Misfortune
>   Weighs down upon our time, disfigures it,
>   Turns it from bad to worse.
>
> And who is not
>   Affected by these wars—
>   By constant warfare, danger, banishment?
>
> And who, this year, is not exhausted too?
>   Who has not seen his blood on a foe's spear
>   —And by a hair's breadth
>
> Eluded death. And so much is at stake,
>   House, home, wife, property.
>
> What is the meaning of it all?
>   A little glory?
>   Pay, or promotion? Or some other gain?
>
> He will see who reads, in the great plan,
>   The fate whereby like dust in wind
>   All our toil dissolves and our illusions too.

This elegy is akin in feeling to the lamentation of Andreas Gryphius in Germany, a hundred years later: 'So now we are utterly, more than utterly, laid waste . . .'

Charles V's battles may look like knightly tournaments compared with the horrors of the Thirty Years War. But war is always 'fire, pestilence and death that strikes through heart and mind'. And Garcilaso composed his poem 'among the weapons of bloody Mars'. In the second Elegy we find him 'in wild Germany' (la fiera Alemaña) and we see Charles in Regensburg, where he had called a Diet in March 1532; at that time the loyal knights of the Empire were assembling there to join the Emperor's advance upon the Turks.

Garcilaso, too, made haste to arrive in time for the campaign. But he had incurred the Emperor's displeasure during his stay in Spain: he had in fact sponsored the marriage of his nephew (son of the Comuneros Don Pedro Laso de la Vega) to the daughter of the Duke of Albuquerque. The bride's father rose in wrath, for to his mind the civil war was still on, and turned to the Empress to have the marriage declared invalid. The Emperor, who allowed no romantic ideas to tinge marriage matters, annulled it on the ground that the pair were minors, and Garcilaso, witness to the marriage, fell into disgrace.

A contract of marriage was a very responsible undertaking for a member of the House of Habsburg, with consequences that went far beyond the feelings of the individuals concerned. When Charles, as Duke of Burgundy, a young man scarcely come of age, discovered his sister Leonora was secretly in love with the Palatine Count of Heidelberg, he tore from her hand a letter she had just received from her lover and, though she was two years his senior, he gave her a round scolding: how could she, a Habsburg princess, so forget herself? It was her duty to serve the dynasty. She should seriously consider the significance of her forthcoming marriage to the King of Portugal. It was a matter of life and death to Spain that Portugal be incorporated in the Iberian unity. And for centuries the Castilian princesses had served this need. Leonora was to marry the widower of her two aunts, Don Manuel of Portugal. Leonora did as she was told.

At the Brussels court, this manifestation of brotherly authority caused great surprise. Cardinal Wolsey's representative wrote to London: 'All the world is taken aback at the uncompromising attitude of the young King, in which signs of future strength of character are unmistakably evident. It is prophesied he will remain tenacious in his views and decisions, and also be careful that the world acquire a high opinion of him.'

Charles was obstinate in Garcilaso's case, too. On his arrival in Regensburg, he refused to receive him and banished him to an island on the Danube as punishment for taking matters into his own hands.

His captivity lasted all the spring and summer of 1532. In the green solitude of his exile he wrote his *Canción tercera* which begins:

> With the gentle sound of
> swift clear water
> the Danube plays around a quiet isle . . .

The Danube flows through this poem a singing river of life:

'Here they heard the mighty Danube rushing . . .' and we see this clear ancient stream flowing mightily on, flowing past Regensburg where the

IV

FROM MADRID TO ANDALUCÍA

Time is an extension of the soul
St Augustine,
Confessions, Book XI, c. XXVI

MADRID

My departure from Toledo was a sort of flight. In the last days of my stay I had tried to paint a picture of the city, but the terseness of the preliminary sketch seemed to snap my brush in two. I broke off in despair only to start again from another viewpoint, dominated by Toledo, dutifully at its service.

The one-time imperial capital now lies so far off the beaten track that the railway line ends there; beyond Toledo the plain appears to stretch out into unfrequented distances. One has to return to Madrid to get a train connection to Andalucía.

Madrid was breathing-space again. The unassuming flatness of the city was like a recovery of selfhood after being a prey to unfamiliar influences.

The personality of individual Spanish towns is so strong that one ought to leave stretches of time between them to enjoy their full effect. Things need to be apart from one another, and the distance that separates them individually is surely the secret of the Creation.

And the spell of a city should be allowed to melt away, one should wait till the mind is itself again before stepping into the sphere of a fresh influence. A mule's trot, a pilgrim's gait formerly divided distances into humanly-manageable proportions; but our present rapid mode of travel forcibly curtails a natural span, cutting out the time we need to pass from one condition of life into another. For the spirit of a place makes great demands and requires our mind to be empty before it will surrender to us. From by-gone days when coming and going was difficult, the Spanish cities have retained their integrity: enthroned in solitary state, they contemplate their realm, the wide spaces. Distance and the bleakness of plains and craggy mountains are the very essence of the Spanish landscape, and wide-open spaces are basic to Spain's soul, filled by day with the powerful light of the sun and at night open to the stars.

Andalucía was the goal of my journey.

For years those names had been calling me: *Ronda—Granada—Córdoba.*

Last winter, turning over the pages of a Rilke book, I found a passage which awoke the cadence of those sonorous names. It was a biography, telling how Rilke once opened an old travel diary in a Russian country house: 'He found a drawing of a towering city with great bridges which made a great impression on him. The city was Ronda in Spain.'

Ronda—it was the sound of it that made me want to paint in Spain.

Ronda, the 'towering city with the great bridges' was the mainspring that set me off on my Spanish journey.

And now I was in Spain, and Ronda was no longer the ultimate purpose of my being there. For unexpected developments had driven Ronda into the back of my mind: since I was in the Escorial library, reading deep into Habsburg history, Ronda had retreated farther and farther away. The magic sound no longer called enticingly, for it held no promise of bringing me face to face with the figures occupying my mind. Neither Charles V nor Philip II had ever set foot in Ronda; it was a heathen place, once a stronghold of the Saracens against Isabella the Catholic, but far from the tracks that brought me to Granada.

In Granada Charles V spent the first happy weeks of his marriage with Isabella of Portugal.

In Granada Charles' parents repose in the royal vault—Joan the Mad and Philip the Fair, and his grandparents, Isabella of Castile and Ferdinand of Aragon.

What riches—all in that one focal point that lay in southern Spain and was called Granada.

BY RAIL TO ANDALUCÍA

The Andalucía express left Madrid at nine o'clock at night. The second-class carriage was full and sleep was not to be thought of. At every station the call rang out: '*Agua, hay agua, Ague helada como la nieve*'— water as icy as snow—and it sounded like a verse of Garcilaso's:

> In the midst of winter, warm
> Is the sweet water of the limpid source,
> But in summer it is like snow
> So icy cold. . . .

Women with earthenware vessels of water came into the compartment, others offered bread and burnous; there were sellers of lottery tickets and newspaper-boys shouting *informaciones* at the top of their voices. Soon the floor was littered with paper, banana-skins and burnous nutshells.

Conversation was about the difficulties of the food situation. Complaints were given the lie, to some extent, by the opulence of the provisions that were unpacked: pots and dishes appeared containing cooked suppers; plates, spoons, knives and forks were handed out, and cold omelettes were consumed with pieces of poisonously red sausage. Roast cutlets and huge white rolls followed. A bottle of red wine did the round, but not literally from mouth to mouth, for my fellow travellers were versed in the art of pouring the liquid into their mouths from above.

I always picture Spain as the land of Don Quixote, but it is Sancho Panza's land, too, I ruminated, sampling the food I was offered.

'There is a lot of hunger about,' said the Señora; 'though it is certainly better than after our war, but the black market is worse than ever before.'

Listening to the conversation that now unfolded, one could have supposed that the majority of Spaniards were wholly engaged in illegal trafficking. 'But it is not only here,' I said, rising to the defence of the land of the knights and saints, 'the war started it off.' 'The war . . .' the conversation now languished in fears of a new war. 'If war comes,' said a young man, 'don't count on me. I shall go to the mountains. . . .'

They asked where I came from.

Austria, I replied, and the word sounded as foreign to the ears of those Spaniards of today as the name of any far-off land 'of which we know nothing' (to quote Chamberlain in 1938). My fellow travellers looked at me with some distrust. How were they to know that through *Carlos Quinto de la Casa de Austria* I was related to Spain? And related to them: we had a common ancestor, *Carlos Quinto*.

The train was taking me to meet Carlos Quinto in Granada. The Andalucía express often crept along at a snail's pace and the stops at stations lasted endlessly. I began to think over St Augustine's words: 'Time is an extension of the soul.' Time and space are so intimately connected, space must be 'an extension of the soul' too. One is only conscious of time and space when they measure the distance from a desired goal. If one is far from the goal, time seems slow and space overwhelmingly wide: but when one has reached it, space and time have no more meaning. . . .

Thus we came to the morning.

'Now we must soon be getting there,' I said to the company, which was just waking up, and we all stretched our stiff limbs.—'Not for a long time.'—'We are hours late.'—'We must be pleased if we get there at all, every day trains run off the rails.'—'The connection to Córdoba no longer exists.'—'I am expected at Granada.'

Names like 'Granada', 'Córdoba' were in daily common use here, but I shuddered every time I heard those prophetic sounds.

The landscape that drew past seemed as bleak as Castile, only more mountainous, more splendid, with a heavier haze in the sky. Barren hills, grey patches of stone, long-drawn-out, dark streaks of mountains on the horizon; sometimes reddish-brown ploughed fields appeared, with low stone dividing walls, and low houses as grey as the stone they were built of.

Slowly, slowly, this grave landscape lit up. Grey-green olive trees drew a shimmer of silver across the hills. Here and there appeared a gleam of bright green winter corn. Pale-rose flowering almonds bordered the roads—all colours unbelievably tender, silver-grey and rose, olive green, earthy brown. . . .

In his book on Spain, Théophile Gautier says one should visit countries in their extremest seasons, Russia in winter, Spain in summer.

The first time I came to Spain was in June and the heat was terrific. I went by car from Portugal through Estremadura, with its completely barren appearance, the towns and villages rising from it like heaps of stones. The sky was white with light dazzling to the eyes. That time, I saw Spain as a land of light and shadow, as T. E. Lawrence saw the Arabs, 'a people of black and white'.

But this early spring scene revealed a wholly new aspect of nature in Spain.

Or was this just *Andalucía*—mild, softly blossoming, and sad?

V

GRANADA

Princess, whose loving found no counter-love.
Crimson carnation in a deep, deserted valley.

. . . .

Granada was your resting-place, Doña Juana,
The window-framed Sierra formed a picture for you,
A snowy picture, cooling your incandescence
With the rushing waters of the Darro as it passed by you.

from *Lorca*, '*Elegy to Joan the Mad*'

IVY IN GRANADA

In Granada it was raining. Mist covered the mountains, water poured down the road and the dark green of the ivy shone out in the rain. Ivy everywhere, on the tree-trunks, on the Alhambra walls and sprawling over Charles V's palace and the Moorish castle, uniting contrasting periods and styles.

I pushed the curtain of ivy aside to read the inscription over a doorway: *Imperatori Caesari Carolo V. . . .*

So there is ivy over your name and over the way you went.

The ivy had a deep still shine and the odour of a gentle sadness rose from the soil. How true it is:

> The glories of our blood and state
> Are shadows, not substantial things,
> There is no armour against fate,
> Death lays his icy hand on Kings,
> Sceptre and Crown
> Must tumble down
> And in the dust be equal made
> With the poor crooked scythe and spade.
>
> (*James Shirley*, 1659)

THE ALHAMBRA

The Parador de San Francisco where I stayed was once a Franciscan monastery, now a guest-house. My room with its corroded dark-brown furniture and whitewashed walls was like a cell, the view from the window its only adornment. Outside was a slope pink with blossom, behind it light brown hills, occasionally a solitary dark cypress.

The Parador lies within the walls of the Alhambra, so that at first, being right inside it, one has no idea of the size of it. It is on a steeply rising hill looking far out into the countryside: there below lies the open green valley of Granada, half-encircled by mountains of volcanic formation. In the background is the ice-shield of the Sierra Nevada, over nine thousand feet high.

Like Toledo, the fortified hilltop of the Alhambra is a natural vantage-point. From early times, no doubt, it was always a lookout and stronghold. The Alhambra is mentioned for the first time in a ninth-century Arabic manuscript: 'The fortress was built at night by the light of burning torches; and the Arabs who saw it red in the light of the torches called it *Al-hambra* (the Red)'.

The powerful four-square towers of the castle recall a Roman fortification; only within is an Arabic world displayed: slender pillars, heart-shaped arches, amber and ivory-coloured marble—in the centre of each of the empty rooms a fountain—from the galleries a view into distance and depth.

The Alhambra's charm is composed of the simplest elements: the water from the fountains—the cool air under the arches—the distances viewed through the windows.

Water, air and a little bit of green—that was sufficient happiness for those men from the African deserts.

To the Mohammedans, heaven is an evergreen garden; there the Lake of the Prophet is to be found 'with water sweet as honey, cold as snow, clear as crystal'. Here in Granada, on the breezy heights of the Alhambra, the Arabs believed they had found a Paradise on earth: water enough and to spare, leafage green the year round. . . .

The Alhambra has the appearance of being built as a temple to fortune, to enclose it and keep it safe; a cage to catch a bird in, a singing bird, to keep it singing on. . . .

Songs of happiness fill the Alhambra and run in charming Arabic lettering along the walls. The signs repeat the word Allah—Allah, who alone bestows blessing and well-being—Allah, the One, the Only, the Exalted, the Mighty, the Beloved. . . .

In the fountains of the Myrtle Court the women of the royal harem bathed. All round the walls run verses from the Koran. Religious belief and sensual enjoyment were intermingled here—two kinds of emotion which the Christian kept apart and Islam united. Nonetheless these rooms have a somewhat ascetic atmosphere, as though the senses were spiritualized, as though in prayer as in enjoyment the same unseen Presence predominated: Allah—O Allah—O Allah . . .

The name varies. Beauty has many forms. The All-Highest has many names, but basically it is the same. And wherever it is honoured the prevailing climate is a beneficial one.

From the Alhambra a path leads between high cypresses to the gardens of the Generaliffe, climbing in terraces up the mountain slope opposite.

Here among cedars and orange-trees lies the Moorish kings' summer residence. There was bubbling, rushing water everywhere, every turn of the path brought anew the sound of fountains. That was all there was to be heard: The murmur of water, the sound of the wind in the trees, and bird-song.

From here, the snowfields of the Sierra Nevada looked like a vision of the other world beyond the Gardens of Life.

Charles V came often during that summer of 1526, finding solace in the shade of the tall cedars. And it is said that he ventured on to the gardens of the Generaliffe to listen to the song of the nightingales which he loved.

I like to think how these scenes filled his mind's eye, how this quiet appealed to him, how he breathed the pure air sweeping over from the Sierra as he walked along this path by the side of his beloved wife, resting in the shade of these trees—for here he found peace.

CHARLES V IN THE GRANADA ALHAMBRA (1526)

The Emperor came to Granada with the Empress on 4th June 1526, to escape from the heat of Sevilla, where their marriage had taken place on 3rd March.

Santa Cruz, the chronicler, describes her as she was at the time: 'The Empress Isabella had a white skin, a clear look, she spoke little and was small. She had large eyes, a small mouth, flat breasts, good hands and a high-set, well-formed throat. . . . She was gentle and more reserved than need be; candid, quiet, devout, inward, not intervening at all.'

The Emperor had a few rooms added to the Moorish palace without disturbing the harmony of the structure; he had a gallery built to the tower with an airy verandah on its top storey, now called the Queen's Boudoir. The room is a sort of balcony over the Darro Valley. The wide window arches look out on three sides: northward to the *Albaizin*, the old Moorish quarter of Granada, eastward to the Generaliffe gardens, and southward to the snowy slopes of the Sierra Nevada.

When Charles V stood here, he will have remembered with gratitude how his grandparents Isabella and Ferdinand reconquered this land from the Moors. It was only thirty-four years ago that on 2nd January 1492 the Catholic Sovereigns made their entry. On that occasion a herald on the highest tower of the Alhambra cried out to the valley below:

'*Santiago—Santiago—Santiago! Castilla—Castilla—Castilla! Granada—Granada—Granada!* For the very exalted and very powerful Lords, Don Ferdinando and Dona Isabel, King and Queen of Spain—who have won back this city of Granada from the infidel Moors with armed might—by the help of God—and of His Mother the glorious Virgin—and of the blessed Apostle Santiago—and with the support of the Most Holy Father Pope Innocent VIII—and the assistance of the great Prelates, Knights and Noblemen of the Kingdom!'

It cost Isabella ten years to reconquer this kingdom; the Reconquista lasted seven centuries; and the fruit of all this toil, the united land of Spain, fell into Charles V's lap, together with this 'pomegranate' of the Moorish Paradise—Granada.

The transition from the Moorish part of the Alhambra to Charles V's quarters is like passing from a southern to a northern landscape. We cross the airy Moorish rooms and enter a whitewashed chamber with a large fireplace which seems curiously out of place, till one remembers that Charles V was born and bred in a chillier climate and was accustomed to warming himself at the fireside.

Over the door leading to the Emperor's quarters there is a white memorial tablet to Washington Irving who lived here in 1829 to write his *Tales of the Alhambra*. There is nothing to show that these rooms were inhabited by Charles V, who spent a whole happy summer here with his newly-wed wife.

The rooms are small with low ceilings, like the burgher houses of the Renaissance in Flanders and Germany. None of the original furniture is left, nothing for daily use. Only the frieze on the wall reiterates the Emperor's motto: *Plus Oultre—Plus Oultre—Plus Oultre*. . . .

A small narrow room, with the ceiling painted Flemish-fashion with fruits of all kinds, was their bedroom. The custodian said: 'Here Charles V and his wife conceived Philip II.' Philip was born on 21st May of the following year. When in Lisbon, he longed to hear the nightingales singing in Aranjuez—they sang here as he lay under his mother's heart before his birth. He loved roses and orange blossom: it was on these his mother's gaze fell when she looked out of the window of her small bedroom.

The view from the room is over the most charming of the Alhambra courtyards, the *Patio de Lindaraxa*. Orange trees raise their blossoms and fruit to the low window-bars. Water leaps and falls in a fountain.

What a picture of peace to refresh one on waking! The Alhambra walls close protectively round the little courtyard and quietness reigns. Here the spirit of man may go free and carefree, for nothing foreign to it will intrude.

THE VICTORY OF PAVIA (1525)

The duties of office pursued the Emperor even during those blissful months.

In his small study at the Granada Alhambra he received news of the death of his brother-in-law, King Ludwig II of Hungary, who fell fighting the Turks.

Here he received the ambassador of the King of France, who had been his prisoner since the Battle of Pavia till he set him free in January 1526.

We must stop and consider this victory, for the Emperor's behaviour after it is a good example of his peaceful intentions and his moderation, and an answer to those who accuse him of striving for world domination. The keynote of Charles V's intentions was not world domination, not the ambition of his great-grandfather, the Emperor Frederick III, but *Austriae est imperare Orbi Universo*. From the notes he wrote at that time it is clear that he wished for peace above all: 'In thinking over my situation, it seems to me that peace is the first thing to be spoken of and the best help God can send me, if He so please. That is something lovely to say but hard to have, for everyone knows one cannot get it without the consent of the enemy. . . .'

The war Charles was referring to was his conflict with the King of France over the Duchy of Milan, that old feudal tenure of the Holy Roman Empire over which the mediaeval emperors had exercised a mild form of sovereignty. Under the Sforza princes Milan had regained a limited independence; and through the marriage of Blanca Sforza to the Emperor Maximilian it fell to the House of Habsburg.

Maximilian defended Milan against Charles VIII and Louis XII of France and lost it to the latter, but regained it in 1512. In 1515 the young King Francis I of France invaded Upper Italy, beat the imperial army at the Battle of Marignon and, to Maximilian's discomfiture, occupied the Duchy of Milan.

The distrust with which Charles V witnessed the machinations of Francis I in Upper Italy was inherited from his grandfather Maximilian, who always carried a small book about with him containing an account of all the misdeeds of France against the House of Habsburg and the House of Burgundy—that attack of Louis XI's on Burgundy to snatch from Maximilian the choicest piece of his wife Maria's dowry, and then the robbery of the dowry of his second wife, Blanca Sforza of Milan. In 1513 Maximilian wrote a troubled letter to his young grandson Charles in which he called the French *les anciens et encoire naturels ennemis de notre maison de Bourgogne.*

When Maximilian died in 1519, he left his grandson Charles a legacy of feuds. In 1522 the imperial armies compelled the French to withdraw from Milan. But this was not the end of the conflict: both sides built up their armies for the next assault. The imperial troops gathered in the city of Pavia.

On 24th February 1525 Francis I, who was in personal command of his army, gave orders to storm Pavia.

An eyewitness, Charles V's chronicler Pero Mexia, described the battle as follows: 'So enflamed were they on both sides that they fought like wild lions. The noise of shouting, the clashes and blows they delivered were so great, it seemed as though the earth trembled. On both sides an immense amount of blood was shed. . . . The fury of the battle lasted a long while before victory was assured; but as God had it in store for the Emperor, it tarried no longer.'

In the tumult of battle the French king was taken prisoner. When Francis I, after fighting so bravely, was led captive and slightly wounded through the streets of Pavia, the cries of victory died down and the Emperor's men stood back respectfully to let him pass.

That same evening Francis wrote his mother a letter to tell her of his misfortune. At the same time he privately gave a courtier a ring, saying: 'Take it to the Sultan.' Two letters to the Sultan were smuggled out of the prison by later visitors. Sultan Suleiman sent answer that he was 'the king's refuge' and 'he would soon advance to the rescue of his brother the King of France'. This was the beginning of the alliance of the Most Christian King with the Sultan of the Infidels.

News of the victory of Pavia reached Charles V in Madrid, where he was recovering from a fever which had kept him in bed for weeks on end. He heard it without any sign of emotion and then withdrew to his private chapel where he remained sunk in prayer for over an hour. Afterwards he said to his entourage: 'Let us thank God for this great victory. May the people celebrate it as I do, inside the churches. There should be no outward expressions of joy, no music or fireworks, for the victory was gained with the blood of Christian men.'

Next morning the Emperor and his whole court took part in a solemn thanksgiving Mass. The people of Madrid went in procession to the shrine of Our Lady of Antocha to join in prayers of thanksgiving for victory.

The Emperor commanded the immediate suspension of all anti-French measures: 'It seems only right (*honnête*) not to go on fighting as long as the King is in my hands.'

The imperial armies in Upper Italy were eager to follow up their victory. Lannoy wrote to the Emperor: 'Sire, God sends each man only one good harvest in his lifetime, and when he does not reap it, it is over.'

And his first Councillor, Gattinara, also suggested he should follow up his opportunity: Dante's dream of universal monarchy was now within reach of realization, the most powerful opponent of the Emperor was a prisoner, the way to supremacy in Europe lay open.

But at this, his hour of triumph, we see the Emperor as Titian painted him in Bologna, quiet, passive; hesitant to take a step that might disturb the blessedness of the hour—the state of mind the Greeks called *aidos*.

'We admit the restraints that *aidos* imposes,' said Pericles to the Athenians.

Aidos is a virtue of humility and is opposed to the sin of *hubris*: the same occasion that invites the impious to acts of insolence brings the God-fearing man to his knees.

The Emperor saw the victory of Pavia, in which he had not himself taken part, as a dispensation of divine Providence; he wished to prove himself not unworthy of such bounty, and therefore wanted to do what was right, not to hurt his neighbour, not to take what was not his. We see him as a Christian victor.

There was no lack of temptations to act on expediency and take advantage of the political situation: King Henry VIII of England let the Emperor know that he was ready to land at Calais in person and to invade Normandy with an army of six thousand men. He sought Charles V's concurrence in a policy that would have meant the partition of France.

On 25th March 1525 the imperial ambassador at Henry VIII's court, M. Louis de Praet, wrote to the Emperor:

'At this moment one may say that Your Majesty holds world-monarchy in your hands, provided this victory over France is turned to good advantage. If the English were to set foot in France, it would be a great advantage for Your Majesty, for it would weaken the enemy and prevent him from doing any further damage, and thus be the surest means to a lasting peace. The whole of Languedoc, Burgundy and the land about the River Somme should be regained. God made the Emperor the arbitrator between peace and war. Such a favourable opportunity should not be lost.'

The Emperor gave an evasive answer to the English king's proposals. Henry VIII's wife, Catharine of Aragon, wrote imploring her nephew Charles not to abandon the way of friendship and affection to her lord and master.

On 26th May the Emperor wrote to de Praet: If the English wished to start warfare at once, the Emperor would advise them to wait till in the eyes of the world there was more justification for such an act; for he could not consider it till then.

The justification for an act of belligerency against France would only arise, in the Emperor's eyes, if the supposition that France would not keep to the terms of the future peace treaty proved correct. But first of all peace must be established.

To Henry VIII's disgust, and to the surprise of the world at large, the Emperor's one concern was the preparation of the peace treaty.

The Venetian ambassador Contarini admired the Emperor's restraint after the victory of Pavia, it reminded him of Pliny's *modestia principis*; the King of France was fortunate in being conquered by a Caesar who desired in the first place the welfare of Christendom.

However, it was not only ethical considerations that determined Charles' political moderation, but also practical ones: the powerful forces of the great Sultan were making their way up the Danube and would soon threaten Vienna; from Italy came letters full of fears of a Moorish assault on Sicily and Naples; the imperial army in Lombardy was in a critical situation owing to lack of money, Germany was in a turmoil through the teaching of Luther, the Anabaptists and the *Schwärmer*—the need of the hour was the consolidation of Christendom.

Therefore, after the victory of Pavia, Charles went to the rescue of his vanquished foe and saved France from the aggression of Henry VIII. And his whole demeanour proved that he was not out to establish the hegemony of Spain but was guided by his views of the *Universitas Christiana*, the co-operation of all Christian states in the common task of warding off the Turkish menace.

Charles V's secretary, Alfonso de Valdés, a humanist and follower of Erasmus, wrote after the victory of Pavia: 'It appears God has bestowed this victory on the Emperor in a wonderful manner, so that he might defend Christendom and fight the Turks and Moors on their own ground, so that the whole world receive our Holy Faith under this Christian Prince and the words of Our Saviour be fulfilled: *Fiet unum ovile et unus pastor.*'

In this declaration of the Emperor's secretary, the Spanish missionary spirit is wedded to Dante's theocratic ideal; it also expresses the high expectations of the group of Italian and Spanish humanists who surrounded the Emperor, seeing him as the reviver of the Roman universal Monarchy, who was, they believed, to put an end to the feudal and dynastic conflicts and establish a democratic *imperium*. For those circles thinking in terms of world-dominion, it must have been something of a disappointment to see the Emperor merely concerned with the ordering of his Empire within a *Respublica Christiana* (the basic idea of a united Europe); and it must have been particularly galling to the ambitious high chancellor, Gattinara, that Charles, the aspirant to world-empire, desired merely 'to possess in peace and quiet what it has pleased God to bestow on me.'

Charles V was no dynamic personality. He only gradually learnt to live up to his own motto of *Plus Ultra* which the Italian humanist Marliano had invented for him. After Pavia he still acted as though his motto were not 'ever further' but 'no more than my own' (his own inalienably, however).

Charles read attentively the letters his rival, Francis I, addressed to him. 'In my misfortune,' wrote the French king, 'there is no other consolation left me but my high esteem of your goodness, and I entreat you to determine in your heart what it will please you to do with me; for I am sure that the designs of such a prince as you are cannot but be compatible with a sense of honour and generosity . . . I therefore hope for indulgence on the part of the Emperor, who can make of the King of France a friend rather than a desperate man. Be assured that instead of a useless prisoner you can count a king among your slaves for ever.'

On 12th August 1525 Francis I came to Madrid of his own free will, to start negotiating the peace treaty. It was a matter of reconciling the viewpoints of victor and vanquished. Charles V had in mind a settlement based on his hereditary rights—he wanted nothing but what was his; but Burgundy was his.

The proposal to cede Burgundy, which had belonged to France for fifty years by now and was French in language and culture, was unacceptable to Francis I, who without ado turned it down.

And now Charles' stubborn insistence on Burgundy threatened to rock the peace that was the purpose of these negotiations with the French king. Erasmus' admonition in *Institutio Principis Christiani*, that 'it is better to renounce a part of one's realm than to keep it in one's possession at any cost', had fallen on stony ground: Charles was not even ready to renounce his claims to a land that was not his at all, but an inherited memory only.

Burgundy was the cradle and burial-place of his ancestors. Charles' aunt, Margaret, had often spoken to the boy about his lost maternal home; when Charles made his first will, on his return to Spain in 1522, he wrote, should he die, he wished to be laid by the side of his grandmother, Maria of Burgundy, in Bruges, or, should Burgundy belong to the Empire again by then, 'in our city of Dijon, by our ancestor Philip, his son John, and Philip the Good'.

The Burgundian centre had for many years been in Flanders, but Dijon, with its Carthusian monastery, where the Dukes of Burgundy lay, remained the ideal centre, the heart of the land. This conception of Burgundy, entirely notional and volitional, caused Charles to forsake all statesmanly caution: he would not admit that the province had now gravitated to France, a national state with a centralized administration. It was an illusion that distracted him from the desirable end of making a friend of the French king and establishing a durable peace.

Charles based his claim to Burgundy on the belief that there was in Dijon a strong *bourguignon* party, that is, *impérialiste*; his House was the House of Burgundy and Burgundy was *son ancien héritage*, his lawful inheritance, the place where his Order was founded (the Order of the Golden Fleece); he bore the name of Burgundy and its coat-of-arms; it was his plan to assemble the Knights of the Golden Fleece in Dijon. . . . Charles' mind was a curious mixture of realism and phantasy; he was equally the grandson of the statesmanly King Ferdinand of Aragon and a descendant of the romantic Philip the Good of Burgundy with his chivalric dreams.

Francis I, to whom the Emperor's claim to Burgundy seemed sheer nonsense, finally agreed to let him have his way—giving in to him as to someone possessed of an *idée fixe*; in addition to Burgundy he undertook to renounce all claims on Artois, Milan and the Kingdom of Naples; he promised to help the Emperor in the fight against the Turks; and in witness to the fact that Habsburg and Valois were now united in friendship, Francis was to marry Charles' sister, Leonora.

In September of that year, the king fell sick in his prison, and the Emperor, who was in Toledo, hurried to Madrid to visit him. A manuscript of the year 1550 describes this meeting:

'When the Emperor came in, Francis I sat up in bed. They embraced and their eyes almost overflowed with tenderness. "Señor, you see me here as your slave and prisoner," said the king. "No, you are free, and my good friend and brother," the Emperor replied. "Above all I wish you to be in good health; this shall be our concern; and whatever else is to happen shall be done as you, señor, wish it."

' "No, but as you command," answered the king, "and I beg you only that there be no third party between you and me!" '

Was this bewitching man to be trusted, Charles must have wondered, and in his straightforward Habsburg way he did not quite know what to make of the Frenchman's insidious smile. 'He will betray me,' was Charles' feeling, 'but I must set him free all the same.'

The Peace Treaty was signed on 14th January 1526. Francis swore on the Gospel to observe all its stipulations. As pledge that he would do so, he was to send both his sons as hostages to Madrid.

On his way home his marriage to Leonora was celebrated at Illescas. The wedding feast lasted all night. Leonora was a good dancer, and Charles made his sister dance Spanish dances for the king's benefit, 'a task she carried out with much grace'. And Charles was careful to see that the couple only danced and spoke together but did not consummate their marriage, for he feared that once over the border, Francis would not keep his promises. In the morning Leonora set off for Toledo to await developments from that vantage-point. In the long run the marriage to Leonora was the only clause of the treaty that Francis did observe.

The Emperor accompanied him on his way. When he gave him his hand in farewell, he asked: 'Do you remember all that you have promised me?'

'Set your mind at rest, Brother,' answered the French king. 'My intention is to keep it all; and if you should hear otherwise, you can consider me a coward and a bad man.' (*Lâche et méchant* were the words used.)

But it was soon clear that Francis did not at all mean to keep to what he had sworn by oath. He had but reached Bayonne when he refused to confirm the treaty. In April he was in Cognac, in the heart of Burgundy, and received tokens of loyalty from the inhabitants. He proclaimed that the Madrid Treaty was an 'imposed peace' and that he therefore did not consider himself to be bound by his word; and he persuaded Pope Clement VII to form an alliance with him—called the League of Cognac, which the Duke of Milan, the Venetian Republic, the City of Florence, the Swiss, and Henry VIII of England also joined, all with the one idea of challenging the Emperor's supremacy in Italy.

Clouet's portrait of Francis I

The French court painter, Clouet, painted Francis I as *le roi politique*, a polished and clever monarch playing with politics out of self-interest, and thus deviating from the conventional idea of politics accepted everywhere in Europe at that time.

Now, though Francis I cut politics adrift from ethics, he went on calling himself *le roi très chrétien*; and his country, France, the land of contradictions, continued to be 'the Church's eldest daughter' although it was the birthplace of the most acute heresies.

Pascal once wrote these paradoxical words: *La vraie morale se moque de la morale.* . . .

One wonders whether Francis was so secure in his own Catholicism that he felt he could set the cause of Christendom at stake and go unpunished for it; whether Christian unity appeared to him so indestructible that he could without misgivings lend support to Turks and German Protestants; and whether he was confident that the Old Faith had such deep roots in his own country (and had such a good defender in himself) that he could without second thoughts foster the new sects struggling into existence the other side of the border.

In Clouet's portrait, Francis' smile is very enigmatic.

THE THIRD FORCE

From his small study in the Granada Alhambra, Charles wrote reproachfully to Pope Clement VII: 'Certain people are saying that Your Holiness has absolved the King of France from the oath by which he promised us to keep to what was agreed; this we do not wish to believe, for it is not a thing that the Vicar of Christ would do. . . .'

The forming of the League of Cognac vexed and upset the Emperor; it was also called *Liga Sancta* or *Liga Clementina* because the Pope supported it. At the very moment when it was so important to uphold the dignity of the Papacy, the Catholic Emperor found himself forced into open opposition to the Apostolic See. He was almost in danger of being confused with the Lutherans who denied the Pope's supremacy, though nothing was farther from the Emperor's mind than undermining the Rock on which the Church was built.

In June 1526, at the Granada Alhambra, Charles V received the ambassadors of the 'Holy League' demanding the release of Francis' sons, though the king had fulfilled none of the conditions of the Madrid Peace Treaty.

The Emperor listened to them, then he stood up and said: 'I have not deserved of His Holiness, Pope Clement VII, that he should conclude a general League against me with all the Princes; it is not in accord with the friendship which united us, nor is it compatible with his dignity to consent to such an ignominious thing. But my hope is in God, that he will justify me, and in this hope I will set up my defence.

'And to you, the King of France's ambassadors, I say that when I gave your Lord his freedom, he gave me his word to carry out everything we had agreed upon, failing which he would become my prisoner again. Write to him and tell him from me that as he neither keeps his word nor returns to prison, I consider him *lâche et méchant*, to use the very terms that were used when he gave me his word and I gave him his freedom; and as you and your Lord now say that I took his sons by force, the only thing to think and to answer is, if I was powerful enough to take the father prisoner, I shall be powerful enough to keep the sons.'

It was a hard retort to a hard blow. The League Francis I had formed behind the Emperor's back made a mockery of his hope for an understanding with the French king; hostilities would break out anew, and that at a moment when all the forces of the Empire were needed for concentrated action against the Turks who had overrun Hungary. At such a time, it was bitter indeed to think that the Pope was his opponent.

In June 1526 Charles received in the Granada Alhambra a sharp letter from the Pope, accusing him of disturbing the peace of Christendom.

This distressed the Emperor, for he felt it to be unjust. He considered with his secretary Alfonso de Valdés how to reply, and the latter composed a letter to the Pope, expressing displeasure in no ambiguous terms. He said the Emperor wished with his whole heart to see peace in Italy and in the world, for only thus could the Turks be conquered and the Lutherans suppressed and brought back to the bosom of the Church. Emperor Charles was prepared to give his realm and his blood in defence of the

Church. But if the Pope put obstacles in the way of those endeavours, and turned at times from a Father into a foe, from a Shepherd into a wolf, then the Emperor would apply to the General Council for a verdict to remedy the difficult situation of Christendom and save the sorely harassed Catholic Faith.

The Universal Council was the Emperor's weapon against the Roman Curia's claims to predominance; on it were centred the hopes of all who desired a reform of the Church; Luther, too, made a request for it to meet, in the hope of obtaining a hearing, and Erasmus supported his request as the only possible means of reconciling conflicting points of view. The Council's function would be to find a common denominator between the orthodox Catholic and the extreme Protestant standpoint, and thus form a higher court of reference over and above the antagonisms.

But Pope Clement VII wanted to avoid open discussion of the religious questions. He had personal reasons for fearing an inquiry into ecclesiastical disorders: there was the fact of his own illegitimate birth, the bribery by which he had secured the Tiara, the trading in ecclesiastical appointments (in the thick of the Reformation storms Cardinals' hats could still be had for the buying)—all these abuses might well, if brought into open discussion, endanger his papal dignity and thus do harm to the Church itself; he turned a deaf ear to the Emperor's entreaty.

On 17th September 1526 Charles had another letter delivered to the Pope, through the Papal Nuncio, Baldassare Castiglione; once more he referred to the Council: 'We beg Your Holiness to call the General Council at some definite place, so that the situation of the Christian religion and the welfare of Your Republic may be deliberated. . . . In this letter we appeal to Your Holiness and entreat Your Holiness to call the honourable Council. . . .' But Pope Clement VII remained disinclined. In exasperation Charles wrote to the College of Cardinals in Rome that if a great misfortune befell Christendom, Clement VII bore the responsibility. . . .

So persistently did he press his claim that in Rome people began to talk of him as the 'leader of the heretics', a 'disguised Lutheran', 'Antichrist', setting himself above the Pope's authority. . . .

Such is the ambiguous situation in which a 'third force' may find itself through attempting mediation. Each of the two poles exerted a strong magnetic attraction and the mediating force was bound in the long run to be drawn one way or the other.

That is what happened to Erasmus. When at last he took up the rôle of

ELECTOR JOHN FREDERICK OF SAXONY SURROUNDED BY
THE REFORMERS

Cranach the Elder, *Museum of Art, Toledo, U.S.A.*

JACOB FUGGER AND HIS BOOKKEEPER, M. SCHWARZ
Duke Anton Ulrich Museum, Braunschweig

intermediary, he found himself a pillar of the Church. And Charles V, when in 1526 he sought a solution in a humanism friendly to reforming trends, without at all intending to, jeopardized the Papacy, and his efforts to act in an Erasmian spirit were swept up and submerged by the Lutheran tidal wave: a year later Rome was sacked.

In that year, 1526, Gattinara wrote to Erasmus saying Christendom was, it seemed, falling into three parts: those that swore by the Pope with eyes and ears tight shut, whether he ruled well or ill; others who equally stubbornly held to Luther; and the third group, which sought only God's glory and the welfare of the realm, and these followed Erasmus in true admiration. From the Emperor he hoped for the eradication of the Lutheran heresy, and Church reform.

Erasmus, like Charles V, was attacked from all sides. Luther spoke of his 'malicious nature', and the Dominicans of his calculating mind and lack of candour. 'It is my fate to be stoned by both sides, and meanwhile my care is for both,' he wrote to the Bishop of Ferrara in May 1525. 'In your land and in Brabant I am considered a Lutheran, and in all Germany, where I live, as so strongly anti-Lutheran that the professed followers of Luther are more furious with me than with anyone else. And it was not through the recent publication of my work, "On the Freedom of the Will", that I first called down this hatred upon myself. . . .'

When Charles heard of Erasmus' *De libero arbitrio diatribe*, he wrote, 'We hope you will proceed with this method of opposition. . . . We have hitherto done all that was in our power for the peace of the Christian Republic: no one can deny it.'

Now, although the Emperor's endeavour to effect a synthesis brought about a most unfortunate clash between himself and papal power again in 1527, and although his threat to impose his ideas by force of arms provoked a rising of his Protestant opponents in 1549, taken all in all, his effort was a creative one. A 'third force' may *ipso facto* be compelled to forgo immediate results, but it has a necessary part to play nonetheless, for it alone is truly constructive, and it alone, in the long run, points the new way into a new age.

FREE WILL OR SERVILE WILL?

The great debate between Erasmus and Luther on the freedom of the will was followed in Spain with the closest attention. At that time Charles had around him a number of ardent supporters of Erasmus, among them his secretary, Alfonso de Valdés, his chronicler, Pero Mexia (who corresponded with 'the most learned men of his time, among them Erasmus of Rotterdam who also sent him a copy of an excellent portrait'), and his chancellor, Gattinara, who used to remark, 'those who curse Erasmus have either not read his books or not understood them.'

This open-minded group of men welcomed with satisfaction Erasmus' definite stand against Luther's disenfranchisement of the human will, for it relieved the Spanish *Erasmistas* of the suspicion of being 'Lutheran'. Moreover, the notion of free will is the pulse of life to a Spaniard, with his acute awareness of human dignity.

So Erasmus had at last made up his mind to oppose Luther in writing, and of all Luther's opinions he singled out for special attack the one underlying his doctrine of justification, that is, the thesis that man's will is unfree.

In *De libero arbitrio diatribe*, Erasmus stated both his own and Luther's standpoint, letting texts chosen from the Bible speak for freedom of the will and divine grace. His old taste for seeking reconciliation everywhere comes out in the recurrence of terms like 'on the one hand—on the other hand . . .', and 'neither—nor . . .'; he admitted that many passages of Scripture were open to various interpretations, others, he said, were quite clear, and among these the precepts for the good life (*bene vivendi praecepta*). And it was with those moral precepts that Erasmus was principally concerned: they formed the basis of his opposition to Luther's predestination theory, which assumed the non-existence of human responsibility, and he declared wholeheartedly for the freedom of the human will on those grounds.

'Let us suppose,' he wrote, 'that what Wycliffe taught was in a certain sense right, and that all we do is not the result of free will but of sheer necessity; but what is more dangerous than to spread such a paradoxical statement among the masses? Freedom of the will received a wound through sin, but it was not abolished. If man had no free will at all, what is the point of saying, "If you will, if you will not"? God should have said, "When I will, when I will not". Why invite people to be converted if they have no will-power whatever? Is it not like calling a man held fast in shackles to "come and follow me"? But why should free will be admitted?—So that the impious who of their own free will deprive themselves of divine grace may be justly accused, and to avoid letting God be the object of scandalous accusations of cruelty or injustice; also to drive despair far from us, and arrogance, too; and to challenge us to bestir ourselves.'

Although Erasmus made his work as conciliatory as he could—'the clause that pleases me is the one that ascribes not the least to free will but the most to grace'—it was an unequivocal defence of free will. Thus he played his part in a decisive hour in upholding man's moral power and his human dignity.

Luther's retort was *De servo arbitrio*. He declared it was clear from Erasmus' diatribe that free will was a 'naked lie', and that 'the thunderbolt of divine Providence completely crushes free will'. From his own extreme position he was not interested in the *bene vivendi praecepti* and he did not hesitate to do away with the very mainspring of moral sanction; he clung obstinately to his thesis that 'all that happens happens of necessity', saying, 'Who, you ask, would trouble now to improve his life? I reply, No one, nor is anyone in a position to do so. Who, you ask, will still believe in God's love? I reply, No one will believe in it or be able to believe in it. But the elect will believe, and the others will go to perdition without belief. . . . Therefore, for the sake of the elect, these things are published, so that they may be humbled and reduced to nothing and thus come to their bliss. Our salvation depends in no wise on our own skill and planning, but only on God's effecting.'

And he concluded ominously: 'In this book I have not set down a string of opinions but have laid down definite assertions, and that is what I do now. I leave no one the right to judge for himself; rather, I counsel all to practise obedience.'

'Definite assertions' that rejected the test of criticism were of course asking for trouble; the Lutherans soon came upon this stumbling-block and were dismayed. Then, a paralysis of the sense of responsibility ensued, as a direct consequence of the 'crushing of free will', and in German lands it was not long before freedom of conscience was replaced by—conscientious obedience.

In later years Luther retreated somewhat from this extreme independence. He often spoke like an Orthodox Russian: 'A cross, a cross is man's lot', and, 'To suffer is better than to act'. But such a basically passive attitude was not up to the task of shaping a world. It was, after all, the Protestant idea of inexorable predestination that made it easy for nineteenth-century positivism to establish its great hold on men's minds. According to Spengler, man has freedom only 'to do what is necessary'. Dialectical materialism is rooted in the denial of the free will—and today we see all Eastern Europe suffering under the infliction of its heavy fatality. Surprisingly enough, it is the natural sciences that show signs of having discovered the way out. Shortly before he died, Max Planck wrote: 'In natural science the conception of freedom breaks in, allowing the religious question to take shape again.' Such a view gives new play to the notion of freedom and to the notion of grace, with the consequence that the relation of world and super-world needs thinking out afresh. So it is that the debate between Erasmus and Luther, which came to an abrupt end in its day, must now be taken up again. But a prerequisite is, for those declaring for freedom to reawaken to a reverence for divine powers, and the propounders of 'necessity' must take freedom of the will into account if the debate is to be a fruitful one and to lead on to a recovery of human will-power under the sign of divine grace.

CHANGE OF CLIMATE

In 1527 there was street-fighting in Valladolid on account of Erasmus' ideas.

Soon it became a risky business to call oneself *Erasmista* in Spain, for the Spanish Dominicans declared that Erasmus was a pioneer of Luther's false teaching. 'Should we who drove Mohammedan fatalism out of Europe open the doors to the doctrine of the enslaved will and faith without works?' wrote Menéndez y Pelayo. 'Catholic dogma is the axis of our culture.'

Luther's work, 'Of the servile will', was a challenge that altered the spiritual landscape of Spain, and reforming humanism now found its direction as a tributary of the main Catholic stream of thought. Pero Mexia, whose humanistic 'enthusiasm' previously had a distinctly evangelical tinge, came to deplore the existence of that 'accursed and mighty Martin Luther, whose false doctrine has kindled and infected the whole world', and he said Luther's teaching was 'the greatest plague the Catholic Church had had to endure since Christ suffered'.

In Germany, too, those not in favour of desperate measures withdrew their support from Luther. Willibald Pirkheimer, the Nürnberg patrician and humanist, complained that Luther's talk was so disproportionate that his impudent, mischievous tongue seemed to have utterly succumbed to madness; the humanist, Ulrich Zasius, wrote that Luther's teaching engendered hostility, brawls, friction, sects and malice. Luther's contemporaries admitted his debt to Huss: 'To Huss and his followers can be ascribed nearly all Luther's false premisses; formerly in Bohemia, now here, they have instigated rioting, insurrection, robbery, arson, murder and the most terrible upheaval of the whole of society.' Sebastian Franck turned away from Luther, a disappointed man, saying, 'Now life is utterly godless as a consequence of the doctrine that faith justifies without works'; and John Denk wrote that the Reformation had been seduced by the devil. Early admirers of Luther such as the humanists John Cochlaus and George Witzel became fierce opponents of his. Witzel deplored the general confusion of minds: 'What is the matter?' he inquired. 'Each section wants to be absolutely right. No one will say, I was mistaken.'

Protestant self-righteousness forced the Catholic side to stiffen its resistance. Discipline was intensified and humanistic works that were not completely in accord with accepted dogma were condemned. The heat of controversy singed the petals of a flowering humanism and many flourishing scientific undertakings withered in the blast. The *changement de climat* was in full swing. M. Bataillon locates it in the years 1556–63, from Charles V's abdication to the end of the Council of Trent, but it was already in the air in 1527 at the time of the Erasmus–Luther conflict. Two temperaments were at daggers drawn, and they stood for contrary spiritual currents that could no longer proceed in one and the same channel; and striking off in opposite directions, ran to extremes. Calvin outstripped Luther in his predestination doctrine, and Ignatius of Loyola saw in a 'corpse-like obedience' to ecclesiastical authority the salvation of the Catholic mind.

The 'third force' had failed to install itself in reality at the right moment. Those who had striven for a settlement and a middle course were inevitably drawn into one or other of the two currents. And it was Erasmus' fate to be accounted a renovator and a rebel by the Catholic side. In 1529, in Paris, Berquin, the translator of Erasmus' works, was burned as a heretic.

The new orthodoxies were no less intolerant: in Geneva, where Calvin had Miguel Servet, the Spanish humanist, burned alive—in England, where Henry VIII sent Sir Thomas More and Bishop John Fisher to the scaffold, there developed those rigid religious attitudes under stress of which the old unity of faith of the western world burst asunder once for all.

In the latter part of his life, Erasmus was on the side of conservatism. In his late work, 'Of the lovely unanimity of the Church', he made one more bid for Church unity, seeking once more to present the ideal of the one hearth to those who had apostatized: in vain—the spirit of the time ran to division.

In 1558 Pope Paul IV placed Erasmus' complete works on the Index of forbidden books.

This Pope's predecessors had judged Erasmus with more insight. Pope Leo X had praised his 'rare and morally impeccable scholarship and his distinguished merits'. Pope Hadrian VI wrote in December 1522 that he gave no credit to those who suspected Erasmus of being a follower of Luther's. And in spite of the hardening of the fronts, in May 1535 Pope Paul III wrote in a Brief that he had always loved the renowned name of Erasmus and esteemed his scholarship highly; he knew what assistance Erasmus' learning could render him in combating the new errors, and in August 1535 he had appointed Erasmus Provost of Deventer.

But by 1558 the Roman Curia had no ear for this Christian-fighter type of religion. Obedience was now all that mattered: humanistic truth-seeking was no longer tolerated.

The first complete edition of Erasmus' works appeared in Basle in 1540, and was dedicated to Charles V.

CHARLES V'S PALACE

The small rooms which the Emperor and his wife occupied in the Alhambra were too modest to constitute a court residence, and the Emperor, who was fond of staying in Granada, decided to build a palace. He built it inside the Alhambra, on top of the hill, looking out like a watch-tower over the countryside.

Many travellers' memoirs find fault with Charles for building his palace inside the Moorish structure and complain that the disorderly mass of the Renaissance building disturbs the delicate Arabic architecture.

Yet, seen from a distance, Charles V's palace harmonizes well with the long lines of the fortress walls; the same reddish-yellow colouring of the stone links the two buildings; and seen from nearer, the places where one wall gives way to another are hardly noticeable, for ivy sprawls over the face of both palaces, Moorish and Renaissance.

It was also said that Charles pulled down valuable portions of the Moorish castle to have his own home put up, but even this seems unlikely, for only the back of the Moorish kings' winter palace was removed—a part of the building never mentioned in any praises of the Alhambra—presumably because it was not such as to strike a song-writer.

Nor is it justifiable to regret that Charles' palace was not built in the Mudejar style (a mixture of Moorish and Gothic); people only build well in the style appropriate to their period, and in Charles V's time the appropriate style was Renaissance.

Some point out that the building is unnecessarily large. Certainly, this palace is an example of the *maniera grande* (which Ortega remarks in the Escorial, too)—that splendid gesture of the high Renaissance which Michelangelo propagated in Italy.

A sense of grandeur was proper to the Renaissance period. New parts of the earth were opening out, new horizons were perceptible, and the Emperor was sovereign over a world-wide realm. There was nothing unseemly in his erecting a structure at the heart of the Alhambra that corresponded to his might.

But it remained uncompleted. The earthquakes that shake Granada from time to time were disliked by the Emperor. He gave up the idea of living here. After his wife's death he never came again. But both desired that after death their bodies should rest here. Charles had the work on the cathedral continued and decorated the chapel which was the final resting-place of the Catholic Sovereigns, in accordance with his grandmother Isabella's wish.

THE CATHEDRAL

The cathedral lies in the valley, as Granada's centre of gravity. It is massive enough to counterbalance the castle, and in it the Cross asserts its exaltation over the Crescent.

Seen from the Alhambra hilltop, it rises powerfully from among the city roofs, broad rather than high, its square tower firm and watchful, as though intent on lasting for ever.

The first stone was laid on 25th March 1523. The plan was Gothic but the building was continued *a la romano*, a style in which the basic character of romanesque architecture in Spain, weighty, severe and simple, was once more stressed.

This massive stone structure has the effect of a condensation of Isabella's nearest and dearest concern—the strength of the Christian Faith: '. . . may he reign, He alone, our Lord and Redeemer.' In perpetuation of her prayer, Isabella rests in the *Capilla Real* opposite the altar, at the side of her husband, Ferdinand of Aragon. Near their tomb is the tomb of their daughter Joan and her husband Philip the Fair. Charles gave his parents the place of honour next to the Catholic Sovereigns.

Mass is celebrated daily before their recumbent figures; when I was there it was Lent, with its silent Masses, so much in unison with the abeyance of natural life, preparing for the Feast of the Resurrection.

The vestments of the three priests celebrating High Mass were purple like the violets on sale at the church door. They offered the old, time-honoured Sacrifice quietly, in all its beauty. When Mass was over an altar-server put out all the candles in the empty chapel except those between the two tombs.

I was glad to be there, so near the heart of Spain. In the presence of those dead, the pulse of eternity is audible. I suddenly understood the power that lies in relics: this chapel meant so much to me, because here lay the ancestors of the kings to whom my heartfelt gratitude is due.

Isabella loved her Castilian homeland: Madrigal, where she was born, Medina del Campo, where she died—she was made of the very stuff of Castile, and Ferdinand was attached to his kingdom of Aragon in the same way. But both sovereigns sacrificed their local loves to the union they had established, with Granada as its crown.

Their monuments are carved in white marble. It was a rare intuition of the Florentine sculptor, Fancelli, to let Isabella's head sink deeper into her marble pillow than that of her husband, Ferdinand of Aragon, 'as though the weight of the crown were too heavy for her head', said Charles on seeing it. And Philip the Fair's head lies without weight on his marble pillow, too, whereas Joanna's presses down into hers, heavy with the melancholy that clouded her mind. . . .

Here she lies, Joanna, Joan the Mad—a name which always made me sad as a child learning history; here lies the mother of Charles V and Ferdinand I, great-grandmother of Rudolf II who died insane in Prague Castle.

JOAN THE MAD

One version of Joanna's story says that she was not mad at all, and that her mother spread the rumour in order to exclude her from succession to the throne: Queen Isabella observed that Joanna was indifferent in religious matters and feared she would neglect the principles that were the very foundation of the Spanish state. Others said that Joanna was kept away from the throne through her father's and husband's ambition and later her son's, though she was in full possession of her reason.

On the other hand, a Spanish doctor, Valejo Nagera, who made a psychoanalytical study of Joanna's mental condition, calls it a case of schizophrenia. And contemporary reports reveal a condition akin to mental disease, with alternating states of exaltation and deep depression. In any case, a person suffering from periodic total incapacity of the will, as Joanna did, was obviously not suited to conduct the government of a large country—such at least was the opinion of all responsible for the welfare of Spain. So we should not think of Joanna as a victim of her relations' power-complexes. She was deeply disturbed in mind by an all-too-painful experience and thus became a stranger to her obligations. She was not mad. Nor was she fit to govern.

Joanna was born in Toledo on 6th November 1479, the most passionate of all the children of that city of intense passions. Clemencin, a chronicler, relates how 'Heaven gave the Queen five children: Isabella, the delicate one, later Queen of Portugal; Prince Don Juan, who died young; Joanna, whose love for her husband (a legacy from the women of her family) finally deprived her of her reason and of the sceptre; Maria, Queen of Portugal after Isabella's death; and Catharine, Queen of England, illustrious for her piety and misfortune'.

Isabella called her children, 'my angels', and taught them to love music. Prince Juan played the harp, and it seems likely that Joanna could play the mandoline, for the instrument is mentioned in an inventory of her belongings.

At sixteen years of age Joanna was a serious, melancholy girl, subject to fits of deep depression. She was distressed at the thought that she possessed no physical charms and was often jealous of her good-looking sisters. The strict religious discipline her mother imposed made her low-spirited.

At that time the Catholic Sovereigns were thinking of securing their united kingdom against French aggression by a *rapprochement* with the House of Habsburg. And Emperor Maximilian met them half-way by also preferring to stop France from pressing beyond her own frontiers. It was therefore to their mutual satisfaction that a double marriage was agreed upon: Maximilian's two children, Philip and Margaret, were to marry Joanna and Juan, the children of the Catholic Sovereigns.

At the beginning of 1496 Ferdinand equipped a fleet to take the Infanta

Joanna to Flanders; the same fleet on its return journey was to bring Princess Margaret to Spain.

In September of that year Joanna landed at Middelburg in the Netherlands, where she remained a few days to recover from a stormy crossing. Then she went on to a place called Liera, where she waited a fortnight for her bridegroom to arrive. Philip was meantime at Landeck in the Tyrol, hunting chamois with his father Maximilian.

Quirini, the Venetian ambassador, gives a picture of Philip the Fair in his Memoirs: 'Philip was handsome in figure, strong and healthy, skilful in duelling, practised in the art of riding, prudent in warfare, and capable of great exertions . . . He loved justice and took pains to see it was observed. He was religious and true to his word. Gifted with unusual intelligence, he easily understood all sorts of matters, but he did not have a ready answer nor did he act with decision; he always followed the opinion of his councillors, and gave them his confidence. It was his nature to be influenced by people he liked.'

In his chronicle of Philip the Fair, Lorenzo de Padilla wrote: 'Philip was tall, strong and supple, with a clear rosy complexion and fair hair. His eyes were startling in their noble generosity and kindness.' Padilla also mentioned that Philip had the most handsome fingernails he had ever seen.

In Flanders the following verses were sung in the streets and alleys:

> *Sa face redonde*
> *Cler, pure et monde,*
> *Comme le soleil;*
> *Pourquoy tout le monde,*
> *Ayme sa faconde*
> *Et son appareil.*

Pirenne, the historian, writes that the enthusiasm which Philip aroused was astonishing: 'He was the first really popular Regent of the Netherlands.'

The marriage contract had been concluded by proxy months earlier, and Joanna's long-awaited husband finally turned up on 16th October.

The young people fell in love with one another at first sight. Philip was eighteen and Joanna seventeen years old. They were filled with such an irresistible desire to embrace that they did not wait for their wedding in church but got the Court chaplain to marry them that very evening and slept together that night.

128

The solemnization of their marriage took place a few days later, on 20th October 1496, in Lille.

The chronicler continues: 'Dona Juana loved her husband passionately, but he did not respond to her feelings in like manner.'

A simple statement, yet it is the whole of Joanna's story in a nutshell. To love without meeting with love in return is a common occurrence; but in each individual case it is a new and bitter experience. And the more whole-hearted the surrender, the deeper the shock. To give oneself heart and soul and then discover one has thrown oneself into the void is mortal agony, a loss of very selfhood. Only through 'the marriage of true minds' are bodies truly wed.

But Philip soon recovered from his first intoxication and turned to pursue his pleasures, neglecting his lovesick wife.

Meanwhile, Queen Isabella was awaiting the return of the Spanish fleet, bringing Princess Margaret, Don Juan's bride, to Spain.

It arrived on 8th March 1497. Ferdinand and Isabella welcomed Margaret and were delighted with their lovely young daughter-in-law. Isabella asked the Spanish escort how Joanna fared and heard from the Admiral that 'Philip was a gentleman, good-looking, lively, high-spirited and of a kindly disposition' and she could not have married her daughter 'to anyone better endowed by nature or who loved his wife more dearly'.

Don Juan's marriage to Margaret was celebrated with great festivity. When the newly-married couple came out of the Cathedral doors, after the wedding in Burgos, both fair and tall, full of youth and innocence, to the onlookers they appeared like a pair of angels.

Once more the magic spell that impelled the Austrian and the Spanish blood to unite caused Don Juan and Margaret to find such delight in one another that it was soon clear the young prince was overdoing his strength. Isabella tried separating the pair for a while, but they yearned for one another so deeply that they had to be reunited. Isabella advised Margaret to be more reserved, and Don Juan's confessor warned him of the danger of giving way to his temperament. It was all in vain: here was life intent on spending itself.

In Salamanca, Don Juan caught a fever in his weakened condition, and died on 4th October 1497.

Margaret was left behind to bear her child, who was stillborn a few months later.

Now the succession to the Castilian throne went to Don Juan's eldest sister Isabella, wife of the King of Portugal. The Catholic Sovereigns invited the young couple to Castile to receive the Cortes' oath of loyalty. But the princess died soon after giving birth to a son, who was christened Miguel.

This child was now the hope of Ferdinand and Isabella, for they had to admit they had been mistaken in their son-in-law Philip. Ferdinand observed with suspicion the latter's friendship with the King of France, Louis XII. Instead of carrying out the combined wishes of his father Maximilian and his father-in-law Ferdinand, Philip came to terms with Louis XII and behaved more like a French vassal than the heir to the Habsburg lands.

The rumours that reached them from Flanders were very disquieting to Isabella: the Archduke gave his wife no money; she had not enough to pay her servants and give alms; she felt isolated and alone in the midst of the light-hearted Burgundian court.

At the beginning of 1498 Isabella sent Father Matienzo, Prior of the Monastery of Santa Cruz, to Flanders, to discover how things really were.

In August he wrote from Brussels: 'Today we spoke with the Archduke and later with the Archduchess too. They gave us a friendly welcome, as it appeared to us. I explained the reason for my visit to the Archduchess, she found it very entertaining. She is so kind, so beautiful and blooming and so far advanced in her pregnancy that Your Highness would be consoled if you could see her.'

In a later letter the Prior wrote: 'Today I spoke with the Archduchess for the third time and begged her to tell me something about herself, so that I could report to Your Highness. She replied she had nothing to say, that she had written to Your Highness herself. I must confess to Your Highness that the Archduchess was little pleased with my coming. . . . I said I had not come to hold an inquisition over her life and that I only put down on paper what she herself told me. . . . I do not know whether it was my coming or her lack of piety that led to the fact that on Ascension Day, when two confessors called on her, she confessed to neither.' (Joanna did actually fear something like an inquistion from the Spanish monk, and to his vexation she confessed to an unknown French priest.) In his last letter, Father Matienzo wrote that Joanna had 'a hard, rough heart' and was without any kind of piety, and that she set up a passive resistance to his own efforts, as to those of other priests, to induce her to return to the Faith. On 16th November 1498 Joanna gave birth to her first child, a daughter, who was baptized Leonora, after Emperor Maximilian's mother, Eleonor of Portugal. Maximilian did not come to the baptism, thus expressing his annoyance over Philip's independent policy towards France, which crossed his own plans.

We have a picture of Joanna at this time, by a Flemish artist: it shows a very feminine, tender face with a slightly veiled look and her attitude is shy and modest. The picture of a young life uprooted, with no one to love her and guide her. . . .

On 24th February 1500, on the Feast of the Apostle Matthias, Joanna gave birth to a son in the Prinzenhof at Ghent. He was called after his great-grandfather, the Duke of Burgundy—Charles.

A few months later, messengers from Spain brought the news that the two-year-old Prince Miguel had died, and thus the succession to the Castilian throne passed to Joanna. It was the desire of the Catholic Sovereigns, the messengers reported, that the Archducal pair should come to Spain as soon as possible to have themselves recognized as heirs to the Kingdom of Castile and Aragon.

Philip found all sorts of excuses for delaying the journey, and Joanna could not be persuaded to travel without her husband. The chronicler Zurita describes the Archduke at that time as 'more given up to pleasure than is wise'.

On 15th July 1501 Joanna gave birth to her third child in Brussels; a daughter, Isabella.

Towards the end of 1501 Philip finally agreed to set off for Spain. At that time there was peace between the Emperor Maximilian and the King of France. Philip and Joanna therefore travelled by land and arrived at Blois at the beginning of December, where they had a hearty welcome from the French king. The ensuing festivities came to an end when Joanna refused to accept a medal which the French king sent them as a sign of their vassalage as counts of Flanders. The French queen was deeply offended by Joanna's brusque behaviour. And on Sunday when she came out of church with her guest, she did not, as usual, give Joanna precedence, but went out first. Joanna was in no mood to accept humiliation: she lingered in the church while the queen waited for her outside. This incident was the occasion for a hurried departure and gave rise to violent scenes between Philip and his young wife.

On 29th January 1502 they reached Fuentarrabia. During the long, arduous journey through Castile, Philip fell ill and they did not reach Toledo till May. On 22nd May, in the Cathedral, they were sworn in as presumptive heirs to the throne, in the presence of the Catholic

Sovereigns, the higher clergy and the Grandees of Spain. In the Church of San Salvador they took the traditional oath to observe the laws, customs and privileges of the land.

Philip did not feel at all comfortable at the solemn, strict court of Castile. The Spanish women were too honourable and virtuous for him and he sighed for the merry, rosy beauties of Flanders and Austria where the girls were easy-going, whereas here they passionately defended their virginity. The whole land was like a convent. It was more than he could stand.

He and his boon companions decided to go home. He announced that urgent government business called him back to Flanders and made an immediate return necessary. But at that time hostilities had broken out afresh between Ferdinand of Castile and the King of France, and Ferdinand said his son-in-law could not possibly cross the enemy's territory. Then Isabella pointed out to him that Joanna was in no fit state to travel, being pregnant again. But Philip remained obstinate. When his plans became known, the Cortes of Castile sent him a petition to stay, 'for it was unprecedented for a Prince to put himself in the hands of the enemy while the subjects of his land were at war with the King of France'.

Notwithstanding, Philip left Madrid on 19th December 1502, and went via Lyons and Perpignan, fêted all the way, to Innsbruck, where he met his father and cried, *Oh, du mein Österreich!*—'Beloved Austria!'

Meanwhile, Joanna suffered greatly from the absence of her husband, 'without whom she knew neither rest nor joy'.

On 10th March 1503, in Hernares, she gave birth to her fourth child, her second son, who was baptized with the name of Ferdinand. In his baptismal address the Bishop of Malaga praised the Archduchess, 'who is so blessed by God that she brings her children into the world without pains and has received a husband who gives her such happiness as has never before been seen'.

Joanna was no sooner up and about again than she expressed the wish to join her husband. But war with France made a journey over land impossible at the moment. Joanna demanded to be allowed to travel by the sea route and Isabella promised to have a ship equipped as soon as possible; meanwhile she was to be patient. Joanna was distressed beyond all reason by the delay. Isabella brought her to Segovia and had her strictly guarded in case she tried to run away. The daily disputes with her refractory daughter were wearing her out and she fell ill. The doctors sent Ferdinand, who was warfaring, a report of the queen's indisposition, in which they also described the state of the princess: 'She sleeps badly and eats little, sometimes not at all. She is very low-spirited and thin. Sometimes she will not speak. This condition can only be remedied by love and kindly persuasion, or else by fear. She does not listen to entreaties and kind words; and if one makes her do something, she is so angry that sometimes the least compulsion upsets her, and it makes one sorry to attempt it, and no one dare do it.'

When Joanna learnt that Isabella had received a letter of Philip's requesting the return of his wife (the letter bore the signature of three-year-old Charles), she went completely wild. As Isabella refused to let her travel, Joanna attempted to prepare her departure secretly, with the help of her Flemish servants. When Isabella heard of her plans, she had her daughter taken to the fortress of Medina del Campo where she was held like a prisoner by the Bishop of Córdoba. Pedro Martyr the chronicler relates: 'She raved like an angry lioness at being put under guard and accused her retinue of a conspiracy to keep her forcibly separated from her husband, and she stormed helplessly.'

On a wild November evening she managed to escape from her rooms and got as far as the castle gates. She commanded the guard to open and when he refused she shook the locked door in desperation and beat it with her hands till they bled. The old bishop hurried to the spot and tried to calm her. Joanna would not leave the gates. Her lady-in-waiting begged her at least to put on a coat, for it was cold, but Joanna was deaf to all entreaty. The queen was told, and although she was still unwell she came at once. 'The respect which the Princess always had for her mother induced her to go back to her quarters.'

Once there, however, she rounded on her mother with the most bitter reproaches. 'She spoke so disrespectfully and so little as it beseemed a daughter that if I had not been aware of her mental state I should never have suffered such speech,' Isabella wrote to her ambassador in Brussels.

This mental condition, to which Isabella's unbending attitude had much contributed, first developed a morbid character during those months of imprisonment. Joanna's screams echoed through the Medina fortress. It was then that people started calling her 'Joan the Mad'.

On 1st March 1504 Joanna finally left Medina del Campo and went to Laredo to embark. But she had to wait two months longer till the weather improved. At the beginning of June she landed in Flanders.

Joanna found her much-longed-for husband cool and indifferent. Indeed, she had known the long separation would estrange him. There was reason for his coldness.

'When she heard that Philip had a mistress, a lady of the nobility who was very beautiful and whom he greatly loved, she was seized with such a fit of anger that she rushed up to this friend of his like a wild lion and tore her hair and scratched her face.' The chronicler Estanques who related the episode added: 'Prince Philip would not put up with this and went to the princess and spoke to her with many harsh words and much scolding, and it was said that he beat her. And as Dona Juana was a delicate woman, she suffered greatly under the rough treatment of her husband, till she fell ill and almost lost her reason.'

This incident was passed from mouth to mouth and was a subject of comment in all the courts of Europe. It was said Joanna surprised the lady in Philip's arms; others said the scene had taken place at a court banquet, Joanna boxed the lady's ears and Philip humiliated his wife in the presence of the ambassadors, and swore aloud not to have any more to do with her.

Yet Joanna bore her husband two more children. Strong sexual attraction still brought them together though they were sworn enemies. Joanna's disappointed love turned sour and she lived in a continual state of irritation and opposition. 'I wanted her to take her share in ruling the state, but she said No to everything. In order not to provoke her continually, I let her do what she liked,' Philip wrote to his parents-in-law in justification of his actions, for he no longer let her function in the government.

And Joanna herself had begun to cut herself right off from court life. The surrounding world became unreal, only her bed-chamber had reality for her, for Philip sometimes came to her there. She dismissed all her Flemish ladies-in-waiting and her only servants were a few Moorish slaves; Philip could not bear the sight of them.

A chronicler found lenient words for Philip: 'Youth is so eager for pleasures of all kinds and specially for women, when their heart is given, that even if the queen had been the most distinguished woman in the world her husband would have deceived her, on account of his youth and through the counsel of the young people around him, so that she suffered greatly from jealousy and for three years knew not a moment's tranquillity, and was like a damned soul or someone out of her mind.'

Poor Joanna! It was never an easy matter to keep a man's love. He falls for the glowing cheeks and ardent eyes of a stranger, and his wife's lot is to endure it all with patience and affection.

134

JOAN THE MAD
Anonymous master of the Flemish School, late 15th century, *Brussels*

BURIAL OF COUNT ORGAZ
El Greco, *Santo Tomé, Toledo*

Now Joanna's love was a sort of instinctive urge to self-preservation, unscrupulous and blind, and Philip henceforth spoke of his wife as 'the terror'. Estanques the chronicler wrote to her mother that 'she only wanted to be near her husband, loving him above all measure, so that she never thought whether her presence was pleasing or unpleasing to him'.

In Joanna's case, it was certainly a feeling of insufficiency in herself that caused her to be in a continual state of fear lest she lose her husband to a woman more worthy of him. Joanna called Philip 'the fairest of all husbands'—and she was, as she knew, by no means 'the loveliest of women'.

A modern psychiatrist would have pointed out to her how from her childhood upwards she had always felt nature had her at a disadvantage. But no psychological treatment could have helped Joanna's mind to regain a poise it had never possessed.

I suffer, Joanna would have replied, I suffer. Call my sickness what you will, I suffer. She was wrecked on her emotions.

The news from Brussels made Isabella very sad, and roused Ferdinand against his son-in-law whom he held responsible for the unhappy course of Joanna's marriage. Isabella fell ill with worry, she feared that Joanna's irritability was a symptom of the mental disease her mother had suffered from. And Joanna was now heiress to a realm which reached beyond the ocean. When Isabella felt her end drawing near, she added a clause to her will: in case Joanna was incapable of ruling, King Ferdinand was to conduct the government till Prince Charles was twenty years old.

Isabella died in Medina del Campo on 26th November 1504. On the same day Ferdinand had his daughter proclaimed Queen. The heralds announced: 'Castilla, Castilla, for Queen Dona Juana, our Sovereign!'

But Ferdinand was not prepared to leave the government to his daughter, whom he knew to be wholly dependent on her husband. In the Cortes which he summoned in 1505, he had himself recognized as Regent of Spain and announced for the first time that Joanna was incapacitated by illness from governing the realm herself. He began to negotiate with the French king and persuaded him to conclude a treaty wherein Louis XII declared his readiness to come to the assistance of Ferdinand, should Emperor Maximilian and Archduke Philip claim the Regency of Castile. To give substance to the treaty, Ferdinand married the French king's nearest relative, Germaine de Foix, on 25th August 1505.

The news caused great consternation in Brussels. Maximilian and Philip immediately attempted to parry the stroke. They drew up a document addressed to the people of Castile, expressing disapproval of Ferdinand's treaty; but when they gave it to Joanna to sign, she refused, on the plea 'that she would never do anything against her father'.

Now Joanna was faced with a difficult conflict between wifely love and daughterly loyalty. In Philip and Ferdinand's rivalry, Joanna supported her father.

In September 1505 Joanna's fifth child was born—a daughter, Maria. Philip was determined to claim the Castilian throne, and he drew up a manifesto calling upon the people of Castile to refuse obedience to Ferdinand.

But Ferdinand was quick and crafty (his political skill aroused Machiavelli's admiration); when he heard of Philip's plan to come to Spain, he obtained from Louis XII an assurance that he would be refused transit through France. Now Philip had no alternative but to face the sea voyage despite heavy winter storms, and he sent his envoy ahead to inform Ferdinand that he was claiming Castile for himself and his wife. Ferdinand had few supporters in Castile (where he remained Ferdinand of Aragon, and the people never forgave his second marriage), so he concluded a treaty with Philip's envoy in Salamanca in which it was laid down that the kingdoms of Castile, León and Granada should be governed by Ferdinand, Philip and Joanna together.

Meanwhile, Philip and Joanna took ship on 8th January 1506. In the English Channel they met a heavy storm, the sails of their ship were awash and fire broke out on board. Everyone was in mortal fear—except Joanna, who remained perfectly calm, saying, 'a king has never yet been drowned'. She put on her robes of state, 'so that if the ship should go down she would be recognized and given a worthy burial.' Philip, meanwhile, thought only of his children whom he had left behind in Flanders.

They finally landed in England and were invited to Windsor by the English king. There Joanna met her sister Catharine, who did all in her power to entertain them. 'But Queen Joanna would take part in no festivities,' wrote Pedro Martyr, 'and spent her time in solitude in darkened rooms.'

At the end of April, they disembarked at La Coruña. Philip came with a great following and was welcomed by the Castilian Grandees as Lord of the land. Soon his supporters were 'strong enough to conquer a country'. Philip now attempted to exclude Joanna from all public business, for since she landed in Spain she was wholly for her father. She frustrated every one of Philip's measures by refusing to sign anything without her father's concurrence. Towards her husband she showed nothing but opposition, extending it to his following too, and she spoke of his friends as 'those Flemings with no business in Spain'.

Encouraged by the support of the Castilian nobility, Philip declared he did not consider himself bound by the Treaty of Salamanca, and gave Ferdinand to understand that he himself was sole ruler of Castile. But when he proposed to the Grandees that they regard Joanna as mentally deranged, they insisted on speaking with her themselves. Joanna received the Admiral of Castile and Count Benavente in her room, darkened as usual. The conversation lasted ten hours, and the admiral sought in vain for signs of the mental weakness Philip attributed to her. 'The Queen never gave any reply that was not sensible,' said the admiral after the meeting, and advised Philip not to part from Joanna and not to have her shut up, as that would make a bad impression on the people.

So Philip and Joanna entered Valladolid together under one baldachin. Joanna had her face veiled and remained absent from all the festivities in their honour. On 1st July she received the oath of allegiance of the Cortes, Philip was recognized as her lawful husband and Charles as her lawful son and heir to the throne.

Philip, however, pursued his plan to have her excluded from the government, for her antagonism blocked every decision of his. The Austrian ambassador, Fürstenberg, wrote to Emperor Maximilian at that time, that 'the greatest enemy our Gracious Lord of Castile has to deal with is, apart from the King of Aragon, the Queen, His Grace's wife; she is worse than I can describe to Your Majesty'.

Philip rode by Joanna's side like a prisoner. In spite of the perpetual stress and strain of their life together, and Joanna's unloving ways, her jealousy remained undiminished. She would tolerate no feminine influence in her entourage and often rode at Philip's side as the only woman in a following of many thousand men. Thus they rode from city to city through Castile, to receive homage as King and Queen.

Ferdinand accepted defeat for the time being and withdrew to his possessions near Naples.

Philip now felt he was sole sovereign and free to act independently, without taking any notice of Ferdinand's orders or Joanna's objections. He allotted the fortresses of Segovia, Jaen, Plasencia and Burgos to his favourite courtiers and disowned the men appointed by Ferdinand. In Burgos, his first act consisted in driving Ferdinand's illegitimate daughter, Juana of Aragon, out of house and home.

Arbitrary actions such as these came to an abrupt end when Philip suddenly succumbed to a fever on drinking a glass of cold water after a game of ball, and in a few days, on 25th September, he died at the age of twenty-eight.

During the seven days that his illness lasted, Joanna never left his bedside. She nursed him day and night, and herself tasted the medicines prescribed for him. She remained composed and tearless the whole time and her tranquillity astonished her entourage. Only when death occurred did she break down, she covered her husband's body with kisses and was not to be parted from him. In the end she had to be carried into her room, where she lay on her bed all day as though frozen, without undressing or sleeping.

Philip's body was embalmed meanwhile, and taken to the neighbouring Carthusian house at Miraflores.

And now began the period during which Joanna sank into melancholy. Sorrow drowned her mind and ruled it unchallenged.

Every week she went to the Carthusian monastery and had Philip's coffin opened, and embraced and kissed her beloved dead. Perhaps he was merely asleep? At that time Joanna believed Philip was only apparently dead, that heathen women had bewitched him and that he would soon begin to breathe again. When the miracle did not occur, at the end of December she decided to fulfil Philip's last wish and bring him to the royal crypt at Granada.

At the beginning of January 1507 the funeral procession set out on a wintry Castilian night, for Joanna would only travel by night, saying, 'It does not become a woman who has lost the sun of her life to see the light of day.'

Four bishops and many priests and monks accompanied the procession. Joanna, who was in an advanced stage of pregnancy, took her four-year-old son Ferdinand with her.

Her jealousy outlived her husband: on her route she stopped only at monasteries, not convents, so that no feminine influence might disturb his rest. In Torquemada she was overtaken by labour pains and gave birth to a daughter, whom she called Catharine. She remained in Torquemada till Easter. In all those months she had not given a thought to government administration, and to all questions she answered, her father would see to it.

When Joanna heard of the arrival of her father (who had stayed away in Naples during all the previous months), she and the entire procession turned to meet him. The meeting took place on the border of Castile and Aragon. A chronicler relates: 'So great was Juana's joy that tears sprang to her eyes and she knelt and kissed her father's hands. A whole night long they spent in conversation. King Ferdinand said that as sovereign she ought to command what was to be done; she replied, that was his office and she would never again cease to be his obedient servant. At dawn, the King departed. Dona Juana waited till evening to follow with her dead husband's body.'

She gave up the idea of going to Granada and accompanied her father on his travels through Castile. But when she learnt that his goal was Burgos she declined to follow, saying 'she would never again set foot in the city where her husband died'. So she remained with her children in Arcos. She began to neglect her appearance and became more and more melancholic. The Bishop of Malaga, who had remained with her, wrote to Ferdinand: 'She has become very quiet. For a long time she has not said an angry word to anyone. Since she came here she has not changed her shift. It is said that she still sleeps on the floor.' The letter is dated 9th October 1508.

In the course of the following year, Ferdinand heard that certain Grandees were planning an alliance with Maximilian to have nine-year-old Prince Charles declared ruler of Castile. In order to prevent Joanna from being taken captive by the supporters of this party, Ferdinand had her brought to Tordesillas, and henceforth Joanna was to live there, for nearly fifty years, like a prisoner.

Tordesillas was a mediaeval castle, once the abode of Alfonso XI of Castile, a fortress almost windowless on the outer side, but with an airy inner courtyard. In this gloomy place Joanna lived with her youngest daughter Catharine, the girl sharing her mother's solitary life till her marriage to the King of Portugal. Philip was buried in the neighbouring monastery of Santa Clara, which Joanna could see from a window; this proximity to Philip's last resting-place was reason enough for Joanna to feel at home here.

Charles visited his mother each time he came to Spain, and as his son Philip grew up, he too came to Tordesillas from time to time. After his betrothal to Maria of Portugal he presented his young bride to Joanna. She invited the young people to dance before her, and thus the visits of her grandchildren sometimes provided a little entertainment to relieve the monotony of her life.

Philip was much distressed by Joanna's indifference, not to say hostility, as regards religious matters, for the fact that Joanna never went to Mass and refused all spiritual counsel might have made her suspect of heresy;

this terrible secret was not to be allowed to reach the public ear—hence the silence that surrounded Tordesillas more and more densely.

Before Philip went to England to marry Mary Tudor, he entrusted Joanna's spiritual welfare to Francisco de Borja. Father Francisco was able to retrieve Joanna's mind from the dull state of brooding in which she remained sunken. He read her passages from the Gospel, and she listened readily enough, at last.

When she died in spring 1555, Charles V was in Flanders, and he thought he heard her voice calling him.

THE GENERALIFFE GARDENS

The Generaliffe Gardens are a work of artistry set out before the mountain-world of the Sierra Nevada. Seen over those trim box-hedges and straight pathways, the untamed landscape is but the more grandiose, and the natural wild background shows up the skilful planning of the gardens; each enhances the other.

The Arab's fondness for ornament is his retort to the inapprehensible desert. The beginnings of geometry are like the magic circles man drew in the sand to claim his shadow back from immeasurable distances. Those hedges and flower-beds are cut to human measure, the symmetry of their forms has a civilizing effect; this is no place to run wild in, but a space in which to recollect oneself.

These are royal gardens, the gardens of men whose life was governed by rules and obligations.

In a place like this, one has the impression that the evil of our time consists in a lack of form, a hatred of formalization and all grading of values.

These are kings' gardens, stiff and formal, reminiscent of Spanish ceremonial, which sprang, as all formality does, from a concern for right behaviour, being an agreed subordination to the discipline of style. When we speak of Europe, what we mean is simply such a concern for form—a concerted endeavour to become something better, a constantly renewed effort, an ever-new achievement in art.

IN THE ALHAMBRA

The Arabic atmosphere casts its spell slowly but surely; like the Spanish afternoon indolence, it stands for—inactive being. Leisure takes on a higher meaning here, breathing through the halls of the Alhambra. It is like that leisure of the soul which St Bernard called 'God's mode of action', 'the highest of all activities'.

An Arabic inscription on a fountain reads: 'I am a liquid sphere, transparent and finely spun, in me Creation is reflected.'

All the verse inscriptions sing the Alhambra's praises: 'I am richer in promises of bliss than any other building on earth.' 'I am a garden that daily adorns itself with new splendour. Here a soul dreams a lovely dream, the moon draws near and speaks to it, the stars stand still instead of passing through the firmament.'—There are inscriptions reminiscent of Arabic mystical poetry: 'I am the house of love. The roof and doors of this house are poetry and melody.' 'It is the house of love: one that knows no bounds and no end . . .'

'Blissful moment when we sit together in the palace, thou and I, two bodies and one soul, thou and I. . . .'

It is the Song of Songs that comes to mind:

A stream bordered with garden;
Water so fresh never came tumbling down from Lebanon.
North wind, awake; wind of the south, awake and come;
Blow through this garden of mine, and set its fragrance all astir.
Into his garden, then, let my true love come, and taste his fruit.
The garden gained, my bride, my heart's love; myrrh and spices of
  mine all reaped;
The honey eaten in its comb, the wine drunk and the milk that were
  kept for me!
Eat your fill, lovers; drink, sweethearts, and drink deep![1]

THE SACK OF ROME (1527)

The Emperor remained in Granada till the beginning of December. He spent Christmas with his wife in Toledo. Then he rode to Valladolid for the opening of the Cortes and sought to obtain financial support for the maintenance of his army in North Italy. This mighty sovereign's money troubles were very grave indeed: the imperial armies that gained the victory of Pavia were without pay and were consequently in a state of insurrection. But the treasury was empty and the Castilian deputies told the

[1] The Old Testament, Song of Songs, Knox translation. Burns & Oates, London.

Emperor they could support him with weapons but not money.

So he approached his brother, Ferdinand, who raised four thousand mercenaries for him in Germany, mostly Lutherans. Under the leadership of George Frundsberg, 'the dear father of the soldiers', this company came to Italy and joined the imperial troops under Connétable Charles de Bourbon. (This Bourbon had turned against Francis I of France in 1523, over a property dispute, and had entered the Emperor's service.) Frundsberg fell ill, and Bourbon, who had no pay for the men, could not assert his authority. The soldiers went ravening through the land and soon they were the terror of Italy. On their way to Rome they received a friendly welcome in Siena only.

The Emperor's directives were to induce the Pope to dissolve the 'Liga Clementina'. At the beginning of May, Bourbon and his unruly rabble arrived before Rome and demanded of the Pope a declaration that he was prepared to renounce his hostile policy towards the Emperor. But Pope Clement VII refused to act under compulsion and had the city gates closed.

Thus the clash of views between Emperor and Pope came to a head. The differences were spiritual ones (the Emperor himself fluctuating between strictly orthodox Catholicism and a leaning towards humanistic reform), and the explosion produced was violent. On 6th May the imperial troops stormed Rome. Bourbon was wounded as he scaled the city walls and died a few hours later; there was now no high command and the undisciplined armies plundered the Eternal City for three days on end, like the Vandals who once laid Rome waste. The Lutheran mercenaries vented their wrath on the 'Roman Babel'. Many works of art and literary treasures were destroyed, halls of the Vatican were turned into stables. The Pope's Swiss Guard fell in his defence to the last man. The Pope was taken prisoner and locked up in the Castel S. Angelo on the Tiber, with a number of Cardinals.

The news reached Valladolid on 22nd June when the city was busy celebrating the happy birth of an heir to the throne.

On 21st May Empress Isabella, her face veiled as Spanish ceremonial required, gave birth to a son. When the Emperor took the new-born child into his arms, he called out: 'May God, our Lord, make a good Christian of thee; may God, our Lord, give thee His blessing; may God, our Lord, enlighten thee to govern well the realm thou shalt inherit.'

Accompanied by singing children in white, the prince was carried to the church of San Pablo for his baptism. There were many who expressed the wish he should be called Ferdinand. The Duke of Alba pressed the point at the very font, but the Emperor gave his first-born child the name of his father, a father he hardly knew—Philip.

Ferdinand's representative, Martin de Salinas, wrote to the king, 'The Empress is doing well and so is the Prince; and the Emperor is so cheerful and happy and so delighted with his son that he thinks of nothing but plans for festivities.'

Bands played music in the streets, oxen were roasted on the market-place, and white wine and red wine flowed from two great barrels as in Utopia. At night fireworks soared to the sky and dancing went on till early morning on the squares.

News of the sack of Rome reached the Emperor as he was watching a tournament. He immediately stopped the proceedings, ordered court mourning and sent the General of the Franciscan Order to the Pope in Rome with a written message, in which he expressed his dismay over what had taken place, never having intended it; and he gave his assurance he would set the Pope free without delay. Nonetheless the Pope was held prisoner in the Castel S. Angelo for seven months, and the imperial troops remained nine months in Rome, till finally plague and hunger drove them out. Among the congratulations that reached Valladolid on the occasion of Philip's birth was a message from the captive Pope.

Sandoval reported that Charles V was glad to hear Rome had been stormed. But the Emperor's reaction was not malicious joy, simply a feeling that 'integral justice' had spoken. He said: 'I well perceive that it has all come rather as God's judgement than as my direction, my decision, or my will, or through any human agency at all, and that Christ himself, on whom we set all our hope, took up the defence of our cause.'

Alfonso de Valdés shared his lord's view of the situation in two works he published at that time. In his dialogue on 'The things that occurred in Rome', he said the Emperor was not responsible for what had happened, 'for it all obviously happened as God's judgement, punishing a city where to the scandal of the Christian religion there reigned supreme all the vices the wickedness of man could invent; in order to arouse Christian people by means of this chastisement to remedy the evil that afflicted them, and to make us open our eyes and live as Christians, proud as we are of the name.'

In the other work, *Lactancio*, he likewise justified the storming of Rome as God's punishment. In all Christendom there was no land so badly governed as the Church States. Church reform was the only means of altering the corrupt conditions, and a Council ought to introduce this reform. Valdés directed his appeal for a Council not to the Pope but to the Emperor, saying: 'Indeed the Emperor needs very good counsel, for if he succeeds this time in reforming the Church (for everyone knows how very necessary it is) from this service rendered to God he will reap the greatest renown in this world that ever a Prince attained to; and to the end of days it will be said that Jesus Christ founded the Church and Emperor Charles V renewed it.'

At that time the Papal Nuncio at the imperial court was Conte Baldassar Castiglione, a personal friend of Charles V's. He spoke of the Emperor as 'the best Christian he had ever known', and only half-heartedly stood for the hostile policy of Pope Clement VII. The fall of Rome, however, induced him to give the Pope his whole-hearted support. He wrote a sharply worded protest to Valdés' anti-Rome pamphlets, and he called on the Emperor for the purpose of persuading him to forbid both works, which, he said, were full of heresies.

The Emperor replied he had not read them, but he considered Valdés too good a Christian to write false doctrine; he would have the works examined by the Ecclesiastical Council.

The Archbishop of Seville declared Valdés innocent of the accusation of heresy (and we see how friendly to reform ecclesiastical circles in Spain were at that time still. The only exception was the Dominican Order which was fiercely opposed to Erasmus). This merely started Castiglione off on a personal attack on Valdés. 'New reformer that you are,' he wrote him, 'new lawgiver, improver of the holy Councils, new censor of morals, you say the Emperor ought to reform the Church, while he holds the Pope and the Cardinals prisoners! Do you think the badness of the priests is sufficient excuse for stealing the treasures of the Church?'

But in spite of his efforts, the Roman Curia accused Castiglione of glossing over the sack of Rome out of regard for the Emperor; in fact, the Pope censured him for deliberately concealing the Emperor's wicked intentions. Castiglione was a sensitive man and suffered considerably on this account; soon after he left the papal service to remain at the Emperor's court.

In the castles and cities of Spain a romance was sung reflecting popular feeling about the sack of Rome:

Sad was the Holy Father—fearful and distressed,
In the Angel's Castle—on a battlement,

No Tiara on his head—covered with sweat and dust,
He saw the Queen of all the world—in the hand of strangers.
The Cardinals were captives—the Bishops in chains,
The churches desecrated—the Crosses robbed.
The haughtiness of Rome—subdued by Spain.
Through the fault of the Shepherd—the sheep are damned,
For the Bark of St Peter—broken and mastless,
Has gone adrift—the compass wavers,
The water pours in—it will have to be reefed,
Through the fault of the pilot—who guides and steers it.
O Holy Father—on thy exalted See,
Behold, thy power—is transient!
O Founder of Heaven—grant us peace,
For peace is good.—When Christians are without it,
The Moors rejoice—the sects increase,
And justice dwindles. He who has power
Gobbles up the other—like sharks in the seas.
Might now rules—might is right. . . .

THE PEACE OF CAMBRAI (1529)

Charles V's hegemony in Italy now provoked Francis I to form an
alliance with Henry VIII of England. Both monarchs came forward as the
protectors of the captive Pope. It was a good opportunity for them to
join forces against the all-too-powerful Emperor. Henry wrote to Charles
that he withdrew his friendship on account of what had happened in
Rome. 'For a short time ago your people plundered the Holy City of
Rome and made prisoners of the person of our Holy Father together with
the Cardinals; they have robbed the churches, threatened bishops, clergy
and monks with knives and performed many horrible and inhuman acts. . . .'

Francis wrote likewise: 'You allowed the city that is the seat of the
Holy Apostolic See to be stormed and all possible misdeeds and sins to be
committed. . . .' And he declared war on him again.

The Emperor remarked to the French envoy who brought him the
declaration of war: 'I wonder that your lord has so soon forgotten his
oaths, in pledge of which he gave me his two sons as hostages, and that
he should stain his honour in such a villainous manner. If he cannot keep
his word, he should return to Spain.'

Francis I thereupon replied to the Spanish envoy in Paris, Granvelle, that if the Emperor said he had done something that no nobleman would do, to obtain his freedom, he challenged him to a duel.

All through 1528 hostilities continued between Francis I and Charles V in the form of defiant letters back and forth. Meanwhile the French and the imperial troops were fighting in Italy. The French took possession of Genoa under the leadership of their general Lautrec; they captured Pavia and advanced upon Naples. During the siege of Naples plague broke out in the French army, Lautrec died, and only a few of the besiegers remained alive. Fortune was again on the side of Charles V's troops: in June 1529 they recaptured Pavia and were the victors in a sea-battle over the combined French and Genoese fleets; the Doge of Genoa, Andrea Doria, entered the Emperor's service.

Exhaustion compelled both sides to sue for peace. As the two unreconciled rivals preferred not to meet, it was Louise of Savoy, the Queen Mother, and Charles' aunt Margaret, Regent of the Netherlands, who mediated the Peace of Cambrai. It was concluded on 3rd August 1529. Francis I renounced his claim to Naples, Milan and Genoa and undertook to pay indemnities to the amount of two million ducats; Charles V released the French princes; and Leonora, who had been waiting three years in Toledo for her marriage to be consummated, was at last to become French queen.

The question of Burgundy remained open: the land was attached to France, but Charles maintained his claims. Actually, this situation suited Charles well enough: it was principles rather than facts that interested him. So long as his right was recognized, he could treat the existing state of affairs as accidental and not finally binding.

The same tendency was noticeable in his attitude to the religious question: so long as an actual separation had not occurred, and the ideal of the unity of all Christians still held sway, he was content with promises and short-term solutions.

Soon after, Leonora accompanied the two sons of Francis I to France and was united with her husband.

But hers was a life of disappointment and neglect. On his return from Madrid, Francis I had fallen in love with young Anne de Pisselieu, later Duchesse d'Étampes. A sketch of her done by an artist of the school of Clouet shows her as a fresh, lively, bright-eyed girl, and her smile was to bewitch the king for a life-time. A portrait of Leonora done in the same year reveals her as not without charm: but she did not please her mate and lived like a nun, loyal to a husband who was enjoying himself elsewhere. Happiness was not an ingredient that was considered important in the royal marriages of those days. Marriage was an indissoluble sacrament, it was a commandment to be observed, and that was the beginning and end of it. It was in support of this view of marriage as an indissoluble sacrament that Leonora's aunt, Catharine, opposed a divorce from her husband, Henry VIII, King of England. 'As long as I live,' she wrote to her nephew Charles, 'I shall consider myself the true and lawful wife of the King, my lord.'

At that time it was certain that Catharine, who had turned forty, would not provide her husband with any further heir to the throne. Henry VIII was thinking of marrying young Anne Boleyn in order to have a son. He commissioned his Prime Minister Wolsey to set about obtaining the annulment of his marriage with Catharine, on the grounds that he, Henry, had been betrothed to the widow of his brother against his will and had married her without regard to the scruples of his conscience.

Wolsey implored Catharine on his knees to renounce her rights and to withdraw to a convent. But Catharine refused to let her marriage be declared invalid. In vain Wolsey strove in Rome to obtain from the Pope permission for an annulment; at that time Pope Clement VII had turned 'imperialistic'; it was said he feared the Emperor 'more than anything on earth' and he was therefore not inclined to take any step against the will of the man who was master of Italy.

Charles would not hear of the dissolution of the marriage, for it would mean that his aunt Catharine had lived for twenty years in concubinage with Henry and that her one surviving child, Mary, was a bastard. He put pressure on the Pope, who then rejected Henry's application for annulment.

Whereupon Henry VIII determined to marry Anne Boleyn, regardless of the Pope, thus putting into question the Holy See's authority in such matters. He now abandoned the Apostolic Catholic Roman Church (although he had referred to it as 'his Mother' in his anti-Luther book), and made himself head of a national Church of England.

Holbein's portrait of Henry VIII presents him as the very incorporation of that new self-dependent England under totalitarian rule: a swaggering figure filling the picture with his bulk, one fist set on his hips, the other resting on his dagger; his gaze is impenetrable and self-assured. Whoever opposed the king's will did so at the peril of his life: two of his wives died at his hand, as did Sir Thomas More, John Fisher, Bishop of Rochester, and many pious monks and laymen who remained true to the mediaeval conception of order, according to which the final verdict in religious matters was not the king's but the Pope's.

The portrait is also a living picture of that 'third power' that throve and grew to maturity on the conflicts between Habsburg and Valois, lending its weight now on one side now on the other in continental strifes, a constant obstacle to the establishment of continental unity.

It is one of the paradoxes of history that Charles V, whose whole purpose was the building up of European unity, should unwittingly have played his part in separating England from Rome, that is, from Europe.

The Peace of Cambrai was concluded without any account being taken of Henry VIII's interests. It more or less drove England out of Europe. Henceforward the British Isles were to build up new spheres of influence outside Europe.

THE BOLOGNA CORONATION (1530)

On 16th September 1528, in a speech before the court in Madrid, the Emperor explained why he had decided to set out on his long-postponed journey to Italy: he was going to be solemnly crowned Emperor by the Pope (which would entitle him to be termed *Imperator Romanorum*), and also to obtain from the Pope his consent to the calling of a General Council; and thirdly, he had to deal with the Turkish menace. He declared he was not interested in trying his fortune in foreign parts but only in safeguarding his heritage, and (according to Erasmus) he said any prince who took possession of what was not his was a tyrant.

The Emperor met with no difficulties this time, the Cortes gave its consent to the costly journey; for his proposal to persuade the Pope to reform the Church was acceptable, as was the plan to fight the Turks. In Spain Charles V had achieved this, that the term *patria* had broadened out to mean the unity of Christendom and its concerns. So he departed with the goodwill and financial support of the Cortes and on 27th July 1529 embarked at Palamos near Barcelona. The Empress Isabella remained behind as Regent of Spain.

It is said that in the seven years Charles spent in Spain he became a Spaniard. The bond that united him to Spain was wrought in those years; but along with this there had ripened in him the universal imperial idea now to be made effective by the coronation.

According to La Roca's description, 'The Emperor's entry into Bologna was done with a pomp and majesty worthy of his lord. With no less splendour the Pope awaited him, in full pontifical attire with the Tiara on his head.'

The Emperor knelt down before Pope Clement VII and kissed his foot. The Pope had forgiven him the months of captivity; he drew him to him and kissed him on both cheeks.

The scene was reminiscent of another meeting of Emperor and Pope, when in the Church of St Mark's the Hohenstaufen Emperor Frederick Barbarossa knelt at the feet of Pope Alexander III, who with tears of joy drew him up and gave him the kiss of peace.

In Venice, in the Doge's Palace, hangs a picture showing Pope Clement VII and Emperor Charles V together, in that unanimity which is the very foundation of the idea of *Sacrum Imperium*: Christ's representative on earth and the monarch, governing the spiritual realm and the earthly realms in unison.

The harmony so finely depicted in the painted scene did actually reign in Bologna from December 1529 to the end of March 1530. The abode of the Pope neighboured the Emperor's and they spent hours every day in friendly conversation. The Emperor conscientiously noted on a piece of paper the themes to be discussed, in order not to forget any important point.

Meanwhile, the old iron crown of Lombardy was brought from Monza and on 22nd February 1530 the Pope set it on Charles' head. The solemn coronation ceremony took place two days later, on the Emperor's thirtieth birthday. He received the insignia of sovereignty from the Pope's hands: the sceptre, that he should rule over his subjects in accordance with the Christian religion; the sword, that he should defend Church and Empire against all enemies; and the orb, that he should govern the world in piety and equity.

Heterodox men like Alfonso de Valdés and other members of Charles' retinue were amazed to see the truly religious devotion with which the Emperor complied with the archaic ceremonial. Actually, nothing could be more native to the Emperor's religious sense than those profoundly symbolic acts of submission and exaltation. Before the Offertory, the Emperor presented the customary thirty pieces of gold, and he served as deacon, handing the Pope the paten with the Host on it and the water-vessel. 'He did it all in so fine and edifying a manner as though experienced in such matters and much practised in them.'

After the coronation the Emperor held the Pope's stirrup and they rode side by side through the festively decorated streets of Bologna, among the excited crowds sinking on their knees before the representatives of spiritual and secular authority. 'Under one baldachin the two great luminaries of the world shone out like sun and moon.' Heralds threw the people gold coins bearing the inscription, *Carolo Quinto Imperatore*. On the triumphal arches were seen, beside the Habsburg arms, pictures of the Imperator Caesar Augustus, of Caesars Titus and Trajan, Marcus Aurelius and Constantine the Great—predecessors and prototypes of Charles V's.

Brusasorci painted a picture of this ceremonial ride of the Pope's and Emperor's under one baldachin, amid pointed swords and lances, in a fresco now in the Casa Ridolfi in Verona. The Emperor is shown in profile as Giotto painted his figures, his head raised, his expression tense and earnest. Pope Clement VII is gazing at the Emperor in amazement, like a father beholding his son grown unexpectedly mature; or rather, startled and taken aback like a sober man looking at a drunkard, for the Emperor as depicted here is in a trance.

Sandoval gives us the account of an eyewitness, Bishop Jovius. At their first meeting, the Pope gazed at the Emperor for a long time, 'and he appeared to him manly and full of majesty; for he had been described to him as rough and wild in appearance, looking like a true Goth, as coarse as his own soldiers; and now he saw the opposite; and found in him no trace of cruelty or haughtiness and found him (as he later said) worthy of a great imperium'.

An incident during the coronation caused a good deal of comment. As the Emperor was on his way from his palace to the cathedral, a balustrade fell just after he passed it. Superstitious people said: 'That means no other Emperor will ever be crowned by the Pope again.' And indeed Charles V was the last Roman Emperor crowned by the Pope; and afterwards the religious divisions wiped out the oecumenical significance of the imperium. After Charles' abdication, when Ferdinand was to be crowned Emperor, Pope Paul IV declined to recognize him because his consent had not been obtained before the election. (He was a Neapolitan and as such unfriendly to the House of Habsburg.) Ferdinand recalled an Electors' Union verdict of the year 1338, 'that the election of the Emperor was independent of papal endorsement'. The Great Schism of those days had made such a verdict necessary, and now another and deeper schism rent Christendom apart: since the Peace of Augsburg that ended the wars of religion, Ferdinand was sovereign over Catholics and Protestants, which meant a *de facto* recognition of the Lutheran faith to which Rome did not subscribe. Thus papal consent to the imperial election was not to be expected. And from that moment the title of Emperor began to lose its supra-national content, though it continued to be borne by the House of Habsburg until 1806, when Napoleon, dreaming of a new unity of Europe under French leadership, and using the magic of the term *Imperator* for the weaving of his own spells, compelled Emperor Francis II to renounce the old imperial title.

THE DIET OF AUGSBURG (1530)

Crowned and anointed, conscious of divine consecration, and utterly possessed of his sense of mission as the protector of Christendom bound by God to re-establish the unity of the Faith, the Emperor left Bologna for Augsburg, via Trent, Bolzano, Innsbruck; he reached it on the Vigil of Corpus Christi.

On the morning of the Feast, which was one he dearly loved, Charles received Holy Communion, and after High Mass walked for two hours behind the Blessed Sacrament through the streets of Augsburg, kneeling at the open-air altars erected along the route; children scattered their spring flowers, the June air was full of incense, the Feast of the Lord's Body was once more being celebrated on German soil. All the princes of the Empire were invited by the Emperor to take part in the procession, but not all had come: the Elector of Saxony and the Landgrave of Hesse remained away. It was thus the Emperor returned to Germany after nine years' absence to restore order. But he had been too long away in Spain. 'For with the advance of time,' as Machiavelli wrote, 'if the disease was not recognized and treated in its early stages, it will be easy to diagnose but hard to remedy.'

But Charles' year-long preoccupation with Spanish and Burgundian affairs was on the side of destiny, too, for time has to ripen before a settlement is possible. A bridge can be built only when the two supporting banks are firm.

In 1530 or thereabouts, the two opposite viewpoints stood in clearly defined relation to one another, and the work of mediation could now begin.

A lot had happened since the Worms days: in spite of the edict against him, Luther had spread his doctrine without let or hindrance and had driven out the old form of worship in many places. The Protestant princes had confiscated Church property and many priests had married. New articles of faith—false ones, as the Emperor held—had taken root and were dissolving the religious unity of the realm. The Emperor hoped to be able to persuade all well-intentioned men that religious unity was at that time a political necessity as well, for the defence of Christendom against the Turks was just as much a Protestant concern as a Catholic one.

But it was not only political considerations that made the Emperor ready to come to terms with the Protestants at Augsburg. In the seven years he had spent in a busily reforming Spain, he had realized that a renovation of Church conditions such as Cardinal Jiménez had carried out was also an urgent need of Germany's. The seven years in Spain were the length of time needed for the spirit of Erasmus to prevail in both humanistic and ecclesiastical circles: the Emperor's supporters had become 'Christian fighters'. Gattinara, a very sincere man, had died on the way to Augsburg. But Alfonso de Valdés, who took up the Emperor's defence at the time of the Sack of Rome, was now in Augsburg and considered the moment was ripe for his Emperor to become the renewer of Christ's Church.

So Charles V went to the Diet of Augsburg with the intention of bringing about a moderate reform of the Church in Germany and uniting all devout Christians in this purification of the Faith. He rejected Luther's doctrine unconditionally, as in the days of his youth at Worms; but he was prepared to lend an ear to justifiable reforming demands.

At the beginning of the Diet of Augsburg the desire for reconciliation was expressed on both sides. Melanchthon, the leader of the Lutherans, had set down the twenty-eight evangelical articles of faith in a document termed the *Confessio Augustana*, and Brück, chancellor to the Elector of Saxony, had made a book of it which he handed to the Emperor; it contained the statement that the evangelical orders were ready to meet the Emperor in his intention to restore Church unity.

But the Emperor's joy at such testimonies of good-will on the Lutherans' part soon turned to perturbation as the twenty-eight articles came to light during the discussions: they raised the most fundamental religious questions, only to provide quite independent solutions for problems such as original sin, justification and free will; they discarded sacraments and Church ordinances—e.g. confession, religious vows, fasting; they set up a new doctrine—the doctrine of justification through faith alone; they altered the liturgy, and even the Canon of the Mass. All these articles raised so much dust and were in such basic disagreement with Church doctrine that the Catholic theologians had no alternative but to reformulate the principles of the Roman Catholic religion in order 'to be sure of their own souls', as St Teresa put it later.

Charles V was tireless in his endeavours to mediate. Melanchthon praised the patience, kindness and courtesy of the Emperor during the long and often heated debates which went on for months on end. 'More glorious than any triumph of the Emperor's is his self-control,' wrote Melanchthon. 'He never shows a trace of haughtiness or harshness. In spite of all the efforts of his opponents to put him out of countenance, he has up to now given us a kindly hearing.' And Luther, who was being kept informed of the progress of events, spoke of the 'wonderful rare gentleness of the Emperor': 'pious good Kaiser Karol sits like an innocent little lamb among many such sows and dogs, indeed among many devils'.

Pious Kaiser Karol gave his confidence to the Lutherans' assurance that they acknowledged the Apostles' Creed and therefore were part of the 'holy Catholic Christian Church'. Melanchthon enhanced the Emperor's hope for a peaceful settlement; he assured the Cardinal Legate, Campeggio, that 'We have no dogma which deviates from the Church'.

Nonetheless, Melanchthon held fast to Luther's justification dogma. There was an ambiguous trait in Melanchthon, a sort of double-dealing that was far more destiny-laden than Luther's blunt contentions to which a straightforward answer could be given. But Melanchthon touched up Luther's demands and kept quiet about the special preferences of his patron, the Elector of Saxony. 'Sweet' Melanchthon's apparent acquiescence deceived the Emperor as to the fundamental discrepancies.

Cochläus, the humanist, co-drafter of the Catholic reply to the Protestant 'Augsburg Confession', observed that Melanchthon was a wolf in sheep's clothing: 'What happens is that Melanchthon with his pleasant approach outdoes Luther,' he said; 'and the more moderate he is in his doctrine, the more does he constitute a danger to the Church's cause.'

Melanchthon, divided in himself, was like a quicksand offering no secure basis for steady constructive work; and thus the Augsburg endeavour to reach agreement was soon to collapse in its turn; the damage to the structure of the Church was terrible.

In Rome it was observed that the Lutherans had abandoned common ground and it was useless to go on negotiating. Campeggio termed

153

Luther's doctrine *questa Diabolica peste* and advised the eradication of *questa Diabolica secta* with fire and sword. Charles' old confessor, Loaysa, wrote him from Rome: 'The stubbornness these heretics display pains me to the depths of my soul. . . . The right rhubarb for their remedy is force, that alone remedied Spain's revolt against its king.'

But Charles not only desired to avoid civil war in Germany, but knew it was absolutely necessary to avoid it. In view of the Turkish threat, he took the initiative himself: he induced Campeggio to propose extensive concessions to the Pope, such as toleration of laymen's Communion in both species, and marriage of the clergy; he persuaded princes, councillors and theologians to come to terms over certain articles, so that Erasmus (the Grey Eminence behind the Diet of Augsburg) could be told that 'now only the *Canon Missae* is controversial'. But the question of the restitution of Church property gave rise to violent dissension. The fact emerged that the political and economic interests of the Lutherans had begun to oust the religious ones. Behind the Protestant theologians there were quite a number of princes and notabilities whose motives were purely egoistical. The particularism of the German princes was in fact an open obstacle to the clearing up of the religious problem.

As Charles V was aware, the men who made such a fuss of their conscience never put it to their conscience whether it was right to destroy Christian unity at such a moment. On 8th September he told the notabilities who appealed to their Christian conscience that he, too, had a conscience and a soul to save, and he had a greater responsibility before God than they had.

In view of the 'acute stubbornness' of the Protestants, the conciliatory attitude of the Emperor stiffened. In annoyance he told the assembled notabilities that everything would remain as it had hitherto been. It was a bestial error to deny the freedom of the will. Faith without charity could not make men blessed, or all true culture would fall to pieces, as was already happening; stolen Church property was to be restored.

By this time a reconciliation was possible only if the deviators returned to the common body of truth. The Emperor suggested that a change of heart was needed, and gave them till 15th April of the following year to think it over. Between now and then, they were not either to practise or to spread their innovations.

The dissidents thereupon withdrew to Schmalkalden and in December 1530 founded the 'Schmalkaldic Liga' which sought reinforcements at the French and English courts and formed the first political front of the

Reformation, paving the way for the coming wars of religion. From that time, Charles V looked upon the disloyal princes as rioters, rebels against the unity of Faith and the unity of Empire. Under pressure of their opposition, the peace-seeking Emperor was moulded into the Mühlberg warrior.

The more clearly Charles V saw the possibility of a friendly settlement recede, the more his hopes for reunion centred upon the calling of a Council. After all, it was clear from Church history that a Council was always the means of preserving Christian doctrine intact. A universal Council would liberate traditional truth from any temporal disfigurement and provide the cure for which all souls were longing.

How confident Charles was that the Lutherans would bow to the authority of a Council! The decisions were to be reached by the most enlightened and learned theologians of the day: as it appeared to the Emperor, those unversed in theological matters would accept the verdict of the initiated as a matter of course. He wrote urgently to the Pope, begging him to propose to the erring the calling of a Council within a certain time limit, under the condition 'that they gave up their errors in the meantime'. And he added: 'If there were to be no Council, then Germany, the most powerful and most bellicose land in Christendom, would be in great peril.'

Charles' preoccupation with religious matters was organic to his imperial vocation; such a mingling of spiritual and worldly concerns was in accord with its theocratic character. It was his conviction that the Emperor's bounden duty was to play his part in the salvation of the world, and therefore he represented a trend that Marsilius of Padua had instigated in the first half of the fourteenth century, assuming the validity of Councils. But he never accepted Marsilius' anti-papal political teaching, for defence of the Church's cause was a privilege and an obligation, whatever Marsilius might say. Nonetheless, the reformed Catholicism which Charles stood for since his return from Spain was bound to bring him into opposition with Pope Clement VII, who rejected the means to reform by refusing to call the Council.

Apart from his personal feelings, Pope Clement VII had valid reasons for disliking the idea, remembering the extreme powers the late mediaeval Councils had allocated to themselves. The desire to avoid schism had produced a sort of super-ecclesiastical court-of-law; in the years 1414–18 the Council of Constance propounded the clause that a Council assembled in the Holy Spirit possessed its authority through Christ and that all, including the Pope, must obey its verdict; and the Council of Basle declared in 1431 that a Council was above the Pope.

The Church did not accept the decrees of the Councils of Constance and Basle; but it was popularly supposed that a Council was entitled to give a verdict on the Pope as well as on other matters. Fear of public opinion was certainly an inducement to Pope Clement VII to veto the plan.

Loaysa wrote to the Emperor from Rome, 'When I pronounce the word "Council" in his presence, I might be speaking of the devil himself.' And Clement VII continued to prevaricate.

Why this overgreat zeal to criticize the Church, he pondered: had not St Augustine said that evil was not in things but in ourselves? Of course there were bad servants of the Lord, sinners and hypocrites among the prelates; the devout were always a minority; of course there were abuses in the Church; wherever the spirit was at work in matter, the inevitable corruption of all that is earthly set in. But what were those temporal weaknesses beside the eternal truths? They remained as ever unassailable. In the Pope's opinion the structure of the Church should not be meddled with.

Erasmus, working loyally away at the slow reformation of hearts and minds, likewise began to think with some scepticism of the idea of a Council to perform the miracle of unification. The spotlight was no longer upon him; at Freiburg he lived the retired life of a scholar and followed the progress of the Diet of Augsburg from a distance. But both Catholic and Lutheran members of the Diet were in correspondence with him and he counselled both sides to be conciliatory, though sometimes in vain.

'We have defined so much,' he wrote, 'which might without any danger to our salvation have been ignored or left undecided. . . . The main thing needed in our religion is peace and accord. These can come about only if we are content to define as little as possible and leave every man free to make his own judgement.' And the passage written in 1524, in his work on free will, now had special significance: 'It were better devoutly to do honour to the mysteries than to discuss the inexhaustible dogmas. . . . And indeed much is reserved for the time when we shall no longer see as in a mirror and in riddles, but God's countenance will be revealed to us in all its glory. . . .'

But the young Emperor was in no mind to harken to his mentor's sententious observations. He waited impatiently for the calling of an official debate on spiritual matters, which was bound, he thought, to lead to unanimity. Confidently he proclaimed the calling of a Council within a year, although the Pope had not yet consented. But Charles held it was necessary and would therefore take place.

CHARLES V AND THE RISE OF CAPITALISM

Golden Augsburg, the scene of the first Protestant Confession, was also the city in which Germany first experimented with the new economic ideas based on individualism. Melanchthon wrote that 'Augsburg is a German Florence and the Fuggers are equal to the Medici'. And, as a matter of fact, the rise of Augsburg to prosperity coincided with the rise of the Fugger family. The Fuggers were originally weavers who made their wealth in trade, and weaving and commerce were the sources of Augsburg's prosperity. Trade in furs and luxury articles, especially jewellery, flourished in this opulent city on the River Lech. As a chronicler relates, 'Anno 1519 there was lavish display among the burghers and the craftsmen. Their clothing was luxurious: men and women wore marten-skins, velvet and damask, precious rings, pearls and golden chains such as are not to be found in any city in the German lands.'

Ulrich von Hutten saw this increase in material goods as an evil for which he held the 'crazy shopkeepers' responsible. The Fuggers were to his mind allies of the 'Römlingen', exploiting Germany for their own ends. He wrote: 'Did not the Fuggers hitherto seek out all possible means, lawful or not, to exclude all other merchants dealing with Indian wares in order to relieve the Germans of their money by importing merchandise either superfluous or damaging to health and morals? Is it not robbery, when they flood Germany with a coinage that does not contain the value that it ought to have? Is it not also robbery that they have obtained a similar monopoly for indulgences, benefices, dispensations and other papal privileges as for earthly goods, and when they flood all Germany with Roman as with Indian trumpery?'

But Dante's attack on the usurers who lent out money in order to claim it back at high rates of interest was sharper still.

Those usurers whom Dante placed in the Inferno for putting their own profit before the common weal, were the first representatives of early capitalism, and paradoxically enough it was the Church that provided it with growing-room.

The late mediaeval Church, with all its duties, tithes and indulgences, constituted a highly developed financial complex with money-brokers as an essential element. And it was money-shortage that turned princes into promoters of great credit concerns. The Fuggers were bankers to Popes and Emperors, and Augsburg was a centre of European money traffic. In his 'Table Talk', Luther said: 'The city of Augsburg can produce thirty tons of gold in three weeks; that the Emperor cannot do.'

In actual fact, the Emperor was dependent on the financial support of the Fuggers for nearly all his undertakings. Jacob Fugger was perfectly entitled to remind him of it, when in 1523 he wrote to him in Spain: 'It is common knowledge and a matter of fact that Your Majesty would not have been able to secure the Roman crown without me. . . .' As a good businessman Fugger was anxious to recover his loans in Spain, and his agents gained the lease of the more profitable of the Spanish iron-mines. It is believed to have been the representatives of the Fugger brothers who obtained the Toledo Mandate from the young Emperor. This mandate, which Charles promulgated in Toledo in May 1525, gave them complete financial freedom of action. In fact, it granted to the holders of the monopoly for mining products the express right 'to sell their iron-ore and metals at the highest price they could obtain.'

It was the spirit of the Renaissance, a spirit of freedom, that had paved the way for the new attitude to finance. Charles V helped it to assert itself on the economic level while seeking on the political level to maintain a mediaeval Christian conception of society.

In Augsburg, the city councillor and humanist, Konrad Peutinger, represented the new economic liberalism. He demanded that no barriers be put in the way of trading companies: 'Every merchant may sell his wares as he can and will.'

This view found an unexpected opponent in Luther. In his 'On Salesmen and Usury' he wrote: 'I may sell my wares only as dear as I ought and as is right and fair.'

Thus we have the paradoxical situation of Luther, the pioneer of individualism, making a stand for the mediaeval attitude to usury, whilst Charles V, champion of Christian solidarity, favoured individualistic economic freedom, i.e. unlimited free trade, which Karl Marx (unwittingly echoing Luther) termed 'conscience-less'.

While Charles was defending the old common Faith at the Diet of Augsburg, his financial agents were selling the lease of the quicksilver mines in Spain to the highest bidders. The highest bidders were the

Fuggers. Charles V raised them to the status of hereditary counts.

Now in granting mining monopolies to the Fuggers and Welsers of Augsburg, Charles V was fostering a price-policy favouring the business-manager alone at the cost of all others concerned, and thus he was one of the founders of capitalism in Germany. He had no idea that the encouragement he gave to untrammelled profit-making was to let loose on the world the very forces which would contribute most powerfully to the disintegration of Christian unity; he could not know that in the twentieth century those forces would produce a crisis threatening to blow up the globe.

CHARLES V AND THE TURKS

At the very time Charles V was preparing for his Coronation in Italy, Sultan Suleiman the Great and his Janissaries were laying siege to Vienna.

To appreciate the danger that threatened Vienna in that autumn of 1529, we have to recall what happened when the fall of Constantinople was the prelude to the rise of Osmanic power in Eastern Europe.

On 24th May 1453, after a siege lasting seven weeks, Sultan Mohammed II gave orders to take Constantinople by storm. The cry of the Janissaries, *La illah illallah* (there is no God but God) mingled with the entreaties of the Christians, *Kyrie eleison* (Lord have mercy on us). The last Greek Emperor, Constantine XI, was slain and his head was set up on the pillar of Constantine the Great. The famous church of Hagia Sofia, 'Divine Wisdom', was plundered, the altars desecrated, the holy pictures trodden underfoot. The surviving inhabitants were sold into slavery. With the fall of Constantinople the millennium of the Byzantine Empire ended, and the hearth of Eastern Christendom was demolished.

The same fate threatened the West in the autumn of 1529, when Sultan Suleiman, the Great, the Mighty, the second Solomon, carried the assault of Islam upon the Christian world to the very gates of Vienna.

On 21st September there appeared before the walls of Vienna the vanguard of the Osmanic armies, the 'runners and burners', the 'ravagers' (the Germans called them the 'sackmen'). They had laid waste villages and towns on their way. 'The sackman strangles, spikes and cuts to pieces man, woman and child,' as a contemporary chronicle relates, 'grievously murdering the people, and that in the most merciless manner, with children cut out of their mothers' wombs and thrown away or spiked. . . .'

The city of Vienna was defended by Austrians, a few German imperial troops, Hungarians, and Spaniards, under the command of Palatine Count Philip of the Rhine and Count Nicholas of Salm. The city gates were walled up and barricaded, with only one left open for sallies.

On 26th September, the Janissaries began digging under the walls right and left of the Kärntner-tor and mining them, and they set roofs alight with fire-arrows. 'It rained cannon-balls and arrows.' On 9th October two mines on either side of the Kärntner-tor exploded and made a breach of which the besiegers rapidly took advantage to storm the city. But the attack was repulsed. Twelve thousand bodies of the enemy filled the breach.

On 11th October the walls near the Kärntner-tor were once again mined and breached. The assault came in three waves and each was thrown back. Suleiman's journal reports on that day the loss of some martyrs in the holy war.

On 12th October the wall between the Kärntner-tor and the Stuben-tor collapsed. A troop of Spaniards immediately filled the gap. Sultan Suleiman rode round the city and found it ripe for storming. On 14th October, in the Turkish camp, when the call to prayer went out, the order for a major attack was given at the same time. Simultaneously, news was spread abroad that Emperor Charles and King Ferdinand were approaching.

The hope of reinforcements warmed the hearts of the beleaguered: when the enemy attacked, assault after assault was repulsed. From the battlements of Vienna it was seen how the Pashas had to drive the Turkish troops to the assault with blows and sword-strokes; many said 'they would rather be cut down by the hand and sword of their warlord than by Spanish nozzles and German spits'.

After a day of bootless assault, Ibrahim, the Sultan's commander-in-chief, gave the command to strike the tents.

What the Janissaries could not carry away with them they set on fire; old people and priests were thrown on the fire, boys and girls were taken off into slavery. On the next day the villages round the Kahlenberg were mere heaps of smoking ashes.

Sultan Suleiman, self-styled the 'Lawgiver', had hoped to impose his law on Vienna. He was the author of a work called *Multeka*, the 'Trumpet of the Holy War', in which he made war on Christians an obligation for all, and commanded that they be either converted or made to pay poll-tax; those who resisted were to be pursued with fire and the sword, their trees were to be felled, their fields laid waste. Suleiman had announced that he would turn the spire of St Stephen's Cathedral in Vienna into the most lovely minaret of all Islam, and have the faith of Mohammed proclaimed from the top of it, in the imperial city and throughout all Germany; he would command the bells to be silent for ever.

On 15th October the bells of St Stephen's rang out over the roofs of the dauntless city. 'In the morning, the Te Deum was sung in the Cathedral, at a solemn High Mass in honour of the Holy Trinity. Bells, silent since September, together with the cathedral organ, with gongs, cornets and flutes from St Stephen's Tower, cannon on the city walls, all lent their voice to the general rejoicing at deliverance from the menace of the Turkish yoke.'

The withdrawal was accounted for in various ways. Among the people the rumour went round that Ibrahim, the Grand Vizir, had parleyed with King Ferdinand behind the Sultan's back, and had been promised the Hungarian crown if he could persuade the Sultan to break off the siege— but there is no trace in the state archives of any such bargain. It was also said that Sultan Suleiman had a dream directing him to withdraw. The stalwart defence of the city of Vienna had given the mighty Sultan his first taste of a fateful 'thus far and no farther'.

'At the walls of Vienna the land-devouring tides of Osmanic invasion in Germany broke for the first time' (von Hammer).

In October 1530 (while Charles was at the Diet of Augsburg) King Ferdinand sent his ambassadors to Constantinople to start peace negotiations. They were received by the Grand Vizir Ibrahim, who as favourite of the Sultan considered himself his equal.

Ibrahim enquired caustically as to the present position of Charles and Ferdinand, 'and he called the King of Bohemia and Hungary nothing but simply Ferdinand and the Emperor nothing but King of Spain'.

The fact that neither Emperor Charles nor King Ferdinand were present in person at the defence of Vienna made Ibrahim despise them. And Ibrahim put his finger on what was a real weakness in Emperor Charles' method of governing: his constant absence from his crownlands. For when he was in Spain, he was missed in Germany; when he was in Germany, he was lacking in Spain, not to speak of the Netherlands and his Italian possessions.

Ibrahim made playful reference to the unsuccessful beleaguering of Vienna, saying his Emperor had gone forth in person to seek out Ferdinand, and, and as he had not met him in the open, he had gone on to the lovely city of Vienna, which was worthy to be the seat of an Emperor; as Ferdinand had, however, disappeared, his Emperor was put out and let the runners and burners loose on all sides to show that the real Emperor was there, and damaged the walls a little, as a souvenir of his visit. As he had not come conquering but purely on a visit, he had not taken any heavy cannon with him, and the cold had induced him to depart.

But Ibrahim knew very well that the imperial army had checkmated his ambitions, and his acid remarks gave him away: 'Charles fancied he was Emperor because he had put on the cap and crown; the real imperial title lay in the sword.' Machiavelli held the same view.

Suleiman guessed he had met his master in Charles V, an opponent against whom all his conquering schemes were to break to pieces. The two would have to come to terms.

Ibrahim gave Ferdinand's ambassadors to understand that the Sultan's peace negotiations had Charles V alone in view, but not as Emperor (Suleiman did not intend to share the title of Emperor with any other sovereign, there should be only one Emperor on earth, as one God in heaven). He was prepared to go to encounter him into the heart of Germany.

The Emperor was in the Netherlands, but returned to Germany at the end of January 1532 in view of Suleiman's threatened campaign. In his Memoirs we read that 'the Emperor went to Germany for the third time, for the purpose of seeing how the heresies could be remedied and to build a bulwark against the Turks, for news had come that they were advancing with strong forces to destroy Germany'.

In April 1532, when Suleiman once more approached Vienna, the Emperor was in Regensburg, where he was waiting—in Garcilaso de la Vega's words—'till the Danube was favourable for bearing the ships to Vienna'.

The Diet that had assembled to deal with the religious conflict now turned into a gathering of all available forces to drive out the Turks. On 9th August 1532 the Emperor wrote to his wife in Spain: 'Now that it is certain that the Turks are advancing upon Germany, many lords and knights from all parts of the Empire, and above all from our Spanish realm, have come together here to take part in the fight against the Turks.'

He wrote in his Memoirs: 'For lack of time the religious problems had to remain in the state in which they were.' The imperial armies, composed of Germans, Italians, Spaniards and Netherlanders, set out for Vienna with the Emperor and his brother Ferdinand at their head.

Sultan Suleiman had meanwhile advanced into the Burgenland and laid siege to the small fortress of Günz. But the Janissaries did not succeed in raising their red banners with the white inscription, 'There is no God but God, Mohammed is His Prophet', over the battlements of the castle. In view of the stalwart resistance of this place Suleiman cooled in his desire to submit Vienna to a second siege. Instead of facing the Emperor's army he set off for the Austrian province of Styria, 'along ways as heavy-going as the Last Judgement', he wrote in his journal. The Turkish tide was on the ebb, but it was not subdued. Suleiman had merely withdrawn his forces. Nonetheless, as Robertson wrote in his biography of Charles V, there was no little honour in this his first attempt at an encounter of arms with an opponent such as Suleiman, and it was very praiseworthy to have compelled him to retreat.

The Emperor remained in Vienna till the beginning of October. Then he went through Styria to Italy, where he met Pope Clement VII for the second time in Bologna.

The main theme of their conversations was the Turkish danger. It was essential to take strong measures against the pirate Chaireddin Barbarossa, for he was in the service of the Sultan and made the Mediterranean unsafe for Christian ships. The Pope agreed to equip some ships and to put them at the Emperor's disposal for his proposed attack on the Turkish fleet.

At the end of April 1533 the Emperor was back in Spain.

In May of that year King Ferdinand sent a fresh embassy to Constantinople to negotiate a peace treaty with the Sultan, saying the Emperor was prepared for peace if the pirate Chaireddin gave up harassing Christian ships and coasts.

The messengers were once more received by the Grand Vizir Ibrahim, who this time used still more presumptuous language. He boasted that he had been right up to the gates of Vienna and had ridden round the city walls. Charles had meanwhile gone to Italy, had threatened the Turks with war and the Lutherans with a compulsory return to the old doctrine, had come to Germany, and had accomplished nothing. It was not the mark of an Emperor to begin something and not to finish it, or to say something and not do it. He had announced a Council and not kept to it. If he (Ibrahim) wished, he would set up a Council today, he would put Luther on one side and the Pope on the other and force them into Church unity.

But it was not as simple as that. The religious and political problems which Charles V had to settle were far too complex to be properly dealt with at a word of command. Power can of course enforce order, but the result is a stark and frigid one, with no further growth possible.

In times of transition, growth goes on unseen but so rapidly that any fixation can be damaging. Charles V's policy of restraint and delay certainly best corresponded to the dominating need for change—and it was precisely the attentive ear he lent the conscience-problem that contrasted most sharply with the despotic spirit of Islam, and distinguished him as essentially a European ruler.

And the same is true of his tendency always to seek a motive for his actions in bygone days, a trait which particularly provoked the Grand Vizir. Picking up a letter of the Emperor's he said: 'This was written by no wise and moderate prince; with pride he enumerates his titles, including those he cannot claim; how dare he term himself King of Jerusalem? Does he not know that the great Emperor is Lord of Jerusalem, not Emperor Charles? Does he want to snatch my Lord's land from him, or merely to insult him?'

Those were notions of a kind to leave Charles quite unaffected. While his opponent saw merely the present factual state of affairs, Charles was conscious of another dimension, he was aware of a whole space of time, and every moment was inextricably related to all the past and future. Indeed, his sense of eternity often made him blind to transient conditions, like Don Quixote he saw the world lit with the splendour of the ideal that fired him. In the realm of ideas, that was enduring which was intrinsically true. Of course he was King of Jerusalem, for he was the Christian Emperor. The Kingdom of Jerusalem, which Godefroi de Bouillon had founded in the First Crusade and which was lost again a few years later, was the heart of all Christendom. On the other hand, the Holy Sepulchre meant nothing at all to the Infidels, their shrine was Mecca, not Jerusalem. For all that the Kingdom of Jerusalem was in the hands of the Mohammedans, it was not really theirs.

In June 1533 Ferdinand's ambassadors concluded a separate peace with Suleiman. But Charles V was planning to carry out a scheme he had had in mind for a long time, and to make his own attack on the Infidels. From Spain, and with the support of that loyal Spanish base of his, he now set to work to prepare for it.

GRANADA CARNATIONS

Here, in Granada, the one-time cross-currents of Moorish and Christian life achieved harmony. The *pension* in which I now lived was on the Bibarrambla Square which was once the jousting-ground of the Moorish kings.

In the morning I looked from my window over the empty square and saw women in black and young seminarists on their way to early Mass. Next came the flower-sellers to set up their stands. And soon it was all a blaze of red and pink—carnations.

Nowhere have I seen such splendid carnations, large, compact, full carnations with a lasting-power as though the substance of eternity was contained in their petals. For five pesetas I had bought a dozen dark red ones some days earlier, and every morning they glowed out at me unchanged, as though they had pulled off a victory over time.

It is said that Charles V brought the carnation to Spain from Tunis. In his *Hortorum libri*, Father Rapin, S.J., called Charles 'the conqueror of the African carnation'.

That is only a legend, of course, for carnation-designs adorn many an old Spanish manuscript. But it is always the single field-pink that is figured there, not this multi-petalled bloom, its blossom-heart bursting with vigour.

It is certainly true that Charles V brought a specially lovely carnation from Africa to Spain. It was his favourite flower and in his Yuste garden he had carnations of all sorts and colours among the great variety of plants from distant lands which he acclimatized there.

Many of the flowers that bloom in our gardens come from the East. It is said that lilac, one of the joys of spring in Vienna, was brought there by the Turks.

Legend has it that the carnation was the Tunis laurel, and this is peculiarly apt, for Charles' Tunis victory was a victory over the Moorish foe, and yet from that Islamic land he brought back the flower that is to-day the most characteristic blossom of Spain.

TUNIS (1535)

Life and death were at stake when the Tunis carnation was plucked. . . .

The preparations for the attack on Tunis filled the thirty-fifth year of the Emperor's life. In August 1534 Chaireddin Barbarossa captured the city of Tunis, drove out the Arabic king Muley-Hasan and used the place as a base for sallies against Sicily and Naples. It was feared that the Turkish fleet would next drive on to Rome.

To deal with this menace was part of the great imperial duty of keeping the Turks at bay. It was one that affected the whole body of Christendom with all its members, and Charles V called upon all Christian princes to play their part. To the French and English kings, too, a request was sent to supply at least a few galleys, but both Francis I and Henry VIII declined to follow the Emperor's initiative. Thus this Christian offensive against the marauding Turks went forward without any support from France or England.

Notwithstanding, the advance upon Tunis developed into a veritable Catholic enterprise. The fleets which assembled in Barcelona in March 1535 were composed of various nationalities: from Italy came the Pope's ships, from Genoa, Andrea Doria with a host of galleys, from Lisbon, led by the Infant, Don Luis, the Empress's brother, came the Portuguese fleet, King Ferdinand sent an élite-troop of German mercenaries, the Spanish fleet in all its strength lay at anchor before Barcelona.

The Cross was set up in all the ships, and banners were hoisted with pictures of the Virgin Mary, St John and St James. When the Grandees asked who would be commander-in-chief, the Emperor replied, raising a crucifix, 'He whose standard-bearer I am!' The enthusiastic response of all present was beyond words.

The Emperor imposed on himself all the ascetic rules which the Crusaders of old adopted when they set out for the Holy Land: three days before departure he withdrew to the Monastery of Montserrat where he fasted and prayed and received Holy Communion. On the evening before they sailed the Blessed Sacrament was carried in procession through the streets of Barcelona.

On 30th May Charles V himself led his troops—not against Christians but against the Infidels who threatened the western world.

This was old crusading country: it was before Tunis that St Louis, King of France, had met his death; before Tunis, the knight and mystic, Ramón Lull, had been stoned by the Infidels.

The united Turks and Moors put up a stiff resistance, particularly at Fort La Goletta. The siege lasted three weeks. Undeterred by the smell of cannon-shot, the Emperor went about among his troops to put fresh heart in them: 'O my soldiers, O my Spanish lions!' The Spaniards fought like lions, and the rest were filled with the same spirit. On 14th July the imperial armies took La Goletta by storm.

On 20th July, in intense heat, the march on Tunis began. The rough life, lack of water, and sandstorms put a great strain on the Emperor's powers of endurance; 'We die of heat and thirst', he wrote to his sister Maria.

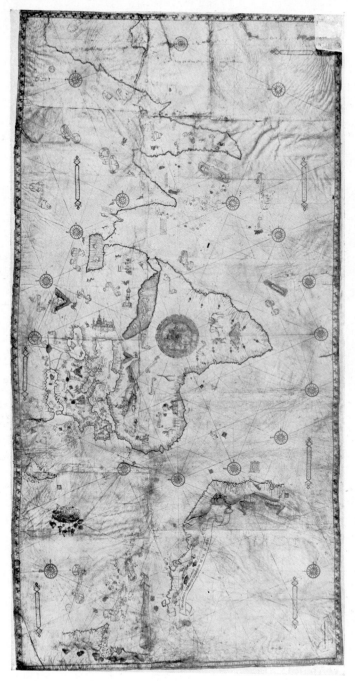

MAP OF THE WORLD
About 1502–1506, *Bibliothèque Nationale, Paris*

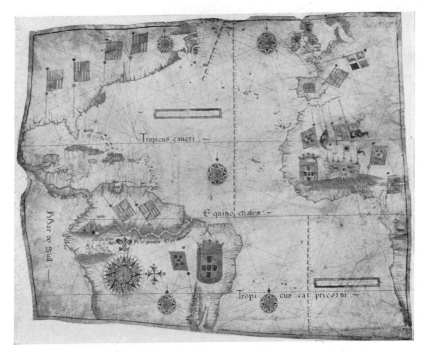

PORTUGUESE MAP OF THE COASTS OF THE NEW AND OLD WORLDS
Probably the middle of the 16th century, *Bibliothèque Nationale, Paris*

VOYAGE ON THE INDIAN OCEAN WITH ASTROLABE
Bibliothèque Nationale, Paris

On the march the imperial troops were surprised by a large band of Moors. The Marques de Mondéjar, who led the defence, was wounded by a lance and fell; the Emperor spurred his horse and took over the leadership crying, 'Santiago'. His knights sprang after him, and in serried ranks attacked with such vigour that the enemy fell back. On 31st July the Emperor entered Tunis.

Among the rich booty were weapons marked with the fleur-de-lis, as direct proof of the French king's assistance to the Turks. In addition, letters came into the Emperor's hands showing that Francis I had supplied the Turks with information about the imperial preparations for war. These were the doings of *le roi très chrétien*. The Tunis victory met with a great response throughout Christendom and particularly in Italy. When the Emperor's fleets landed at Messina they were welcomed with jubilation. There were triumphal arches and gates of honour everywhere, lauding him. Santa Cruz the chronicler made a note of the inscriptions: 'Charles V, invincible grandson of the divine Maximilian, illustrious saviour of the fatherland, best and bravest prince, conqueror of Africa; who with astonishing speed drove off the Turks; who increased the Empire and restored peace. To him do the senate and people of Messina dedicate these triumphal arches.' 'To the founder of tranquillity and peace, to the divine Charles the Fifth, to the preserver of the Christian Republic, in memory of glorious deeds in Africa! From the people of Messina.' At a city gate two pillars were erected representing the Emperor's own badge-token: the Pillars of Hercules, and among garlands of flowers the words: 'From the rising of the sun till its setting.' This manner of expressing the people's admiration was like an echo from Hohenstaufen times, when the Sicilians welcomed their ruler, Emperor Frederick II, as the 'invincible', 'the most mighty hero, greatest of the princes of the globe, the wonder of the world and its admirable transformer'.

Stupor mundi. Sol invictus.

We may wonder whether, in the Cathedral of Palermo, Charles pondered over the sarcophagus of the last great Emperor of the Middle Ages, and over the fate of the Staufers whose fall had meant the decline of the Empire.

Transformer of the world.

Was it a transformation from a holy world into a worldly one, with the Empire going to ruin because its essence was spiritual, foredoomed to failure if its Christian character were lost? The whole significance of the *Sacrum Imperium* lay in its subordination to the order of holiness. A devotion to higher reality was its very *raison d'être*. And when its attention turned exclusively worldwards, it lost its inmost soul.

But now, throughout the Empire and throughout the western world, there reawakened an awareness of Christian foundations. At Tunis, many nations had fought together under the one banner of the Cross: the Christian community was at last within sight—or so it seemed.

Hope shone like sunshine about the Emperor as he rode through the streets of Palermo, while Sicilian women and girls strewed flowers along his way.

CHARLES V IN ROME

From Palermo the Emperor went on to Naples, where honours continued to shower upon him. He spent the whole winter there and liked it. Some time after his abdication, in a lighter moment he once told how he had had his first grey hairs removed after the Tunisian campaign, in order to make a good impression on the beautiful Neapolitan ladies.

The farewell banquet that the Viceroy of Naples gave for the Emperor in March 1536, which was attended by the flower of the Italian nobility and the most beautiful women of Italy, was described by contemporary chroniclers as one of the most representative feasts of the Renaissance.

Rome, too, received the Emperor with triumphal arches. The Pope had a *via triumphalis* erected right through the Eternal City, which greeted the Victor of Tunis as its Caesar, as *coronatus magnus et pacificus Imperator Romanorum*. At the doors of St Peter's Church a banner recalled the Emperor's Christian mission: 'Emperor Charles V alone is today the ever-active Defender of the Christian Faith.'

And after Tunis Charles V really did deserve this title. He had fulfilled his Christian duty up to the hilt and now he hoped to find due acknowledgement on the Pope's part. For now was the time to ratify the order of the *respublica christiana* and furnish it with safeguards. But the disturbing spirit of the moment was Francis I. For the Emperor's successes were not at all to his liking and he had meanwhile invaded Savoy and openly laid claim to the Duchy of Milan.

Thereupon the Emperor requested the Pope to make a statement on the subject of the *invasor reipublicae christianae*. It was an impossible situation to have the Pope continue to treat Francis I, the friend of the Turks and of the schismatic King of England, on the same level as himself, the Emperor. A neutrality as between good actions and bad ones was not admissible.

In a memorandum Charles V addressed to the Pope he requested him to observe justice and be mindful of the 'continual good works of the Emperor'; he should no longer tolerate the hostile actions of the French king; he should support with all his authority him who laboured for the peace of Christendom.

The whole of Holy Week was filled with negotiations, but Pope Paul III evaded the Emperor's demands. As ruler of the Church States and as political realist, he did not conceive of the world in terms of universality and unity. Was it perhaps the English Cardinal Wolsey who first broached in Rome the new theory of 'balance of power'? At all events that was the principle Pope Paul III now stood for. The revival of the idea of united Christendom through Charles V meant to the Pope quite simply a Habsburg hegemony in Italy. Charles V's intentions might be of the purest, in practice his conception led inevitably to that *monarchia* and *tyrannis* which the Pope as well as Francis I feared. In the eyes of Pope Paul III, the Emperor was well on the way to be *conquistador* of Europe, able by force of arms to compel recalcitrant sections to conform. Therefore the Pope was on his guard. He refrained from vouchsafing his moral support, and thus, at the very moment when Charles was occupied in restoring the idea of *imperium* to its old Christian context, the Pope rejected it. His motive was that it was bound to come into conflict with the heightened self-awareness of individual states and was therefore no longer in the interest of Christendom as a whole.

The date of that historic moment was Easter 1536, in Rome: the day when the Pope stood as representative of 'progress' and 'champion of European freedom', while Charles emerged as standard-bearer of 're-action', determined to compel Europe to accept a no longer presentable conception of *imperium*.

Today, a devaluation of positive ideas has set in, and young historians are at pains to demolish the bastions of the past—and among them the ideal of the *Sacrum Imperium*.

But when Professor Heer declares that the Staufen dynasty's aim to maintain the old Carolingian Salic order was the most reactionary thing in Europe, he is parting company with his own roots; the Staufens by no means stood for a *status quo* in regard to the Carolingian Empire, whose chief concern was to find a *modus vivendi* within the Church's order of salvation. Owing to the Gregorian exaltation of the Papacy, their problem was quite a different one: it was to seek freedom from papal patronage.

While he was in Rome Charles V desired to restore the original interdependence of Papacy and *imperium*. The intrinsically international character of the latter was once again a reality, needing but the endorsement of its spiritual nature by the Pope, whose blessing would establish it on its Christian foundations again. If Charles V is to be called 'reactionary', it is in a very profound sense of the term. For (to quote Eugen Rosenstock) 'the prefix "re-" means the revival of a basic right, a restoration of things to their natural condition'. There are fundamental principles at the back of any culture, 'laws' that promoted its birth, but they may fall into oblivion, or be rejected or misinterpreted: such oblivion or rejections or distortions have to be heavily paid for, in terms of weakness, spread of error, and loss of intrinsic substance. And Charles V's evocation of a Church and Empire in harmony was not un-contemporary but was rather a 'blessed looking back' to the basic laws of Europe's very existence. To the god-fearing Crusader of Tunis, the cause of Christendom was his own. He was convinced that in defending the Empire he was contributing to the welfare of all Christendom. So it seemed to him most unfair that the Pope should refuse his recognition and support in the hour of crisis.

To all appearances *Imperium* and *Ecclesia* were in complete agreement: Emperor and Pope assisted at the solemn Easter High Mass in St Peter's, each on his raised throne, and at Communion the Emperor received the Sacrament from the Pope's own hand; they left the church together. But more was needed, and the Emperor decided to take steps to induce the Pope to adopt the only right attitude, as he saw it.

On Easter Monday, before Mass, in the presence of the College of Cardinals and the French and Venetian envoys, the Emperor asked the Pope's leave to say something, and the Pope assented.

And now, in a speech lasting an hour, the Emperor laid bare his heart's concern. First he gave an account of his efforts for peace, efforts that were continually checked by the French king. For when he was in Worms trying to bring Luther back to the Faith, Francis I threatened Italy; and Francis I had broken the Treaty of Madrid in order to start a new war. Notwithstanding, he concluded the Treaty of Cambrai on terms favourable to France, and now Francis I had invaded Savoy. . . . Nonetheless he, the Emperor, wished to keep the peace and was prepared to invest the son of the French king with Milan if he would commit himself to the necessary assurances. But were Francis I to reject this peace offer, there would be war. In war, victors and vanquished would be so greatly weakened that they would not be capable of defending Christendom from the Turks. The sects would spread and men would rise against their masters. If Christendom was to be spared that fate, there was one way open: a man-to-man fight between Emperor and King. 'To avoid the shedding of Christian blood I offer the King a duel, on foot or mounted, on land or water, or even without armour, with sword or fist.'

'No, no duel', the Pope objected, and sought to bring the excited Emperor to silence; he had to turn down the duel, for the death of one of the two would cause more disaster than a war; he called upon both princes to keep the peace: should one of them oppose peace, he would declare himself against him.

The Pope's words, anticipating the 'Locarno spirit', appeared to satisfy the Emperor, for he cried: 'I kiss Your Holiness' hand for that reply!'

In his speech the Emperor had spoken the whole time of the *respublica christiana*, never of the 'Empire', paying lip-service to a conception of total community with the *imperium* as part of it. But he took it for granted, all the same, that his Empire was the core of the concern, with rights of leadership.

And we may well ask whether the term *respublica christiana* really had a separate meaning of its own.

The 'Roman spirit' forced Charles V to a political moderation not without its vein of self-will and pride. To the French ambassador, the Bishop of Mâcon, who declared he had not understood the Emperor's speech because it was in Spanish, Charles V replied: 'The Señor obispo will understand me if he chooses, and let him await no other answer from me but one in my Spanish tongue, which is noble enough to deserve to be spoken by the whole of Christendom.'

'*Et voilà*,' the French might say, 'he talks of *respublica christiana* and means Spanish world-monarchy,' and they were doubtless filled with the same misgivings as the modern French about the Germans: 'They say Europe and mean a Europe under German hegemony.'

The Pope may have hesitated to distinguish between Charles V and Francis I because, as he saw it, each of them was a prey to the spirit of the times and the will to power. However that may be, the Pope's reserved attitude towards the victor of Tunis had more to it than the mere withholding of a decoration: by not supporting the Emperor's idea of himself as regent of the western world, he stressed the special rôle of the Papacy in the government of Christendom. It was actually a return to the policy of Pope Gregory VII who had endeavoured to establish the Church as a universal Christian realm above the *imperium* and the different kingdoms: once more God's Kingdom was to be set high above the kingdoms of the world, and there was to be *no* alliance between Pope and Emperor, *no* co-operation of the Emperor in the government of Christendom, *no* revival of the idea of *imperium*.

Age-old rights were denied; Charles found himself expelled from the Church's Eden, and in his wake the entire lay world went too. Mediaeval human-kind grew and throve under the very shadow of the Holiest of Holies, but henceforth laymen were to be confined to the secular sphere. The Pope (like Luther) drew a dividing-line between God and the world. Whereupon the Platonic impulse of the Renaissance flagged, charity grew cold and humanism degenerated—after a period of flowering as a product of Church culture.

There ensued an estrangement between Pope and Emperor which, a decade later, led to that curious partial settlement known as the *Interim*.

SIENA AND ARLES (1536)

It must have been a relief to the Pope to see the last of the exacting Emperor. He remarked to Granvelle that he had observed in Charles an 'admirable attitude', and Granvelle wrote to Venice that the Pope had been 'quite imperial', but he did not stir from his neutral position. The Emperor considered the Supreme Pontiff had left him in the lurch, he felt disappointed and thrown back on his own resources. His mother died at this time. He and his army left Rome and went north to deal with Francis I alone.

When he came to Umbria his low spirits revived. 'Now we are at home,' he cried, 'let each go as he will.' There were no lurking dangers there, it was all Ghibelline country. When he was handed the keys of Siena, he said he knew he and his would be well received 'in this city that was always so loyal to the Holy Empire'.

Ben venga, Carlo Imperadore (welcome, Emperor Charles), shouted the people as he rode through the narrow streets, *Viva Carlo Quinto*. He commanded his retinue to keep close together so that no one should be hurt by their horses' hooves. *Imperio, imperio*, called the crowd, *imperio*. Those were sweet sounds indeed; he checked his horse and stopped, smiling at the people who shouted *imperio* in his ears. To him the word had a ring of *com-*

munità, or *communione dei cristiani*—'Christendom'. It made him extremely happy. He bent down from his saddle, picked up a child and kissed it.

In the dappled black-and-white cathedral he heard a solemn Mass. The food for the banquet was borne to the palace by a hundred pages in procession. In his speech as City Father he called the citizens of Siena *fidelissimi dell' Impero*. Outside the palace walls the people tore souvenirs off the baldachin under which he entered the town.

On the steep Piazza the Emperor witnessed the festive games that were put on in his honour. Trumpets played *la sonata imperiale*, small-mortar fireworks went off, the town seemed ablaze with rejoicings; 'the whole time the city gates stood open, and nothing happened', says the chronicle.

The Emperor was at his ease in Siena. Maybe the pure Umbrian sky reminded him of Castile.

Dwelling *permanente nella santa e dolce dilezione di Dio*—ever in holy sweet enjoyment of God—as St Catherine of Siena said, how simple life became! But others preferred multiplicity and division. They desired not the Highest, but to have their own way.

From loyal Siena, Francis I's betrayal looked like sheer bad faith and a scorning of holy world-order.

But Francis I had no notion of anything more integral than—France: Habsburg supremacy was simply a menace to his own country. Imperial sovereignty in Northern Italy was a case in point: it meant much-to-be-feared world domination, a situation that must be overthrown by any means whatever, even with the assistance of Turks and Protestants. Whatever served this end was fair play to Francis. He acted instinctively, implicitly, for reasons of state. So that Charles, after Tunis, after Rome, now found himself compelled to act in self-defence. He conducted the campaign against *le roi très chrétien* in person.

The Emperor determined to carry the war into the enemy's territory. It had started with the French invasion of Savoy. He and his army drew out of Siena and proceeded along the Mediterranean coast to Nice, and thence northwards towards Aix-en-Provence.

Charles V regarded this French province as old imperial territory, and fondly supposed he was entering into his own, as in Siena—or so it appears from a letter to his brother Ferdinand, dated 16th January 1523, shortly after he became Emperor, in which he said it would be necessary to put 'our enemy' Francis under the imperial ban 'on account of the lands he usurped which belong to the Empire, such as *le royaume d'Arles*, *Dauphiné, Lyonnoi*, etc. . . .'

L'ancien royaume d'Arles was part of the south-west portion of Lothair's Empire until 855, when he divided his realm among his sons. Charles the Bald, King of France, conquered the Rhône region but was unable to retain it and appointed Count Bosco of Vienne as Duke of Burgundy, ruling the kingdom of Arelate. Duke Hugues made Arles the centre of his domains, but Arles still termed itself *ville impériale* and would admit no other sovereign but the Emperor. But that was centuries ago. Charles' notion of history did not take account of changing times and varying circumstances.

France had long since acquired and assimilated that ancient portion of Burgundy, and Charles V came merely as *invasor reipublicae christianae*, and it was an outrage. The resistance that he encountered in the *ancien royaume d'Arles* soon opened his eyes and put an end to the dream.

The French destroyed harvests and stores as they withdrew, so that the Emperor and his army of fifty thousand men entered a waste land. It was August and the thirsty troops fell like locusts on the orchards. They were seen in the vineyards drinking the juice of unripe grapes from their helmets. Dysentery broke out. 'Drink, drink,' the natives heard, as the German soldiers staggered on, dazed with fever, under the ardent sunshine.

The Emperor sent the Marquis del Vasto and a vanguard on to Arles, in order to spy out the country. The Arlésiens thought the Emperor himself was advancing and opened a terrific cannonade. Del Vasto reported that Arles was too strongly fortified to risk a siege. The Emperor then struck Arles out of his calculations, writing to Henry of Nassau, who was fighting the French in the Netherlands, that the approach to Arles was *très difficile* and it was impossible to set up camp there 'owing to the great poverty of the soil'.

In Aix-en-Provence, he was faced with the possibility of being surrounded and starved out. Medical supplies were lacking and an epidemic raged among the troops. A withdrawal was inevitable. With greatly decimated forces he reached Genoa in October 1536, and thus concluded this most bootless expedition of his.

COMPASSES, CHARTS AND SOUTH AMERICA

At the end of December 1536 the Emperor returned to Spain and was welcomed home by the Empress. In February 1537 he called the Cortes in Valladolid to discuss the French war, which was proving very costly. The city prepared great festivities for him, but he was unable to take much part in them owing to a severe attack of gout. In his hours of enforced leisure he took up astrology, so his chronicler Santa Cruz reports. 'He used to converse with his first cosmograph, Alonso de Santa Cruz, and asked many questions regarding the philosophy of nature and the spheres, and wished to know all about the courses of the stars; and with his lively intelligence and applied concentration, he mastered it all much more rapidly than others with more time to give. And he wished to have explained to him the instruments and clocks he carried with him, Arabic and Latin ones, how they were made and what they were for; all that he learnt, as he intended to do.'

The instruments that aroused the Emperor's curiosity were mostly nautical ones to guide seafarers on their way over the ocean, such as the *astrolabium*, an astronomical instrument of measurement, indicating the position of a ship according to the direction of the polar star, and above all the magnetic needle that pointed north, 'a small instrument of tremendous effect', as Bacon described the compass. The Emperor's interest contributed to the improvement of these instruments and thus indirectly eased and stimulated the voyages of discovery.

He spent many hours bent over his charts, and it was only with maps that he could follow the course of his war with France. His Empire was so widely scattered, it was only as charted that he could see it all at once. The rectification of the first maps and charts was made by Mercator of Duisburg, and thus the Emperor's interest fostered the development of geography, too.

It is easy to see why he liked them so much: under his very eyes, known frontiers shifted, and new lines had to be drawn in to show the coasts that were daily being discovered and the lands accruing to the Empire. The heavenly spheres, the constellations, the round world—it was all a wonder and half a miracle still, at the time of the Renaissance, but the explorers made it come true. Charles himself witnessed the transformation of Ptolemy's flat static world into the round, rotating world of Copernicus—a change that awoke the earth from its millennium sleep: so it was not the centre of the universe? It was no longer fixed and stable? 'The Emperor asked many questions and wished to know all about it.'

The first heraldic representation of South America in Europe occurred in a festive procession of Emperor Maximilian's, when, on the occasion of his son Philip's marriage to Joanna of Castile, he had the arms of the

Spanish lands carried through the German cities, and among them there figured, for the first time, the new Indies.

In 1518 the financial support Charles, as young King of Spain, gave to the Portuguese Magellan contributed to the first voyage round the world.

Mexico was conquered by Hernán Cortés in the years 1519–22, Peru by Pizarro between 1530 and 1535. Ramón Menéndez Pidal saw the growth of a realm overseas, during Charles V's reign, as 'the most gigantic step in the living fusion of humanity'; for the conquest resulted in a merging of new lands and peoples with Europe—body, mind and soul. The Spaniards arrived not as champions of their race but as fighters for the Cross, in whose sign victors and vanquished united.

The *conquista* was hard, as all conquest is; but Charles' intention was to give the New World the same ethical foundation as Europe had.

As early as 1517, a Dominican Friar, Bartolomé de Las Casas, pressed the Emperor to send *agricultores y no conquistadores* (planters, colonists, not conquerors) to the New Indies, and foster peaceful penetration of the land by means of Christianity and agriculture. In his writings he pilloried the Spaniards' cruel methods of exploitation and pleaded for humane treatment of the *Indios*, because they were *señores de su albedrío*, masters of their own free will. And eventually human rights did prevail in the New Indies, thanks to the Catholic principle of free will and the recognition of the transcendent worth of each individual soul.

During the summer of 1537, which Charles spent in Spain, Pope Paul III confirmed the human rights of the *Indios* in a Bull: forbidding any enslavement of the natives and any exploitation of the vanquished by their conquerors.

These orders were often transgressed, it is true; but they set the norm for colonial development. The Christian Faith, the guiding principle of Charles V's *imperium*, became basic in South America, too. Charles sent priests and missionaries to accompany every expedition. They preached and spread Christianity throughout the new realm. In return for these spiritual benefits, the new lands sent gold, silver and precious stones which helped to defend and maintain the Catholic Faith in Europe.

Charles V let the Germans play their part in the opening up of the new continent. The rich Welser family of Augsburg were the first Germans to send ships to the New Indies. In 1528 they obtained from the Emperor the exploration rights in Venezuela—as payment for debts incurred, it was said—and they expected quick returns from the new land in which the legendary *El Dorado* was supposed to lie. In the lease they signed, Antony and Bartholomew Welser undertook to build two towns (*pueblos*) and three forts, and to employ fifty masters of mines; they also undertook to treat the *Indios* well and convert them to the Christian Faith. In return they received administrative rights in Venezuela, a monopoly of imports and exports, and the right to choose their own collaborators. And unhampered by customs duties and competition, the Welsers pursued a policy of wholesale exploitation. The yield of gold and metal was less than they expected, and they attempted to cover their expenses by charging high prices for the import of livestock and merchandise (there were neither horses, cows nor sheep, pigs nor chickens in South America). In Venezuela the cost of living rose rapidly and the Spanish colonial authority wrote to the *Consejo de Indias* (the Indian Council in Seville) complaining that horses cost six times more in Venezuela than on the neighbouring island of La Española.

Venezuela was largely roadless and difficulties of transport accounted to a large extent for the high prices charged for imported livestock and merchandise; but the Spanish held the Welsers and their profit-making policy responsible for the high cost of living, and in 1546 the son of Bartholomew Welser's chief business representative was murdered in a revolt against Welser domination.

Another victim of dissatisfaction was Philip von Hutten (Ulrich's cousin). He had gone to Venezuela at the age of twenty-five, taking part in an expedition organized by Governor Hohermuth (from Spires), to find 'that most rich land which is said to be in the interior'. He wrote to Bernard von Hutten: 'God knows, it was not out of greed for gain that I decided to set forth on this journey, but because of an extreme desire that has possessed me for a long time; and I should not have died happily if I had not seen the Indios.'

In 1540, by a decree of Charles V's, Philip von Hutten was appointed Captain-General of Venezuela. Soon after, he set off on a new expedition into the interior of the country, and, on his return journey in 1546, he was robbed and killed by a Spaniard who had stepped into his shoes during his absence.

But the cause of this murder was not, on the Spaniards' part, merely a matter of professional jealousy and national rivalry; the dry commercial spirit of the Welsers was taken as an insult: the Spaniards as colonists felt they had obligations to fulfil, standards to maintain, and they were conscious first and foremost of being representatives of the Christian

Faith. True, the Spaniards in Venezuela were no less greedy and unscrupulous than the Germans—and a contemporary chronicler called the Welsers and their staff 'the most inhuman of all inhuman people'. But whereas Spanish acts of violence were admittedly deviations from the Christian ideal they acknowledged, the question of ideals never entered into the calculations of the hard-headed Welsers, and they did not consider it was part of their business to convert the *Indios* or carry out social obligations such as colonizing the land and building cities; they merely pursued their own financial interests and (to quote a remark of Karl Marx about later developments), they replaced 'an exploitation under cover of religious and political illusions with open, shameless, deliberate, sheer exploitation'. In other words, they totally disregarded the Convention. The Spaniards protested loudly. The German venture in Venezuela failed owing to its blindness to non-commercial considerations.

We have a proof that the Spaniards were not hypocritical in their belief that they were in the New World to found a spiritual unity based on the Catholic religion; we see it in the ultimate results of their colonizing efforts in South America. In spite of all the outrages committed, the Spaniards did succeed in winning a whole continent for Christendom; out of a variety of races they founded the great family of the *Hispanidad* with the Catholic Faith as its basic principle.

Philip II continued the Spanish missionary enterprise, and when the Indies Council in Seville advised Philip to give up the Philippines because they produced no income, he replied: 'Although the income from those islands is insufficient to maintain one simple hermitage, if one single person there upholds the name and the worship of Jesus Christ, it is reason enough for me to send out the whole income of Spain to spread the Gospel. The search for precious metals is not the sole task of kings.' It was in this spirit that the New Indies achieved intrinsic membership of the European community.

NICE AND AIGUESMORTES (1538)

At the beginning of 1538 a truce was reached as between Charles V and Francis I, after two years of wearisome fighting in Provence and Picardy. Both sides were exhausted and accepted with relief the arbitration of Pope Paul III, who for all his seventy years travelled from Rome to Nice to reconcile the old rivals.

But coming to terms was no easy matter: Milan was the bone of contention. The French proposed that the Emperor should recognize Francis I's youngest son as ruler of Milan; this was acceptable to the Emperor only on condition that Francis I should first afford practical assistance in the form of weapons to fight the Turks, and should also support him in his difficulties with the Protestants. But Francis wanted to have Milan at once. No, the Emperor had him told, the French king must first give practical proof of his friendly intentions.

During the negotiations, King and Emperor never met, their ministers and the nuncios took counsel together in three separate headquarters. The great discrepancies made Francis' sister Margaret exclaim, Charles and Francis were so unlike that God would have to remake each in the image of the other to bring them to an understanding.

But mercifully there was still a higher *praetor*, and both monarchs finally submitted to the Pope's desire for peace; on 18th June an armistice was concluded for ten years.

At last, perhaps at the express wish of Queen Leonora, who had accompanied her husband to Nice, Emperor and King met. If the marriage ties between dynasties were not sufficient to prevent wars, they did make the resumption of friendly relations easier.

Now there was peace throughout the Empire, true peace based on mutual confidence. The Emperor, who never fought shy of a battle when necessary, was now ready for complete agreement. It is true, as his confessor Glapion once remarked to Aleander, Charles had one fault, and that was, he found it hard to forget an insult. And how often Francis I had abused his confidence. What deliberate hurt he had done him. But when the French king visited him on his galley, and embraced and kissed him, saying, 'Brother, you see me your prisoner a second time', all previous hostility was forgiven and forgotten. Emperor and King remained embraced for a long time, till Queen Leonora came and laid her arms round her husband and her brother with the words: 'This is the treasure that is of most worth to me in the whole world.'

'It was like a dream that we saw with our eyes open,' an eyewitness reports, 'so does God let us know that He it is who guides men's hearts as it please Him.'

Aiguesmortes, where the meeting took place, was once a Mediterranean harbour. King Louis the Saint had embarked here on his Tunis crusade. But in course of time the waters of the Rhone had silted up the harbour and Aiguesmortes now lay two miles inland. *Aquae mortuae,* 'dead water' is the meaning of the name, for the sea had withdrawn and the place was now deserted and cut off, like Ravenna, or Bruges.

But life returned to Aiguesmortes on that day, a life of pomp and splendour. Next morning, when the Emperor went ashore with his following, there were beating drums and a flourish of trumpets. He was received by the royal princes and bowed low to them, but Francis I advanced rapidly and drew him to him, and Emperor and King went arm in arm through the jubilant crowds, accompanied by Queen Leonora, Madame d'Étampes, Margaret of Navarre and the French and Spanish courts. 'The jewels and gold-embroidered robes glittered in the sunshine. This vision was the more enchanting to the eyes of the people for the fact that the splendid clothing was worn by persons of high rank, which was much appreciated at that time.'

The town hall was decorated, and a banquet with the most exquisite dishes was held there. The Emperor particularly enjoyed the oysters, fresh from the Bay of Marseilles.

After the meal the Emperor withdrew for a siesta. But barely an hour later his sister Leonora knocked on the door, and behind her came the French king, exclaiming: 'Well now, Brother, I hope you have had a good rest.'

'The magnificent meal made me sleepy,' answered the Emperor, putting his clothes on.

Francis handed him a precious ring. Charles had no present ready, and took off the Golden Fleece which he wore, laying it about the king's neck; who then took off his Cross of the Order of St Michael and gave it to the Emperor. Wine was brought in and all drank the health of the two monarchs.

Now it was possible to speak intimately and on easy terms of the things that mattered. With a smile, the French king fell in with the Emperor's wishes; yes, he would help him to fight the Infidels, yes, he would support him in bringing the apostasized back into the bosom of the Church. That same evening, Charles wrote confidently to Ferdinand, saying: 'I am sure the King will give the deviators to understand they have our true and utter friendship, and will help and persuade them to return. I have a clear impression that without this act of confidence, coming together and talking things over, it would never have been possible to be friends.'

Next morning both sovereigns were together at Mass, in a room that was turned into a chapel. Each was accompanied by his own choir and they sang in turn; those present said that the imperial singers were the better musicians.

After a breakfast lasting several hours, Francis accompanied the Emperor back to his galley. 'Never and nowhere have I spent such pleasant hours,' said Charles. Francis assured him 'that the Emperor's cause and his own were now one and the same'.

They were to remain on good terms for several years. In the long run the Emperor was to be disappointed again, but one thing Charles V learnt from the inability of the French king to keep his word: not to demand the impossible. He had to admit that a real partnership with France was out of the question and all he could expect was a periodical truce.

'Rivalry with Francis was the thorn in the flesh that goaded Charles and proved him,' wrote the Venetian Ambassador Michieli.

Francis I, who felt his security to be constantly exposed, who chose as his badge the salamander, symbol of restless fire, gave Charles a taste of life as something spontaneous and irrepressible. But of course the high-flown promises of this treacherous friend of his were not to be taken too seriously. From the flames of the salamander he returned to his normal life, an older and a wiser man. So in the last resort Francis I's unreliability had a positive value for Charles V, stimulating and enlightening rather than otherwise.

FRANCISCO DE BORJA'S CONVERSION

Here, in Granada, a stone cross recalls the last journey of the Empress Isabella who died in Toledo on 1st May 1539. The Emperor withdrew to the Hieronymites' monastery near Toledo, and wrote from there to his sister: 'Over this heavy loss I feel all the sorrow and distress which you can imagine, and there is nothing that can console me so well as the contemplation of her good Catholic life and her holy religious end.'

The memorial cross stands on the road along which the funeral procession passed on its way from Toledo to Granada Cathedral. According to ancient custom, the coffin was opened before entering the city, and it was Isabella's chamberlain, the young Marqués de Lombay, who had to declare that the coffin did in fact contain the body of the Empress. One look was enough to show him the frailty of all earthly things. He exclaimed: 'Had I not accompanied the bier all the way from Toledo, I could not say that this was the Empress.'

Twelve-year-old Prince Philip was present, and he broke down, we are told.

This scene is known as the moment of the Duke of Gandia's conversion. A few years after, he entered the Jesuit Order and was later canonized. In his life of Francisco de Borja, Padre Ribadeneyra described the moment when the Duke 'recognized the vanity of all that the world prizes so highly; and it inspired him with disdain for all that is transient, and with a good, efficacious desire to know what is true and enduring and to bring it about, be it at the cost of great hardship, suffering and persecution.'

That same evening, when the Duke left the cathedral to go home, in his heart he had uttered these words: 'What shall we do, Soul, what shall we seek? Have you not seen, Soul, how the brightest and most precious things of earth end? If death treats earth's splendour so, who can resist him? That same death has his arrow directed at you. Were it not well to die to the world in life, in order to live with God in death. Give me, O God, give me Your light, give me Your Spirit. . . . Nevermore, never will I serve a master who can die on me.'

On his return to court, the Duke informed Charles of his design to enter a monastery; the Emperor replied he had the same intention.

JOURNEY THROUGH FRANCE

In the La Sisla monastery near Toledo the Emperor spent many hours in his cell lost in prayer, 'while seven candles burned round his couch which was covered with black cloth'.

He now developed the habit of withdrawing frequently to his own room to give himself up to prayer and meditation. The whole atmosphere was desolate, said an English envoy.

The idea of seeking his peace in a monastery was no doubt a consolation to the Emperor. But with the letters of condolence that reached him from all over the world there came news of fresh conflicts, as though the world were incapable of rest. The Turks were hard on the Austrian borders again, Barbarossa was harrying the Mediterranean from Algeria; in the Netherlands, and in Italy too, serious riots had broken out.

There was to be no breathing-space—he had to set off with all speed to be wherever danger threatened his realm.

At that time Charles V and Francis I were so united that the latter invited him to travel across France. Many advised the Emperor not to ac-

FRANCIS I, KING OF FRANCE
Titian, *The Louvre, Paris*

ANNE DE PISSELIEU, LATER DUCHESS OF ÉTAMPES
Clouet, *Musée Condé, Chantilly*

LEONORA, QUEEN OF FRANCE
Spanish School, 16th century, *Musée Condé, Chantilly*

[183]

cept the invitation, suspecting the French king of some new trick. As La Roca reports, 'but in that high-minded way of his the Emperor brushed aside all warnings and gave his own idea of what the French king would do—in which he was completely right, his reception in Paris being in accordance both with the greatness of the guest and that of his host'.

The Emperor knew that in his political transactions Francis I was not guided by any chivalric sense of honour, but that in his personal affairs this was paramount. Francis I was *le roi chevalier* in spite of all, and he was therefore to be trusted. Francis I's two sons, as boys hostages in Spain for years on end, came to meet the Emperor at Bayonne and accompanied him to Bordeaux and Poitiers and on to the Castle of Loches where Francis I was awaiting him. The next stage took them to Fontainebleau where Francis I had a great hunt put on for the Emperor's entertainment. During the hunt the younger of the French princes sprang up to the Emperor saying, '*Maintenant l'Empereur est notre prisonnier*'.

But it was not imprisonment the Emperor had to fear, but rather a spate of grand social events. Francis I proved himself a royal host indeed: there were banquets, hunts and tournaments in rapid succession, and Charles wrote to his brother Ferdinand that it was almost too much of a good thing.

At the beginning of January, Emperor and King entered Paris together. The whole city came out to meet them. The people rejoiced at seeing the two monarchs united, for it gave them a sense of security. The Rector of the Sorbonne came with sixty doctors of theology and an equal number of doctors of law and medicine, the four presidents of the *parlement* and the city dignitaries with their standards, the higher and lesser clergy with crosses and church banners—and thus accompanied, Emperor and King rode to the cathedral of Notre Dame where High Mass was celebrated.

That same evening, during the banquet, sixty noblemen waited at table and the sons of the French king handed the Emperor his napkin and fingerbowl. Queen Leonora sat opposite him and the banquet proceeded in an atmosphere of complete harmony.

Afterwards there was a masked ball. The Emperor was 'pale and serious' and considered thoughtfully the black masks that bowed to him.

The court poet, Clément Marot, had composed a poem for him:

> *Or est César qui les Gaulles conquist,*
> *Encore un coup en Gaulle retourné.*

Non point en main le glaive mais l'olive. . . .

Bien heureuse est la gent qui n'est point mort
Sans voir premier votre ferme unité,
Qui le repos de tant de monde porte!
Viens donc, César, et une paix apporte
Perpétuelle entre nous et les tiens. . . .

The verses expressed the Emperor's own feelings and we may suppose he let the poet know he was pleased with them.

'Without poetry,' as Francis I was fond of remarking, 'life is very death.'

The Emperor was much impressed with Paris: 'Other cities are cities,' he said, 'Paris is a world.' He stayed in the Louvre; his bed-chamber had been done up with crimson damask for the occasion and was henceforth known as *la chambre de l'Empereur*. At night there was a girl to warm his bed for him.

The Emperor was adaptable to the *moeurs* of the French court. He did not turn a hair when Madame d'Étampes, Francis I's mistress, frequently occupied his sister's place. He took pains to please the duchess, for he was aware that she ruled not only the king's heart but also his counsels.

At a banquet where Queen Leonora was absent and Madame d'Étampes was hostess, Francis I said to Charles: 'You see this beautiful lady; she advises me to keep you here for as long as you do not declare the Treaty of Madrid to be null and void'—for the Emperor still claimed Burgundy.

'If the advice is good it should be followed,' he replied.

And that very evening he sought to gain the lovely lady Anne's favour. After the meal, when the duchess poured deliciously scented water over his hands out of a small golden jug, as it were accidentally he let a diamond ring fall to the ground. Madame d'Étampes picked it up and cried in admiration: 'What a wonderful gem!'

'It is yours, Duchess,' replied the Emperor, 'the hands it lies in are too lovely for me to dare to take it back again.' Madame d'Étampes accepted without more ado.

Whether it was on account of the diamond or his regardful manner of paying court to her, the Emperor won the lady over and she became one of his most ardent supporters, her influence at court working in favour of enduring friendship between Francis I and Charles V. Matters went so far that later she was accused of having imparted state secrets to the Emperor. It was not purely political calculation, however, that induced him to establish good relations with his sister's rival, he earnestly desired peace with France and anybody who shared this desire was an ally worth gaining.

Doubtless, Francis I's extra-marital relations were not to be glossed over, he was indeed an impossible creature—a regular Turk, a gormandizer, loving pomp and circumstance inordinately. But he was also *le roi artiste, le père des lettres et des arts.*

Francis I informed his friend and brother of the treacherous schemes of the city of Ghent, which had offered him its fortifications and the County of Flanders.

'*Discipliner cette ville de Gand,*' said the Emperor, '*discipliner le Gand.*' Give Ghent a lesson. On the Feast of the Holy Trinity he set off, and Francis accompanied him as far as Cambrai. The two monarchs parted cordial friends. Charles rode on to punish Ghent and Francis I returned to Paris to find that entertaining the Emperor had cost him four million *écus.*

Titian's portrait of Francis I

Titian painted his portrait after a medallion, without ever coming face to face with his model. The portrait is nonetheless true to life.

For there is more to a personality than appearances show, there is also the way it impresses the world around it. Now Titian was very sensitive to personality, and what he rendered in painting Francis was his colossal *joie de vivre.* It is a trick of modern historians to want to debunk myths and see through ideologies—but the disguise is often genuine and to tear it off is to disfigure the subject. Sometimes there is nothing underneath at all— for, as Antiquity knew, the mask itself is *persona.* . . .

In Titian's picture of the 'myth' of Francis I, we see the French king as his contemporaries pictured him, as typifying the Renaissance feeling for life's abundant possibilities. Leonardo da Vinci, who was a friend of Francis I's, said that painting is *cosa mentale*—a thing of the mind—and any rendering of a personality is a mental process with the 'myth' as starting-point. Thus history might be described as the evocation of a saga, and portrait painting as making the invisible visible.

GHENT (1540)

In Brussels, Charles received further news of the rebellion in his birth-place, Ghent. For two years the city had refused to pay taxes and was now in open revolt. 'The people of Ghent,' says a contemporary report, 'are hard to rule owing to their intemperance and their inclination to rebellion and rioting.' The rebels had torn up the constitution which Charles as young Duke of Burgundy had granted, and wanted to turn their city into *une ville de commune*; and they had tortured and beheaded loyal members of the council.

According to some, it was Luther's doctrine that was the cause of the revolt. At that time Luther already had many supporters in Flanders and Brabant, who constituted an element of social unrest. Like the Anabaptists of Münster, the people of Ghent wanted all goods to come to the community. As the report says: 'This was the occasion for everyone to plunder as much as he could.' They intended to set up a revolutionary democracy in the County of Flanders, and they had turned to Francis I for protection as he had the reputation of being ready to assist the Emperor's enemies. Ghent was Charles' birthplace and its behaviour made him extremely angry. The world he lived in was the hieratic world of St Thomas Aquinas, a world stratified into princedoms, powers, dominions, thrones, and every revolt against the secular law he held to be an infringement of divinely willed order. He proclaimed that he would enter Ghent as sovereign, 'in one hand the sceptre, in the other the sword', and he advanced on it with a large escort followed by thousands of serfs. The city was appalled and yielded without a blow being struck.

The Emperor exacted stern justice: he declared the people of Ghent 'guilty of disloyalty, rebelliousness, and *lèse majesté*' and had sixty of the chief rebels taken prisoner and fourteen condemned to death. Nine were beheaded then and there, in the fish-market. The city lost all its privileges, its gates and fortifications were to be torn down; the popular feast of St Lievin, which broke into Lent, was suppressed; community property was confiscated, and the great tower-bell of the cathedral, named Roland, was taken down.

The bell bore the following inscription: 'When I ring with all my powers: Triumph; when I tinkle: Storm.' The bell had rung at Charles' birth, and now it had summoned Ghent to rebellion. It bore the name of the hero who was said to have lost his life in Charlemagne's service—Roland, whose pillars stood in the cities of northern Germany, watching over the royal peace of the market. The bell Roland had been disgracefully misused; it was therefore condemned to silence. It is said that Charles' severity struck the people as so just that he did not forfeit any of his popularity.

No doubt Machiavelli would have approved. In the seventeenth chapter of *Il Principe* he wrote: 'A prince should not fear the accusation of cruelty when it is a matter of keeping his subjects together in unity and loyalty, for with only a few examples of severity he will be more lenient than those who out of too great leniency give free rein to every disorder, a troubled well-head from which proceed murder and rapine.'

The solemn apology of the city was proffered on 3rd May; the Emperor was on his way to Mass when the prisoners approached him bareheaded, with halters on their necks, and threw themselves at his feet, crying, 'Mercy, Your Majesty!' Then came the City Fathers and the scribes who implored Maria, the Regent, to obtain from Charles a remission of his stern verdict. The Emperor gave his reprieve.

It was this kind of spontaneous act of pardon, *un atto umano e pieno di carità* (a human act full of charity) that Machiavelli praised in the *Discorsi* (III, 20). 'For in the last resort an example of humanity and leniency can do more than violence,' wrote that intrepid connoisseur of political life.

VIEW OF SIERRA NEVADA

Opposite the castle-hill of the Alhambra, the old Moorish quarter, Albayzín, climbs the slopes of Mount San Miguel.

The way up leads through narrow odorous alleys, a way of penance and humiliation, for the pestiferous stale air of centuries hangs among the walls of this the poorest quarter of Granada. Women sit in the open doorways, naked children play in the filth and refuse.

If you can endure it, you eventually emerge onto an open space from which the whole sweep of the plain of Granada is visible. And opposite—directly facing—is the dazzling white chain of the Sierra Nevada mountains, enthroned like a symbol of other-worldly majesty beyond all basenesses.

A higher order, another world. The redeemed creatures that dwell in such clarity will not be looking back to the valley—hence their aloofness. Themselves light, the gloom knows them no more.

Such purity—is it unattainable on earth, we ask, and Plotinus answers us: 'It is attainable in beauty, and the way leads on to those heights that sparkle yonder in their solitude. And at last, solitude flies to solitude, abolishing all intervening space, and attains to union. . . .'

The Sierra Nevada glitters icily under the southern sun.

Meanwhile Holy Week was approaching and I wanted to spend it in Seville. I selected the most rapid conveyance, the 'autoferro' which was supposed to cover the journey in five hours. I was now literally leaving Ronda away to the left. But the trip to Seville lasted twelve hours. Towards evening the small motor-train stuck mid-way. What had happened? A train ahead of us had run off the rails, it might be hours before the line was clear again, all night at the very least.

My fellow travellers, students going home for their Easter vacation, took it in good part. They went out into the open and started dancing.

The young men sat in a circle on the grass and beat time by clapping, while the girls danced *Sevillanas*, charming rounds with graceful arm movements and an inimitable turning of the head to look back over their shoulders—'sparkling glances heavy with the scent of orange-blossom . . .'.

Someone started to sing. *Coplas Andaluzas*, Andalusian folk-songs rising and falling in Arabic half-tones.

Twinkling tremulously and softly, the stars shone down from the velvety darkness of the night sky.

VI

SEVILLE

Why dost thou seek another way
than this royal way,
which is the way of the Cross?

(Imitatio Christi, II, 12, 28)

One's first impression of a city is often a disappointment. A look around before real contact has been made is bootless. One has a certain idea of how it is likely to appear—a mental picture often traceable to the mere sound of the name, and reality is expected to conform.

But the reality is always entirely different.

You look forward to a wonderful new experience—and it begins by being dull and flat, like scenery on a half-finished stage. You had pictured a coherent whole, and you have to accept it piecemeal, as though a kaleidoscope picture had splintered into a myriad fragments, with items such as a railway station, a porter, the inside of a taxi, a drive through uncommunicative streets, a revolving door, the face of a hotel porter, a form to fill in, stairs or a lift, a strange room. Here was journey's end, but it was not the goal.

In expectation, all was quiet and still—in actuality all was loud and noisy.

'El programa', called the street sellers, 'el programa para la Semana Santa'. Seats for sale for Holy Week. On Seville's open places hammering and sawing were in progress, stands were being erected for the Holy Week processions and chairs were placed along the pavements.

But Holy Week should be quiet and meditative, I thought within myself, as I walked with some distaste through the noisy streets. The cathedral? A low building, a disconnected tower. I contemplated the slender, tall Moorish tower standing haughtily beside the shapeless mass of the cathedral, as though declining to draw up the heavily crouching structure with it into the blue sky of Seville.

The Alcázar? On a level with the ground! O, for the red towers of the Alhambra! On an open space there were orange trees bearing fruit and blossom, both at once. The scent of orange-blossom, called *azahar* in Arabic—*azahar*, coming across in soft ravishing waves—I was won over: how sweet it is, I thought; how soft the air. It is springtime and I am in Seville.

THE CATHEDRAL

The cathedral of Seville, which looks so insignificant and low from outside, has inside all the proportions of a Gothic cathedral in height and depth. The nave is so large, you are lost in it, yet it carries you on up to the high altar, splendidly enthroned on carpeted steps, like a symbol of the abundance of the divine Heart.

The Capilla Real sparkles in a shimmer of gold and silver, like a jewel. I sat engrossed, in speechless delight. Truth to tell, it was purely aesthetic enjoyment, but as St Francis de Sales said, such a state of mind is not lacking in religious devotion, 'though the soul in profound silence speaks no word and is not praying'. So much beauty and quiet were sheer bliss.

Before the steps leading up to the high altar there rests in a silver sarcophagus the body of St Ferdinand of Castile, who took Seville from the Moors in 1248.

In the blaze of Isabella the Catholic's achievements, one tends to overlook the merits of her ancestors who drove the Arabs out of Spain, step by step. But it was only step by step that the spiritual ground could be regained, assuring the hardly won unity of the state.

It is no doubt this missionary zeal which accounts for the character of the religious figures that are carried shoulder-high through the streets of Seville during Holy Week. The symbols of the Christian faith could not be too emphatically imprinted on the minds of people who had lived so long without them, hence the solemn realism of the figures of Christ and the sheer beauty of the Mother of God, in appreciation of the fact that it is through his senses that natural man apprehends best.

PALM SUNDAY IN SEVILLE

During Holy Week in Seville, the figures of Christ and His Mother are carried out of the Church into the open air and set up for people to look at and remember. Likewise Philip II was surrounded in his bedroom by religious pictures, 'so that the pictures should come to his eye and through his eye to his heart, and that he should not lose sight of what was so important', as Fray Joseph de Siguenza relates.

'Through the eyes into the heart,' I murmured to myself as on Palm Sunday I went from church to church and saw the statues of the Saviour and the Virgin Mary adorned for their exodus.

The Seville churches with their chalk-white or yellow walls are not attractive outside, but inside they glow with the gold of the altars. The Virgin Mary is clothed in velvet and silk, a silver crown with rays hovers over her head, diamonds and precious stones sparkle on her fingers, red carnations form a great carpet at her feet. . . .

The Mother of our Lord is the central figure of the Seville Holy Week. She is the great bearer of suffering, the infinitely patient one, in her the people relive their own most profound experience of life: suffering motherhood.

Each church has her as its own patron: *Virgen de los Dolores, Virgen de la Amargura, Virgen de la Angustia, Virgen de la Soledad . . . Virgin of Sorrows, Virgin of Bitterness, Virgin of Anguish, Virgin of Solitude . . .*—and souls find consolation in those Madonna statues: Virgin of Sorrows, Virgin of Refuge . . .

It is because the heart of the divine Mother is a refuge that men's gratitude clothes her figure so richly, and that is why there are shimmering pearls about her neck, precious rings sparkling on her fingers, and a gold-embroidered coronation-robe round her shoulders—

> Mystical rose
> Tower of ivory
> House of gold . . .

The realism with which the Christ-figures are rendered is at first sight unattractive: Christ the Man, Christ as a person stands as though physically present in the churches of Seville. Those statues are not symbols but in intention real representations of the divine Life. Christ's Passion is depicted so literally that it is often terrible to look upon. And yet it was so: so He suffered, so He was bowed down under the burden of the Cross. . . .

Jesus de la Pasión

The faithful pressed round one life-size figure of Christ to kiss its foot. A verger pressed a slip of paper into my hand. I read: 'I am the way, the truth and the life. Whoever believes in me, were he dead, will live.'

Jesus del Gran Poder
Jesus of the great power.

IN THE GARDENS OF THE SEVILLE ALCÁZAR

In the late afternoon the churches were full to overflowing, the faithful crowded round the confessionals as though the entire city was fulfilling the Catholic duty of Easter confession.

I went from church to church but in Seville I could not find the meditative quiet I sought. I decided to spend the rest of Holy Week in Córdoba.

And now, as Seville was to be left behind, I finally visited the Alcázar in which Charles V's marriage to Isabella of Portugal took place in March 1526.

But even this historic connection with Charles V could not make the palace live for me, for it is built in Mudejar style, the style which made use of Moorish elements in buildings erected after the Moors had been driven out of Spain. The imitation of Arabic forms was successful in this case because the ornamentation is not in carved stone but stucco work. That is why it all seemed so stereotyped. Only in one room was I made conscious of the presence of authentic life. 'This is the *Salon de Carlos Quinto*,' said the museum guide, and the sound of the familiar name filled me anew with unspeakable pleasure and a secret pride.

From the *Salon de Carlos Quinto* a few steps lead down into the Alcázar gardens, like an oasis, green and full of bubbling water.

And like an Arab in the desert I drank in the sight of green leaves and spray that afternoon. St John of the Cross tells us in his hymns that the beauty of nature leads us to the Creator, and in March the first roses are out in the Alcázar gardens. It was March when Charles married Isabella. The sun-dappled shadows of the trees in their tender spring greenery fell then as now over the garden paths, and the fountains murmured as they do today.

I saw the Emperor on those garden paths as though the surroundings on which his gaze once fell gave back his picture through intervening time, as one may meet someone's gaze in a mirror without seeing them in person.

But this was the first time that the Emperor's presence gave me the impression of being transparent, as though he deliberately withdrew behind himself, as much as to say, Only the end is important, only the Highest *is*.

VII

CÓRDOBA

You need not hesitate to declare that
the highest good is concord of souls.
For where harmony and unity prevail,
the virtues must be present too. It is
the vices that strive asunder.

Seneca, 'De Vita Beata'

CÓRDOBA

Córdoba is a city to be alone in, it does not oppress with its mystery like Toledo, it does not thrust its beauty upon you like Granada, it is not exhausting like Seville at Easter—it is uncommunicative and so reserved that one has an impression of void, as though it were emptied of all the substance that once made it a centre of Arabic life and, two hundred years before Christ, one of the capitals of Roman Spain.

Under Córdoba lies the Roman city of *Colonia Patricia*, sunk eighteen feet down in the earth. In Córdoba you stand on Roman foundations, and something of that tension-free tranquillity of pre-Christian times pervades the atmosphere. Córdoba is very still and quiet. It was, one felt, the undramatic flatness of the place that caused its sons to be philosophers: it is the birthplace of both Senecas, of the Arabic philosopher Averroës and of the Jewish philosopher Maimonides. Averroës strove to bring religion and philosophy into unison; this trend of his philosophy was adopted by Albert the Great and Thomas Aquinas, and his influence on Master Eckhart was such that the latter was accused of Averroism. Maimonides influenced Goethe through Spinoza and through Goethe helped to determine the modern German outlook on life. Córdoba lies on the flat banks of the River Guadalquivir. To the north, the chain of the Sierra Modena with its broad dark slopes runs parallel to the river. To the south, the view lies open, over undulating reddish-brown ground and the light green of spring cornfields.

The old Roman bridge straddles across the river on short, sturdy arches and the country people come and go as they have always done, women with waterpots on their heads as in paintings on classical vases, men with the breadsack lightly slung over their shoulders, and the heavily laden donkeys that pass unwearyingly from shore to shore. Looking towards the town with your back to the bridge, you will observe a low citadel crowned with pinnacles and battlements, and over the castle walls there rises a tower all pilasters and balustrades to the top, where great bells hang from high arches, ringing out the hours to the open sky—the Mesquita Tower.

THE MESQUITA

In Moorish times the Córdoba Mesquita, next to the Caaba in Mecca, was the largest mosque of the Osmanic world. When Ferdinand III

197

reconquered Córdoba in 1236 the mosque was turned into a church. Since then it is known as the Mesquita Cathedral.

Inside, one is at first put out by the innumerable slender pillars, bearing red and yellow painted double arches, running off in all directions, but without giving an impression of space—rather the contrary, like one of those labyrinths spacious in appearance owing to cunningly placed mirrors. Only the different colouring of the pillars—now of rose marble, now pearl grey, now greenish, now violet—show that there is no optical illusion here but a truly great expanse. And the focus of this perspective of fleeing pillars is—Mecca, far away in the east.

After a time one distinguishes a number of structural intersections: they compose the Christian choir, built at the beginning of the sixteenth century by bishops zealous to complete the transformation of the Mesquita into a cathedral. At the heart of this forest of pillars, sixty-three of the marble stems were felled, and here the high altar and choir were erected.

The result is a hybrid: two different styles cross and mingle indecisively, two different attitudes of mind give conflicting accounts of themselves. Charles V stopped in Córdoba on his way to Seville, and this is what he told the bishops: 'If I had known what this was, I should not have allowed the old structure to be touched; for you have built something which could have been put up anywhere on earth, and have destroyed something which was unique in the whole world.'

When the Arabs conquered Córdoba, they had no aesthetic qualms to keep them from razing to the ground the Christian church of San Vicente which stood here in Visigoth times. Yet it must have been a structure of great purity of style, for the few Visigoth fragments incorporated in the Mesquita reveal a clear and simple design.

An Anglo-Saxon tourist near me was lamenting 'the barbarism of the Catholics', while I mourned for the Visigoth temple of San Vicente and stood in admiration before the foundation-stone of a great basin, still showing traces of a cruciform design. The Arabs eliminated the horizontal arms of the Cross, but even the fragment left still has a power of compulsion, conjuring up a vision of the earlier romanesque church. To build the Mesquita the Arabs used the material at hand, and this accounts for the fact that the capitals of the pillars are as various as the flora of different epochs: Corinthian capitals unfold their rich fan-crowns, making the columns look like young ferns. The Visigoth capitals weigh heavily upon their slender supports—Gothic ponderosity as against Moorish delicacy.

In the Mesquita prayer-niches the original Arabic ornamentation has been preserved: it is byzantine, like the earliest Christian art. This Mihrab of Islam has something the same atmosphere as a romanesque church in Ravenna with its early Christian mosaic, 'classical' in character—the east is indeed the wellhead from which the western world sprang.

Those arabesques inlaid with dull gold and red and blue enamels were like a link with the east, knitting together separate and diverse things in beauty.

GOOD FRIDAY PROCESSION IN CÓRDOBA

Here no stands were put up for visitors, the people brought their own seats on to the streets each afternoon, to wait for the beginning of the processions which according to old custom occupy the evenings of Holy Week.

On Good Friday afternoon I sat among the crowd on a small square above which rose the Mesquita Tower. Every quarter of an hour, from the top of the tower sounded the beat of great wooden clappers, for 'the bells had flown to Rome', they were silent on account of Christ's death.

Between the rows of chairs the youth of Córdoba walked up and down, girls in long black silk dresses and the traditional lace mantilla, with still, regular features; the young men behind them in their Sunday best.

The Mesquita Tower looked down benignly on the flock of the faithful passing to and fro under its watchful eye, like a patriarch looking proudly upon the host of his children and children's children in whom his blood lived on, his soul and mind. This one-time minaret had become a Christian bell-tower, just as the one-time Moorish capital was now a Christian city.

It was already growing dark when mounted police cleared the way. A procession of solemn boys marched sedately by to the sound of drums. Then the small square was suddenly full of candlelight: figures in violet robes and pointed hoods bore lighted wax candles, others carried silver crosses inlaid with ivory. A number of men brought forward on bended shoulders a figure of the Mother of our Lord. Barefoot women penitents followed dragging large wooden crosses. Then came a carriage with a recumbent figure of Christ among red carnations. The higher clergy, dignitaries and city elders walked behind it while a band played a funeral march.

It was a strange kind of music, Andalusian, consisting of few notes with a simple melody that recurred and was at once sad and joyous. It struck me as infinitely beautiful. I closed my eyes to catch the last strains of this melancholy yet happy-making music as it faded into the distance. Here the memory lived on of suffering endured for love. In Thee alone is a new heaven and a new earth. In Thee is resurrection and our salvation.

At one with the people around me, I followed the crowd that accompanied the Christ-figure to the church in which it was at home.

EASTER AND MUSIC

After the long Lenten silence, the return of the sung Mass is a good symbol of the resurrection of life. Spanish church music is very lovely—the organ never blares out but quietly accompanies the course of the Holy Sacrifice.

I found a book here that gave me great pleasure: *La música en la Corte de Carlos Quinto*, by Higinio Anglés. Now as I picture the Emperor's life I hear the soft accompaniment of viol and lute, *viol da gamba* and recorder.

Charles V had three permanent groups of players: one in Madrid, one in Brussels, the third in Vienna. On his journeys and campaigns he always had his Flemish choristers with him for church music, as well as drums, kettledrums and fifes for ceremonial marches, and 'players on the flute' for his chamber music. In Spain he had a band of Spanish musicians that played folk-tunes.

Those old Spanish tunes are atonal and yet melodic, their range seems somehow richer than classical music. Their melodies wander through all possible pitches and keys, like a spirit freed of earth's burdens roaming through the celestial spheres. Unpredictable as life itself, those tunes know no harmonic ending and break off suddenly; they are curiously crude and solemn, and yet they give immediate satisfaction as songs sure of themselves, for each successive harmony seems to contain all possible resonances, as a contented heart contains all happiness.

SENECA'S *CONCORDIA*

It was Seneca that brought me back to the Reformation.

In his *De Vita Beata* I came upon a phrase setting out the basic problem that occupied Charles V all his life long. It ran: 'You need not hesitate to declare that the highest good is concord of souls, for where harmony and unity prevail the virtues must be present too. It is the vices that strive asunder.'

Concordia, unanimity, was of great concern to the Emperor. Apart from the landscapes he gazed upon and the rooms he lived in, we find the man most surely in this, the goal of his endeavours. And it was Seneca who made it plain to me.

Concord as a virtue, discord as a vice: a notion Seneca shared with the leading thinkers of the Middle Ages. St Bernard distinguished between two sorts of human will, the *voluntas propria* and the *voluntas communis*.

By *voluntas propria* he meant self-will, self-seeking as the root of all sins and all errors.

By *voluntas communas* he meant the common will, which he identified with neighbourly love, raising selfhood out of its self-imposed limitations into fellowship with the community.

In the same sense St Thomas Aquinas stressed the primacy of universal will over private will; he saw good in the subordination of private will to universal will, and evil in the rejection of universal will by private will.

According to Plato, evil comes of our old nature's resistance to the Light which is the end and purpose of life. Evil is whatever blocks our endeavour to reach the Highest. And Schelling, through whom German idealism returned to a classical and Christian mode of thought, wrote that 'self-assertion is not in itself evil, it is evil only in so far as it deliberately parts company with its necessary counterpart, Light—or the universal will. It is in this departure from Good that sin consists.'

From that standpoint the post-Reformation period, with its aggravated individualism, was a period of sin because it exalted the individual will at the cost of the universal will; and the twentieth century, with its sense of collectivity, may be taken as a period of revival, a revival of the universal will—producing power-systems and inhumanity only because, in the course of centuries of de-Christianized humanism, an awareness of man's higher nature had flickered out, and thus the will-to-community worked blindly, not under the sign of grace.

If modern thought does not know what to make of the present-day shambles, where the *voluntas communis* is concerned, it is because our western world is guided by an Anglo-Saxon conception of life, rooted in Protestantism and remote from the modes of olden Europe. As Ernst

Troeltsch put it, Protestantism let loose the 'most violent forces of the free personality', forces which of their very nature, which is anarchic, were incapable of establishing true order, that is, communal order.

Today's problem is not so much that of 'a meeting of West and East' (for today's East is merely the child of yesterday's West), but of a meeting of the western mind with the mediaeval conception of order and the mediaeval disposition, which were suppressed by Luther's and Calvin's Reformation and Voltaire's Age of Enlightenment. It is a matter of bringing the Western mind back into contact with its own pre-Reformation foundations.

A re-birth of the suppressed values of our own history would bring about a renaissance in which those values prevailed.

A renaissance becomes a necessity when the spirit of an age declines to admit what is new, or rather, to take on something old which was once suppressed but now suddenly produces new shoots.

And the miracle of Europe is its capacity for producing new blossoms on old stock.

Dare we see, in the wild blossoming of our present reality, hope of new joyful service to the community by all—a new *concordia*?

In modern biology, an order is visible today reminiscent of Christian order: for in the living communality of all organic things the part serves the whole unreservedly; and the whole serves the part; but if a part tries to make itself independent and strive for its own advantage alone, there is a disturbance in health, a dissonance in the rhythm of life.

Freely given service in love is life's recipe for countering domineering self-will—it is the evangelical recipe which inspired Luther's finest utterance, calling upon us 'to serve our neighbour for nothing'.

Maybe the religious division of Europe is due to neglecting the real Luther, the one who tells us 'that a Christian man does not live in himself but in Christ and in his neighbour, in Christ through faith and in his neighbour through love'.

They are words that place Luther in the Catholic Christian tradition which he would surely never have abandoned of his own accord, had not the majority of the German princes used his evangelical zeal, from 1521 onwards, to pursue their own political ends, just as in 1933–45 the National Socialists canalized the German people's love of country and nostalgia for the past to feed their own ambitions.

'It is the vices that strive asunder.'

The causes of the Reformation lie deeply embedded in Church history.

Efforts to renew the Christian faith were constantly in evidence through-out the Middle Ages. But the reform movement turned to revolution only through a combination of factors: the particularism of the German princes, discontent with feudal conditions, and the anti-Rome feeling in eastern, non-Latin Germany.

On top of it all came the invention of printing which for the first time gave the broad masses of the people access to the written word, with a shattering effect comparable to that of broadcasting in our day: in 1520 it was the printed word, in 1933 the spoken word, that shook Germany's foundations.

DISCUSSIONS ON RELIGION

From Diet to Diet, from discussion to discussion, Charles V endeavoured to realize the highest good, the concord of souls.

But the opposition lacked a true desire for unity. Much argumentation brought the protagonists not one step nearer to agreement, it served rather to reveal how far removed the Protestants already were from the Old Faith. Their misunderstanding of the Mass (which Luther in the *Schmalkaldic Articles* termed 'the greatest and most horrible abomination of the Papacy') showed how remote they were from appreciating the mysteries of the old religion. The dissensions that arose on the subject of the Catholic dogma of transubstantiation, that is to say, the enduring presence of the Blessed Sacrament of the Altar in the consecrated Host, indicated how fundamental the difference was between the old religious conception and the modern intellectual one. For although Luther was of the opinion that he alone was called by God to give a verdict, nonethe-less he approached ultimate mysteries with intellectual arguments; and no words are more appropriate to the situation than these from the *Imitatio Christi*: 'Of what use is it for you to quarrel over the high matters of the Trinity if you are not humble, thus incurring the displeasure of the Trinity?'

The new critical attitude, based on pure reason, was bound to falter at belief in the Blessed Sacrament. Melanchthon, the rationalist, declared that on the question of the Sacrament of the Altar agreement was im-possible.

The Protestants had begun to lose contact with those fundamental depths which are of the very nature of religion.

St Catherine of Genoa, who lived only a few decades before the Reformation storm, found the right words to convey an idea of the perpetual presence of Christ in the consecrated Host, saying it gave out 'rays of love', and she called the Sacrament of the Altar 'the heart's most proper food'.

But the Protestants banished those rays of love from the cathedrals and churches.

REGENSBURG (1541)

The Diet of Regensburg in 1541 opened with the most glowing hopes for unity. The Pope sent as his representative Cardinal Contarini, a kindly man, friendly to reform. The Protestant theologians' mouthpiece was Melanchthon, who was generally considered to be conciliatory. Perhaps reconciliation could be reached this time; 'we both have but one Gospel', said Charles V.

The Emperor himself prepared a little book to serve as a basis for mediation: 'On the settlement of the religious issue.' And he himself appointed the theologians who were to conduct the discussions and insisted that they should 'go about their work without fear or passion, and do it with naught but the glory of God in view'. The Protestant theologian Bucer assured the Emperor: 'If God so will, we shall meet in the truth.' But it was not love of the truth that inspired the participants in these debates: all the theologians present were in the service of the princes and only repeated what their lords said. Melanchthon and Bucer represented the interests of the Protestant state-rulers; Dr Eck, the mouthpiece of the Catholic side, championed the intolerant attitude of the Bavarian dukes; it soon came to 'bad, defiant, rough words'.

In the thick of the fray, amid clashing opinions, stood Charles V endeavouring to carry out Erasmus' last wish for 'the loving harmony of the Church'.

From Regensburg Melanchthon wrote: 'In spite of all the pomp and ceremony, the Emperor's modesty is wonderful and so is the mildness of his replies . . . the true virtue of Emperor Charles lies in his desire to bring to light true pious opinions and in his express instructions to explore the truth. The Emperor's intention is the best; he desires unity and the reformation of abuses.'

An agreement was of serious import to the Emperor. He declared he would carry through 'a Christian reformation' even if the Pope were disinclined for it, for unity would be 'to the honour, the good and the welfare of the Empire'.

But unity was precisely what many participants in the Diet wanted to prevent. Contarini's secretary wrote to Rome: 'The Emperor's enemies inside Germany and out of it, fearing his greatness if he should unite the whole of Germany, are beginning to sow tares among the theologians. Elector John Frederick of Saxony and Francis I have achieved that no further agreement can be reached on any article.'

The secret contact of Francis I's men of confidence with the Protestants was one of the most harmful elements at the Diet—and the Thirty Years War was to come of it. Melanchthon was often seen in conversation with Calvin.

Calvin was in Regensburg as representative of the city of Strasbourg, and his political activity suggests that, in spite of his ejection from French territory, he remained loyal to the French king, for by fostering the Protestant cause he was working against the Catholic Emperor on behalf of the French crown, which desired a prolongation of the German religious differences.

One way of making the situation worse was to arouse national passions against Rome. Calvin put a document into circulation in which he adopted the tones of a German patriot and warned 'his Germany of the bloodthirsty Roman tyranny and its bepurpled, godless company'. He advised Melanchthon not to yield.

And in fact, as the discussions proceeded, Melanchthon became more and more obdurate. For a while the Protestants consented to the reintroduction of Confession, and the Emperor was already rejoicing over this victory on the path to unity; but in the end Melanchthon rejected all the Emperor's proposals on the side of agreement and peacemaking.

Giustiniani, a Venetian, wrote from Regensburg: 'The princes favour Lutherism, not out of zeal for the faith but because the religious cause is a means of drawing the people on to their side against the two feared brothers (Emperor Charles and King Ferdinand) . . . thus nearly all German princes are against the House of Austria.'

For it was not only the Protestant princes who were ill disposed towards the Emperor, the princes of the Old Faith were no better: the Dukes of Bavaria made earnest protests to the Emperor for not proceeding more sharply against the Protestants; they complained of his 'all-toogreat mildness, gentleness and consideration' and of his 'dilatoriness'.

They advocated violent measures and offered the Emperor their armed forces and their lives to eradicate the Lutheran sect with the sword. But the Emperor replied 'he did not want to start any war'.

He did not want to start a war because, as in 1530 when he was in Augsburg, the Empire's external enemies were threatening again: Sultan Suleiman was advancing on Vienna. The Emperor told the Bavarian dukes that it was his duty to fight the Turks. 'And,' he added, 'it is useless to make war on the Protestants, for even if they were beaten they would not give up their opinions.' Thus, yet another discussion-meeting had yielded no results. But so long as people met and talked, the will to understanding was still alive. And in spite of all disappointments, Charles V stuck to his resolution to attain to concord of souls through the voluntary collaboration of all Christians. He did not want to start a war, he wanted to persuade and convert.

ALGIERS (1541)

The months of fruitless endeavour in Regensburg roused in the Emperor an urge to action. He determined to carry out a well-considered plan to attack the Turks from Africa by seizing the Moors' base of Algiers.

On occupying Algiers, he could divert Ottoman attention from the Empire; and at the same time the south coast of Spain would be secure, for in recent years there had been a number of raids by Moorish pirates. Spain was in favour of an attack on Algiers.

But it was now autumn. Andrea Doria, experienced in these matters, advised the Emperor not to risk an undertaking, at that time of year, that depended on the support of the fleet. Charles V, who usually looked up to Doria, now an old man, as to a father, was so engrossed in his plans that he had no ear for advice.

Accompanied by the Duke of Alba and Hernán Cortés, the conqueror of Mexico, and with a retinue of many galleys of German, Spanish and Italian troops, he embarked in Genoa at the beginning of September.

On 20th October the North African coast was in sight. But the stormy sea made landing difficult. A part of the ships had to remain at sea, the others drew up to the shore and were at once attacked by the Moors. The galleys' cannons drove them off and the landing finally took place on 23rd October.

On that same day the Emperor advanced along the coast with his army and encamped at a small oasis, the 'Spring of Palms'. 'The Germans were very eager to fight,' wrote an eyewitness of the campaign, 'they crossed themselves and kissed the earth.' And their fighting spirit was soon put to the test. That very night the Moors made a raid on the camp. 'The Emperor was in great danger,' the same witness tells us, 'but he showed neither fear nor terror, his expression and colour were unchanged and he remained in his whole manner as imperturbable as on days of good fortune.' In the skirmish he called out to his German troops: 'Fight by my side like Germans for your Faith, your Emperor and your Nation!'

The Moors were driven off. But on the next night a hurricane arose, causing great disaster to the fleet. As the storm grew ever fiercer, the Emperor said to his despondent staff: 'If only the galleys can hold out till midnight! For then the monks and nuns in the Spanish monasteries and convents rise to pray for the success of my enterprise. Then God will be with us.'

It was Sandoval who reported those words, which show what sort of a Catholic Charles was: the communion of saints was a reality for him, he put his trust in the power of prayer and humbly believed that the petitioning of men and women devoted to holiness would be more effective than his own. We see, too, how closely Charles was identified with Spain —and in hours of need, as we know, he drew spiritual strength from the thought of Spain, the Mystical.

But the elements won the day, the storm wrecked over a hundred ships with their crews, munitions and stores.

The Emperor was badly shaken. 'His Majesty was nearly desperate and more despondent that he had ever been seen before.' 'With tears in his eyes,' says the chronicler, 'he informed his staff of the loss: "It is not without reason that you see me so distressed, for with my own eyes I witnessed how a great number of noble men who had come from all nations to fight the Infidels with me, went to their death. And now there is no ship left for us to return to Christendom, no shelter to keep us dry from the rain, no food to feed us, no powder and weapons, and thus I am in no position to take that city. My friends, there remain only divine consolation and godly counsel."' The situation was perilous indeed and the Emperor soon came to himself. It was his strength of mind that kept the army together, for the storm had not only wrecked the ships, it had also broken the soldiers' spirit, 'for nothing makes them more superstitious than a bolt from the blue', as La Roca wrote.

And indeed it did seem as though the Algiers campaign took place under an unlucky star. The continual rain put firearms out of use, tents were lacking for shelter at night, and, most serious of all, with their insufficient provisions the fighting spirit of the troops deteriorated. The Emperor had his horse slaughtered to provide food for his men. They ate the fruit of palm trees, and toads. For days on end the Emperor marched on with his army, under constant attack from the enemy, endeavouring to recover contact with the scattered fleet.

On 28th October he reached Cape Matifou where the remaining ships were assembling and they managed to get some supplies ashore. But the whole artillery had been jettisoned during the storm. The heavy losses induced the Emperor to break off the campaign—it is said he did it against the wish of Hernán Cortés, who had overcome far greater obstacles in Mexico.

But he no longer felt inclined to force events. 'Thy will be done,' he was heard saying during the retreat.

While they were embarking the storm blew up again and delayed their departure. The soldiers were afraid the Emperor would leave them behind in the enemy's country, so he embarked last on the last galley.

At the beginning of December he landed in Cartagena. In Germany the rumour went round that he had been drowned in the surging Mediterranean before Algiers.

A PAUSE IN SPAIN

Whenever fortune struck him a blow, the Emperor felt the need to withdraw completely in order to regain his peace of mind, and so it was after the Algiers disaster.

Fray Martin de Angelo reported thus: 'That monk tells . . . how the Emperor when he was returning home from Algiers and his journey to Italy, withdrew to La Majorada, a little monastery in the neighbourhood of Olmedo, remaining there a number of days. And on Friday in Holy Week, at mealtime, he walked up and down an avenue of very lovely cypresses in the monastery garden and asked what was being eaten in the monastery; water and bread, he was told; and he said, they were to bring him two pieces of bread of the kind the monks were eating, and a jug of water; and he ate and drank as he stood, walking up and down; and on that day he took no other food.'

The monks' bread and water, the peace of the monastery garden, the sun from Spanish skies, gave the Emperor renewed vigour. There were hostile tendencies to encounter, physical disabilities to ward off, depressing money troubles to deal with; new conflicts loomed on the horizon, but under the heavy burden he bore he grew ever stronger.

Francis I calculated that the Emperor would be exhausted after the Algiers misadventure and judged the moment ripe for the undermining of Habsburg domination. Early in 1542 he threw five army units against the imperial boundaries and the Emperor found himself involved in his fourth and last war with Francis I.

The new war posited fresh expenditure. The Emperor summoned the Cortes to discuss means of raising money. The forthcoming marriage of Prince Philip with the Infanta Maria of Portugal was to bring many thousands of gold ducats into the empty treasury; but more was needed. The Spanish representatives promised their support. Far from blaming the Emperor for the great losses of his ill-timed campaign, they offered to continue the fight with the Moorish pirates themselves, and to raise the means for it.

Spain was now completely loyal, supporting the Emperor in all his undertakings and never leaving him in the lurch, even in defeat. Others might term the Algiers enterprise an error of judgement—the Spaniards were quick to see the necessity for this very campaign.

A bad attack of gout forced the Emperor to rest for the time being. While he was laid up, he wrote to his sister Maria: 'Time will teach me what I have to do. May God guide me.'

Maybe he had begun the attack on Algiers too hastily. Maybe the storm was God's punishment for his unreasonable act. There shall be no more ill-considered actions, said the Emperor to himself, from now on every step should be taken with circumspection.

It would be two years before the money question was settled, he wrote to Maria. He laid orders for new weapons from Germany and sent ships with Spanish troops to the Netherlands. All through 1542 he took counsel with the representatives of the Spanish cities as to the possibility of raising money to finance the impending campaign.

In spite of the influx of gold from the New Indies, the Emperor's sources of income were, in relation to his widespread obligations, comparatively restricted, and we see this lord of a world-wide realm bent over his accounts, worried by the gap between debit and credit.

His perpetual money troubles brought him into closest contact with his Spanish lands. The various local Cortes taught him how hard it was to obtain ready money, and in the end it was always the Fugger banking house in Augsburg, under faithful Anton Fugger, that advanced the sums required.

When during a pause in their lifelong fighting Charles V once asked Francis I how much money he was able to obtain from his subjects, he replied: 'All I want' (a policy that ended in the French Revolution). And on that occasion Charles V must have recalled with perplexity the trouble he had to persuade the Cortes to make new concessions.

The credit of six hundred thousand ducats which Anton Fugger put at his disposal in 1535 to finance the Tunis campaign was exhausted long ago and not repaid; a new loan would be necessary. Legend has it that once, when the Emperor was his guest in Augsburg, Anton Fugger burnt a credit note of his in the fire on the hearth. Whether it was consumed in flames or entered in the account was all the same in the long run: Anton Fugger never got back any of the ready money he advanced him. It is true the Fuggers drew large incomes from the Spanish mines owing to highly favourable contracts, but these only partly covered the Emperor's debit account. In fact, the whole Fugger business became more and more involved in the Emperor's fortunes, and creditor and debtor were mutually dependent and had to stand or fall together. Thus Anton Fugger saw himself forced to save his sovereign from bankruptcy again and again.

The whole of the sums raised went on warfaring expeditions; in comparison with the extravagance of the Renaissance princes, Charles V was modest in his personal requirements; he had long ago discarded the gold-stitched clothes he used to like so much as young Duke of Burgundy, and since the death of his wife he dressed Spanish-fashion in plain black.

Of Charles' ancestor, Rudolf of Habsburg, it was recounted to his disfavour that he always wore a plain grey coat, and in the same way Charles' unostentatious appearance caused wagging tongues to call him niggardly and mean. Thus Contarini spoke of Charles' *occi avari*, his 'miserly eye'.

The people of the Renaissance expected their lords to display *magnificencia* and Lorenzo *il Magnifico*, Francis I, and also Sultan Suleiman the Splendid corresponded to their idea of luxury and extravagance and thus appealed to them far more than the Emperor, impeded as he was on all sides by money troubles. Liberality and a generous style of living were considered princely virtues, and any pettiness was a vice.

Machiavelli took a stand against this attitude, praising the thrift of Charles' grandfather, Ferdinand of Aragon, in the sixteenth chapter of *Il*

Principe: 'Thus it is high wisdom to be accounted a skinflint, for it cannot do more than give rise to fault-finding talk, rather than try to gain a name for liberality and be dubbed a thief for it. . . .'

This was no doubt Charles' view, too. Strict economy was a basic principle of his.

Sastrow, mayor of Naumburg, wrote in his memoirs how once the Emperor reached the town in a rainstorm and had taken off his magnificent velvet cap to keep it dry: 'How deserving of pity is an Emperor who pours out tons of gold in warfare but lets his head grow wet in order not to spoil his cap!' Another version of this incident tells how the Emperor asked his servants for a blanket 'in order to protect his fine clothes'. Nothing of the sort was told of Francis I.

INSTRUCTIONS TO PHILIP (1543)

At last he was ready to leave for Germany. A whole series of complications had arisen: Gelderland, a frontier region, had gone over to the French; Francis I had invaded imperial territory; the Protestant princes were growing more and more insubordinate. In view of these difficulties, the Emperor made a contract with the King of England that was to compel Francis to give up his alliance with the Turks.

Spain, praise God, was at peace, the Emperor could go away and leave it in the hands of his sixteen-year-old son, Philip, without any misgivings at all.

Early in May 1543, while waiting in the harbour of Palamos near Barcelona for a favourable wind to carry him to Genoa, he wrote down a number of instructions for his son, Philip—his so-called 'political testament'. These pieces of political counsel reveal something of his frame of mind, for at that time he felt he was at a turning-point in his life.

'My son,' he wrote, 'as my past endeavours have brought me some suffering, and as I was a short time ago in danger of death and do not know what God's will has in store for me, it seems well to advise you as to all that may occur in such a case; but owing to the continuous uncertainty and variability of earthly things, it is impossible to give you firm commands for ruling, and so I can only pray the divine indulgence and goodness that rule these realms to guide you in this holy task.'

In Sandoval's chronicle the Emperor's counsels to his son fill seventeen pages: he commends to Philip the men whom he set at his side as counsellors, he begs him always to act justly and impartially, to make no decisions out of personal inclination, annoyance, or passion, and to let mercy rule in judgement, after Christ's example; he should always be quiet and dignified, never do anything in anger, and beware of flatterers as of fire itself.

Shortly before his departure the Emperor added a postscript: 'It is a great trouble and concern to me that I have to leave you my Empire in such a state of need. For I do not know how we shall survive. All things lie in God's hand, and not for my merits, but only of His grace, I entreat Him to help me. For the journey I am now undertaking is the most perilous for my honour, my good name, my life and my means. But without this undertaking I could secure your heritage for you even less surely, nor could I remove from you the danger that I am now going to encounter. Honour and repute demand that I set forth, and no one knows what will come of it. For much time has gone by, money is limited and the enemy is on the watch. Hence our life is imperilled and our means too. But as things are, I must risk both. In what concerns life, God will appoint in the way that serves Him best; I shall be left with the consolation of having lost it in doing what I had to do.'

Those words show to what an extent his sense of vocation possessed the man, involving him in duties not to be overlooked. They also throw light on Charles' way of proceeding, which was sometimes impulsive, sometimes circumstantial: he went straight at a thing that 'had to be done', but hesitated when he was not sure if it was in accordance with God's will —enduring the whole weight of responsibility that freedom of the will incurs.

This accounts for the end of the postscript, the Emperor frankly admitting that he was at a loss—a very human admission! Moments of confidence are short and far apart, and a man's normal state is one of indecision, doubt, perplexity. 'Perplexity is an inherent part of the existence of man,' said Heidegger. And then the soul longs for the salvaging of truth and a clear view of the right way.

A profound honesty speaks in the Emperor's confession of uncertainty: 'I ought to tell you much more, my son, only the important things to say are so obscure and full of doubt that I cannot counsel you decisively, for I am myself still undetermined and largely unenlightened. Indeed it is one of the main objects of my journey, to gain clarity on what we have to do. Remain in the will of God, and let all else alone, while I too endeavour to carry out my obligations and commit myself into the hands of Him who

I pray will grant you His bliss when you have ended your days in His service.'

Let us recall for a moment St Teresa of Avila's words about the 'special care' God takes to enter into contact with us, and the 'so gentle and penetrating touch of His love', to which we must be sensitive in order to be aware of supernatural guidance. She advises that in moments of indecision we ask, like St Paul, 'What do you want me to do, Lord?'—'and almost always the soul will answer the light touch aright and do with determined will what it is told'.

So it is clear that a determined will has nothing to do with arbitrary judgements but arises from a conscience on the alert, and so long as a soul has not established contact with its own inherent and highest principle, it is bound to grope in obscurity and remain without counsel.

THE EMPEROR IN GERMANY (1543)

After months spent in thinking things over, the Emperor found the inward certainty he sought in the performance of the tasks awaiting him in Germany.

At that time, the Protestant theologian Bucer described him in the following terms: 'The Emperor is clear in mind and firm in the pursuance of his plans. He does everything with astonishing mobility, answering in German and mustering his troops himself. Imperial are his words, deeds, look, demeanour, his very gifts—everything, in fact. Even those nearest to him are amazed at his present freshness and energy, his strictness, severity and majesty. This Emperor could accomplish a great deal, did he elect to be a German Emperor and a servant of Christ.'

Bucer was (like Hutten) obsessed with the idea of a national *imperium*. But Charles V stood for the universal *imperium*, like the German emperors of the Holy Roman Empire in the Middle Ages. He was a servant of Christ, not of his own appointing, but in the form which the Christian religion had created in the course of centuries. Bound by tradition, he protected and preserved the German religious tradition as well, for the Church's best safeguard is the continuity of her institutions.

The first task that now confronted him was coming to terms with the Duke of Cleves, who had deserted and made an alliance with the King of France. In the Duke's Gelderland ruled that same spirit of rebellion that

Ghent had incited in the country of the lower Rhine. Like Ghent, Gelderland was to be forced into submission.

The Emperor assembled his troops in Bonn; he had brought a thousand Spaniards and Italians with him, experienced soldiers who proudly exhibited their storm-tattered, bullet-ridden colours. Again he took on the high command himself. 'He is said to have smiled when he caught sight of himself on horseback, all in iron and gold ornament like his horse. He was seen flying up and down the ranks, ordering this, improving that; with his own hand giving Hans von Hilchen his flag; and so he advanced upon the Duke of Cleves' lands.'

The first attack was directed at the rebellious city of Düren. The Emperor promised immunity from punishment in return for a voluntary surrender, but Düren was strongly fortified and considered itself impregnable: it refused to submit and was to pay heavily for its act of defiance. Rebels could not hope for mercy; like Dante, who condemned them to the deepest hell, Charles V considered them wicked men. Judgement would be inexorable. The imperial cannon balls soon breached the city walls, Düren was stormed and after a terrible blood-bath reduced to ashes. The Emperor saw to it that women and children were saved.

Once more, as at Ghent, forceful means attained their object; the harsh fate of Düren served as a warning to others, and the deputies of the Jülich and Gelderland cities streamed into the Emperor's headquarters to convey their submission. In Jülich, a woman handed over the keys at the city gates, because all the men had flown. At Venloo, the Duke of Cleves submitted and came bareheaded to sue for pardon on his knees. The Emperor, for whom treason was the sin of sins, remained unmoved; only some days later, when the Duke had sworn to maintain the Catholic faith in the lands left him, was he reprieved.

It must have occurred to the Emperor that it would be a fine sight to see all the Protestant princes on their knees. Ranke states that it was at that time that Charles formed his design to end the German religious rift by subduing the Lutheran princes. To his chronicler, Jovius, who accompanied him on his Cleves campaign, he said: 'Write down those past deeds quickly, for soon you will have fresh work, greater work to do.'

With coverage to the rear, the Emperor could now devote himself to his second task, which was to drive the French off imperial territory. Francis I had wantonly broken the truce and invaded Luxembourg.

Once again Charles rode to encounter his old enemy. They had fought and embraced and fought again—as though conflict and reconciliation

POPE PAUL III
Titian, *National Museum, Naples*

THE SURRENDER OF
BREDA
Velázquez, The Prado, Madrid

were complementary sides of a life-long relationship flowing like the tides between love and hate. Now it was the turn for war. The Emperor was truly up in arms, for the French king had formed an alliance with the Turks again, and in the Battle of Nice the French had borne the banners of the Crescent against the imperial troops. Francis I had offered the Sultan Toulon as a base for his fleet—it was said that he let a mosque be put up in Marseilles at the very moment when the Turks were invading Hungary. Francis I's behaviour was not to be tolerated, and the Emperor determined to give him a thorough drubbing. He said he would dictate peace terms to the beaten king in Paris itself, just as he had dictated them to the captive king in Madrid. He turned to the Pope, requesting him to condemn Francis' dealings with the Turks, 'whose fleet he has harboured in his realm where they live like barbarians, to the great scandal of all Christendom and to the scorn of our holy religion'.

But the Pope showed no inclination to risk a break with France for the sake of condemning her Turkish policy; 'Otherwise there is the danger that Francis I, who does such appalling things, might himself turn Turk, like the King of England.' He continued to treat Charles V and Francis I on the same footing and lauded both as firm supporters of the Christian cause.

The Pope drew a dividing line between religion and politics, just as Machiavelli described it. Within his realm, Francis I defended the Catholic faith against all the assaults of Lutheran doctrine. And as for his political alliance with the Turks, had not Charles but recently formed an alliance with the schismatic Henry VIII of England?

It was true, the Emperor had made an agreement with the English king early in 1543, for common action against France, and Henry was at that moment engaged in opening a second front based on Calais.

France's precarious situation aroused concern in Rome. Exaggerated reports of the Emperor's victory over Cleves provoked fresh fears as to his imperialistic intentions. An anonymous letter that was passed round in ecclesiastical circles reminded the Curia that the Roman Church was the glory of Italy and the true pledge of her liberty.

Meanwhile, the Emperor laid siege to Landrecies, a fortress in Hennegau. On 28th October Francis I set up his headquarters ten kilometres west of Landrecies, ready, it was rumoured, to fight a decisive battle.

The Emperor was prepared to present his bare chest to his opponent. This time it should be a duel, and the old conflict should be settled from man to man. He went to Confession and Holy Communion, to be in a state of grace on approaching the sacrifice of his life. He heard two Masses daily. His determination was impressive as he prepared his army for the mortal encounter. However, on 4th November, in the early morning, under cover of darkness, Francis withdrew with his troops—without trumpets or drums. The French soldiers took the bells off the supply-mules to make sure their escape would not be heard.

The Emperor remained in the field the whole autumn, in spite of bad weather and attacks of gout. To his private entourage he said: 'All my life long I have done all I could to remove the religious rift in the Church and to deliver Christendom from the Turks, and Francis I did all he could to strengthen the Turks and perpetuate the religious rift.'

In Germany Francis I now had himself termed the 'protector of German liberties', and his agents spread the view that Charles V's sovereignty meant submission to the 'ignominious Roman yoke'. They gave currency to the phrase: 'Better a Turkish Germany than a papal one!'

And the great Sultan Suleiman advanced upon Vienna.

THE DIET OF SPIRES (1544)

Early in January 1544 the Emperor hastened to Spires where he had called a Diet to consider the costs of the French war and anti-Turkish defence. He stopped for three days in Cologne where the archbishop had shown Protestant tendencies and permitted Lutheran preachers to preach, let Mass be said in German and Communion be given in both species. The Emperor persuaded the archbishop to abandon these practices; the archbishop followed him to Spires.

At the beginning of 1544 Spires was a completely Protestant city. The Venetian ambassador Navagero wrote to Venice: 'Spires is wholly Lutheran. No more is Mass said. The churches are in any case not very numerous, and in none of them are pictures to be seen, not even a picture of our Lord Jesus Christ. The walls are whitewashed, in the middle there is a pulpit from which the Gospel is preached daily, which the whole town comes to hear. The preacher receives an official salary. He wears ordinary clothes; he is married. He consecrates the bread and wine and frequently distributes Communion in both species. In speaking of the Papists, as these people call them, they use highly insolent expressions.'

With the arrival of the Emperor and his court, the atmosphere of Spires became that of the Old Faith again. In the venerable cathedral where St Bernard had his vision of the Virgin Mary, the *Salve Regina* rang out anew. On 14th February the Diet was opened with a High Mass in the cathedral. Of the Electors, who had all arrived, only the Elector of Saxony remained away from Mass. And now the Emperor hoped to win the Pope over to his side. In his conviction that he was defending the Christian cause, he insisted to the Papal Legate that Pope Paul III could now no longer give his preference to Francis I, the Turks' friend, but should declare himself for the Emperor. Was it not right and proper, Charles pursued, for the Pope to take up a definite attitude in regard to the French king? It vexed him that Francis still bore the title 'très chrétien' although openly supporting the foes of Christendom. And in spite of this the Pope did not excommunicate him but rather continued to show him favour—and Charles V felt like the obedient brother who had stayed at home and done all the work, only to witness the prodigal's cordial welcome on his belated return!

'I have served you faithfully so many years,' wrote Charles. 'I conduct these heavy wars of defence alone. Is it not time that I should receive support?'

But the Pope's reply was evasive—and support was evidently not forthcoming.

It came, unexpectedly, from the Protestants. After a few mutual concessions the German princes voted unanimously in favour of supporting the Empire against France, and a few weeks later they voted for common action against the Turks, too. Then Charles V told the Papal Legate he would restore religious unity in Germany whether the Pope liked it or not.

Those words found a great response in the Protestant camp. In March 1544 Luther wrote: 'The latest development is the alliance of Pope, French and Turks against the Emperor.'

And in fact those were the three powers that opposed the Emperor's endeavours in the cause of union. But the fourth and greatest obstacle, the particularism of the German princes, seemed to have completely melted away; on 12th March they declared the King of France to be 'the common foe of Christendom and the German nation' and promised the Emperor to prove themselves 'in word and deed' the enemies of the king.

Charles V was very pleased. 'It was truly a great victory,' said Granvelle, his chancellor, 'and it was more than the Emperor ever expected, that Germany, where the King of France boasted he had so many friends, should declare itself against him.'

It was the alliance of Francis I with the Turks that brought about this astonishing unanimity. It had become known in Germany that in honour of his Turkish alliance Francis had coins stamped with the fleur-de-lis on one side and on the other the Crescent, and the inscription: *Non contra fidem, sed contra Carolum* (not against the Faith but against Charles), or as others had it, *Amicus fidei et inimicus Caroli* (the Faith's friend, Charles' enemy).

French gestures of this kind duly swept public opinion over to Charles' side. All over Germany a saying of the French king's was repeated, arousing much patriotic feeling, to the effect that Francis had no more ardent wish than to 'have his horse drink at the Rhine'.

So much for that, said the Germans, and rallied to their Emperor. For a moment, at the Diet of Spires, it might have been possible to unite the Germans permanently. They were threatened from east and west and in the hour of common peril they flocked fearfully round their shepherd. And the Emperor was now frankly determined 'to carry out the Christian reformation' soon, which stirred the Evangelicals to fight for him with might and main.

Spring had come. The Emperor conceded the Protestants the right to hold their church services in the cloisters of the Dominican Church which was otherwise used for Catholic worship. To the envoy of the Landgrave of Hesse he had it said that so long as he was Emperor he would be his gracious Sovereign; he consoled Catholics and Protestants alike with hopes of a 'future free Christian general Council' which would settle the differences of opinion that divided them; until then all should leave the religious feud alone and 'each should stand on terms of friendship and Christian love with the other'.

Charles V had to muster all his diplomatic skill to keep the precarious union together. The Catholics declared he gave way to the Protestants all the time; in Bavarian circles there were promptly whispers to the effect that the Emperor had turned Lutheran, but Charles assured them that he was still, and forever, the religious and Catholic prince he had always been, and if he now did something against their will it was because he could not do otherwise. (It might be inferred from this that Charles' tolerance towards the Protestants was not genuine; but the remark can be taken simply as oil poured on troubled waters.) Both parties left it to the Emperor to close the proceedings. He laid down that civil peace was to be maintained unbroken; there was the question of the ecclesiastical property confiscated by the Protestants—it was adjourned; help to fight the Turks was to come from a general tax—a 'common penny'. The Protestants were provisionally afforded equality of rights with the Catholics; if for

218

any reason the Council were to be prevented from sitting, a German Diet would settle the religious and ecclesiastical question in the following year.

The Emperor had achieved what he wanted. On the very day of the closing of the Diet, he left Spires and went to Metz to join his army and carry on the campaign against France.

The German princes did actually raise an army and the Elector of Brandenburg led it to Hungary to fight the Turks. Young Duke Maurice of Saxony rode with it.

But the fair weather was not to hold: selfish interests were too strong. The springtime of Spires only lasted so long as the Rhineland was threatened and the Turks stood at the gates of Vienna. When the Emperor made peace with France and the Sultan withdrew—no doubt feeling that the limits of his expansion had been reached, the concord broke.

The closing speech of the Diet of Spires had not been well received at the Roman Curia, and Pope Paul III wrote a letter of reproof to the Emperor recommending him not to assume rights of his own in religious matters; negotiations on spiritual questions were to be excluded from the agenda of a Diet; let him not follow in the wake of that godless Henry IV or Frederick II, or he and his lands would suffer the fate of the Jews and Greeks, over whom God's judgement broke.

Titian has shown us what Pope Paul III was like. The painting depicts him in his old age, bowed with the weight of years, and does it in so lively a manner that when it was hung up to dry, passers-by are said to have genuflected. It is like a portrait of Solomon, full of sober wisdom: 'O folly of the children of this world!' it seems to say, 'How laborious is the office of the Supreme Shepherd!'

He followed Charles' reforming activities very closely, for it was not clear whither they were tending. He certainly feared he might become the 'leader of the heretics' again, as in 1526.

And indeed it would have been very easy for Charles to copy Henry VIII's example and make himself head of a schismatic national church at Spires. It was a moment that served to show up his flawless integrity: he did not seize hold of the political advantage that was offered, he did not want governance in Germany at the cost of the Faith to which he was deeply devoted and duty bound.

Notre ancienne religion, he used to say—a phrase heavy with a sense of tradition and youthful loyalty preserved.

Now Protestant historians accuse Charles V of sacrificing the ecclesiastical unity of the German nation to the interests of Habsburg world monarchy. But the ecclesiastical unity they have in mind would be in Luther's name. And it would have eradicated from German soil the old religious roots that are today, shyly but surely, sending up new shoots, into a new springtime with a commonalty of its own, and new understanding in the light of the old love.

THE MARNE CAMPAIGN AND THE PEACE OF CRÉPY (1544)

Meanwhile the imperial army had retaken Luxembourg, 'the key between Germany and France'. In June 1544 the Emperor assembled his troops in Metz; German, Italian, Spanish and Dutch cavalry and infantry, cannon, horses and wagons. At the beginning of July this well-appointed army with the Emperor in command rode off across Champagne; it was said that Francis I was at Châlons-sur-Marne.

On this historic ground, where the united Romans and Visigoths beat the Hun King, Attila, 'the scourge of God', in 451, there might be another decisive battle to fight. But, we may well ask, what was the decision that had to be reached by such drastic means, and why were the two Christian rulers, Francis I and Charles V, at war with one another? Their rivalry really amounted to a quarrel between royal brothers as to their heritage from their common ancestor, Charles the Great, whose Frankish Empire was divided among his nephews at Verdun in 843; King Ludwig the German received the eastern part (Germany), King Charles the Bald the western part (France), while the eldest, Lothair, became Emperor, with the middle portion as his realm. It stretched from the Mediterranean to the North Sea and in that middle kingdom lay Siena and Milan, Strasbourg and Cologne; in the old *regnum Burgundiae* lay Lyons, Arles and Avignon. Burgundy itself was divided between Emperor Lothair and King Charles the Bald. The Lotharingian imperial house died out in 875, the imperial crown passing to the German line of the Carolingians.

Under its own dukes, Burgundy gained a certain degree of freedom from France and Germany. But the House of the Dukes of Burgundy had now expired, and the nationalistic policy of the Valois kings in France put in question the old dynastic heritage. Valois and Habsburg now had to face the question of frontiers, and that old no-man's-land of Lotharingia was a standing bone of contention. The possession of Milan, Burgundy, Lorraine, Luxembourg and Flanders was at issue, too.

220

The imperial army met with little resistance on its advance. The tactics of the French were to let the enemy penetrate far into the country and then cut off supply routes. It was a device that soon proved successful: 'Hunger will drive and beat us out of France on behalf of the French,' a German mercenary wrote home. Navagero, who accompanied the imperial court, reported to Venice in July: 'Here bread costs four times more than in your Signorie. Wine and oats are unbelievably dear. I and my household would have been without bread on several occasions had I not brought a good supply of zwieback with me.'

The first serious encounter with the French took place at the fort of St Dizier, but it surrendered after a short battle on 9th August. (Certain Frenchmen accused Madame d'Étampes of letting the plans of the fort and those of the cities of Epernay and Château Thierry fall into the Emperor's hands.)

Francis I did not take part in the battles, he lay ill at a castle not far from Paris. He was in a state of despondency and despair, saying he would place no obstacle in the Emperor's way and wanted only to die in St Denis by the tombs of his ancestors.

In Paris, the army advancing from Germany awoke such panic that it might have been the Huns on the warpath again. A pacifist party distributed posters worded: *Non habemus regem nisi Caesarem*. The Emperor was now only two days' march from Paris.

In view of the present danger Francis I pulled himself together and prepared to parley; he rode to Paris and made a speech saying that he would rescue his people of Paris, if not from fear, at least from disaster.

On prend la France dans Paris, King Louis XI had said, and Emperor Maximilian had certainly passed on to his grandson his hereditary enemy's remark. Nonetheless the Emperor stopped in front of Paris. The shocking condition of his army made it improvident to attempt to take Paris alone. He sent the son of his chancellor Granvelle to Henry VIII (who had meanwhile invaded Normandy, as agreed) and challenged him to advance on Paris. But Henry VIII was merely engaged in besieging Boulogne in order to add to his possessions around Calais. He sent a message to say he could give no support.

Such unreliability on the part of his ally made Charles turn back to his royal brother-in-law: Francis I petitioned for peace.

Negotiations went on privately for a time. Queen Leonora's confessor, a Spanish Dominican, went from one camp to the other, bearing proposals for peace. Francis I returned to his old plan, the one he had put forward in Nice, namely to marry his youngest son, Duke Charles of Orleans, to the Emperor's daughter Maria, or to a daughter of King Ferdinand; one would bring Milan as her dowry, the other the Netherlands.

Once Francis I had given his word that he would withdraw from Savoy and render assistance against the Turks, Charles V accepted the terms proposed.

Whereupon, one day, the Duke of Orleans appeared at the imperial headquarters at Crépy and placed himself at the Emperor's disposal.

Navagero told the Signorie how the French king explained matters to the Duke. He said, 'My son, you are now twenty-two years old. You have seen that all the wars I conducted and all the dangers to which I exposed myself were for your sake. It was God's will that all those wars reached the upshot of which you are the witness. I have resolved to give you to the Emperor as his son and servant. Honour him as your father and obey him as your lord. I give you my blessing and admonish you by virtue of my old age, and entreat you as your father, that if the Emperor should order you to take up arms against me and my kingdom, you should do it without hesitation.'

The French envoy who presented the prince to the Emperor, said: 'Here is the prisoner whom the King, my Lord, sends to your Majesty.' 'Not my prisoner,' answered the Emperor, 'rather my son, and as such I welcome him,' and he accompanied the words with a smile full of *dolcezza*.

Peace was signed on 18th September in Crépy.

In the treaty each opponent chivalrously returned to the other all he had taken from him since the truce of Nice. Francis I committed himself to helping the Emperor against the Turks; he renounced all claims to Savoy, Naples, Sicily, Artois and Lorraine. And the Emperor finally renounced that dearest dream of his, cherished since early youth, of regaining Burgundy.

Burgundy was Charles' great concession to the peace. Years of warfare had taught him at last that his claims could not be sustained, and his grandmother's dowry must remain under French sovereignty.

The ceding of the Netherlands or Milan as a dowry was a second concession the Emperor made to the cause of peace; and not under pressure, after defeat, but at the very moment he had reached a position of supremacy.

The court considered it excessive. Granvelle, the chancellor, was in despair. The Spaniards showed their displeasure, saying the French king could hardly have gained more favourable terms had he penetrated with his army into the heart of Castile. Henry VIII said outright: 'If his Majesty were the prisoner of the French he could hardly have concluded a more damaging and disgraceful treaty.'

The imperial court consoled itself with the thought that 'between the cup and the lip' much can happen. Some said the Treaty of Crépy was a ruse of the Emperor's to enable him to withdraw from France unscathed.

Modern historians still puzzle over the terms of it. Maurenbrecher took the view that only the prospect of a German war made the Emperor accept such a surprising pact. Others hold that his compliance was due to his failing health, and that peace with France was such a necessity that he was ready for any concessions. With the winter coming on, and still no signs of the financial help promised by the German princes, the difficulty of keeping his army fed, deep in hostile country, determined him to seek agreement with Francis.

The question remains whether Charles V was really driven to conclude the Peace of Crépy by sheer necessity—that *necessitá* of Machiavelli's that created its own laws. Was he really seriously thinking of depriving his son of his inheritance of the Netherlands or Milan?

No doubt the Emperor was honestly ready to bestow one or the other on the Duke of Orleans. As Navagero wrote to Venice: 'The tokens of favour which the Emperor showers upon the duke are beyond all imagination. He desired that they should eat together. He has him with him continually and speaks to him in a familiar way and laughs with him more than is his custom. Once or twice he even paid him a visit in his room.'

'The prince is full of kindness and liveliness,' wrote Navagero, 'and he is as courteous as he is modest.'

Courtesy and modesty were the characteristics that the Emperor most prized in a young man, and his liking for Charles d'Orléans was without doubt genuine.

The duke accompanied him to Brussels where in October the peace was celebrated in great style. Queen Leonora, accompanied by Madame d'Étampes, also came to Brussels and both ladies took part in the festivities.

The Emperor treated the French king's mistress honourably and at one banquet placed her on his right-hand side, while his sister, the French queen, sat on his left.

It was said that Madame d'Étampes had played a considerable part in bringing about a peace treaty. It lay in her own interest to strengthen the position of the Duke of Orleans as against that of the Dauphin and his mistress Diane de Poitiers. Diane had expressed the opinion that the Dauphin contemplated overthrowing his father, and Madame d'Étampes, 'whose insolence he could no longer endure', was to be murdered. The lady no doubt felt she could be sure of a safe corner at the future court of young Duke Charles.

Such abundant and splendid meals caused the Emperor to suffer a bad attack of gout. When the Admiral of France visited him for the ratification of the Treaty, his arm was almost paralysed with gout. As he made the effort to sign the document with his stiff, painful hand, he said: 'You observe, Admiral, that I shall certainly keep all the points: for he who cannot wield a pen can wield a lance still less.'

'On that day,' wrote La Roca, 'the French who accompanied the Admiral had so great a desire to see the Emperor that they stood on tables and benches, some of which collapsed under them. When a chamberlain objected, they shouted, excitedly, "Let us see the bravest and most fearless prince that ever lived!"'

But in France the Dauphin protested against the Peace of Crépy which so strongly favoured his brother.

There was a secret clause in the treaty by which Francis I undertook to support Church reform 'whether by a Council or by other means', and when religious unity was only to be gained by way of violence, to turn the troops destined for the Turks against the heretics.

The Emperor had four months in which to choose between the Netherlands and Milan, and four to eight months to decide on Charles of Orleans' bride.

King Ferdinand declared himself opposed to any cession of the Netherlands. The Emperor agreed to marry Ferdinand's second daughter to Charles and to endow them with Milan. This displeased the Spaniards, who were distressed at the idea that if the Emperor considered ceding Milan now, he would have one day to face giving up Naples and Sicily.

The Emperor had bad attacks of gout during the winter and postponed an official decision.

We do not know whether the eighteenth chapter of Machiavelli's *Il Principe* was then in his mind: a chapter on 'loyalty and good faith', in which the following passage occurs: 'One has to be a fox to scent the snares and a lion to scare the wolves. Therefore a wise ruler cannot and dare not keep faith when it is to his disadvantage, and when the reasons that induced his original promise no longer exist. Were men all good, these would be no good precepts; but as they are base (*ma perchè sono triste*) and would not keep faith with you, you need not do so either. How many peace treaties, how many promises have been broken for a trifle, on account of the perfidy of princes, while the one who could best play the fox was the one who came best out of it all.'

Perhaps the moment had come to play the fox. But it is a waste of time to ponder whether Machiavelli's seductive counsels did or did not prevail over the probity of Charles V's conscience in those critical hours: fate intervened and took matters out of his hands. On 9th September 1545 the young duke Charles d'Orléans died of a fever. (He was hunting with his father and brother in the Fontainebleau forest and had drunk 'a glass of cold water' after the hunt, or so it was said. But some declared that the Dauphin's wife, Catherine de Medici, had poisoned the ambitious duke, and there were others who suspected an intrigue from the imperial side.)

However that may be, the event saved the Emperor from an awkward predicament. Milan remained part of the Empire. It was Francis who came to the conclusion that 'the reasons which induced his original promise no longer existed', for instead of providing armed assistance against the Turks he became involved in fresh negotiations with Schmalkaldic quarters. If such practices did not quite shake the foundations of the Peace of Crépy, they certainly made the settlement of the religious problem in Germany more difficult—and that was now the Emperor's main concern.

Charles V foresaw political trouble in his dealings with the Protestant princes, and on this account we may assume that he earnestly desired peace with France. He desired it so eagerly that he had been ready to make a very great sacrifice for it, one which on mature reflection he felt unable to carry out. If the man's spontaneous impulse and his considered views were at variance on this point, we are left with the plain fact of his desire for peace with France; for he needed it to attain to his highest aim and endeavour, religious unity in Germany.

BEFORE THE SCHMALKALDIC WAR (1545-46)

The peace with France allowed the Emperor to devote himself wholly to the German problem. Pope Paul III recommended stronger measures against the Protestants and promised all support. But Charles V felt that it came rather late and the moment was not the right one; the Council was at last about to sit, and stern action against the Protestants should be avoided just then if their participation was to be secured. The voluntary co-operation of the Protestants was a prerequisite if conclusions of general validity and bearing were to be reached. And for the same reasons that Erasmus refused the Cardinal's hat which Pope Paul III offered him in 1535, Charles V now refused to enter the service of papal politics; he wanted to make one more attempt to reach understanding in an amicable spirit.

But it was too much to hope for in 1545. The situation was rife with stresses and strains.

In the middle of May the Emperor came to Worms, still in a poor state of health. He wore his arm in a sling of black silk, but his aches and pains did not stop him from immediately getting into contact with the Protestant civil authorities. It was a matter of obtaining Protestant assent to the conclusions to be reached at Trent, for without it there was no hope of re-establishing a unity embracing all who held the Christian creed.

But in Protestant Worms the prevailing opinion was that 'the time had come to overthrow the man of sin, the Antichrist, the Pope, who had set himself in the temple of God; his crafty grasp must be broken and that of his following, too'.

Public opinion was in a state of insurrection against all that was Catholic on account of Luther's latest piece of invective, 'The Papacy founded by the Devil'. It bristled with vulgar calumnies and accusations. In challenging terms, Luther called upon the Protestants 'with all available weapons to attack Pope, cardinals and the whole ulcer of the Roman Sodom and to wash their hands in their blood'.

The Emperor was indignant and dubbed it 'a raging piece of defamation'. But there was no point in trying to stem a rising tide of hostility by prohibitions. The damage was done and the Protestants simply adopted Luther's tone.

John Sleidan, the chronicler of the Schmalkaldic union, delivered two litigious speeches before the assembled authorities, demanding concrete action against Rome. The Pope was the Antichrist who was ruining Germany; the Emperor was the Pope's vassal and he should 'liberate himself from the Pope's tyranny and mastery'.

Faced with such intransigence, the Emperor kept his distress to himself. He betrayed no loss of self-control, even when he heard that Lutheran supporters had broken into a Catholic church, intent on disturbing the

Mass, and that a preacher had preached against the Pope from the pulpit. He knew that these fighting spirits were merely the tools of certain powerful men who pulled the strings behind the scenes. It was with those men that he had to deal.

For all the tense atmosphere, the Emperor kept firmly to his resolution to pave the way for the religious and political unity of Germany. The Council of Trent was to establish religious unity; he himself desired to bring about political unity.

At the end of March 1546 he had a talk with the Landgrave of Hesse to induce him to send a delegation to the Council.

The Landgrave called the Pope 'the wicked usurper' and said that he had no hope of the Council doing anything; he was now engaged on reforming his land himself. As he praised the reformation that 'Cologne made with godly zeal', the Emperor interrupted him: 'How was the good lord to go reforming—he knew no Latin, he had not done more than three Masses in his life . . . and did not know the Confiteor.' 'Reforming,' the Emperor remarked, 'does not mean accepting a new faith.'

Those who call Charles V 'a disaster for Germany' and regard him as the originator of the Schmalkaldic War should ponder over the Emperor's plans for the unity of the realm. He discussed them with his brother and the South German authorities in that same year, and they witness to the fact that he wanted to avoid an imposed solution and hoped for the voluntary accession of the Protestant princes to his conception of the realm.

This was a federation of all German territories, regardless of religious differences, under imperial rule. A government subvention would make the Emperor financially independent. The imperial crown which the House of Habsburg wore with honour, was to be hereditary. A standing army was to be raised to assure the safety of the realm (for like Machiavelli Charles V considered that mercenaries, fighting only for their pay, made bad soldiers). To finance the project the Emperor planned to draw half the Papal and episcopal annual incomes from German ecclesiastical properties. The union was to be the foundation-stone for a 'good honest settlement of the religious question'.

Bavaria's negative attitude was an obstacle from the start. Duke William of Bavaria expressed the view that a connection with the Rhine Electors and others at a distance was not capable of realization, and the religious split prevented an alliance between Catholics and Protestants.

But Charles had come to the conclusion that the religious difference was due to political disunity. If political unity could be restored, and the power of the supreme state authority be enhanced, then religious unity would come about of its own accord.

However, Bavaria was strongly ecclesiastical and did not take to the Emperor's statesmanly manoeuvres. Moreover, the old Wittelbach envy of Habsburg hegemony certainly biased Duke William's estimation of the situation: he refused to comply, adding 'that the two Houses of Austria and Bavaria should not let one another down', meaning that they should remain equal. Like the Elector of Saxony, the Duke of Bavaria could not bring himself to admit the hegemony of the House of Habsburg.

According to Maurenbrecher, imperial statesmanship dealt with the German Protestant problem as with any other form of power-politics, and indeed Charles V saw more and more distinctly that the Reformation question in Germany had become a political one. Henceforth his endeavours were concentrated on keeping the *evangelium* and the princes' political aspirations apart.

'With no army and only a small number of attendants' the Emperor went on to Regensburg in April, having invited the Protestant civic authorities and Protestant theologians to meet him there 'to achieve a true Christian agreement and reformation'.

But a bloody crime startled all concerned into awareness that it was already too late, a fresh wave of intolerance had broken out. A certain Spaniard, Juan Diaz, a theologian, had become a Protestant in Germany, and at the beginning of the discussions his brother Alonso, a lawyer, had him murdered by his servants, on the grounds that 'he would rather see him dead than a heretic'.

The Erasmian age was over.

Luther had died on 18th February 1546. But the Protestant princes still used his doctrine as a pretext for asserting their own authority.

Charles V was gradually coming to the conclusion that 'the great pride and obstinacy' of the protesting princes would have to be countered with the naked sword. His present intention was to perform in Germany what he had succeeded in doing in Spain in 1522: eliminate the mediaeval feudal tendencies that threatened the unity of the realm and were prejudicial to the Emperor's authority. The old conflict between the sovereign and the estates should now be resolved in favour of the sovereign.

Meanwhile the Council of Trent was beginning to draw up resolutions that were to be valid for all Christendom. In the spring of 1546 the Schmalkaldic League assembled in Frankfurt to protest against the Council's forthcoming decisions, declaring that they would oppose them by force of arms. The rebels elected the Landgrave Philip of Hesse and the Elector of Saxony to be their leaders.

This declaration of hostility determined the Pope to enter into an alliance with the Emperor early in June and promise him military support.

On 20th June the Emperor proscribed the two leaders as 'vassals guilty of perjury and neglect of duty'. He wrote to his sister Maria: 'You know I wanted to avoid using force as far as possible, and did all I could to bring the Lutherans and other erring folk to a pacification. But now I see there is no other means but to stand up to these mistaken people with armed force; and I have made up my mind to declare war on the Elector of Saxony and the Landgrave of Hesse, as disturbers of the common peace and of justice, contemptuous of the authority of the Holy Empire.'

That was the end of peaceable plans for the union of the realm. But the Emperor never abandoned them; he hoped that victory over the rebels would establish him incontestably as sovereign of the German people, and place him in a strong position to deal with the religious as well as the political situation.

So when he stated in his letter to his sister that his forthcoming conflict with the rebel princes was 'for religion's sake', it was indeed true.

Henceforth he made no secret of the fact that he intended to take proceedings against any of the princes who, under cover of Lutheran doctrine, sought to undermine imperial prestige and obstruct religious unity. The proof that till then he had hoped for a peaceful settlement lay in the fact that he was completely unprepared for war: he was in Protestant Regensburg with no cover or protection. The Emperor's capacity for remaining serene under trying circumstances was once more evident. Disquieting sounds certainly reached his ear, but meanwhile he was celebrating the marriage of two of his nieces. In a leisurely mood he waited for his troops to come up, making their way as best they could through Protestant lands. And to those weeks belongs his love-affair with Barbara Blomberg, mother of the future Don Juan de Austria. 'The Emperor and his Papists are merry,' wrote a Schmalkaldic observer in Regensburg, 'banqueting and dancing as though there were no troubles in sight.' The supporting troops from the Papal States arrived, and so did Spanish and German mercenaries. Maurice of Saxony placed himself in the service of the Emperor, who acknowledged him as Elector (and soon after he received homage as such in the lands of his notorious cousin).

The Landgrave of Hesse raised an army of fifty thousand men and opened hostilities. The Schmalkaldic side accompanied its offensive with a shower of derogatory pamphlets and cartoons, depicting the Emperor as 'hangman and executioner of Antichrist, the devil's bailiff in Rome'. Circular letters described him as 'the Pope's journeyman at the head of a lot of people who knew nothing of Christian doctrine and thirsted for German blood'. One of these circulars said 'the tyranny of the Spanish Inquisition was nothing compared to what would be done in Germany if it put itself at the mercy of the Papists; and the tyranny of the Spaniards would know no end. Indeed it was less hurtful to lie a captive of the Turks, who leave people in freedom as regards their religion and faith, whereas those tyrannical tyrants ruled right into men's consciences and likened themselves to God.'

Minimizing the Turkish peril was a line taken by French subversive activities; for although Francis I was 'already quite feeble and near his death', he continued to back Protestants and Turks alike against the Emperor. At the beginning of 1547 he wrote to his ambassador at the court of the Elector of Saxony to do all in his power to make the Elector go on fighting. This was his last express wish, for he died on 31st March.

All through the Schmalkaldic War, Charles V never lost sight of his ultimate aim, which was the unity of all Germans in the old religion, till this eventually brought him into conflict with what had been his most cherished project—a general Council.

The Council of Trent turned down Luther's justification doctrine early in January 1547, and defined Christian justification as a man's inner transformation and renewal by means of grace and the co-operation of his free will.

Although it was essential to have a definition of the objective nature of free will and the efficacy of good deeds, in terms comprehensible to all, the Emperor begged the Pope to delay publishing the Tridentine conclusions, in order to give him time first to break down the political resistance in Germany before starting on clearing up the religious question. He wrote in the same strain to his brother Ferdinand: he was anxious that the religious settlement should be left till after he had re-established his authority throughout the realm.

The Pope was none too pleased with the Emperor's interference in ecclesiastical matters, and his victories on the Danube made him fearful of an increase of imperial power, entailing a threat to Farnese power in Italy; and in January 1547 he terminated his alliance with the Emperor and recalled his troops from the imperial army.

CHARLES V IN AN ARMCHAIR
Titian, *Munich Art Gallery*

MAXIMILIAN II
Antonio Moro, *The Prado, Madrid*

'It was from the beginning His Holiness' intention to involve us in this undertaking and then to abandon us in it,' said the Emperor, in some anger. The fact that the Pope was leaving him in the lurch although the campaign was far from being successfully concluded, caused him to utter some very strong words, saying, 'he would in future honour St Peter only and not St Paul; he hoped to bring the war with the Protestants to a satisfactory conclusion even if the Pope disapproved, for all that he had gout in one arm and blood-letting in the other'.

When the Pope heard how angry the Emperor was, he had the Council transferred to Bologna as a punishment, though the pretext was an outbreak of plague in Trent.

The Emperor then continued fighting for his conception of Empire—a prerequisite, he believed, for the reinstating of religious unity.

MÜHLBERG (1547)

All through the summer of 1546, during the months of the Danubian campaign, the Emperor grew and grew in stature till he attained to heroic proportions. He was by nature highly strung, his fearlessness was a product of his dauntless spirit.

'When he was being armed, it was observed that he trembled all over. But when he was ready he was calm, and so full of mettle that it looked as though he were flaunting the fact that no Emperor had yet been shot down.'

He was on the march with his troops for weeks on end, spending the night under canvas, on horseback all day long in spite of his pangs of gout. 'Field-life suits this prince particularly well,' wrote a Venetian envoy, 'he is at all times cheerful and animated' (*e in quel tempo tutto allegro, tutto vivo*). As he advanced, the rebel villages and towns yielded and the people ran to meet him, calling him 'Father'—'for' as La Roca reported, 'only the great were against the Emperor, among the people he was *amadissimo*, much loved'.

In spite of the 'most appalling agitation' on the part of the Protestants, the population of South Germany remained true to the Emperor; slumbering in the depths of simple people's minds lay an old yearning for the Emperor of the World, asleep in the mountains, who was to return, bringing justice and peace. Was this he, at last, ready to protect the poor and the weak from misery and oppression? 'Wherever the Emperor goes, all give in to him,' wrote the humanist J. U. Zasius. 'Never has such an advance been seen.'

Like Emperor Maximilian, Charles called his soldiers his sons. 'He was friendly and unaffected with his men and so close to them in battle that they joyfully died for him at all times.'

At Ingolstadt the Emperor and his troops met the artillery fire of the Schmalkaldic side. Under a shower of bullets he rode to each group in turn to encourage the men. (In the army it was believed that a word of the Emperor's was a protection against enemy gunfire.) To the Landgrave's challenge to surrender, the Emperor gave answer, 'he would remain in Germany, dead or alive'.

King Ferdinand wrote that he ought not to expose his imperial person to such mortal danger. Charles retorted: 'It was not the moment to set a bad example.'

There is a soldiers' song of this period that was sung by his troops:

> *Der Kaiser ist ein ehrlich Mann,*
> *allzeit ist er der vorderst dran*
> *zu Ross und auch zu fussen;*
> *seint wohlgemut, ihr Landsknecht gut,*
> *da sprach der edle Kaiser gut:*
> *wir wölln uns nit ergeben.*

The Emperor is an honest man,—always to the forefront,—on horseback and on foot;—Be of good cheer, good soldiers all,—the noble Emperor spoke right well:—we never shall give in.

In spite of heavy fire the imperial losses were slight, 'so that many believed in a miracle'.

When the cannonade started, the Emperor had his cavalry dismount and take cover, a measure that had never been adopted before. The first trenches were dug in that campaign. The Emperor noted in his Memoirs: 'Those who were in the trenches were absolutely safe.'

The encounter ended indecisively. The weather broke, and dysentery spread among the troops. Winter came early, with heavy frosts, and the southern troops, particularly the Italians, suffered from the cold spell. Scenes occurred like those described by Tolstoy in *War and Peace*: soldiers sitting motionless round a burnt-out fire, all dead, frozen to death in the snow.

The Emperor found winter quarters for his troops in the southern

German cities that had surrendered to him; he himself took quarters in Ulm.

Here he accepted the surrender of further cities: Strasbourg submitted; Anton Fugger came to Ulm in order to obtain favourable conditions for Protestant Augsburg. Duke Ulrich of Württemberg came to Ulm in person to plead pardon for his rebellion. In Württemberg the peasants put white cloths with red Burgundian crosses in their windows.

By March 1547 the Emperor was master of all southern Germany. He now reassembled his army and advanced upon Saxony, where the Schmalkaldic troops had withdrawn.

In the Emperor's Memoirs we read: 'Having reached Nördlingen, the Emperor felt so unwell after the hardships he had endured that he had to take a few days' rest. But as a longer delay might prove fateful, he set out in a litter and got as far as Nürnberg, which received him in exactly the same manner as those who had never been members of the League nor hostile. He had a relapse and was forced to remain there longer than he had planned. Nevertheless he made a great effort and got as far as Eger, carried in a litter.'

There he met his brother Ferdinand and Maurice of Saxony, with their troops. They drew on together towards Meisen, but did not encounter the Schmalkaldic army that had camped there the previous night. The Emperor was eager for a decisive battle with the Electors and set off in their pursuit.

On 23rd April he reached the Elbe. He concluded that the enemy were encamped on the opposite bank. He gave his troops a few hours' rest, but soon after midnight had the reveille sounded. The Elector of Saxony's troops were superior to the imperial ones in number and their position was more favourable. 'But what is an advantage of number and position when courage is less,' wrote La Roca. The Spanish soldiers threw themselves into the water and swam across bearing their swords between their teeth; they seized barges to serve as bridges, and in no time the two banks were connected; the main body of the imperial army crossed the river at a shallow reach.

Shouting 'Santiago', 'España', and 'St George for the Empire', Spaniards and Germans hurled themselves into the fight, and by evening the battle was won. Elector John Frederick of Saxony and Duke Ernest of Brunswick were taken prisoner and brought before the Emperor.

'Most gracious Emperor,' the Elector began, trying to make a deep bow (he was the stoutest man in Europe), 'I am your prisoner——': the

Emperor cut him short: 'Am I now your gracious Lord and Emperor?
Formerly you called me otherwise,' for the Emperor knew that he always
spoke of him as 'Charles of Ghent' or 'Charles of Spain', whereas that
was precisely what he was not: not Charles of Ghent or Charles of Spain or
Charles of Austria, but the Roman Emperor. And it was as Emperor that he
constituted a focus of attraction with a radius far beyond national bounds.

The high treason of the Elector merited the death penalty. But as Don
Luis of Avila observed after fighting in the Mühlberg campaign at the
Emperor's side, 'the Emperor began to incline more and more to mercy,
out of pity for such a great prince in such great misfortune, and he decided
not to carry out his original resolution to have him beheaded'.

When the Landgrave of Hesse, who was fighting the imperial troops in
the neighbourhood of Halle, heard of the Elector's defeat he surrendered
unconditionally. He, too, was taken prisoner.

Pale and sick with his gout, the Emperor replied to the congratulations
of his followers with a 'God has conquered'.

Now his opponents were in his hands. The question remained, whether
the Empire was on that account safe from treason and rebellion. And
whether the Old Faith was now out of danger.

The evening shadows that spread over the Mühlberg woods fell darkly
across the Emperor's path.

INTERIM (1548)

Although North Germany remained unsubdued, the Emperor stopped
the war in order to turn his attention to a peaceful settlement of the religious problem.

'In war there is only one result, the final result,' said Clausewitz. It is
stated in terms of victory and defeat. But Charles V was not seeking to
subjugate but rather to reconcile. His counsellors recalled to his mind the
example of the Caesars, warning him that a victory once gained must be
followed up till the enemy is completely subdued, but the Emperor
merely replied: 'The Ancients had only one aim: Glory. We Christians
have two aims: Glory, and the salvation of souls.'

And the salvation of souls was not to be achieved by violent measures.
Men's consciences must be won over and convinced by clearly-formulated
resolutions. That was what the Emperor awaited from the Council of
Trent.

But now the Council sat in Bologna. In January 1548 the Emperor had his envoy in Rome protest at the 'so-called Council of Bologna'. Pope Paul III was, however, not prepared to lend an ear to the Emperor's protest at that moment. His son, Pierluigi Farnese, Duke of Parma and Piacenza, and a friend of the French, had been murdered on 10th September 1547 by Gonzagan and Dorian guards, that is, families hostile to the French. Thereupon the Emperor had Piacenza dealt with according to imperial law, in retaliation for the Pope's disaffection during the Schmalkaldic War (Contarini described Charles V as 'revengeful'). The Pope then retorted by occupying Parma in the name of the Church. Ottavio Farnese, married since 1538 to Charles V's natural daughter, Margaret of Parma, essayed to regain Parma for the Emperor. Henry II of France came to the Pope's assistance and relations between Pope and Emperor were so strained that Charles V could hardly hope to obtain the Pope's consent to the transfer of the Council from Bologna to Trent. Yet only if it sat in Trent were the Protestants willing to be represented, and the participation of the Protestants was for the Emperor an essential condition if the two sides were to come to terms. There was nothing for it but to take independent action; the result was the compromise settlement of the Diet of Augsburg in 1548: the *Interim*.

It should be regarded as a highwater-mark in Charles V's career. It is the sum of his endeavours, the most hopeful plan that existed for closing the gap between old and new forms of belief and bringing German Christendom back into the *ecclesia una, sancta, catholica et apostolica*. But it had to be done in a Church renewed, one that had rid herself of all temporal dross and satisfied justifiable Evangelical claims. The Emperor wrote in his Memoirs: 'In spite of all, the Diet came to proper decisions in the direction of reunion, and so far as religion was concerned a *modus vivendi (um modo de viver)* was adopted that was to be valid till the Council sat in Trent again. So that everything that could be decided was decided at that time.'

The resolutions of the *Interim* represented in Charles V's mind the outside limit of what could be done at that moment.

The Augsburg Diet was solemnly opened on 1st September 1547. All seven Electors had appeared and nearly all the ecclesiastical and secular princes. The Venetian envoy mentioned the 'immensely great awe' with which they approached the Emperor. In his opening speech he spoke of the 'gracious fatherly affection he had shown for the Holy Empire of German nations from the beginning', and he reminded those present of 'the necessity for peaceful Christian measures to get rid of the most disadvantageous, harmful and distressing division and rift of the German people, and restoring concord and agreement'. The victorious Emperor spoke as though neither war nor victory had occurred. Those present imagined how the Schmalkaldic side would have spoken and acted had the fortune of war favoured them. Charles did not demand the compulsory return of the new sects to the old Church; he required them to send a representation to the Council of Trent, and the Council would put through all the reforms desired. The despondent princes agreed to accept the decisions of the Council. A token of their defeat, the captive Elector John Frederick of Saxony was in the Emperor's retinue in Augsburg, with all his corpulence like a bear in chains.

'By Jove, that was a fierce Diet,' wrote Sastrow in his memoirs. The imperial army was encamped in the flat country round Augsburg—German and Spanish mercenaries and the armed following of the German princes. The traffic in the streets of Augsburg was tremendous. The Emperor lived in the Fuggers' house, of which the lofty arches of the inner courtyard are still standing. The Diet was busy dancing. Sastrow tells of the gay life of the princes and of King Ferdinand's jolly court: 'Ferdinand danced with his guests, leaping prodigiously, and buffoons capped one another's remarks most amusingly. But his brother was another matter, he gave no banquets, and hardly had he come home from Church, he dismissed his relatives and sat down to table alone.'

The Emperor took the Diet extremely seriously. Evening was approaching. A severe attack of gout reminded him of the transitoriness of life. He could not wait till the Council had reached its conclusions, he felt his job must be done at once.

The insecurity of temporal affairs had brought it home to him that plans can provide only short-term respite, and there is no point in seeking solutions to last a millennium: what matters is to find the right answer to the challenge of the moment. The concessions he wanted to make the Protestants were concessions to the present situation, concessions to German unrest, which was a fact that had to be faced. His orthodoxy was rooted, as ever, in what was eternal and enduring, but he no longer saw Church discipline as something rigid and set, nor religion merely as law, but as the Way, the Truth and the Life. Surging life, if it was frustrated and hemmed in, would burst asunder the whole structure of the Church.

'But let them marry,' he urged the Pope, in support of the Protestants' request for married priests, 'grant them Communion in both species.' On

236

those two points the Pope was not wholly unrelenting; but on the question of justification (whether by faith alone, or by faith and good deeds), where the Emperor sought some kind of conciliatory formula, the Pope forbade any compromise, for it was a fundamental element of Church doctrine.

Charles V's attitude in Augsburg foreshadowed St Francis de Sales' remark that 'God is not mean'. In his desire for unity he overlooked the strict meaning of the word 'dogma'. It was at the moment urgent to find common ground, and the twenty-six articles formulated by a commission of Catholic and Protestant theologians set up by the Emperor were given a terminology such that each could find what he wanted in them. On the strength of this draft, an agreement was reached in February 1548, which was intended to hold good for the time being (*ad interim*), that is, till the Council reached its conclusion.

This 'declaration of His Imperial Roman Majesty on how things are to be as regards religion in the Holy Empire until the decision of the General Council,' formulated the Christian Faith in the Catholic sense, but used Protestant modes of expression: the Old Faith was to be renewed by using the language of the day, as though the Reformation was merely an attempt to put divine Truth out of Latin into sounds and syllables comprehensible to all. The seven Sacraments were endorsed 'on Scriptural authority', with chapter and verse from the Bible. On the justification question, stress was laid on the merits of Christ's Passion, by means of which man obtains forgiveness of his sins and renewal in the Holy Spirit, 'and thus an unjust man becomes just'; but 'merciful God does not deal with man as with a dead weight, but draws him with His will when he reaches the years for it'. Good deeds were recognized as necessary, 'as long as they issue from love', but not in the sense that heaven could be gained by good deeds alone. 'The altars, vestments, sacred vessels, banners, crosses, candles, statues and paintings' were to remain; 'but they were to be simple reminders, and no godly honour was to be done them. And no superstitious crowding to statues was to be allowed.' 'Likewise the *Horas canonicas* and the godly singing of Psalms, which was commended by the Apostles themselves, were in no wise to be got rid of, but were praiseworthily to be retained in the Church.'

The main Church Feast-days were to be observed according to ancient custom, and all seemly processions, too. The saints were still to be held in memory and also the dead, 'for it would be a horror', ran the imperial declaration, 'not to remember the dead in the Church, as though their souls had gone with their bodies'.

237

It was very ancient, primitive religious feeling that found utterance in the following clause: 'The blessing of objects is not to be despised, when they are, by means of blessing and prayer, prepared for the use of men; but only in so far as the effects are attributed not to the creature of itself but to divine power.'

The spiritual power of the Church and the primacy of the Papacy were endorsed. Holy Mass was, of course, accepted; not only as a renewal of Christ's sacrifice of Himself, but also as memorial or thanksgiving. And finally, the Protestants were conceded the chalice for lay Communions, as well as married priests. The thorny question of the restitution of Church property, which had been the stumbling-block at all other discussions, was passed over.

The Emperor's reforming intentions come out clearly in a corollary clause: 'In what concerns the discipline of priests and people, it is of urgency to get rid of the scandals which have largely caused the disorders of our day, on account of which His Imperial Majesty has made a useful reformation of the Church, which no one favourable to our holy religion and common peace will look down upon but will rather help to the utmost to forward.'

Charles V was very pleased about the *interim* settlement. And the tenacity with which he held to the agreement reached showed that he found this temporary solution highly satisfactory. He was no theologian and remained completely unaware of the fundamental weakness of the *Interim*, blurring over all doctrinal differences as it did. He believed he had brought about the longed-for conversion of the unrepentant by means of a formal recognition of the Catholic form of worship—by persuading them to observe Church ceremonies and fasting rules, and to reintroduce the Feasts of Our Lady and of the Saints, and above all his beloved Corpus Christi Feast. If the old customs were now secure, and the old prayers and petitions—surely there was nothing more to worry about?

The *Interim* was a makeshift. Charles V's methods of conversion anticipated a word of Pascal's addressed to a later doubting generation: 'Act as though you believed, taking holy water . . .'

The Emperor had confidence in the power of habit. By dint of practice the old religious rites would come alive again. Outward observance was conducive to inner concordance.

The *Interim* had a platonic kernel, too, for 'beautiful form is the reflection of truth', said Plato.

The Church's liturgy is the splendid adornment of the Faith, bestowing invisible blessing through visible things, schooling men's minds to contemplation. Its symbolism speaks directly to the mind, as immediately as colour and music. Statues and pictures are gateways into the infinite, they lead through appearances to deep wells of life; they are images that point to the Origin and Author of all things. In the forms of the Catholic Faith there is platonic wisdom inferring the identity of Beauty and Goodness. The outward form is beautiful to the degree that it participates in supreme Beauty, and it is good because it is conducive to Goodness: Beauty lends wings to the spirit, that they may carry it to its true home.

Pictures and images are symbols of ultimate reality; as the *Interim* put it, 'no divine worship was to be given to those objects', for they are but traces and shades of divinity; 'they should serve as reminders only'—reminders of transcendental things.

The Catholic Faith in its liturgical form meant a tremendous lot to the Emperor. Prayer, and worship of the Blessed Sacrament, were all-important, and a reasoned understanding of the Scriptures was in a different category. It was the reverent silence at the moment of Consecration, and the people's humble responses at Benediction, that counted. Thus defiant souls were to be won back by the sheer beauty of the old form of worship, and it was to bring them slowly but surely into communion with the rest, a communion where love and concord would prevail.

The Emperor was very proud of his *Interim*. All the more bitter was his disappointment when it pleased neither Catholics nor Protestants. With Duke William of Bavaria at their head, the Catholic authorities resented the request for toleration of innovations in their lands. And among the Protestants, only the Electors of Brandenburg and the Palatinate gave it their support. Maurice of Saxony prevaricated, and the captive Elector John Frederick declared against such a 're-erection of the Papacy'. But Charles V was determined to put it through. He stormed the Pope with appeals for support, and Pope Paul III showed himself not disinclined. Whereupon the Emperor decided that the Catholic strictures were not justified; it annoyed him not to have the backing of his own side, and in a sharply worded address to the ecclesiastical princes, he made it clear what he thought of people who turned down the *Interim* solution.

'My intention always was to bring back our opponents to accept our true religion,' he said, explaining that the innovations were not binding on the Catholic authorities. 'What has occurred provokes us to say, like Christ, You are pure, but not all of you,' and he went on to hint that the Bavarian chancellor, Leonard von Eck, was undermining the cause of unity for the sake of a few pieces of silver: 'seeing the trend of things towards agreement, he seizes the opportunity to raise obstacles, for his purpose is to promote discord, and his life and well-being depend on it.' 'Now in your reply you put a construction on my words that I never intended, saying I favour the Lutherans. I cannot love them, for they believe neither God nor Luther nor the saints. You should consider yourselves and your own interests, and accept this good means to concord and public peace for your own sakes. It was on your behalf that I laboured; bear in mind the support you received, and see how you can make the best of this victory God granted me. Therefore be of one mind, and I will help you, as I have hitherto done, and persevere with you in the cause of our holy religion.'

He went on to speak of the reform of the German clergy, for the corruption of the priests was a main complaint of the Protestants. He laid it down that the Ecclesiastical Council of Cathedral Chapters was to promote proper behaviour among the clergy, and that provision should be made for diocesan visitations, the foundation of Chairs of Theology for the training of suitable candidates for the priesthood, and the building of hospitals and hospices.

The archbishops, bishops and prelates present admitted the moderation and equity of the Emperor's reform proposals, and declared themselves to be essentially in agreement.

But in Rome such summary dealing with ecclesiastical matters was not approved of. The Curia complained that the Emperor went beyond his mandate as a layman. Charles was so sure he was doing the right thing, he had not even sought the Pope's consent beforehand. Actually there was nothing revolutionary about his proposals: they were strictly in accord with that combined secular and spiritual authority on which the Spanish monarchy was based, and the *Imperium* too. Direct intervention in ecclesiastical affairs was always a prerogative of the Catholic Sovereigns of Spain.

Pope Paul III still hesitated to declare for the *Interim* and the reform plan; but when Charles entreated him not to jeopardize his efforts to restore unity, in August 1549 he finally authorized his bishops in Germany to accept the *Interim*.

Meanwhile the Emperor had taken pains to obtain the assent of the Protestants. But the very fact that he negotiated instead of dictating made the princes presumptuous once more. Of those who had previously rejected the *Interim*, only the Landgrave of Hesse consented to change his mind; hoping no doubt to purchase his liberty at the price, he wrote to the Emperor that he accepted the *Interim* for his Land. Maurice of Saxony still refused to do so. The Emperor, thinking Melanchthon was at the back of the Electors' reluctance, grew extremely angry with him and felt instinctively how half-hearted his support was.

To appease the Emperor, Maurice of Saxony persuaded Melanchthon to attend further discussions to decide how the reintroduction of Catholic ceremonies was to be made acceptable to the new groups. One could not simply turn down the Emperor's decrees out of hand.

Melanchthon termed Catholic Church customs, such as Latin anthems, candles, pictures of saints, adorned altars, fasts and feast-days—*adiaphora*, which is Greek for 'intermediate things', things neither good nor bad in themselves, but being 'indifferent', they were not opposed to Holy Scripture.

But the Lutherans were well aware that something intrinsic clung to the visible forms of the Faith, and for decades past they had banned Catholic rites from their churches as 'outward show-ceremonies'. They could already claim the right of established custom: 'The people have been accustomed to the present church order for many years now.' Young Count Palatine of Zweibrücken could honestly say, 'he knew no other religion than the one he was born and bred in'—meaning the Lutheran one. The cities most vehemently opposed the reintroduction of Anointing at death, and the Feast of Corpus Christi. The priests' white surplices, now becoming customary again, were soon taken for a symbol of 'papistical idolatry' and compulsion in conscience matters.

While the Catholic authorities remained dissatisfied with the reforms decreed by the Emperor, the great mass of the Protestants were definitely anti-*Interim*. There was an epidemic of derisive verses, lampoons and cartoons, satirical woodcuts, and even comedies, throughout the realm. Verses such as the following passed from mouth to mouth:

> *Hütet Euch vor dem Interim,*
> *Es hat den Schalk hinter ihm.*

'Beware of the Interim, there's mischief afoot.' It was dubbed an offspring of hell:

> *Mir, Lucifer, ist ein Kind geboren,*
> *Von meiner Frauen Päpstin auserkoren,*
> *Zu dieser Geburt sind mir zur Hilfe kommen*
> *Meine geistlichen Diener, die treuen und frommen*
> *Kardinäle, Erzbischöfe, Bischöfe, des Papst Offizianten . . .*

'I, Lucifer, have had a child—born to me of my papist wife.—And at the birth there came—to our help my clerical servants, the loyal, pious—cardinals, archbishops, bishops, the Pope's dispensers . . .'

And some of the attacks on the 'enemies of the evangelii' were intended for the Emperor, too:

> Herr Gott in Himmel steh uns bei
> Und straf des Kaisers Tyrannei
> Und steuer seinem Toben!
> Er macht sich Gott im Himmel gleich
> Und stiess ihn gern aus seinem Reich,
> Das sieh, o Gott, dort oben!

'Lord God in heaven, be our aid—and quell the Emperor's tyranny—and control his raging!—He thinks he is as good as God—and would fain drive Him from his realm.—O God on high, observe it!'

It was the spirit of Ulrich Hutten, now many years dead, that inspired such invective. He figures in a *Dialogus etlicher Personen vom Interim* as a fierce opponent of the *Interim*, intended as it was 'to reinstate the wickedness of the devil, abomination, idolatry and blasphemy'.

And Melanchthon, the vacillator, though he had recently admitted in a letter that '. . . already as a boy I used to watch the ceremonies with special pleasure', now began to inveigh against the *Interim*. He called the Emperor's decree 'a patched-up thing, with good and bad mixed up together', and in a pamphlet, 'Thoughts on the Interim by the reverend highly-learned Master Philipp Melanchthon,' he disapproved of the reintroduction of the Sacraments, and especially Confession, for it was not good 'to burden consciences with this dangerous and unnecessary load'. '*In summa*,' he said, 'there are so many abominable abuses in papal custom that we are terrified to speak of them.' He also denounced Masses for the dead, which the Emperor had so warmly commended, and came to the conclusion 'that the Interim in many of its articles is contrary to right doctrine'.

Other Protestant pamphlets 'against the Interim and the papistical Mass' circulated the phrase: 'All church services founded on human worship without God's word, or in opposition to it, are idolatrous.' The Mass was 'mere human trumpery and a pet sin of the devil's.' A new matter-of-fact spirit was chilling men's minds and blinding their hearts to the symbolic power of old Church customs. In Protestant Germany this rejection of the external forms of the Faith was to bring about a rapid deterioration of all the visual arts.

'Nothing is so tender nor so easily clouded as reverence for God in the hearts of men,' Melanchthon once wrote in Augsburg. The traditional manner of venerating God, the old Church forms so intimately connected with sowing and harvest-time and the seasons of the year, was an inward bond that Luther loosened and Charles V would gladly have restored. But now the Protestant theologians tore it asunder for good and all.

For the whole agitation against the *Interim* came from the theologians who were in the service of the Protestant princes, and not from the people. Magdeburg, 'God's chancellery', issued a writ challenging all Christians to oppose the *Interim*.

The Emperor now proceeded to enforce the acceptance of his decree. Those Protestant princes who rejected the *Interim* were told 'that they would soon see a thousand Spaniards in their land'. In Ulm he had the preachers against the *Interim* put in chains and taken away. More than five hundred Protestant clergymen were relieved of their office. Constance was compelled to submit by force of arms. In Spires the Protestant preachers were driven out and all necessary measures taken for 'peace and justice in Germany'. In Augsburg, however, a riot occurred in St Ulrich's church, and in Ulm, Strasbourg, Nördlingen and many other places there were tumultuous demonstrations. Protestant resistance was concentrated in the north, in Magdeburg, which was strongly fortified. When the Emperor heard of the cities' hostility, he said: 'So much the greater their disgrace, and if they start rebelling again, it may well happen that the rods that lightly chastise them will turn into thwacking sticks.'

'Freedom of the Estates and of Evangelical doctrine were things of the past,' wrote Ranke, 'and the whole method of government that the Emperor now adopted developed the character of a hideous imposition of violence. . . . An all-penetrating will now made itself felt throughout Germany.'

Charles gave proof of an all-penetrating will and an extraordinary degree of energy because he whole-heartedly believed in the *Interim*. He was convinced that in the long run it could prove to be a bridge permitting a return to unanimity. He upheld the *Interim* because he felt that concord of minds could be realized only on a basis of common religious customs.

Thus in addition to being a religious settlement the *Interim* was a formula for common behaviour, in fact *um modo de viver*.

The Munich Portrait of Charles V

Titian's portrait in the *Haus der Kunst* in Munich was painted in 1548. The artist was then seventy years old. He came to Augsburg to paint the Emperor at his zenith of power. His chief work of that period was 'Charles V at the Battle of Mühlberg', and presumably he painted the seated portrait at the same time, with the Emperor dressed simply but regally in black, his only decoration the Order of the Golden Fleece about his neck, his feet resting on a red carpet. The picture must have been painted when the Emperor, in a moment of respite, visited the painter in his workshop to see how the equestrian portrait was getting on and recover a little from the exhausting proceedings of the Diet, among pictures and painters' paraphernalia. We see him as he would have sat there at his ease, a little weary, but composed, as though the cultivation of his spiritual life was not relaxed even when concentration on external events was demanded of him.

This portrait is complementary to the equestrian one, as though Titian felt an urge to express the paradoxical personality of his subject in two quite different studies. One is veiled in a legendary twilight, the other is matter-of-fact, and together they compose a synthesis of Charles V's character, for he was at once idealist and realist, a dreamer and a man of action, offspring of the Renaissance and of the Middle Ages.

In the Mühlberg picture he is dressed in armour with plumes in his helmet, but here his clothes are attractively modern and comfortable. There he was Don Quixote pursuing a forgotten dream, here he is the statesman who read Machiavelli for pleasure; there, he gazed into the distance fearlessly, with the gaze of a man whose integrity is absolute because his conviction is unconditional; here he gives you a searching, slightly apprehensive look, as a man does who knows he is vulnerable and needs to be on his guard all the time.

It is a picture that explains why many of his contemporaries found him unduly reserved, and in his eyes there lurks a trace of that dry, often biting humour of his.

Other remarks of contemporary observers cross one's mind: the Venetian envoys, Baduero and Mocenigo, said he was an erotic type, 'who in the opinion of his doctors and his entourage was much inclined to sensual indulgence'. According to them, the Emperor was fond of 'women of high state and low', *donne di grande ed anche di piccola conditione*.

But Eros played a very subsidiary part in Charles V's life. Melanchthon's view was nearer the mark, when he praised the exemplary married life of the Emperor. 'His private life is full of the most honourable examples of continence, self-control and moderation. Those strict standards that used to prevail in the home life of the German princes is now only to be found in the Emperor's own entourage'; and later, in an obituary notice, he wrote that the Emperor had been 'a retiring and moderate lord'.

The most delightful estimation of Charles V comes from Luther: 'We have a pious Emperor,' he said in his Table-Talk, 'he has a padlock to his heart. I reckon he does not say as much in a year as I in a day.' It was precisely in their religious piety that the two great opponents were alike.

Many contemporaries traced his paradoxical nature to the complex hereditary factors with which he was endowed: from his grandfather Ferdinand of Aragon he inherited his political sagacity, from Isabella the splendid scope of his plans, from his great-grandfather Charles the Bold he inherited his courage, and from Maximilian his love of art. His confessor Loaysa found 'indolence and a passion for glory' to be his main faults; in 1530 he wrote to him from Rome: 'May you succeed in overcoming good-living and time-wasting, your natural foes.'

Charles V was not one of those men who have to wrestle with their vital urges in order to master them: his will grew instinctively out of his devotion to his ruling idea.

And this emotionally coloured will-power of Charles is to be understood in the light of his pre-Reformation type of mind. For it was Luther who created the rift between nature and will-power, with his doctrine about the corruption of human nature and the incapacity of the will to control the appetites, a rift which struck right through German Protestant philosophy, till we find in Kant a fundamental opposition between inclination and will, supposing nature, being evil, not to be able to will the good with the emotions concurring.

Charles V's sense of duty was not the result of an inner conflict against his own nature, it was the fulfilment of his nature. When he was a young Emperor of twenty-five, Contarini said of him that *solo si diletta di negoziare e stare nelli suoi consigli* (his one delight was diplomacy and councils). His duty was his pleasure.

Charles V wanted most deeply to do what he conceived to be right: the weariness evident in the Munich portrait is due to the insufficiency of his physical constitution, which found the heavy demands his beloved duties made on him too much of a good thing. He forced himself not to lag behind his own ideal, and thus his portrait is a sort of allegory, showing true humanity as the fruit of spiritual endeavour.

DIVERGENT VIEWS ON THE SUCCESSION
(1548–51)

And now, within the circle of his own family, the Emperor fell into disagreement with his brother Ferdinand, that brother whom he had often called his other self, so compliant was he and so amenable to his wishes. For decades he had patiently played second fiddle, but now the separatist tendencies of the day came into the foreground. As recently as 1541, a Venetian named Giustiniani had lauded the unanimity of the brothers on the occasion of the Diet of Regensburg, saying: 'The Emperor is the heart and the King is the breath of life, breathing as the heart requires.'

But the question of the successor to the imperial title now gave rise to a difference of opinion. Since the proclamation of April 1521, when Charles transferred the hereditary Austrian lands to his brother, Ferdinand was patently heir to the Empire. But now the House of Habsburg had a Spanish as well as a German line, and who was to be Emperor after Ferdinand?

The Habsburg brothers were agreed on the desirability of making the imperial crown hereditary. Charles V knew from bitter experience what was involved in an imperial election: the crown was venal nowadays and cost ever-increasing concessions to the prince-electors who were continually engaged in restricting imperial power. In view of this it was essential to secure the imperial crown to the House of Habsburg. Charles V had his son Philip in mind as successor to Ferdinand, whereas Ferdinand, with the support of the German princes, wanted his own son Maximilian as his successor on the imperial throne.

The negotiations began during the Diet of Augsburg in 1548. It was not only the desire to further his own flesh and blood that made the Emperor insist on his plan; during the last years he had been carefully observing his nephew Maximilian as a prospective son-in-law. Maximilian had been with him since 1544, and was now enjoying the merry social life of Augsburg, so vividly described by Sastrow: '. . . young princes were to be seen lying on the floor in the homes of royal and noble ladies, for it is not the custom for them to sit on benches or chairs, but a rich carpet is spread out in the middle of the floor where you can comfortably sit or lie. And this is done not without hearty kissing and hugging.' Maximilian thoroughly enjoyed himself. In his levity and love of pleasure he took after his grandfather, Philip the Fair. And he was easily influenced, which might imperil his religious orthodoxy. The Emperor had not spent a life-time fighting for the Catholic Faith in order to have his work undone by a weakling. No, it was Philip, his dutiful son, who was the rightful heir to the imperial throne.

Charles V took various measures: he sent Maximilian to Spain to marry his daughter Maria, and Maria's good strict Catholic influence would keep him on the right path; during Philip's absence, Maximilian was to be Regent of Spain. Philip had set off for Flanders to be sworn in as heir to the Netherlands; and the Emperor was also planning to present him to the German princes as his candidate for the imperial throne.

In mid-August, Charles V left Augsburg and travelled through Ulm to Spires, where he embarked and went down the Rhine to Cologne and then on to Brussels, which he reached at the end of September. 'It was the ninth time that he made this journey and the eighth time that he came to the Netherlands; after meeting the Queen, his sister, in Louvain, he went to Brussels to see to his own affairs and to the affairs of state,' so we read among the last entries in Charles V's Memoirs.

On 1st April 1549 Philip arrived in Brussels. His father received him with great festivity. Triumphal arches were erected in the streets, and platforms on which allegorical scenes were acted; there were marchings and popular entertainments of all kinds. 'Philip, Hope of the Century,' ran the welcoming inscriptions, 'Philip, future Heir to the Globe'. Solemn Masses were sung in the old church of St Gudela. The Emperor set aside his thrifty Habsburgian habits and gave splendid feasts and banquets which recalled the magnificence of the old Burgundian court.

The celebrations and acts of homage continued throughout the provinces: in Louvain Philip was sworn in as Duke of Brabant, in Ghent as Count of Flanders.

Philip's recognition as heir of the Netherlands dashed Maximilian's hopes that Charles V would give him Flanders as a dowry for his daughter. But the Emperor elected to bestow Maria of Burgundy's inheritance on his first-born. (Yet had Maximilian been the one to be acclaimed in the Netherlands, many a future conflict might have been avoided.)

In the hours the Emperor dedicated daily to his son's political education, he drove it in to him that this key position in Europe must be retained at all cost. He called Flanders 'a stronghold of steel', 'a shield that enabled him to meet attacks from England, Germany and France far from the heart of the monarchy'. He advised Philip to work incessantly for peace, but never to give up his Flemish possessions. (Philip's later policy in Flanders was based on his father's counsel.) And he was to see that he kept the Duchy of Milan, 'the gate of Italy', 'that gem of my crown'.

The Emperor remained in Brussels till May 1550. Then he went by ship up the Rhine to Spires, and thence to Augsburg, where a new Diet was to regulate the succession question.

On his Rhine journey the Emperor began to write his Memoirs. It was a happy moment, he could settle down to it as a man who has done his duty and can now look back on his work in peace. His son Philip, with whom he was greatly pleased, would soon take over the government; the *Interim*, with which he felt satisfied, would bestow religious concord on the Empire, and the Emperor could start his Memoirs in the exalted state of mind of a Seventh Day of Creation.

He dictated them to his secretary van Male, in French, which was the language he knew best. Van Male, an ambitious humanist, persuaded him that it was necessary to have the manuscript translated into Latin, 'a language which relates it at once to Livy, Caesar, Suetonius and Tacitus'. Both the draft and the Latin translation are lost. A Portuguese translation forms the basis of the versions now current. The many transcriptions made of the original assuredly account for the detached style of the text, which is written in the third person; it contains a sober enumeration of journeys and campaigns. But that was like Charles V: his whole person was engaged.

In Augsburg he continued his notes. He worked with van Male for four hours a day. The chronicler Snouckaert reports that at that time the Emperor also worked with van Male at the improvement of a number of prayers and psalms that he had composed himself in hours of stress. He was an intensely religious man who sought to give expression to his feelings in his own individual way. But with no sign of a break with tradition—one of those prayers that has come down to us, the *Protestation de Emperador*, is a confession of his love for the Catholic Church.

The Emperor was once more staying with his friend Anton Fugger. Van Male wrote in a letter from Augsburg, '*Aestivamos in Hortis Fuggerici*': 'We are spending the summer in the Fugger gardens. . . . The Emperor tries to pass the time, captivated at any rate by the pleasantness of the spot, even though the general confusion is no guarantee of any real happiness.'

The cool shade of the gardens must certainly have been a relief after the strain of state business, for the negotiations over the imperial succession were heated. Blind with paternal pride, Charles V fought for his son Philip. And on Philip's behalf he took part in all the banquets and festivities and did all he could to make his son known to the German princes. However, they showed no great interest in this serious, reserved boy, considering him haughty and foreign. And Philip for his part was repelled by their noisy behaviour and heavy drinking. It was simply differences between the Spanish and the German character that came to light, but precisely those differences were now beginning to cut people off from one another, because the underlying, unifying current of the common Faith was no longer the determining factor, keeping the body of Europe together as one.

But in 1529, when, as a student at the Sorbonne, Ignatius of Loyola was attacked on account of his religious zeal, he could still retort, 'It is hateful to find fault with a Christian man at a Christian university because he follows Christ and would bring other men to Christ.' The accent is on the words, *un hombre cristiano en una universidad de cristianos*—a Christian at a Christian university. Whereas today we should say, 'A Spaniard at a French University', implying that here was a stranger among men with a different cast of mind—but at that time he was still 'a Christian among Christians'.

From now on, however, national idiosyncrasy would be stressed as though it were something fundamentally different in each case.

In September 1550 the French envoy wrote from Augsburg that 'the King of Bohemia (Ferdinand) cannot bear the supremacy of the Spaniards in Germany, and he finds support on all sides, for he is much liked throughout the land, whereas the Spanish prince is hated by all lands, his own too, barring the Spaniards'.

In spite of Ferdinand's and the princes' discouraging attitude, the Emperor stuck to his plan of assuring the succession to Philip: only the Spanish line of the House of Habsburg could perpetuate the idea of a Christian Roman Emperor, for it was only in Spain that the Catholic Faith lived on unbroken, and at that moment Spain alone actually possessed the power to make the idea of the universal Empire prevail.

As Ferdinand persisted in his opposition, Charles V said in pique, 'he would soon show Ferdinand which of the two was Emperor'. Ferdinand finally had to yield. On 9th March 1551 he signed a capitulation in which he fell in with the Emperor's wishes: he undertook to obtain from the Electors, later on, that Philip be elected Roman Emperor, and he also promised on Maximilian's behalf to agree to Philip's succession.

Charles V had imposed his will, but he was conscious of silent disapproval and felt the negative atmosphere. The Diet broke up in low spirits, and the royal brothers parted, estranged.

MAXIMILIAN II (1564–76)

By a curious stroke of fate, it was Charles V's somewhat despised nephew who was to be the only one really to succeed in carrying out the Emperor's much-cherished *Interim*. Maximilian remained all his life a confirmed *Interim* man. He always took Communion *sub utraque*, never *sub una* (on his deathbed he omitted Communion in order not to pain his beloved wife and his strictly Catholic sister by observing 'utraquistic' custom to the end). It is remarkable that until the very last he rejected the finality of the religious split and, like Charles V, only tolerated the Evangelical church-order *ad interim*, 'until a general Christian reformation and a God-blessed settlement of the religious question in the German nation'.

While opposition was hardening on all sides, he represented once again the spirit of reconciliation, and sought, like Erasmus and Charles V, a *via media*. He counselled the Church 'to make use of quiet and peaceful ways, rather than strict and harsh measures', and desired 'freedom and mild treatment for the erring'. Religious matters ought not 'to be settled with the sword'. The ordering of religion which he intended for his own lands, was an order based on 'common work', which would reawaken 'love of one's neighbour, which has unhappily grown very cold'. Thus, as he hoped, 'the division would be healed, and with the help of divine grace a good common Christian discipline could be steadily reintroduced into life and doctrine'.

His conciliatory efforts made him the true spiritual son of Charles V, whereas the Emperor's real son, Philip II, represented the uncompromising spirit of the Counter-Reformation. Philip II and his Spanish theologians were the life and soul of the Council of Trent which reaffirmed Roman Catholic dogma; whereas Maximilian laid no special emphasis on dogma and considered that the healing of the religious divisions depended on mutual concessions. His endeavours to have the lay chalice and married priesthood accepted found in Philip II a more determined opponent than the Pope, for the latter had in 1564 allowed Maximilian to take Communion under both species.

True to the *Interim*, Maximilian wanted those two matters to be universally tolerated in the Church, saying, 'the married priesthood is an urgent need in all Germany' and the means to revive the Catholic Faith.

But Maximilian had no success with his plea for a married priesthood. His readiness to compromise found no support on the Catholic side. He was dubbed 'a secret Protestant'—and yet nothing could have been more Catholic, in the all-embracing sense of the word, than his desire for unity; he was accused of ambiguity—and yet nothing was more single-minded than his will for conciliation; his weak character was a subject of complaint —but it requires great strength of mind to conclude a true compromise, for it always involves a certain relinquishing of private interests.

And the Protestants were equally dissatisfied with Maximilian. As at the time of the *Interim*, defamatory verses went the round in Germany:

> *Da du empfingst die güldene kron,*
> *hast du das evangelion*
> *zu schützen vielen zugesagt.*
> *Denk ob es denn auch Gott behagt,*
> *wenn itz die hur von babylon*
> *gefürdert wird durch deine kron.*

('When you received the golden crown—you promised many to protect the Gospel.—Think whether it is pleasing to God—when now the whore of Babylon—is supported by your crown.')

Like Erasmus, Maximilian complained that the Lutherans called him a Papist, the Papists a Lutheran. The spirit of the times was one of thesis and antithesis, incapable of grasping the urge to wholeness that inspired Maximilian and the synthesis that had been the goal of Charles V's never wholly realized endeavours.

Maximilian was a living example of synthesis for a whole decade. Mildness and consideration marked his reign. He wished to attain to the higher reaches of concord by dint of sheer kindness. He forbade his preachers to scorn the Lutherans, and he would not countenance the use of the hideous word 'heretic'. 'I cannot and will not tolerate it,' he said.

'I want them to come to terms,' he repeated again and again, and he hoped that it would be possible, for he considered that the 'Augsburg Confession' (formulated by Melanchthon in 1530) was within the Catholic Church. Like Charles V, he could not grasp the dogmatic divergencies and hoped all would turn to unity, if only the Lutherans would once more 'use the old-founded *observances* and spiritual *rites* and burning lights again'.

The *Interim* died with Maximilian. His sons were brought up in Spain; his heir, Rudolf, who resided in Prague as Emperor Rudolf II, was in the spiritual succession of Philip II.

Rudolf no longer had the elasticity to seek out a new basis of understanding between Catholics and Protestants. The contrast between the ideas that prevailed at the Escorial where he grew up, and the heretical tendencies at home in Bohemia, was too much for him, and he broke under the strain. Incapable of finding a solution, he sank into melancholy, and in 1612 died insane in Prague Castle. On 23rd May 1618, the Thirty Years War began with the rebellion of the Protestants in Prague and the ejection of imperial government officials, who were thrown out of the windows. All conciliatory voices were now to be drowned in the din of battle.

THE COUNCIL OF TRENT (1545-63)

The great Council on which Charles V pinned all his hopes for a final settlement of the religious rift was opened in Trent on 23rd December 1545, 'in the name of God and to the honour of the Pope'. The Emperor had suggested Trent, 'for the Germans beg that it be allowed to sit in Germany, and Your Holiness might choose Trent for it, considering it a German city although it is actually already in Italy. . . .'

The Emperor had rejected the idea of a German national council, 'for', as he wrote to his brother Ferdinand, 'the more the German nation is on its own, the more it will incline to error'. The General Council was to remind the Germans of the supra-national character of the Christian religion.

The Emperor did not live to see the conclusion of the Council, the very existence of which was due to his own tenacity. It was not to fulfil hopes for the restoration of unity, but it did reaffirm the Catholic Faith and reinforce it at those points most vulnerable to Protestant attack. The justification of man by means of his good works as well as his faith was strongly vindicated.

Over against the one-sidedness of Lutheran doctrine, the Council restored the total conception of revelation; to the *sola fide* of the Protestants it replied whole-heartedly, 'faith and works'. And 'and' is important, connecting the two intrinsically, for from a right mind come right deeds; over against Luther's servile will, the Council asserted man's aptitude to distinguish between good and evil, thus stressing the freedom and responsibility of the human will; over against the limiting of Christianity to the Bible it reaffirmed the Word of God and Church tradition, another 'and' that salvaged the Greco-Latin heritage of Christendom and the inspiration of the saints. And thus the Council of Trent was, after all, the means by which the old religion, to which Charles V had dedicated his life, came into its own again.

But after the Council of Trent, the Church's field of activity was the narrower. It was already the period of the Counter-Reformation, when the spiritual unity of Europe broke up and melted away. The cracks grew ever wider, and in the seventeenth century we hear the tones of concern of men such as Bossuet and Leibniz, in a renewed endeavour to join up the jagged edges. 'The hope of reconciliation was lost,' wrote Leibniz on the Council of Trent, 'no one dared ever to open his mouth again, for fear of being taken for a heretic.'

And henceforth religion and intellectual endeavour were to go their separate ways.

At first it seemed as though a new accord of mind and soul had indeed been discovered, and the abundant fullness of the Faith found outlet triumphantly in Baroque art. But all too soon its spiritual content evaporated in ostentation and ornament.

The Baroque high tide ebbed because reason and emotion had parted company and faith was no longer nourished by life as a whole. In fact, the old religion was now but a fraction of human existence instead of being its *raison d'être*, and the atomizing process spread to all sides of life. Hölderlin's plaint applies to the whole of the western world: 'Is it not like a battle-field where hands and arms and fragments of limbs lie scattered about and the life-blood is spent, running away into the sand?'

. . . The Emperor saw it all coming: the overstressing of individuality, discord among men in lieu of harmony, life all made up of disconnected bits and pieces—he saw it coming and strove to the last to ward off the evil. His son's ships sank in the storm which the new independence let loose. 'I sent them out to fight men, not natural forces,' said Philip II on hearing of the wreck of the Armada, a wreck that was the prelude to the decline of old Catholic Europe and the rise of the Protestant West.

God permitted the storm. God permitted the wreck. For there is a time for discord and a time for harmony. There is a time when salvation depends on differentiation—the salvation of life as such and its capacity for growth, and there is a time when only concord can foster new growth.

Perhaps the storm that rose in Charles V's time, a storm with which Philip was to wrestle all his life, is now dying down; perhaps the tendency to individualization has run its course, and nature itself will now bring healing in the shape of harmony between the parts and the whole; and in view of the annihilation that threatens us, we can but hope for an upsurge of mercy and loving-kindness among men, till at last love predominates and clenched fists relax.

There is a time for fighting, and a time for peace.

INNSBRUCK (1552)

The turn of fortune that struck Charles V in early 1552 was so heavy in consequences that one is tempted to pause and probe into the causes of it.

Machiavelli would have said it was due to his tendency to be content with half-measures, and Machiavelli hated nothing more than half-measures. He despised the *via del mezzo*. In his *Discorsi* we read: 'Men always choose the middle way, the most damaging of all; for they take it to be neither quite right nor quite wrong.'

With the *Interim* the Emperor had tried to give things a turn for the better. But the resistance his solution met with forced him into measures hardly consonant with the intended 'God-blessed compromise'. For although the *Interim* was proposed in the conciliatory spirit of the *via media*, its imposition by violence turned it into an instrument of extreme reaction and intolerant harshness.

'Violence is power externalized,' says Hegel's *Logic*.

The very fact that the Emperor was compelled to use force to impose his ideas shows that the ideas themselves remained outside ones, he had not succeeded in making them acceptable to the Germans. The Protestants said the Emperor had 'a hypocritical false heart'.

Maurenbrecher repeated the accusation, observing that the Emperor, 'making doubled-faced promises of a council, attempted to override the Protestant princes by means of this formula', and his German policy in the *Interim* years provoked Ranke to call him 'equivocal, utterly calculating, avaricious, implacable and unrelenting'.

It was in fact a curiously mixed policy, at once conciliatory and tyrannical. The original intention, and its actual realization, were two different things, showing all too clearly how the author of the *Interim* vacillated between Erasmus and Machiavelli. Finally he determined on the decided attitude Machiavelli required of his prince, but only in order to enforce the *via del mezzo*, Erasmus' middle way, a policy which was bound to undermine his position of power. Moreover, in imposing the *Interim* he was himself unfaithful to its spirit, and it all culminated in dire punishment for unresolved disparity.

In northern Germany, rebellion smouldered like a badly extinguished fire. The old bishopric of Magdeburg, historic bulwark of Lower Saxon opposition to Rome and now a stronghold of the Lutherans (the Spanish called it *el Alcázar del Protestantismo*)—Magdeburg put up a bitter resistance.

The Emperor commissioned the Elector Maurice of Saxony to outlaw the city.

But Maurice only pretended to do so; actually, he took the rebels into his service, and agreed on common action against the Emperor with the Protestant authorities and the French. He issued proclamations inviting rejection of 'the bestial servitude of the *Interim*', and with the envoy of the French king he concluded a highly treasonable treaty, ceding the imperial cities of Metz, Toul and Verdun (which King Henry soon took possession of) in return for a large quantity of Judas money, which he spent on raising troops to fight the Emperor.

Meanwhile Charles V spent a quiet winter in Innsbruck, without any apprehensions. His daughter Maria and her husband Maximilian, with their little daughter Anna, had passed through Innsbruck on their return from Spain, then he was alone again. He was not at all well: his gout was worse than ever on account of the cold winter, and he was short of money, in fact his chancellor Granvelle wrote to Brussels that he had not got 'a single kreuzer'.

It was a bad time to receive news of the Elector of Saxony's defection.

Although his sister Maria, Governor of the Netherlands, wrote from Brussels mentioning rumours of negotiations between the French king and Maurice of Saxony, he would not credit it: Maurice, his fellow-in-arms at Mühlberg, a traitor? There could be no question of it! Maurice on the Protestant side? Impossible! It was only the other day Maurice had heard Mass at his side: Maurice was his best friend. . . .

But this time the Emperor proved a bad judge of character. Maurice really was advancing against him. By the beginning of April he stood before Augsburg with an army of thirty thousand men. His goal was Innsbruck, 'to catch the fox in his lair', as he said. The Emperor was taken off his guard and had to admit that the situation was critical. On 4th April he wrote to his brother: 'I am at this moment bereft of an army and without any esteem whatever. I therefore feel compelled to leave Germany, for I have no one who will take my part but many opponents who already hold the power in their hands. All things considered, and commending myself to God, in this hour I see but one choice: to endure great disgrace, or to expose myself to great danger. I prefer danger, for it lies in God's hand to ward it off, to disgrace, which is public.'

In the midst of his preparations for flight the Emperor remembered his spiritual offspring, his Memoirs. The precious document could not be allowed to fall into the hands of the enemy, a reliable messenger should convey it to Spain. He addressed a few words to Philip:

'This history is what I wrote as we sailed up the Rhine, finishing it in Augsburg. It is not as I wished it to be, and God knows that I did not write it out of vanity. If He feels He is offended by it, my offence was done in ignorance rather than with evil intention. Such things are always displeasing to Him. I could wish He would not be angry with me on that account just now. Reasons enough there are indeed. I hope He will appease His wrath and save me from the difficult situation in which I find myself. I was at the point of burning it all: but I hope, if God gives me life, to shape it in such a way that He will not reject it; and in order that it should not be lost here, I send it you to be kept in safety and not opened, till . . .

In Innsbruck 1552. I, the King.'

The sentence remained unfinished. Perhaps he had no time left, or his people were urging him to hurry.

On 6th April he rode out of Innsbruck by night to escape to Flanders, 'where,' he said, 'he had most power at the moment and most means of assistance'. But in Allgäu he found the streets already blocked by a hostile militia; so he turned round and went back to Innsbruck.

So dilatory in the face of danger! But wherever thou art, thou art in God's hands.

Maurice was already advancing through North Tyrol. He stormed the Ehrenberg Pass, and the road to Innsbruck now lay clear before him. Ferdinand, Lord of Tyrol, had forgotten to blow up the bridges and Maurice saw the Emperor as good as his prisoner. But luck was against him. A mutiny broke out among his troops and this delayed him for a day. And just as, according to legend, an angel once rescued Emperor

256

Maximilian from St Martin's rock where he had taken a wrong turning, and brought him safely back to Innsbruck, now a guardian spirit led Emperor Charles out of peril. He was a sick man, and loyal hands bore him on a litter, at night, by torchlight, over the snow-bound Alpine passes, across the Brenner to Bruneck, and thence to Villach on the River Drau. Here, under cover of the dense forests of the Carinthian mountains, and among loyal countrymen, he desired to wait till his strength returned and his star rose again.

Elector John Frederick accompanied the court as a prisoner and the Emperor set him free on the way to Villach. As the Elector expressed his gratitude, he said in German, 'he needed no thanks, for he had let him go free, and he wanted to be and to remain the gracious Emperor to his dear folk and to their sons'.

The Landgrave Philip of Hesse was still kept captive. Sepulveda, the chronicler, reports that the Emperor was advised to get rid of the Landgrave by poisoning him; a Spaniard had brought an Italian poison from Milan for the purpose. But he replied, nothing was more unworthy of a prince than to murder by poison. (If Charles V at times adopted Machiavelli's sagacious political methods, he never imitated the latter's hero, Cesare Borgia.)

Meanwhile, Maurice of Saxony, the Duke of Mecklenburg, and William of Hesse, had entered Innsbruck, accompanied by the French envoy. The troops bore the fleur-de-lis among their colours.

The high-born lords plundered like common soldiers. Maurice took possession of the Emperor's belongings and the Duke of Mecklenburg was no loser on this occasion either. Even King Ferdinand's property was not spared, the dukes appropriating his guns and fowling pieces.

On 26th May Maurice concluded a truce with Ferdinand, and agreed to go on to Passau where a congress of princes was to take place. In spite of the armistice, Maurice and his troops rode through the Tyrol and Salzkammergut, plundering and murdering. Churches were stripped bare, tabernacles broken open, whole villages laid in ashes. Once in Passau, Ferdinand persuaded Maurice to lay down his arms. In return, Maurice demanded unlimited religious freedom for the Protestants, and the freeing of the Landgrave of Hesse.

The Emperor, when presented with the conditions of the treaty, spurned them in anger. Freedom of religion for the Protestants? That meant declaring the *Interim* null and void. Never. Free the Landgrave? That meant letting loose the greatest mischief-maker. Not on any account.

Ferdinand himself hurried to Villach to talk things over. Only by granting them complete equality and freeing the Landgrave of Hesse were the Protestants to be induced to take part in common action against the Turks, who were once more threatening Vienna. These arguments finally persuaded the Emperor to accept the Passau Treaty, which was the equivalent of a peace with Maurice of Saxony and a recognition of the new sects—but on condition that it had validity only till the next Diet, when the whole matter would be gone into.

But the chivalrous knight in Charles V suffered deeply on account of that forced flight of his, his hard-won consent to the treaty and helpless position. A Venetian envoy once said, the Emperor would rather let the world go to ruin than do anything under compulsion. Not to be able to act of his own free will was a terrible infliction. He was determined to regain his freedom.

Messages went to Spain, Philip would have to scrape some money together; the Duke of Alba should come to Villach immediately. Faithful Anton Fugger wrote yet another credit note, for money was needed, lots of it. Charles V had to make an appearance and obliterate the disgrace that had befallen him. And he had to regain the cities which Maurice had so shamefully traded with France.

METZ (1552)

'The Emperor's luck is given to rising just when you think it is down for good,' said the Italians.

At the beginning of August the Emperor was in Augsburg at the head of an army; in September he was in Alsace. He set up his headquarters at Landau in Alsace, where he received reinforcements. An attack of gout delayed his advance. His sister Maria wrote in concern to tell him he ought not to start a campaign in the autumn. But Charles was all agog to vindicate his honour and restore his realm. He had received his inheritance whole, and he was determined to lay it whole in his son's hands. As his condition did not improve, he sent the Duke of Alba on to Metz to open proceedings. At the end of November he reached Metz himself and took over the conduct of the siege. In storm and rain the old warrior was out in the field. From the fortress the French could watch him mustering his troops at dawn on a capering white horse.

Metz had meanwhile been strongly fortified by the French and it was splendidly defended by the Duc de Guise. The siege proved very costly. Cannon-balls and gunpowder were shot off in vain, the powerful city walls stood firm and the damp chilly weather affected the fighting-spirit of the imperial troops. A cholera epidemic broke out and weakened the decimated army still further. For lack of money, munitions ran short. 'The fortune of war eludes the old,' said the Emperor bitterly, seeing himself obliged to relinquish the siege.

The hardships of the last months and the cold wet winter had completely undermined his health. A bad attack of gout put one arm and both legs out of action. He was carefully borne in a litter to Diedenhofen, where he lay ill for many weeks. His doctors tried to cure him by their drastic measures and caused him violent pain. But the misadventure plagued him worse than the gout. It weighed on him like the shadow of his last inescapable defeat, which he now felt closing in upon him. 'I have often seen him in a worse condition,' wrote the English envoy who was his visitor at the time, 'but never so near death.'

Broken in body and spirit, the Emperor came to Brussels early in February. For months no one was allowed to see him. Months were to pass before he could sign the waiting documents. He had needed victory in order to revive. And it all seemed to be in vain, the long fight and the many troubles. Perhaps God had not accepted his offering. The angel of good succour had deserted him, after lighting him through so many darkened hours. Now the night of the soul bore down on him implacably. In a state of utter apathy, he left all government matters to his chancellor Granvelle and his sister Maria.

And then fortune smiled on him once more, reawakening hope and the old dream.

On 6th July 1553 Edward VI of England died and Mary Tudor succeeded him.

MARY TUDOR (1553-58)

Mary Tudor, Queen of England: the news was like a new flow of life coursing through the Emperor's weary limbs. Suddenly all was well, suddenly all the suffering of the last years was swept away by the wind of hope, all gloom was dispelled by the rising sun, the sun of belief in a world united in one faith.

In his joy at seeing his cherished dream appearing anew over the horizon of his life's evening, the Emperor rose from his sickbed, regained his strength, took on fresh heart with the awakening of fresh confidence; in imagination he saw the map of Europe spread out before him, and his mind embraced the island kingdom and drew it into his dream world. The bonds of marriage should link England to the mainland: *Tu felix Austria nube.*

He would woo the English queen for his son. Mary, betrothed to him in his youth, came at the right moment to save his waning strength, his sinking realm, and all Europe from decline and ruin. Mary Tudor of England. A Catholic England would weight the scales decisively in favour of the *Universitas Christiana.* What a dismal day for the old foes, the rebels, heretics, apostates, doomed to fade from the scene like ghosts at the victorious dawn now about to break over the western world. No selfish national ambitions would henceforth be able to destroy that unity which was bound to come at last, for the salvation of Christendom.

On 30th July the Emperor wrote to his son in Madrid that he should break off his betrothal to his Portuguese cousin (the daughter of Leonora's first marriage) and prepare for marriage with Mary Tudor of England.

Philip ventured to suggest that his father should marry Mary himself. The Emperor replied that his state of health did not permit him to marry again. Then Philip wrote submissively, *La voluntad de Vuestra Majestad sea también la mia* (may Your Majesty's will be mine, too).

With true Spanish frankness, Sandoval observed: 'The queen may well be saintly, she is none the less ugly and old. Like Isaac, Prince Philip let himself be sacrificed in order to do his father's will and serve the Church well.'

It was Charles who took the first step. He sent a private envoy, Simon Renard, to England to make the proposal.

Renard was received by Mary in various confidential audiences, the course of which he reported to the Emperor. 'She replied she had heard from many quarters that His Royal Highness was not as reasonable as Your Majesty and—*que s'il voulait estre voluptueux, ce n'est pas ce qu'elle désire*—for she has reached the age that Your Majesty knows; and has never entertained any attachments or affections.'

The Emperor instructed his envoy to talk her out of her misgivings. What were such trifling objections beside the immensity of the plan! Mary's and Philip's child would inherit a world empire in which the sun of the Faith would never set; this child would bring the world what he himself could no longer give it—the *Pax Christiana.*

Pax Christiana—the Emperor's dream was at last to be realized, what he desired heart and soul would now be accomplished. Peace was at hand. Then he could relax, physically and mentally, for the dream would go on without him.

But it is only in fairy-tales that wishes come true. Life makes no concession to dreams and often has no reward for the most painstaking endeavours—that is the secret law that rules the shaping of men's souls—for the one thing that matters is the growth of the soul. So it comes about that obstacles tend to multiply just when a good thing is about to be realized, as though evil stood at the Lord's command as well as goodness.

The Emperor's plan spurred all the most hostile elements to violent counter-action. Henry II of France felt, like his father before him, that the Habsburgs were encircling him, and promptly invaded the Netherlands. Like the Turkish 'runners and burners', the French troops laid waste villages and fields. In autumn 1553 they were beaten by the imperial army at Mons. But in the following spring Henry again advanced to the Maas. Once more the Emperor took up the challenge: he went to Namur and had himself carried to the battle-field in a litter; he conducted the relief of Renty in person. With his superior forces he was able to drive the French back into Picardy. In the midst of the resulting congratulations he passed the command on to his nephew, Philibert of Savoy; younger hands should now continue his work—he was worn out.

And fresh storms were brewing on the horizon. In England, Mary's intolerance served to nurture the resistance of the Anglicans. In Rome, the Neapolitan Cardinal, Caraffa, mounted the See of Peter in May 1555, as Pope Paul IV.

Many years earlier the Emperor had stopped him from being appointed Archbishop of Naples, and Caraffa had not forgotten it; the new Pope's hatred for all that was Spanish, and above all for Spanish sovereignty in Naples, set the old conflict between Pope and Emperor alight again. The Portuguese envoy was entrusted with the task of reducing the tension between the Curia and the Spanish crown, and the Pope said to him: 'Do you not know the damnable methods of those scoundrels, heretical and godless as they are? The one [Charles] is a schismatic, the other [Philip] is covetous. We shall destroy them and their realm.'

Pope Paul IV had a horror of any interference by secular powers in the spiritual sphere; but he himself constantly interfered in the secular sphere. It looked as though the new Pope wanted to put the last chapter of *Il Principe* into effect and 'free Italy from the barbarians'.

Like Machiavelli, he had *mile ragione di odiare Spagna*—a thousand reasons for hating Spain. He said: 'We shall declare a crusade against them [Charles and Philip], so that the tyrant [Charles] may see the annihilation of this damnable race [the Spaniards] in his lifetime.'

It was clear that relations between Pope and Emperor could hardly be more strained than they were.

Nonetheless, Charles V remained true to the Catholic Church to the end. And to the end he refused to accept the religious division as final. The Diet of Augsburg that met in February 1555, 'in order to cure the highly damaging mistrust that reigns in the realm', gave the final touch to the recognition of religious freedom for the Protestants, as foreseen in the Treaty of Passau. Charles V saw himself powerless, but declined to put his seal to it and handed the responsibility on to his brother Ferdinand.

Towards the end of the Diet, in September 1555, under the presidency of Ferdinand, the assembled princes settled matters by means of the formula, '*cujus regio, ejus religio*', 'whose the land, his the religion', meaning that the ruler of a land had the right to impose his own type of religion on his subjects. There was no longer any question of freedom of conscience for the individual. The 'religious peace of Augsburg' meant nothing more nor less than the permanent separation of the two hostile camps—Catholic and Reformed; it was no peaceful settlement, but rather, weighty with explosive matter, as the future would show. And it involved the unconditional and automatic subordination of the individual to state authority, it meant the end of all the Emperor's hopes for unity, the end of the *Interim*. Common ground no longer existed, and the schism was a reality.

The Emperor had no strength left to dam the flood that inevitably rose. He left it to his brother to do whatever was timely. But he protested vigorously at everything 'by means of which our true, old Christian and Catholic religion is offended, weakened or burdened'; and he chose now to lay down the power he could no longer wield in favour of the old religion.

Before the year was out, he had written to his son in Spain, where he was engaged in equipping a fleet for his wedding expedition to England, asking him to visit the monastery of Yuste and have living quarters prepared for him there. Philip fulfilled this wish, too. He travelled to that remote spot and gave orders for a house to be built adjoining the monastery—the so-called *Palacio del Emperador*. The purpose of the building remained secret, only the Prior was initiated. The rooms were arranged according to the Emperor's own design: he wished to be able to see the high altar in the church from his bedroom (we know that this arrangement made such an impression on Philip that years later he had it incorporated in the plans for the Escorial).

When Pope Paul IV heard of the Emperor's intention to abdicate, he cried, 'He has lost his wits!' Even now, when the Emperor would never more face him as an opponent in this world, the Pope had no kind word for him. He said 'he knew Charles well, he had gone to Spain with him and had discovered his faults: his overweening pride, his lust for domination, his contempt for religion. What other Emperor would ever have held diets and councils in which Lutherans and heretics were represented? God punished the Emperor by letting him die while he was still alive, for he was a madman possessed of the devil, like his mother and sisters, and like Philip himself who lived like a Lutheran and did not observe the laws of fasting.'—Was it madness, or divine folly? The world of men with their wits about them was taken aback on hearing of the Emperor's impending abdication.

'*Consider, brethren, the circumstances of your own calling; not many of you are wise, in the world's fashion, not many powerful, not many well born. No, God has chosen what the world holds foolish. . . .*' (1 Cor. 1. 26, 27).

The Emperor went to Yuste, and the world deemed it foolish.

CHARLES V'S ABDICATION (1555)

The moment had come. On 25th October, a Friday, at three o'clock in the afternoon, the solemn renunciation of the imperial crown took place in the great hall of the castle of Brussels, and the hereditary lands passed on to Philip.

All in black, with the Order of the Golden Fleece about his neck, the Emperor entered the packed hall, leaning on the arm of young Prince William of Orange. All the great of the realm were assembled—the General Estates and State Councillors of the Netherlands, the Knights of the Order of the Golden Fleece, King Philip, King Maximilian of Bohemia, Duke Philibert of Savoy, Archduke Ferdinand of Austria, Queen Maria Regent of the Netherlands, the Dowager Queen Leonora, Queen Maria of Bohemia, the Duchess Christine of Lorraine, the Spanish

Grandees of the imperial suite, all were present when the Emperor took his place on the throne.

First, a member of the State Council read the proclamation, and then, in the breathless silence, the Emperor spoke.

'Dear Friends, the Chancellor has very properly informed you of my decision and of the reasons for it; and I would merely recall to your minds how it is now forty years since my grandfather, Emperor Maximilian, declared me to be of age in this very hall, and almost at this very time—I was then fifteen years old. In the following year my lord, the Catholic King, died, and I became King of Spain. At nineteen years of age I was awarded the imperial crown, to my great joy, hoping as I did to strengthen religion in Germany, my homeland, and to cross swords with the Sultan of the Ottomans. The heresy of Luther and his followers, and the authoritarian demands of some Christian princes, kept me fully occupied, but I spared no trouble in my endeavours to hold them at bay. In the fulfilment of these obligations I travelled to Germany nine times, to Spain six times, to Italy seven times, and I came here ten times. I was in France four times, whether for peace or war, in England twice and in Africa twice. That makes altogether forty journeys, without counting those of less importance which I undertook with a view to visiting my lands. I have embarked on the Mediterranean three times and on the ocean three times, and now it will be the fourth time that I sail on it, on my last journey to Spain.

'Of all the wars that I waged, some were for the defence of the Faith, some for the defence of my rights, others were in the cause of justice, which the imperial crown upholds; but I waged no war out of ambition or hatred.

'I had a long reign, long in troubles and labours; but I assure you that in all that long time nothing has pained me so much—I leave aside Luther's heresy—as parting from you in this hour without leaving you the peace for which I longed. The freedom of my conscience depends on the execution of my decision, a decision I have considered at great length; for the weightiness of state affairs requires a freer hand and mind than mine, tied as they are by pain, for I am greatly plagued by gout. I should have done what I do today many days ago, but for the youth of my son and the adversities of the times, which often compelled me to sacrifice my health in order to maintain yours. The King of France's breaking of the peace, Maurice of Saxony's presumption in raising an army against me, the loss of Metz and Hesdin, the French in possession of Arras—all those were no accidental occurrences, they were certainly effected by the common foe of mankind in order to delay my withdrawal, which I had of course to postpone to make good the damage done. But now, God be praised, things have improved in many respects. Today, with a son like Philip, and a brother like Ferdinand, to whom I can entrust the furtherance of my life's work—and if necessary, its expansion—it would be wrong not to yield—to the one the possession of my lands, and to the other the Empire. It is much that I give you, and much that I commend to you, and above all good mutual relations, which will bear good fruit for both. But even should you forget it all, never let this one thing go out of your minds: the purity of our Catholic religion, over which you will have to watch as over an exceptionally important fortress surrounded by hostile armies; and if the proximity of the enemy has perchance sown tares in you, pull them out, pull them up by the roots before it is too late, for otherwise—you will remember my words again—you will become in misery slaves to your errors, without power to set yourselves free when you desire to. I tell you, I would rather have lost what I was and am, than accept the least error as regard the purity of the evangelical commands. In government, I confess it, I often erred, out of lack of experience, out of excessive confidence placed in others, sometimes out of sheer daring, but never with the intention of wounding anyone; did I inadvertently do so, I beg pardon of all concerned.'

Then the Emperor turned to his son Philip, and once more implored him to hold fast to the Faith of his fathers; he left him a great inheritance; the love he owed it should extend to his subjects too. . . .

The Emperor was too deeply moved to say more. 'Forgive the tears of the old man I am,' he said to those around him. Philip knelt before his father, and promised to do everything as he intended it to be done. The tears flowed down the Emperor's face as he gave his son his blessing.

Sobs were heard all over the hall. The Emperor's sisters wept uncontrollably, 'and all present showed signs of grief, not because of the new lord they gained, but expressing how much he whom they were losing meant to them.'

The Emperor drew his son up to him and kissed him tenderly.

VIII

YUSTE

Nowhere, Beloved, will world be found but within.
Our life passes away by a process of change. And
the outside world grows less and less . . .

from Rilke's 7th Duineser Elegie

I greet the Estremadura sky that reigned over the Emperor's last years. It has a great clarity, a clarity already implicated in another realm. And northwards lies Yuste.

This time I could not go there, for it lies far from any railway station and it was not on my route. But I take as my trusted mentor an old Spanish traveller, Don Pedro de Alarcón, who published his impressions of Yuste in Madrid in 1873.

From his descriptions there emerges an epic landscape, with a forest of cedars, chestnuts and old oaks, such as the nineteenth-century Romantics liked to paint. A steep path leads up the mountain-side among bushes; a great stone cross proclaims that we are now within hail of the monastery of San Jerónimo of Yuste.

In the midst of the solitude we observe on a weatherbeaten wall the arms of Charles V, carved in stone, with that same Habsburg two-headed eagle who spreads his wings across the arms of all the royal and imperial lands.

The coat of arms proclaims how he who withdrew to this solitude 'was, in the world, King of the Romans, King of Germany, of Castile, of León, of Aragon, of both Sicilies, of Jerusalem, of Dalmatia, of Navarra, Granada, Toledo, Valencia, Galicia and Mallorca, of Sardinia and Corsica, the Canary Isles and the Indies, the Islands and Continent of the ocean; Archduke of Austria; Duke of Burgundy, of Brabant, of Lorraine, of Styria, Carinthia and Krain, of Luxembourg, Limbourg, Athens and Patras; Count of Habsburg, Flanders, Tyrol, Landgrave in Alsace . . . sovereign in Asia and Africa.'

Beneath the arms, an inscription runs:

> To this holy house of San Jerónimo, Charles the Fifth withdrew to end his life that he had wholly devoted to the defence of the Faith and the maintenance of justice, the most Christian Emperor, invincible, King of Spain. He died on 21st September 1558.

A life wholly devoted to fighting and serving: so it was indeed.

The Yuste monastery was the poorest one of the Hieronymite Order, which had valuable properties in Spain; in neighbouring Guadalupe, sons of the most distinguished families of Spain served under the same rule. But the remoteness of Yuste attracted the Emperor.

It was in 1404 that two hermits established their cells here. A pious farmer of the village of Quacos presented them with the ground of Yuste, which they turned into arable land. In 1408 they asked the Infanta Don Fernando to obtain from the Pope permission to make a monastery of their hermitage. Fernando took the necessary steps with the desired result, 'as though he had foreseen that this place of refuge would be the last resting-place of the noble invincible Eagle, Emperor Charles the Fifth', as the monastery chronicle puts it.

We may picture it with an adjoining one-storey house, the *Palacio del Emperador*. Over the basement there is a terrace with steps leading up to it, and from the terrace an overgrown garden is visible, which in the Emperor's time was full of blossoms of great beauty and rarity. A fountain murmurs, now as then.

It was here the Emperor was sitting, on that day in August 1558, when he had the Titian pictures brought him, and contemplated 'The Last Judgement' with such intensity that he trembled all over, saying to his doctor, '*Malo me siento*'.

From the terrace you go through the main entrance into the Emperor's quarters. His living-room is on the left, so is his bedroom, and the dining-room and very roomy kitchen are on the right.

Unamuno, who visited Yuste in 1920, found the Emperor's rooms *pobrisimo*, 'miserable', and the bedroom 'small and gloomy'.

Sandoval's report runs: 'The Emperor lived so miserably at Yuste that his rooms looked as though they had been plundered by soldiery rather than adorned for so great a prince. They contained only black cloths, and not even that, except in the room he slept in. And he had only one arm-chair, of so little value that you would not have got four reale for it. He was dressed poorly, too, and always in black. His most valuable possession was a little silver, but he had nothing made of gold.'

These statements of Sandoval, in a 'History of Charles V' written several decades after his death, are traceable to legend. (We have already had occasion to observe how naturally legend embellishes the individuality of a life.) It was a fact that at Yuste the Emperor was very close to the religious life, and thus his contemporaries pictured him as a sort of monk.

But the inventory of his estate shows how splendidly his villa was furnished: precious Flemish Gobelins covered the walls, Persian carpets lay on the floors; in his dining-room there were twelve leather-covered chairs studded with gold nails; in his wardrobe were sixteen quilted silk nightshirts.

The Emperor had a retinue of fifteen, among whom were his trusty major-domo Luis Quijada, his private physician Dr Mathys, his secretaries van Male and Gaztelú, and his confessor Juan de Regla. He had a master of the wardrobe, several chamberlains, four barbers, an apothecary, an Italian clock-maker, and a huntsman to keep his larder stocked.

The inventory also enumerates the Emperor's personal belongings, his books, paintings, maps, clocks (which appeared to the monks to be works of the devil); he had his mathematical instruments there, his astrolabes and compasses; an astronomical ring, several magnifying glasses and crystals, a gold-set stone that was a talisman against bleeding, two bracelets of gold and bone to cure haemorrhoids, a blue stone as protection from gout, nine rings from England against cramp, a number of stones from the Orient, said to be cures for all kinds of afflictions. 'With all those wonder-working stones,' wrote M. Mignet, 'the Emperor ought to have been cured of all his troubles'; but neither they nor all Doctor Mathys' skill could do anything about his painful gout, which only strict dieting could have relieved.

And the Emperor still favoured highly spiced foods. He made not the slightest effort to mortify his liking for meat or to deny himself anything at all. 'I want to be no monk,' he said, for he found (like Erasmus) that the Rule was too strict, particularly as regards fasting. And he went on indulging in the pleasures of the table as hitherto. In the words of his major-domo Luis Quijada, he did nothing 'but stimulate his appetite'.

The whole of Spain contributed to the Emperor's household requirements; daily, a caravan of heavily-loaded mules carried fresh food to Yuste, special messengers brought oysters, soles and crabs packed in nettles from the Atlantic coast, trout from the mountain streams of the Pyrenees, lobster from the Mediterranean, sardines from Portugal. And the Netherlands kept their old lord and master provided with local dainties in the form of liver pies, smoked salmon, herrings and also partridges, 'the best in the world', as the Emperor said.

But nothing went to waste in the Yuste household; when Don Luis de Avila, a frequent visitor, once came later than expected, the Emperor dined alone, eating very little of the roast capon, the main dish of the meal: 'Keep it for Don Luis,' he said to his servants, 'for we may have nothing else that we can offer him.'

When the meal was over, the two old war veterans would spread maps out on the table and grow absorbed in re-fighting the old campaigns.

Don Luis once told the Emperor he was having a fresco painted in his house, showing the Emperor's last victory at Renty and the flight of the

French. The Emperor remarked: 'Don Luis, see that the painter uses moderation in his treatment of the theme, so that it looks like honourable withdrawal, for it was in fact no flight.'

Although the Emperor had renounced all his titles, he remained for all *Emperador, Sacra Majestad Caesarea.*

Charles' *Majestas* lay not in his title but in his person, and was a potency that radiated out far beyond the small immediate circle of Yuste; the abdication had not quenched it.

The *Palacio del Emperador* became the private 'residence' and secret heart of the lands which King Philip now governed. Although, as the anonymous monk of Yuste wrote in his chronicle, 'In order to serve God the better, His Majesty did not busy himself with worldly matters', in actual fact, through written counsels he sent his son Philip or his daughter Juana (ruling in Philip's absence), he played a considerable part in political events. Dona Juana frequently consulted him, and in Yuste there was a constant coming and going of her messengers and state secretaries. Couriers came from the Netherlands, received precise instructions, and hurried back to Brussels. Philip betrayed no great zeal in carrying out his father's wishes, and many a letter was left unanswered. But Charles followed Philip's battles closely, and made available money that Philip badly needed to strengthen his military position in France. When he heard of Philip's victory over the French at Saint-Quentin in August 1557, he expressed his joy but also his disappointment that Philip had not won through personal participation in the campaign.

And Charles followed Philip's contests with Pope Paul IV with the utmost interest. The Pope had concluded an alliance with Henry II of France, whose troops under the Duc de Guise had invaded Philip's Italian possessions. The Pope threatened to excommunicate Philip and have him deposed. The Spanish theologians declared that it was permissible for the king to fight the Pope in the capacity of Sovereign of the Papal States. Under the command of the Duke of Alba, Philip's army beat the united Papal and French troops. The victorious Alba was about to enter Rome, when through the mediation of the Venetian Ambassador (a master of conciliatory diplomacy) peace was declared between Philip and the Pope in September 1557.

Philip agreed to return to the Pope all the fortified places he had conquered, and in the person of his representative, the Duke of Alba, to sue for pardon on his knees. This was done in a solemn ceremony, the Pope absolving Philip, and also Charles, for all actions against the Holy See.

Pope Paul IV accorded his absolution as victor: he proclaimed that 'in the King of Spain he had desired to humiliate the haughtiness of princes who undervalued the obedience they owed to the supreme head of the Church'.

When the Emperor heard of this ceremony he fell into a rage. 'In spite of his gout,' the imperial secretary Gaztelú wrote to Dona Juana, 'the Emperor became very angry about this peace which he found dishonouring.'

To Charles, it was a Canossa; the treaty assured the Pope's position as sole supreme ruler, a position Charles had contested for many years. 'Not a day passes,' wrote Luis Quijada on 26th December,' but the Emperor mutters sullenly about the peace with the Pope.'

Glapion was right when he said in Worms that the Emperor found it hard to forget an injury.

But in spite of his bouts of anger and in spite of his self-indulgence at table, the Emperor lived a devout Christian life in Yuste. And to the companions of his solitude, the Yuste monks and the simple country people, he was the 'holy' Emperor when the end came.

CHARLES V AND FRANCISCO DE BORJA

Among the visitors to Yuste was the one-time chamberlain of the Empress Isabella, the Duke of Gandia, who was now a Jesuit, Padre Francisco de Borja.

Ribadeneyra described the first meeting of Emperor and priest. Both had left the world to dedicate themselves to God, the Emperor in the manner of the layman he was, Francisco de Borja in the school of Ignatius Loyola.

Charles was a Ghibelline and did not like the Jesuits. They seemed to him like a militia that only harkened to the Pope's wishes; and the present Pope was Paul IV, the personal enemy of Charles and his son Philip; he observed the activities of the new Order with some distrust.

Francisco de Borja, who at the time had the supervision of all the Jesuit foundations in the Iberian Peninsula, hoped to override his old friend's prejudices in private conversation. Ribadeneyra recounts how 'when he approached the Emperor he sank on his knees and begged for his hand, and His Majesty would not give it him unless he got up; but Padre

Francisco begged him to let him remain kneeling. And when the Emperor pressed him to be seated, he said to him (as the Padre himself recounted some years later): 'I humbly beg Your Majesty to leave me on my knees, for your resignation affects me as though I were in the presence of a resignation in God. And if Your Majesty will allow me to speak of myself, and the change in my life and my Order, then I will speak to Your Majesty as though I were speaking to God Himself.'

Padre Francisco then told the Emperor how first of all he wanted to enter the Order of Saint Francis, 'for poverty always pleased me, as well as humility and scorn of the world as they are practised in that Order', and yet his decision produced only 'a great dryness and desolation in his heart'; but when he met the *Compania de Jesus*, the Lord granted his spirit a great satisfaction and sweetness, which he took for a sign of the will of God; that is why he joined the *Compania*.

The Emperor listened to him attentively, and replied: 'I am very glad to hear of your life and state. For I will not deny that it astonished me, when you informed me of it from Rome in Augsburg; for it appeared to me that a person like yourself would, in the choice of an Order, prefer the old Orders, proved through many years' experience, to a new Order which is not so widely recognized and of which one hears various reports.'

'Holy Majesty,' said the Padre, 'no single Order is so old and so proved that it was not at one time new and unknown; and the time they were new was not the Orders' worst time. I know that various things are said about the *Compania*: but if I knew anything bad about it or unworthy of our holy religion and its integrity, I would not set foot in it.'

'I believe what you say,' said the Emperor, 'for I always found your lips spoke the truth. But tell me, is it true that in your Order there are no grey hairs?' 'Señor,' replied the Padre, 'when the mother is young, how can Your Majesty have the sons old? And if it is a fault, time will soon cure it.'

Then the Emperor said: 'Do you remember what I said to you in 1542, that I was thinking of retiring and doing what I have done?' 'I remember very well,' said Padre Francisco, 'and does Your Majesty remember that I at the same time told you of the change that I wished to make?' 'Indeed I remember,' answered the Emperor, 'and so we have both kept our word.'

The Emperor then questioned him about his penances and prayers and whether he should sleep in his clothes. 'For I must tell you that owing to my constant illness I cannot do the penances that I intended to do: but above all it seems to me that I would be incapable of sleeping in my clothes.'

To which the Padre replied: 'The many nights on which Your Majesty watched, fully armed, are the reason why you cannot sleep clothed. But let us thank our Lord, who sees more merit in Your Majesty for having spent those nights fully armed to defend His faith and His religion, than in many monks who sleep on pebbles in their cells.'

Francisco de Borja remained in Yuste for three days and came again on several occasions.

'I do not know on which occasion it was,' wrote Ribadeneyra, 'when Padre Francisco was staying with the Emperor in Yuste, and His Majesty asked him whether it appeared to him to be a sign of vanity when a man wrote an account of his own deeds. For he wanted to tell him that he had written down all his journeyings and campaigns together with their causes and motivations; and that it was neither desire for fame nor vanity that had inspired him, but solely that the truth be made known. For the historians of our time which he had read obscured the truth, either because they did not know it, or on account of their own inclinations and passions.'

Ribadeneyra did not report Padre Francisco's answer. But it is possible he said: 'Yes, it is vain, yes, it is serving idols, like all clinging to the past; all that was, however grand the occasion, is as nothing compared to the potency of the present hour: for God is present here and now.'

It is possible that a word from his friend persuaded the Emperor not to continue writing his Memoirs, for they break off in 1549, after the *Interim*.

THE EMPEROR'S BOOKS

Among the books that accompanied the Emperor to Yuste was Boethius' *Consolatio Philosophiae* (in Latin, French and Italian editions), the *Commentarios* of Caesar (in an Italian translation), the *Commentarios* of Don Luis Avila on the Schmalkaldic War; the *Mémoires* of Philippe de Commynes; Ptolemy's great astronomical work and the *Astronomia Imperial* of Santa Cruz; the *Meditationes* of St Augustine; the mystical meditations of Fray Luis de Granada; the writings of St Bernard; a Bible in French; several books on Christian doctrine, a few Books of Hours and Breviaries;

a single romance, *Le Chevalier Délibéré* of Olivier de la Marche (who wrote verses in honour of the Emperor's grandfather, Charles the Bold of Burgundy); and of course the Emperor's little favourite, *Il Cortegiano*, by Baldassare Castiglione.

Those books, bound in red velvet with silver corners, reflect Charles V's main interests: history, religion and natural science, and in the midst of it all, the blue flower of the *idealità caballeresca*, 'The Book of the Keen Knight' and 'The Courtier as he should be'. The Emperor once said to van Male that he owed nothing to his education but everything to his private studies.

It was a fact that Chièvres had told Charles' tutor, Adrian of Utrecht, not to burden the boy with too much Latin; 'a prince should be brought up in the knightly practices of a nobleman, not among books like a scholar'. Thus Charles became an excellent knight, but in knowledge of the humanities he stood a long way behind his brother Ferdinand, who had enjoyed a thorough humanistic education in Spain under the supervision of Ferdinand of Aragon.

Charles had a great respect for his brother's prowess in Latin. When anyone made a Latin speech to him, he used to say, 'This man thinks I am Ferdinand'. But Ferdinand would hear none of this, saying he only spoke Latin *à la mode militaire*.

But Charles filled in the gaps in his education later on. Van Male reported that he read chiefly classical authors, such as Thucydides, Tacitus and Caesar; Sansovino spoke of Polybius as a favourite author of the Emperor's; and in Yuste we find the five volumes of Boethius, 'the founder of the Middle Ages', 'the last Roman and first scholastic', who had conveyed the culture of late Antiquity over into the Christian centuries. In Caesar's commentaries the Emperor re-lived his own warfaring (for he liked best to think of himself as a great commander of armies), and in Thucydides he found that same abhorrence for any too great personal power which he himself had so often experienced at the moment of victory.

In Polybius, Charles found useful directives on wise statesmanship. But in the last great historian of the Greeks, it was chiefly his love of truth that appealed to him, and a remark of Polybius' perfectly expressed Charles' own conception of history: 'I consider no one to be an historian who sets anything above truth.'

The great value the Emperor laid on truthful recording of historical events is shown in an anecdote which Sepulveda, the Emperor's chronicler, reported. He visited the Emperor in Yuste in order to bring his *De Rebus gestis Caroli Quinti* up to date. As he did not want to weary the Emperor with questions, he proposed to read him certain passages; the Emperor was to keep silent if he agreed and interrupt if something struck him as wrong. Charles replied: 'I do not concern myself about what is written of me, others will read it after my death. But if you want to know something, ask me, I shall be glad to answer you.'

The Emperor gave Sepulveda to understand that only an account based on facts is worthy of posterity. He said, 'in the writing of history, he could bear neither lies nor flattery, and he held the Lutherans John Sleidan and Bishop Paul Jovius, whose pens were influenced by passion and greed of gain, for a couple of liars'.

Sepulveda, who did not want to risk being judged a liar, begged the Emperor to confirm an episode he had been told of, which showed the Emperor's nobility of mind in a particularly favourable light. The Emperor replied, he could not remember the occasion. Sepulveda, in concern for his attractive story, asked if he might consult Granvelle and Covos to have the episode endorsed. 'Leave it out,' said the Emperor, 'the thing is not right at all, it is pure invention.'

And since the accounts of his chroniclers did not satisfy him, he wrote his own Memoirs, 'so that the truth be known'.

It was his sense of authenticity that drew him to Philippe de Commynes with that fresh, sharp, sober mind of his, typical of early humanism.

For Commynes took no pains to varnish the unscrupulous will-to-power of his lord, King Louis XI of France, but told with great veracity, for instance, the king's *très grant joye* when he heard of Maria of Burgundy's death in consequence of a fall from horseback.

Some decades before Machiavelli even, Commynes declared that what prevails on earth is not Christian unity but selfish interests in conflict with one another. In the eighteenth chapter of his *Mémoires* we find the following passage: 'It appears to me that in this world God has created neither man nor beast without providing a counterpart to keep him in humility and fear. To the kingdom of France he gave as counterpoise the English; to the English, the Scots; to the kingdom of Spain, Portugal. To the princes of Italy (most of whom possess their lands without any title, unless it was given them in heaven, and that we can only guess), who rule most gruesomely and violently over their subjects, God gave as counterpoise the cities, such as Venice, Florence, Genoa, and at times Bologna and Siena. . . .

'Germany has always had the House of Austria and the House of Bavaria against it, and the House of Austria has the Swiss. It might thus appear that these divisions were necessary for the world and that these contrary things, which God has ordained for every state and for nearly every individual, were needed. One is therefore forced to the conclusion that neither natural reason, nor our feelings, nor fear of God, nor love of our neighbour make us refrain from acts of violence towards one another, or from keeping hold of what belongs to another, or taking it from him, mustering all the force at our command. It is thus probable that God is practically obliged to beat us with several rods on account of our inhumanity and wickedness, and this seems to me right. But the profligacy of princes and their ignorance are very dangerous and much to be feared, for they decide the weal or woe of their subjects.'

As in Machiavelli, in Commynes too the Emperor found, not indifference in regard to good and evil, but a mind aware of the 'depths of Satan' and therefore unlikely to deceive itself with hollow phrases as to the basic evil of his time; for no one can overcome evil who has not made himself aware of 'the deep mysteries of Satan' (Apoc. 2. 24).

It was no doubt as an overcoming of evil and a dam and dyke against the flood of violence, that the Emperor appreciated Castiglione's little book, *Il Cortegiano*, for (according to Sansovino) he often read it with delight. He found in it an atmosphere of courtly culture, art and high morality, a studied way of life and an attitude of mind that greatly appealed to him. In imagination he pictured the lovely rooms and gardens of the Prince of Urbino, and heard the sound of pleasing voices when the perfect nobleman spoke with his perfect lady of painting and poetry, music and love, for here beauty and sensitivity, gentleness and courtesy prevailed.

In Castiglione's book there reigned that same harmony between worldly and other-worldly things that made the Emperor's own life in Yuste so satisfying: the *Palacio del Emperador*, with its Titians, its elaborate table, its stimulating talk, its good books, was, in a modest form, a small Renaissance court; and simultaneously, the monastic atmosphere initiated the Emperor into the religious life.

Gradually he ceased to care to busy himself about his own past. When someone read to him, he chose the works of St Augustine and St Bernard, for only Christian mysticism was able to satisfy his hungry soul; and St Augustine's 'Lord, Thou hast created us for Thyself, and our heart is restless till it rests in Thee', will have struck him as the perfect expression of

THE ARMS OF CHARLES V ON THE WALL OF THE MONASTERY
GARDEN OF YUSTE

LA GLORIA (Detail)
Titian, *The Prado, Madrid*

his inmost feeling. He said he was 'the most contented man on earth and the one who felt most at peace and least inclined to take himself off anywhere else'.

In his commentary on the Song of Songs, St Bernard wrote of the line, 'to his own bower the king has brought me', 'O place of true rest! to which one can really give the name of bower, where one does not meet a wrathful God but feels the efficacy of his goodness and loving-kindness. This vision inspires no fear, indeed it brings sweetness; it arouses no restless curiosity, it satisfies rather; it does not weary the spirit, it calms it, rather. Here in truth is one at rest. God, who is quiet, makes all things quiet here, and in contemplating His quiet one has a share of quietness.'

The Emperor listened attentively to what his confessor was reading, while out of doors, beyond the half-closed shutters, the sun-drenched air quivered over the monastery garden.

DAILY LIFE IN YUSTE

For Charles' spiritual life, Yuste was a culmination. No descent but an ascent to the goal of Christian living, which is to see God. The Emperor came perceptibly nearer this goal in Yuste.

It is true, he did not practise asceticism; and the reports of the Hieronymite monks that at Easter the Emperor participated in the strict penances of the monastery and 'beat himself with rough pieces of rope till he had worn away the knots', surely exaggerate the devout exercises of their imperial lay-brother. Nor is there any trace to be found in him of a Luther-like 'dust and ashes' feeling, no drastic immolation of the creature before the Creator. He was a pre-Reformation Christian and did not keep profane things and holy things apart, for the world was under the sway of the supernatural, and holiness penetrated daily life through and through.

In Yuste the Emperor had his own Rule. Every morning a Mass was said in his private chapel for the repose of the soul of his wife Isabella, and the members of his household attended it. As soon as he awoke, his confessor Juan de Regla came into his room to pray with him. (The anonymous monk relates that the first man to enter his bedroom was his clockmaker Janelo, who wound up the clocks and regulated them.) At ten o'clock his chamberlain and barber came to dress him. When the state of his health permitted, he attended Mass in the monastery church, otherwise he assisted at it from his room, with great devotion. After Mass came the midday meal (years earlier, a Venetian had coined the phrase, *de la messa a la mensa*—from Mass to table—in reference to the Emperor's habits). During the meal his secretary van Male and Dr Mathys entertained him; both were very well-read men and they spoke on historical and scientific themes. Afterwards he sat at the window and his confessor came and read him pages from St Bernard. Then followed a short siesta. On Sunday, Monday and Friday he heard a sermon in the afternoon, 'and he never wearied, however long it might be'. The other days were dedicated to St Bernard and St Augustine, the Hieronymite monk Bernardin de Salinas reading aloud to him. Sometimes he went to Vespers in the church choir to sing with the monks. He had a very good ear and knew the voices of the different monks so well that after evening Benediction he was liable to say, 'So and so sang out of tune.'

He was fond of conversing with his confessor, valuing his great simplicity, clear mind and ripe Christian wisdom. Fray Juan de Regla, who came of a poor peasant family, originally wanted to decline the office of confessor to the Emperor, feeling he was not up to it. 'Be appeased, Brother Juan,' said the Emperor, 'five theologians and canonists relieved my conscience of all past things in Flanders; your concern will only be with what happens in the future.' (What a healthy disposition of soul the Emperor reveals here—no tormenting scruples or over-anxiety!)

One day the Emperor ate with the monks in the refectory. 'His Majesty thanked us very much for everything we gave him, also for the strawberries and fruit which we sent him from time to time and which he valued as much as pearls.'

The letters from Yuste echo the rhythm of its life; Quijada and Gaztelú dispatched them regularly to the secretary of state, Juan Vasquez, in order to inform Dona Juana of the state of her father's health. They are letters full of affectionate concern for him: 'His Majesty feels very well.' 'His Majesty is not quite in order, having eaten too much fruit.' 'His Majesty slept well.' 'His Majesty had a restless night.' 'His Majesty is out of sorts because the sardines have not turned up yet.' 'The suggestion he should eat no fish was in vain: today His Majesty had a sardine omelette prepared for him.'

And the old money troubles cropped up again. 'We are very short of money,' wrote Quijada. 'I had to advance a hundred reales myself.' (The Emperor's annoyance over a money fraud of the *Casa de Contratación* in Seville fills a considerable part of this correspondence; he said the culprits should be thrown into a dungeon.) 'The Emperor is very pleased that he now receives twenty thousand ducats a year for his expenses.'

This eventless life was punctuated by seasonal variations in the menu: 'For the last fortnight there have been cherries which the Emperor always eats at the beginning of his meal.' 'His Majesty is delighted with the strawberries—and consumes them in great quantities; he likes them with a spoonful of cream.' 'The melons have started here, but the local ones are not the best, and His Majesty regrets that the ones in his garden were frost-bitten—but he eats those available, saying a bad melon is anyhow better than a good cucumber.'

'The Emperor feels very well. Two days ago he asked for his gun and shot two pigeons.' 'A medicinal herb called Caleopsis has arrived from Italy and His Majesty has had it planted in the garden.' 'His Majesty is pleased to spend his leisure in having a new garden laid out, with fountains and many orange trees, flowers and shrubs. We shall need more money for these jobs.' 'Life is sparse and dear here. The Emperor is much annoyed that grain was exported to Portugal whereas there is none here and many are dying of hunger.'

And the changing seasons are noted: 'It is snowing and freezing here and it is as cold as in Burgos,' wrote Quijada in January 1558. And in July of the same year he reported: 'It is unusually hot, and in great heat His Majesty always feels well.'

Sometimes the monastic calm of Yuste was disturbed by small events of daily life that tossed up great billows on the calm sea of the passing hours. Fray Joseph de Siguenza mentioned the disrespectful inhabitants of the village of Quacos. Those bad neighbours took pleasure in annoying the Emperor: they caught the trout that were intended for his table, and even went so far one day as to capture his Swiss herd which through an oversight of the cowherd's grazed on the village pastures. That put the Emperor into a furious state and it took every possible form of argument to persuade him not to get his son Philip to inflict severe punishment on the village. Another time the crude villagers threw stones at the fair-haired boy Geronimo 'upon whom the Emperor's eyes often rested with pleasure' (he was later Don Juan of Austria), because he ate cherries from a tree that belonged to Quacos. . . . But the Emperor's disgust at disrespectful, insubordinate behaviour was balanced by his sensitive attitude towards his retinue and servants and his appreciation of their attachment to his person.

'In Yuste his kindness to those in his service was very great,' wrote

La Roca, 'but this was no newly-won virtue of Charles V's, he always treated them like his sons.'

Nearest to him was his sincerely loyal Luis Quijada, who had served him for thirty-four years, accompanying him on his campaigns to Tunis, Aix-en-Provence, Mühlberg and Metz. Now, Quijada's main job was to see that the Emperor did not eat too much food of a sort that was bad for him, and 'he threw himself between his lord and an eel-pie as he would once have thrown himself between him and a Moorish spear' (Stirling).

Sandoval relates that in Yuste the Emperor often joked with his people. He had his cook fetched and said to him: 'Adriano, do not sprinkle so much cinnamon on the food.' The cook answered: 'The major-domo is the culprit because he buys old spice without any flavour.' 'Adriano, Adriano,' said the Emperor, 'ever since I have known you, you have always put the blame on someone else.'

To his baker he said: 'Come here, Pelayo, you are in the habit of getting drunk seven times a week and that is why you do not take the trouble to bake me a bit of good bread that I can eat with my bad teeth.'

These anecdotes may seem too insignificant to quote, but they show the Emperor in a serene mood. He had the cheerfulness of a man who lived at peace with himself and his neighbour.

He liked chatting with the monks and recounting episodes from his past life. Thus he told them that when he escaped from Maurice of Saxony, two Protestant princes came to meet him who begged him, in Maurice's name, to leave them to their opinions and not to take them for heretics, and that they promised him in return, in the name of the whole realm, to advance against the Turks and not to return home till Constantinople was reached. But he answered: 'I do not want so dear a realm, and at such a price I will have neither Germany nor France nor Spain nor Italy, but Jesus Christ alone'—and he spurred his horse on. As a matter of fact, when the Emperor fled from Maurice of Saxony he was borne in a litter. But who was going to mind the old warrior's seeing himself as a knight on horseback, retrospectively? Or depicting himself as a victor over temptations of the devil? He had truly rejected the kingdoms of this world and their glory for the sake of loyalty to the traditional conception of Jesus Christ.

Another time he said to the prior: 'It is very dangerous to negotiate with those heretics, for they advance such effective arguments and have got up their case so well that they can easily deceive people; and therefore

I never wanted to listen to them when they disputed about their sects.' Whereas in fact he had often listened to them and had even sometimes given in to their wishes.

Whether he was for a time slightly influenced by Lutheran doctrine we shall never know, nor whether it was in order to clear himself that he wrote his glowing assent to the Catholic Church at Yuste. His *Protestación del Emperador* opens with the following words:

'Jesus be in my understanding, my well-loved God and Lord: I believe with my whole heart, and I confess with my lips, all that our Mother the Church believes and teaches about You, and all that a good Christian must believe, and I declare that I will live and die in this holy Faith. . . .'

He hoped to end his days in a Spain united in the Faith. But in spring 1558 came news that the Bishop of Seville, Constantin Ponce de la Fuente (whose work on Christian doctrine was among the Emperor's books), had been arrested by the Inquisition in Seville, accused of Lutheranism. With him, more than eight hundred people were handed over to the Inquisition. At the same time Juan Vasquez reported from Valladolid that the Emperor's former preacher, Cazalla, was held captive there by the ecclesiastical court of enquiry because at secret meetings he had expounded the Bible freely in a Lutheran sense. A number of priests, learned legal men, and men and women of the nobility, who had taken part in those secret meetings, were also under arrest.

This was sad news indeed. The Emperor felt he had not escaped to Spain from a world divided on religious issues, had not come to live in a land where hearts beat in unison, only to be harrowed once more by religious dissensions. He was profoundly shocked and wrote to his daughter Juana on 25th May 1558, saying: 'Believe me, my daughter, this matter causes me such pain and such distress that I can find no words for it. . . . While the king and I were absent from this kingdom, such peace reigned, and now that I have come here, in order to retire and seek repose and serve our Lord, in my presence and in yours those same shameful things occur which caused me to suffer and endure so much in Germany, costing me as they did all that labour and expenditure as well as a good portion of my health. . . . I conjure you to attack the evil at the root. For believe me, my daughter, if one does not apply the right punishments and cures from the beginning in order to prevent the spread of such evil, later on neither the king nor anyone else will be in a position to put it down.'

On the same day the Emperor dictated a report to his son Philip, adding in his own handwriting: 'My son, this dark occurrence that has taken place here makes me as angry as you may well imagine. You see what I write to you and your sister on the subject. It is essential for you to give written instructions for attacking the root of the matter, displaying the greatest strictness and inflicting severe punishment.'

Philip did so. Constantin Ponce de la Fuente was thrown into a dungeon where he died soon after; Cazalla was burned in an *auto-da-fé* at Valladolid, after long years of imprisonment.

The intolerance Charles displayed in regard to Lutheranism in Spain was to some extent in the tradition of the Catholic Sovereigns: in Spain any rebellion against the Catholic Faith amounted to rebellion against the state, and Charles merely expressed the will of the majority when he demanded severe punishment for all who deviated. In Germany, too, he had come to see that religion and politics were not to be kept apart, and political unity was possible only when spiritual harmony prevailed. With this in mind he wrote to his daughter Juana: '. . . for there can be neither peace nor prosperity where unanimity of doctrine does not prevail—I learnt this by experience in Germany and Flanders.'

Charles' reactions were but the sharper for that undercurrent of self-accusation, he blamed himself for not having put up a sterner resistance to Protestantism in its initial stages. He said to the prior: 'Padre, nothing could draw me away from this cell but the necessity to punish heretics. But to deal with this common enemy I am no longer required, for I have written to the Inquisition to burn them all, they will never make good Catholics.' And he said he regretted that in Worms he did not have Luther undergo the full punishment for heresy but assured him a safe-conduct even though with bound hands.

The time when Charles V wanted to achieve the 'lovely unity of the Church' by conciliatory means was long past, and the days were distant when Cardinal Jiménez published his multi-lingual Bible translations in Spain; now, the possession of a Bible was taken as a proof of Lutheran tendencies. Charles, who possessed a Bible, received from the Grand Inquisitor permission to retain it; on the other hand, Dr Mathys had to burn his. By about 1558 the change of climate was complete: the universal intolerance had swept up the peace-loving Emperor, too.

And in Yuste the relentless Spanish light began to have its effect on him, a light that permits of no half-tones and no half-measures, and disposes men's minds to belief in one sole saving truth (and even the Arabs of Spain were, of all the branches of Islam, the most inclined to orthodoxy), and thus, at the end, the spirit of place prevailed, and the merciless spirit of the times settled upon long-suffering Charles V, the one-time mediator.

THE END

Belief in eternal life was so strong in Charles V that one might well write 'the passage over' rather than 'the end', when he passed on into that higher reality to which his soul belonged already here on earth. A remark of the Emperor's reported by Fray de Siguenza would seem to indicate that in preparing for the Last Things he experienced that sense of the fullness of grace that St Bernard calls the fulfilment of all Christian endeavour. After the Mass for the repose of his own soul, he said to his confessor, 'he was happy and had a great consolation in his soul which seemed to him to be filled and brimming over with an abundance that he felt in his body too'.

In Yuste the Emperor reached his goal.

A number of historians shed doubt on the authenticity of that pre-dated Requiem Mass. Gachard finds the date, 31st August, inaccurate; according to Siguenza, that was the day on which the Emperor told his confessor how he longed to have his own Requiem Mass. 'Do you think it would be of use to me?' he inquired. 'Yes, my Lord, very useful indeed,' said Fray Juan de Regla, 'for the devout actions performed in our lifetime are of greater merit and more effective than those that are done for us after death.' 'Then everything should be made ready for this afternoon, beginning at once,' said the Emperor. And on the same day, according to Siguenza, there occurred that scene on the terrace, when the Emperor had Titian's paintings brought him and was overcome by an indisposition he was not to recover from. By the evening of 31st August he was no longer fit to attend a religious ceremony. Uncertainty as to the date is not in itself sufficient to put the fact in doubt, the monks were necessarily vague in their reckoning of time, for they had neither clocks nor calendars. Fray de Siguenza wrote his history of the Hieronymite Order years later, from memory, and memory often effects collusions when things in reality happened separately. A stronger argument is the fact that neither Quijada, nor Gaztelú, nor Dr Mathys, though they kept Dona Juana faithfully informed of all that went on at Yuste, made any mention of the Requiem Mass.

285

On the other hand, the major-domo, the secretary, and the physician but seldom refer to their lord's religious life: for Quijada, he was first and foremost the man with the difficult palate; for Gaztelú, the statesman with political interests; and for Dr Mathys, a sick man to be tended. However, on 1st May 1558 Quijada mentioned the solemn Mass for the repose of the soul of Empress Isabella, and Dr Mathys wrote on 1st August that the Emperor had been so weak that he had to be carried into church, where he received Communion seated. It seems unlikely, then, that they would have failed to mention such an improbable event as a Mass for the repose of a soul still this side of death—unless they wanted to avoid causing anxiety to the Emperor's daughter.

In their letters we hear only of the midday meal on the terrace. On 1st September Dr Mathys wrote to Juan Vasquez: 'Last Tuesday, 30th August, His Majesty took his meal on the terrace, where radiation from the sun was very strong. He ate but little and had not much appetite. . . .' Quijada reported: '. . . I think his indisposition comes from the fact that yesterday His Majesty ate his dinner on a covered terrace where the reflection of the sunshine was very strong. He left the terrace with a headache and had a bad night. It may be that this chill and fever have their origin here. . . .'

Gaztelú's report is the same; his letters of the last days of August indicate that at that time the Emperor was wholly taken up in political discussions with Garcilaso de la Vega (the poet's nephew), commissioning him to persuade Queen Maria, who had retired to Cigales, in the neighbourhood, to resume the regency of the Netherlands. Judging from Gaztelú's letters alone, it would appear that at Yuste the Emperor was wholly absorbed in worldly concerns. Only the monks of the monastery were aware of the intensity of his religious life, and for that reason if for no other their reports should not be neglected. Doubtless they exaggerated and took a suggestion for an accomplished fact, and the legend of the Requiem Mass may perhaps be traced to a chat of the Emperor's with his barber, the monks' imagination supplying the rest of the story.

La Roca had the following from Fray Martin de Angelo: the Emperor used to converse with his barber in the morning and often confided his thoughts to him. When one morning the barber found him unusually silent, he asked what he was thinking about: 'I have saved two thousand escudos,' said the Emperor, 'and wonder how I am to defray the expenses for my funeral.' 'Do not worry, Your Majesty,' replied the barber, 'if you should die and we live on, we shall do you every honour.' 'You don't understand,' said the Emperor, 'there is a great difference, Nicholas, when one would see one's way, if the light is brought afterwards or if it is carried ahead.'

The sequel to this story comes in the monks' account of the Requiem Mass: at the beginning of the Offertory he went up to the altar holding a burning candle which he handed to the priest, saying, 'I implore thee, Judge over life and death, that thou mayest accept my soul as the priest accepts this candle'; and then he lay down on the altar steps with his arms outstretched, as though he had utterly died to the world.

The French historian, M. Mignet, remarked that in the last days of August the Emperor was in such a poor state of health that he would not have been up to so strenuous a ceremony, and doubted whether it took place at all, for 'the Catholic Church prays only for those who can no longer pray for themselves'.

And yet in Charles V there existed a curious juxtaposition of temporal and eternal concerns, and he would see no particular difficulty in making present something that actually belonged to the future. He had a great variety of Masses said in Yuste. Fray de Siguenza reported that in the monastery church, apart from the regular Masses for the repose of his parents' souls and his wife's, the Emperor had 'Masses of petition celebrated for his son Philip, that God might send him health and victory, or of thanksgiving, when success was achieved; also Masses for the repose of the souls of Knights of the Golden Fleece who died during His Majesty's stay in Yuste, and for kings and popes; although there were so many of us priests, we were all kept busy with these Masses'. So that it is not wholly improbable that the Emperor had a solemn Mass celebrated for the repose of his own soul after death, the monks taking it for a Requiem Mass. Like the men of the late Middle Ages, Charles was very serious about his preparation for his last hours, it was an important task to which he desired to do full justice.

The end found him ready. In the twenty-one days that his fever lasted, he was so utterly occupied with the thought of God that it filled his servants, spiritual counsellors and friends with devout awe. 'To his last breath,' wrote Carranza, Archbishop of Toledo, 'he was full of a great confidence and joy that deeply stirred and consoled all of us who were present.' When the Archbishop of Toledo reached Yuste, the Emperor had already been anointed.

Carranza was one of the most outstanding of the Spanish delegates at the first session of the Council of Trent; nonetheless he was to end his days under arrest by the Inquisition. Since his return, complaints had been heard that his sermons showed traces of Melanchthon's influence. Carranza's arrival at Yuste brought the tensions of the day right into the Emperor's bedroom.

The prior of the monastery, Fray Juan de Regla, Fray Villalba, Quijada, Dr Mathys, Don Luis de Avila, the Count of Oropeso, Don Francisco de Toledo, Don Diego de Toledo and several monks were all in the Emperor's room when the archbishop arrived. Charles was fully conscious. He had requested that the blessed candles from Monserrat and his wife's crucifix be kept in readiness, and said: 'Read me this psalm, then that prayer, then such and such a litany.' The archbishop took over the prayers. The Emperor asked him to read the *De Profundis* and in the prevailing silence sounded the Psalmist's verses: 'Out of the depths I cry to Thee, O Lord; Master, listen to my voice. . . . If Thou, Lord, take heed of our iniquities, Master, who has strength to bear it? Ah, but with Thee there is forgiveness; I will wait for Thee, Lord, as Thou commandest. . . . My soul waits patiently for the Lord. From the morning watch till night has fallen. . . .'

When the archbishop finished, he sank down on his knees and holding out the crucifix, he cried: 'Here is He who answers for all, there is no more sin, all is forgiven!'

Many of those present shrank at the words, for they struck them as a confession of Carranza's Protestant leanings, Luther's *solus Christus, sola gratia, sola fide* (and Carranza soon had to account for his words before the Inquisition). Don Luis de Avila gave the archbishop to understand it were better he said no more; and he begged Fray de Villalba, the preacher, to speak to the Emperor.

The simple monk then told the story of the patron saint of the day, St Matthew, and of St Matthias, on whose day the Emperor's birthday fell—both Apostles of our Lord, in whose guardianship and intercession he could well find comfort on his great journey. . . . But how strange it was that the major controversies of the day should pursue him to his very deathbed.

To the very last, the Emperor prayed for the peace and unity of the Church: 'Lord, into thy hands I have commended Thy Church'. The last words he spoke were for his faithful servants: 'Luis Quijada, I feel it is the end of me, and I thank God very much, for it is His will. Tell the king, my son, that I beg him to take on my retinue, those who served me right up to my death, and to make use of the barber Gila if he will, and that no visitors be allowed to enter this house.'

The blessed candle was lit and he held it in his right hand; his other hand clutched Isabella's crucifix and attempted to bring it to his lips; with the word 'Jesus——' he breathed out his soul. It was on the twenty-first of September, at two in the morning, before day broke over the mountains, and the stars shone over the monastery from a clear sky.

CONCLUSION

In following the course of Charles V's life, we saw how the failure of his political mission was conducive to an inward-turning. The miscarriage of a life's work may well serve a clarification of the personality and thus be of great value in the spiritual sphere; but in the political field, where a positive idea is at stake, such a miscarriage will produce, first, stagnation, then violent reaction.

Charles V's political mission came to grief the moment the religious peace of Augsburg compelled him to renounce his rôle of arbitrator. In his abdication speech he no longer spoke as sovereign of the western world, but as a man of the Counter-Reformation. His words, 'to defend religion like an exceptionally important fortress' were echoed by St Teresa of Avila in her *Interior Castle*; they are words of self-defence, expressing the spirit of a time that failed to find a formula applicable to all men in common. And where the spirit fails, the sword cuts the knots asunder.

We may see in the fact that synthesis was striven for but never realized, an admonishment to seek once more a common denominator, and a challenge to continue caring for the cause of a united Europe; reminding us that Erasmus' mean, so long submerged, deserves to be salvaged and to play its part in the realization of Europe's mission, which is to arbitrate.

BIBLIOGRAPHY

CONTEMPORARY AND NEAR-CONTEMPORARY
SPANISH HISTORICAL WORKS

Mexia, Pedro, *Historia de Carlos Quinto* (1530; Madrid 1940)

Sandoval, Prudencio de, *Historia de la Vida y Hechos del Emperador Carlos V* (Pamplona 1618)

Santa Cruz, Alonso de, *Cronica del Emperador Carlos V* (1536–51) (published by the *Real Academia de la Historia*; Madrid 1920–25)

Siguenza, Joseph de, *Historia de la Orden de San Geronimo* (Madrid 1595–1605)

Vera y Zuñiga, Juan Antonio, Conde de la Roca, *Epitome de la Vida y Hechos del invicto Emperador Carlos Quinto* (Madrid 1624)

FRENCH COMMENTARY

Morel Fatio, Alfred, *Historiographie de Charles-Quint*, including *Commentaires de Charles Quint* (Paris 1913)

BIOGRAPHIES

Armstrong, Edward, *The Emperor Charles V* (London 1910)

Babelon, Jean, *Charles-Quint* (Paris 1947)

Baumgarten, Hermann, *Karl V und die deutsche Reformation* (1889)

Brandi, Karl, *Kaiser Karl V* (Munich 1937)

Cossio, Francisco de, *Carlos V* (Madrid 1941)

Pfandl, Ludwig, *Philip II* (Munich 1938)

Robertson, William, *History of the Reign of the Emperor Charles the Fifth* (London 1769)

Sans y Ruiz, de la Peña, N., *Dona Juana I de Castilla* (Madrid 1942)

Walsh, Thomas W., *Isabel of Spain* (New York 1930)

Wyndham Lewis, D. B., *Emperor o the West* (London 1934)

RELATED HISTORICAL AND RELIGIOUS
WORKS AND ART HISTORIES

Altamira y Crevea, Rafael, *Historia de España* (Barcelona 1929)

Andreas, Willy, *Deutschland vor der Reformation* (Stuttgart 1948)

Anglés, Higinio, *La musica en la Corte de Carlos V* (Alcala de Hernares, 1557)

Ballesteros y Beretta, Antonio D., *Historia de España y su influencia en la Historia universal* (Barcelona 1926)

Bertrand, Louis, and Sir Charles Petrie, *The History of Spain* (London 1934)

Buchholtz, F. W. v., *Geschichte der Regierung Ferdinands des Ersten* (Vienna 1831–38)

Dilthey, Wilhelm, *Weltanschauung und Analyse des Menschen seit Renaissance und Reformation* (Berlin 1914)

Döllinger, Ignaz von, *Die Reformation* (Regensburg 1846)

Harnack, Adolf von, *Dogmengeschichte*, Part IV, Vol. III (Tübingen 1905)

Jansen, Johannes, *Geschichte des deutschen Volkes* (Freiburg i. Br. 1878, Vol. II, III)

Joachimsen, Paul, *Das Zeitalter der Reformation*, Propyläen Weltgeschichte (Berlin 1930, Vol. V)

Justi, Karl, *Velázquez und sein Jahrhundert* (1888)

Lanz, Karl, *Korrespondenz des Kaisers Karl V* (Leipzig 1844–46)

Lortz, Josef, *Die Reformation in Deutschland* (Freiburg i. Br. 1948)

Marañón, Gregorio, *Elogio y nostalgia de Toledo* (Madrid 1941)

Maurenbrecher, Wilhelm, *Karl V und die deutschen Protestanten, 1545–1555* (Düsseldorf 1865)

Maurenbrecher, Wilhelm, *Studien und Skizzen zur Geschichte der Reformationszeit* (Leipzig 1874)

Menéndez Pelayo, Marcelino D., *Historia de los Heterodoxes españoles* (Madrid 1880)

Oliveira Martins, J. P. de, *Historia de la civilicaçao iberica* (Lisbon 1878)

Ortega y Gasset, José, *Velázquez* (Bern 1943)

Pirenne, Henri, *Histoire de Belgique*, Vol. III (Brussels 1907)

Ranke, Leopold von, *Deutsche Geschichte im Zeitalter der Reformation*, Vols. IV, V (Berlin 1839–47)

—, *Die Osmanen und die Spanische Monarchie* (Berlin 1837)

—, *Die römischen Päpste, ihre Kirche und ihr Staat im XVI. und XVII. Jahrhundert* (Berlin 1834)

Rassow, Peter, *Die politische Welt Karl V* (Munich 1942)

Sainz Rodriguez, Pedro D., *Introducción a la Historia de la Literatura mistica en España* (Madrid 1927)

Srbik, Heinrich, Ritter von, *Deutsche Einheit. Vom Heiligen Reich bis Königgrätz* (Munich 1935)

Trend, J. B., *The Civilization of Spain* (Oxford 1944)

Troeltsch, Ernst, *Aufsätze sur Geistesgeschichte und Religionssoziologie* (Tübingen 1924)

Fernandez de Oviedo, Gonzalo, *Relación de lo sucedido en la prisón de Francisco I* (MSS. 1550, Biblioteca Nacional, Madrid)
Hauser, Henri, *Le traité de Madrid* (Dijon 1912)
Mignet, M., *Rivalité de François I et de Charles-Quint* (Paris 1943)

Clouet's Portrait of Francis I

Pascal, Blaise, *Pensées*, I, Section I (169)
Terasse, Charles, *François I, le Roi et le Règne* (Paris 1943)

The Sack of Rome

Romance on the plundering of Rome. Biblioteca de Autores Españoles, Romances Historicos, No. 1155

Charles V and the Rise of Capitalism

Häbler, Konrad, *Die Geschichte der Fugger'schen Handlung in Spanien* (The story of the Fuggers' business activities in Spain) (Weimar 1897)
Strieder, Jakob, *Zur Genesis des modernen Kapitalismus* (Bonn 1903)
—, *Jakob Fugger der Reiche* (Leipzig 1925)
—, *Das reiche Augsburg* (Munich 1938)

Charles V and the Turks

Hammer, Joseph von, *Geschichte des Osmanischen Reiches*, Vol. I, III, IV (Pest 1829)

Tunis

Gachard et Piot, M. M., *Collection des voyages des souverains des Pays-Bas*, Vol. III: *Expédition à Tunis* (Brussels 1881–82) (including the expedition to Algiers)
Illescas, Gonzalo de, *Carlos V en Tunis* (Madrid c. 1550)

Charles V in Rome

Heer, Friedrich, *Die Tragödie des Heiligen Reiches* (Stuttgart 1952)
Rassow, Peter, *Die Kaiseridee Karls V* (Berlin 1952)
Rosenstock, Eugen, *Die europäischen Revolution* (Jena 1931)

Siena and Arles

Bourrilly, V. L., *Charles-Quint en Provence* (Paris 1918)
Pichot, Amédée, *Charles-Quint* (Paris 1954)
Vigo, Pierro, *Carlo Quinto in Siena* (Bologna 1884)

Compasses, Charts and South America

Häbler, Konrad, *Die überseeischen Unternehmungen der Welser* (Leipzig 1903)
Humbert, Jules, *L'occupation allemande du Venezuela* (Paris 1905)

Menéndez Pidal, Ramón, *Idea Imperial de Carlos V* (Madrid 1940)
Sucre Reyes, José-L., *Le système colonial espagnol dans l'ancien Venezuela* (Paris 1939)

Nice and Aiguesmortes

Albiousse, Lionel de, *Entrevue de François I et de Charles-Quint à Aiguesmortes en 1538* (Vannes 1909)

Journey through France

Burnard, Robert, *La cour des Valois* (Paris 1938)
Champion, Pierre, *Paganisme et Réforme* (Paris 1936)
—, *Le règne de François Ier* (Paris 1935)

Ghent

Gachard, L. P., *Relation des troubles de Gand sous Charles-Quint, par un anonyme* (Brussels 1846)
Straeten, E. van der, *Charles-Quint musicien* (Ghent 1894)

Charles V in Germany

Drüffel, August von, *Die Sendung des Cardinals Sfondrato an den Hof Karls V, 1547–1548* (Munich 1893)
Friedensburg, W., *Kaiser Karl V und Papst Paul III* (Leipzig 1932)
Gachard, L. P., *Trois années de l'histoire de Charles-Quint d'après les dépêches de l'ambassadeur vénitien Bernard Navagero* (Brussels 1865)
Gossart, Ernest, *Espagnols et Flamands au XVIe siècle* (Brussels 1896)
—, *Charles-Quint et Philippe II* (Brussels 1896)
Hecker, O. A., *Karls V Plan zur Gründung eines Reichsbunds* (Leipzig 1906)
Heidrich, Paul, *Karl V und die deutschen Protestanten am Vorabend des Schmalkaldischen Krieges* (Frankfurt 1911)
Pastor, Ludwig von, *Die Reunionsbestrebungen während der Regierung Karls V* (Freiburg i. Br. 1879)
Ribadeneyra, Pedro de, *Vida de Ignacio de Loyola* (Madrid 1598)
Sastrow, Bartholomew, Memoirs, 1520–1603 (Hamburg 1907)
Schütz, A., *Der Donaufeldzug Karls V* (Tübingen 1930)

Interim

Interim, contemporary print (Central Library, Zürich)
Pascal, Blaise, *Pensées, 'Le Pari'* (451)
Plotinus, *An Essay on the Beautiful* London 1792)

Maximilian II

Hopfen, Helmut Otto, *Maximilian II und der Reformkatholizismus* (Munich 1895)

Yuste

Alarcón, Pedro de, *Una visita al Monasterio de Yuste* (Madrid 1873)

Castiglione, Baldassare, *El Cortegiano* (Madrid, Liv. Austral)

Commynes, Philippe de, *Mémoires* (Antwerp 1597)

Gachard, L. P., *Retraite et mort de Charles-Quin au Monastère de Yuste* (Brussels 1854)

Gilson, Etienne, *Saint Bernard* (Paris 1947)

Mignet, M., *Charles-Quint, son abdication, son séjour et sa mort au Monastère de Yuste* (Paris 1854)

Ribadeneyra, Pedro de, *Vida del P. Francisco de Borja* (Madrid 1592)

Stirling, Sir W., *The Cloistered Life of the Emperor Charles V* (London 1852)

Unamuno, Miguel de, *Andanzas y Visiones españolas* (Madrid, Liv. Austral)

INDEX OF PERSONS

Berquin, Louis de *(cont.)*
stood out for freedom of conscience. His works were confiscated in 1522 and he was summoned to recant his opinions; condemned to witness the burning of his books, and himself burnt to death—123

Blomberg, Barbara *(c.* 1527–97), daughter of a citizen of Regensburg, who became the mistress of Charles V in 1546, and mother of Don Juan of Austria—229

Boethius, Anicius, Toquatus Severinus *(c.* 480–525), Roman philosopher and statesman. Consul under Theodoric, King of the East Goths, he was calumniated, imprisoned and executed. Whilst in prison wrote his *Consolations of Philosophy*—275, 276

Boleyn, Anne (1507–36), became second wife of King Henry VIII of England at Easter 1533. In September 1533 she gave birth to a daughter, the future Queen Elizabeth I. Henry, disappointed that the child was not a son, accused her of adultery and had her beheaded—147

Borgia, Cesare (1475–1507), son of Pope Alexander VI, who subdued the Romagna, Umbria and Siena. After his father's death he went to Spain and entered the service of the King of Navarre. Machiavelli's model of the strong prince, who could alone achieve the unification of Italy—40, 57, 257

Borja, Francisco de, Marqués de Lombay, Duke of Gandia (1510–72). Became General of the Society of Jesus in 1565; formerly Chamberlain to the Empress Isabella—95, 140, 181–2, 273, 274, 257

Bosch, Hieronymus *(c.* 1450–1526), Dutch painter, whose work gives characteristic expression to the late medieval fear of Hell; a favourite painter of Philip II's—15

Bossuet, Jacques (1627–1704), French Catholic theologian and preacher, who corresponded with Leibniz on the prospects of the reunion of the Christian confessions—253

Bouillon, Godefroi de *(c.* 1058–1100), Duke of Lower Lorraine, who led the First Crusade and took Jerusalem by storm in 1099. Elected King of Jerusalem, he would accept only the title of 'Protector of the Holy Sepulchre'—164

Bourbon, Charles de, Connétable (1490–1527), Crown Vassal of Francis I, who went over to Charles V in 1525, and fell at the storming of Rome—92

Brant, Sebastian (1458–1521), German humanist, author of Latin verses and German pamphlets, who attacked the immorality of his day in a great satire, *The Ship of Fools.* Deeply Catholic, he nonetheless helped pave the way for the Reformation with his merciless criticism of Church and clergy—57

Bruck, Gregory, Chancellor of the Elector John Frederick of Saxony, and spokesman of the Elector's policy at the Diet of Augsburg in 1530—152

Brusasorci, Domenico de Riccio *(c.* 1516–67), Italian painter of the School of Veronese—150

Bucer, Martin (1491–1551), Protestant Reformer who strove to create unity within the reform movement. Expelled from Strasbourg on account of his opposition to the Interim he came to England at Cranmer's invitation and was given a professorship at Cambridge—70, 204, 213

Caesar, Caius Julius (100–44 B.C.), Roman General and statesman. As Consul became master of Rome. Subdued Gaul 58–52 B.C. —248, 275, 276

Cajetan, Thomas de Vio (1469–1534), General of the Dominican Order. A learned Catholic theologian of the Reformation period, he was counsellor to Pope Clement VII, and was created Cardinal—69

Calderón de la Barca (1600–81), prolific Spanish dramatist, whose numerous works are all deeply imbued with Christian values—27

Calvin, John (1509–64), French Reformer. Strove to put God's Law into effect on earth—123, 202

Campeggio, Lorenzo (1474–1539), created Cardinal in 1517, Papal Legate to Germany in 1524 and from 1530–32—78, 153, 154

Caraffa, Neapolitan noble family of, see *Paul IV*, Pope

Carlos, Don (1545–68), eldest son of Philip II, who showed symptoms of degeneration and was excluded from the succession by his father—4, 87

Carranza, Bartolomé de (1503–76), created Archbishop of Toledo in 1557, he was later suspected of Protestant leanings and imprisoned by the Inquisition. As theologian attended the Council of Trent—287, 288

Castiglione, Baldassare, Conte de (1478–1529), Italian writer and diplomat. In 1525 sent by Pope Clement VII as Nuncio to the Court of Charles V. Author of *Il Cortegiano*, in which he represents the ideal man of the Renaissance as the perfect courtier—40, 118, 144, 276, 278

Catharine of Aragon (1485–1536), first wife of Henry VIII of England and mother of Mary Tudor—112, 127, 147

criticism. He stood out for ideals of culture and reason against ignorance and fanaticism—36–40, 44, 54, 56–59, 63–66, 71, 76, 82, 91, 113, 114, 118–24, 144, 148, 156, 204, 226, 250, 251, 254–55, 271, 290

Étampes, Anne de Pisselieu, Duchess of (1508–85), cultured mistress of Francis I, friendly to Charles V's policies—146, 180, 184, 185, 221, 223, 224

Farnese, Ottavio (1520–86), nephew of Pope Paul III; adherent of Charles V—235

Farnese, Pierluigi (1503–47), son of Alexandro Farnese, later Pope Paul III, who made him Duke of Parma and Piacenza in 1545; he led the Papal party opposed to Charles V—235

Ferdinand I (1503–64), German Emperor 1556–64, inherited Bohemia and Hungary (1526), lost Hungary almost entirely to the Turks; crowned German king, 1531; vainly strove for a married priesthood and Communion under both kinds at the Council of Trent for his hereditary lands—5, 6, 9, 36, 78, 126, 132, 142, 150, 160–63, 166, 173, 180, 183, 205, 222, 224, 230, 232, 233, 236, 246, 249, 252, 257, 258, 262, 265, 276

Ferdinand II, of Aragon (1452–1516), *The Catholic*, King of a United Spain 1479–1516, founded Spanish world-sovereignty through his marriage with Isabella of Castile (1469), the conquest of Granada (1492), Naples (1503), and Navarre (1512)—34, 86, 100, 107, 108, 126, 127, 129, 130, 132, 135, 136, 137, 139, 210, 245, 276

Ferdinand III (1199–1252), Saint, King of Castile 1217–52, reconquered Córdoba, Seville and Murcia from the Moors—192, 197

Ferdinand, Duke of Austria, second son of Ferdinand I—256, 263

Ferrara, Bishop of (Coelius Calcagninus, *d.* 1540), poet and humanist, favoured by Pope Leo X—119

Fichte, Johann Gottlieb (1762–1814), German philosopher—ix, 81

Ficino, Marsilio (1433–99), Italian philosopher, physician, humanist, who sought to establish a synthesis of Christian thought and Platonism—56, 57

Fisher, John (1469–1535), Saint, Bishop of Rochester and Cardinal, executed by Henry VIII for refusing the Oath of Supremacy—123, 147

Foix, Germaine de (1488–1538), second wife of Ferdinand of Aragon—135

Francis I (1494–1547), King of France, who strove for the supremacy of France and waged four wars against Charles V, thus imperilling the religious unity of the Germanies, which only a strong Emperor could have achieved—51, 109, 110, 113, 115–17, 142, 145, 146, 166, 167, 168, 169, 170–73, 178–86, 205, 209, 210, 211, 213–18, 220, 221, 224, 225, 230

Francis II (1768–1835), German Emperor 1792–1806, Emperor of Austria 1804–35, who stood for conservative principles in the era of the French Revolution—151

Francis de Sales (1567–1622), Saint, Doctor of the Church and, since 1922, Patron Saint of Catholic authors and journalists, who was active in regaining northern Savoy for the Church from the Calvinists—192, 237

Francis Joseph I (1830–1916), Emperor of Austria 1848–1916—6

Franck, Sebastian (1499–1543), humanist and priest, who went over to Lutheranism but abandoned it in 1528, in a further search for a dogma-less form of Christianity and religious tolerance—123

Frederick I, Barbarossa, von Hohenstaufen (*c.* 1122–90), German Roman Emperor 1152–90, seen as the ideal mediaeval German Emperor—149

Frederick II, von Hohenstaufen (1194–1250), German Roman Emperor 1212–50, King of Jerusalem and Sicily. Highly gifted, cultivated monarch, interested in all forms of intellectual pursuits, including the study of Hebrew and Arabic—167, 219

Frederick III (1415–93), German Emperor 1442–93. It was during his long, weak reign that the forces which were to come to a head during the Renaissance-Reformation period gathered momentum—109

Frederick the Wise (1463–1525), Elector of Saxony, founded the University of Wittenberg, and although he did not accept Luther's teaching, was responsible for having him brought from Worms to the Wartburg—52, 64

Frundsberg, George (Jorg) von (1473–1528), Imperial Army captain and 'father of the German soldiers'—142

Fugger, Anton (1493–1560), the nephew of Jacob Fugger, banker to Charles V, who, as a convinced Catholic, supported Eck against Luther—158, 210, 233, 248, 258

Fugger, Jacob, 'the Rich' (1459–1525), founder of the Fugger financial empire, creditor to the Pope and to the Habsburgs, who financed the election of Charles V as Emperor—52, 158

Gachard, Louis-Prospère (1800–85), Belgian historian—285

Galerius, Gaius, Roman Emperor 305–11—33

Garcilaso de la Vega, see *Vega*

Gattinara, Mercurino de (1465–1530), High Chancellor and counsellor of Charles V, who saw Charles' realm as the realization of Dante's dream in *De Monarchia*—52, 80, 111, 113, 119, 120, 152

Gautier, Théophile (1811–72), French author and poet, wrote *Voyage in Espagne* (1845) —102

Gaztelú, Charles V's secretary for political affairs at Yuste—271, 273, 280, 285, 286

Gilson, Etienne (*b.* Paris, 1884), French philosopher, authority on scholastic philosophy, at present in Canada—76

Giotto di Bondone (1266–1337), an Italian master of religious painting—150

Giustiniani, Vicenzo (1519–82), historian and priest; member of a Venetian noble family—205, 246

Glapion, Juan (1450–1522), a French diplomat who entered the Franciscan Order and became successively Confessor to Maximilian I and to Charles V; friend of Erasmus—70, 71, 179, 273

Góngora y Argote, Luis de (1561–1627), Spanish poet who developed a grave, ceremonious style of writing known as the 'estilo culto'—27

Granvelle, Antoine Perrenot de (1517–86), Cardinal, statesman under Charles V and Philip II, who, from 1547, performed many of his father's duties—255, 259, 277

Granvelle, Nicholas Perrenot de (1468–1550), Charles V's minister, after the death of Gattinara his most influential counsellor— 80, 146, 172, 217, 221, 222, 255, 259, 277

Greco, El, actually Domenico Theotocopuli (*d.* 1613), Greco-Spanish painter; a pupil of Titian and Tintoretto. His art is the expression of his own type of piety and that of Spain—48, 49, 50

Gregory VII (1020–85), Pope 1073–85, champion of papal primacy. He forbade the investiture of bishops through secular powers and thus came into conflict with the German Emperor Henry IV—172

Gryphius, Andreas (1616–64), German baroque poet—93

Guicciardini, Francesco (1483–1540), Florentine historian and friend of Machiavelli— 58

Guise, François, de Lorraine, Duke of (1519–63), French Commander-in-Chief, who valiantly defended Metz against Charles V—259, 272

Hadrian, Publius Aelius (A.D. 76–138), peace-loving Emperor and patron of art and learning, who raised protective walls against barbarian invasions, and built his own mausoleum in Rome, later known as the Castel S. Angelo—53

Hadrian VI, Pope, see *Adrian of Utrecht*

Heer, Friedrich von, contemporary Viennese historian—169

Hegel, Georg Wilhelm (1770–1831), German philosopher and 'secular theologian'—40, 59, 75, 254

Henry II, of France (1519–59), son of Francis I, who allied himself with the German Protestants and with whom he bargained for Metz, Toul and Verdun. Fell in a tournament—235, 255, 261, 272

Henry IV (1050–1106), German Emperor 1056–1106, who clashed with Pope Gregory VII over the investiture of bishops and submitted to the Pope finally at Canossa in 1077. Fought for the supremacy of the Empire as against the Papacy—219

Henry VIII, of England (1491–1547), succeeded in 1509 and brought about the severance of England from the Continent —65, 111, 112, 118, 145, 147, 148, 166, 169, 215, 219, 221, 223

Henry of Nassau, Count of Dillenburg (1483–1538), Charles V's Commander-in-Chief in the War of the Netherlands against France—174

Hildegard of Bingen (*c.* 1098–1179), Abbess of a convent she founded on the Rupertsberg, near Bingen, Western Germany; a highly gifted mystic who gave poetic expression to her visions—55

Hohermuth, Georg (*d.* 1540), German conquistador, and representative of the Welser interests in Sevilla, he was made Regent of Venezuela by Charles V; undertook a voyage of discovery into the interior of the country—177

Holbein, the Younger, Hans (1497–1543), noted portrait-painter and engraver of the Renaissance—62, 147

Hölderlin, Friedrich (1770–1834), poet of the German Romantic era—1, 253

Hugues (Hugo) de Provence, Duke of Burgundy (928–933)—174

Huss, John (*c.* 1369–1415), Czech reformer who propounded Wycliffe's ideas at Prague University. Preached against indulgences and the Papacy. This led to a rising not only against the Church but against the German middle classes in Bohemia, so that the Hussites were national and social revolutionaries. In spite of King Sigismund's safe conduct, Huss was condemned for heresy at the Council of Constance and burnt—66, 123

Hutten, Philipp von (*c.* 1505–46), German conquistador, who went to Venezuela in the service of the Welsers in 1535, and in

Julius II (1443-1513), Pope 1503-13, founder of the modern Papal States, he opposed Cesare Borgia and drove the French out of Italy to the cry of 'Out with the Barbarians'; patron of Michelangelo, Raphael Bramante—57

Justin, the Martyr (c. 100-165), a former pagan philosopher who, after his conversion, sought to prove the truth of the Christian revelation, by the light of Platonic philosophy; honoured as one of the Fathers of the Church—56

Justin of Nassau (d. 1631), Governor of Breda, natural son of William, Prince of Orange —26

Lachance, P., contemporary French theologian and Thomist—41

Lannoy, Charles (1487-1527), Flemish nobleman and Knight of the Golden Fleece; Charles V's Commander-in-Chief, to whom Francis I surrendered his sword at the Battle of Pavia—111

Las Casas, Bartolomeo de (1474-1566), Spanish missionary in Peru and Mexico, who championed the natural rights of the Indians—176

Laso de la Vega, Pedro, Spanish nobleman who took up the cause of the Comuneros and contended for their leadership with Padilla. He gradually abandoned his comrades and finally went over to the loyal Grandees—92, 93

Lautrec, Odet de la Foix, Vicomte de (1485-1528), Field-Marshal to Francis I— 146

Lawrence, Thomas Edward (1888-1935), 'Lawrence of Arabia', organized the Arabian war of independence against Turkey (1916-18), author of *The Seven Pillars of Wisdom*—102

Leibniz, Gottfried Wilhelm (1646-1716), philosopher and encyclopaedic scholar— 253

Leo X (1475-1521), Pope 1513-21, second son of Lorenzo de Medici. A typical Renaissance prince, a highly cultivated patron of the arts, it was his scheme for financing the building of St. Peter's in Rome by the issue of a special Indulgence which became a pretext for confessional disaffection throughout Europe—54, 56, 57, 64, 69, 77, 124

Leonardo da Vinci (1452-1519), Italian painter, sculptor, builder, natural scientist, the first technician, the most all-round genius of the Reformation—185

Leonora (1488-1558), Queen of France, sister of Charles V. First married to King Manuel of Portugal, she was widowed within two years and then married Francis

I of France at the express wish of her brother—36, 94, 115, 130, 146, 179, 180, 183, 184, 185, 221, 223, 263

Leovigildo, the last Arian King of the Visigoths in Spain (d. 586)—34

Livy (Titus Livius) (59 B.C.-A.D. 17), famous Roman historian—33, 248

Loaysa, Garcia de (1479-1546), General of the Dominican Order, Charles V's Confessor 1523-30, Ambassador to the Holy See 1530-32, and, finally, a member of the Regency Council in Spain and Cardinal— 154, 156, 245

Lope de Vega (1562-1635), Spanish dramatist, wrote at least 1500 plays—27

Lorca, Garcia Federico (1899-1936), Spanish poet, shot by nationalist soldiers in the confusion of the Spanish Civil War—103

Lorenzo I, de Medici (*il Magnifico*) (1449-92), ruler of the city state of Florence 1469-92; a poet and scholar, he was a lavish patron of artists, especially of Michelangelo—57, 210

Lothair I (795-855), Roman Emperor 840-55, eldest son of Louis the Pious—220

Louis IX (1214-70), Saint, King of France 1226-70, consolidated the power of the throne against the feudal lords and the Church; led the Sixth Crusade—166, 179

Louis XI (1423-83), King of France 1461-83, fought Maximilian of Austria and gained Burgundy and Picardy after the death of Charles the Bold, Duke of Burgundy—110, 221, 277

Louis XII (1462-1515), King of France 1498-1515, conquered Milan in 1499 but lost it again in 1503. In alliance with Ferdinand of Aragon, conquered the kingdom of Naples, but Ferdinand later ejected him—109, 130, 131, 132, 135, 136

Ludwig the German (804-76), German King 843-76, by the Treaty of Verdun (843) received the eastern third of the Empire— 220

Ludwig II of Hungary (1506-1526), King of Hungary 1516-26, died fleeing from the Mohacser battlefield—109

Luis de Granada, Fray (1504-88), famous Dominican preacher and author of numerous mystical works, including 'What a Christian has to do'—275

Lull, Ramón (1232-1316), Catalonian mystic, poet, missionary and champion of the Catholic Faith. Worked for the conversion of Islam. In his *Ars Magna* he endeavoured to deduce all knowledge from the highest principles—46, 166

Luther, Martin (1483-1546), German reformer. Originally an Augustinian monk he found in St Paul's teaching a trust in divine grace which he turned into his 'justification' doctrine which is contrary to Church doctrine. By refusing to revoke his opinions he caused the splintering into confessions of the religious life of Europe. His translation of the Bible is a landmark in the German language—39, 42, 54, 56, 57, 59, 60–78, 81, 82, 87, 112, 118, 119, 120–24, 151, 152, 153, 158, 163, 170, 172, 186, 202, 203, 217, 226, 228, 230, 243, 245, 252, 264, 284, 288

Machiavelli, Niccolò (1469–1527), Florentine writer on historical subjects and political philosopher. Worked in the Florentine state chancellory, but withdrew to the country when the hated Medici were reinstated. He composed his works in the hope of freeing Italy from foreign rule—38, 40, 41, 42, 43, 44, 57, 58, 151, 162, 187, 210, 215, 223, 224, 225, 227, 254, 255, 257, 262, 277, 278

Mâcon, Charles Hérnard, Bishop of, French diplomat, envoy of Francis I at the meeting of Charles V with Pope Paul III in Rome in 1536—171

'*Mad Joan*', see *Joanna*

Magellan, Ferdinand (1480–1521), Portuguese explorer in the service of Spain—176

Maimonides, Moses (1135–1204), Jewish physician and theologian, who based Old Testament doctrine on Aristotle and whose endeavours to bring reason and revelation into harmony influenced St Thomas Aquinas and the Renaissance neo-Platonists—90, 91, 197

Male, van, private secretary to Charles V—80, 248, 271, 276, 280

Manuel I (1469–1521), King of Portugal 1495–1521, promoted voyages of discovery. Father of Charles V's wife, he married Charles' sister, Leonora, as his third wife—85, 94

Marañon, Gregorio (*b.* 1887), contemporary Spanish physician, scholar and writer—92

Marche, Olivier de la (1435–99), Chamberlain to Duke Philip and Charles the Bold of Burgundy, governor of Philip the Fair; wrote his memoirs—276

Marcus Aurelius Antoninus (121–180), Roman Emperor 161–180, who endeavoured to bring a kindly and humane spirit into imperial administration—150

Marcus Fulvius Flaccus, Roman Consul, 125 B.C., popular tribune 122 B.C.—33

Margaret of Austria (1480–1530), General Regent of the Netherlands 1507–30, daughter of Emperor Maximilian I; widow of the Infant Don Juan of Castile and of Duke Philibert II of Savoy. She brought up Charles V and three of his sisters in Brussels—4, 114, 127, 128, 129, 146

Margaret of Navarre (1492–1549), sister of Francis I of France, Queen of Navarre, poet and writer, chiefly remembered for her romantic novels and mystical verses. A patron of humanists, she gave refuge to persecuted Calvinists at her court at Nérac. Some of her works were declared heretical at the Sorbonne. Later, out of affection for her royal brother, she gave her complete allegiance to the Catholic Church—179, 180

Margaret of Parma (1522–86), Regent of the Netherlands 1559–67. The natural daughter of Charles V and Joanna of Gheenst (?) she married, first, Alessandro de Medici, and later, Ottavio Farnese—235

Margarita Teresa of Spain (1651–73), Infanta, married Emperor Leopold I—28

Maria of Austria (1528–1603), Charles V's daughter, who married Maximilian II and whose 15 children include Rudolph, the later German Emperor, and Anna, fourth wife of Philip II—4, 6, 21, 247, 255

Maria of Burgundy (1457–82), daughter and heir of Charles the Bold, she married Maximilian of Austria; died as the result of a fall from horseback. Mother of Philip the Fair and Margaret—4, 114, 247, 277

Maria of Hungary (1505–58), sister of Charles V, who married Ludwig II of Hungary (he fell at the Battle of Mohacs 1526); Regent of the Netherlands 1530–56—187, 229, 255, 258, 259, 263, 286

Maria of Portugal (1526–45), daughter of King Juan III of Portugal and Catharine, youngest sister of Charles V; the mother of Don Carlos—4, 127, 166, 209

Marliano, Luis (*d.* 1521), Italian humanist and counsellor to Charles V, who appointed him Bishop of Tuy, in Spain—113

Marot, Clement (1495–1544), French court poet, influenced by Erasmus. Persecuted after 1526 on account of his suspected Lutheranism, he fled to Margaret of Navarre, 1533, then to Venice. Francis I received him back into favour, 1536. He composed occasional verses to celebrate the meeting of Francis I and Charles V in Nice and Charles V's journey through France. In 1542 he had to take flight again on account of his verse translations of the Psalms—183

Marsilius of Padua (1290–1342), writer on Church and State affairs, who belonged to the Ghibelline party and founded the Conciliar movement. In *Defensor Pacis* he questioned the primacy of the Pope and the assumption that no one can call him to order—155

Martyr, Pedro, Spanish chronicler of the first half of 16th century—22, 35, 133, 136